HANDBOOK OF BEHAVIORAL ECONOMICS

Volume A · 1986

BEHAVIORAL MICROECONOMICS

To Leah and Lois

HANDBOOK OF BEHAVIORAL ECONOMICS

BEHAVIORAL MICROECONOMICS

Editors: **BENJAMIN GILAD**
STANLEY KAISH
Rutgers University
Newark, New Jersey

VOLUME A · 1986

 **JAI PRESS INC.**

Greenwich, Connecticut   *London, England*

Library of Congress Cataloging-in-Publication Data

Handbook of behavioral economics.

    Includes bibliographies.
    Contents: v. A. Behavioral microeconomics—
v. B. Behavioral macroeconomics.
    1. Economics—Psychological aspects—Handbooks,
manuals, etc. I. Gilad, Benjamin.   II. Kaish,
Stanley, 1931-
HB74.P8H36 1986   330'.01'9   86-10315
ISBN 0-89232-539-9 (Set)
ISBN 0-89232-700-6 (V. A)
ISBN 0-89232-701-4 (V. B)

Copyright © 1986 JAI PRESS INC.
36 Sherwood Place
Greenwich, Connecticut 06830

JAI PRESS INC.
3 Henrietta Street
London WC2E 8LU
England

MB

ISBN: 0–89232–700–6
ISBN: 0–89232–539–9 (set)

Library of Congress Catalog Card Number: 86-10315

Manufactured in the United States of America

CONTENTS

PART III: THE THEORY OF THE FIRM

Section A: Entrepreneurial and Managerial Behavior

Section B: Intra-Firm Considerations in Productivity

Section C: Extra-Firm Considerations in Productivity

Section D: Industrial Organization

CONTENTS

LIST OF CONTRIBUTORS

Paul Andreassen

Department of Psychology
Harvard University

Bruce J. Caldwell

Department of Economics
University of North Carolina
at Greensboro

Richard M. Coughlin

Department of Sociology
University of New Mexico

William T. Dickens

Department of Economics
University of California,
Berkeley

Randall K. Filer

Department of Economics
Hunter College
The City University of
New York

Robert Forsythe

Department of Economics
University of Iowa

Roger S. Frantz

Department of Economics
San Diego State University

William Gerin

Department of Psychology
Columbia University

Benjamin Gilad

Department of Business
Administration
Rutgers University, Newark

Sebastian Green

The London Business School

Amyra Grossbard-Shechtman   Department of Economics
                                   San Diego State University

Donald C. Hood   Department of Psychology
                                   Columbia University

F. Thomas Juster   Director of the Institute
                                   for Social Research
                                   University of Michigan

Stanley Kaish   Department of Economics
                                   Rutgers University, Newark

Philip A. Klein   Department of Economics
                                   Pennsylvania State University

Howard Kunreuther   Department of Decision Sciences
                                   The Wharton School
                                   University of Pennsylvania

Harvey Leibenstein   Department of Economics
                                   Harvard University

Alan Lewis   School of Humanities and
                                   Social Sciences
                                   University of Bath

Shlomo Maital   Faculty of Industrial Engineering
                                   Technion – Israel Institute of
                                   Technology
                                   Haifa

John J. McGonagle, Jr.   Vice President
                                   Helicon Group
                                   Allentown, Pennsylvania

James N. Morgan   Senior Research Scientist
                                   Institute for Social Research
                                   University of Michigan

Stanley Schachter   Department of Psychology
                                   Columbia University

Julian Simon

College of Business and
Management
University of Maryland

Martin Spechler

Department of Economics
University of Indiana

Burkhard Strümpel

Professor of Economics
Free University of Berlin
Berlin, West Germany

John F. Tomer

Economics and Finance
Department
Manhattan College

W. Fred van Raaij

Department of Economics
Erasmus University
Rotterdam, The Netherlands

Karl-Erik Warneryd

Stockholm School of Economics

Sidney G. Winter

School of Management
Yale University

E. Yuchtman-Yaar

Professor of Sociology
University of Tel Aviv

PREFACE

The impressive development of classical economic analysis over the past 200 years has been accomplished with the use of extremely simple assumptions about the behavior of the human actors on the economic scene. The consumer maximizes his or her utility; the business firm, its profit. Today we know that powerful results can be obtained from analysis using these assumptions, but we also know something about the limits of those results for explaining the actualities of the economic world.

The limits show up, for example, in the current confusions and uncertainties of macroeconomists about government policies for combating underemployment and inflation. For lack of empirically founded theories of how economic actors actually make decisions in the face of uncertainty and complexity—where the assumptions of global rationality are no longer even approximately valid—neoclassical economics provides us with little help in understanding business cycles or the longer movements of economic development.

At the level of the business firm and the consumer, classical theory gives few hints as to how real human beings make real decisions in a world that rarely provides them with the data and computational resources that would be required to apply, literally, the theory of the textbooks. We need empirically valid theories of how business organizations operate, of how investment decisions are actually made, of how the levels of salaries and wages are determined, and of the growth and sizes of business firms.

In sum, we need to augment and amend the existing body of classical and neoclassical economic theory to achieve a more realistic picture of economic processes as well as a more accurate understanding of the equilibrium toward which these processes move.

Behavioral economics is the name we give to the research enterprise that seeks to meet these needs. It is no new thing. Alfred Marshall of *Industry and Trade* could well have labeled himself a behavioralist. And, of course, behavioral economics can claim John R. Commons, Thorstein Veblen, Joseph Schumpeter, George Katona, and many other distinguished economists of past and recent generations.

But behavioral economics, with its emphasis on the factual complexities of our world, has not always appeared as attractive as the axiomatized certainties of marginal analysis and subjective expected utility. Classical and behavioral economics have stood apart, eying each other nervously and suspiciously. They have put off the synthesis that we shall need to fully grasp the economic world around us.

I am encouraged, at the present time, by what I perceive as a strong ground swell of interest in behavioral economics and in closing the gap between behavioral and classical theory. With enough patience and diligence in exploring the empirical realities of economic processes, and enough ingenuity in modeling these processes, we will be able, in time, to return economics to the real world. I welcome this volume as a survey of the work that is carrying us in that direction.

Herbert A. Simon
Carnegie-Mellon University

INTRODUCTION*

Economists have known about psychology since Adam Smith's day. Indeed, it is possible that they were more aware of it then than now. From Ricardo on, the mainstream has gradually moved away from Smith's broad view of the full human experience to its present ascetic state where the bare bones of rationalism dominate and very little human flesh is to be seen covering them. For the past hundred years or so some economists have been warning other economists that they had better make provision to include psychology in their field or it would be in trouble. By and large, although the warnings were acknowledged, they were ignored when it came to the serious work of economics. Veblen's place in the history of thought is as an iconoclast; Mitchell is accused of empiricism without theory; J. M. Clark is better known for his work on the accelerator theory than on behavioralism. Rather than becoming more behavioral, mainstream economics opted for the positivistic point of view that the reality of the assumptions doesn't matter—only the results.

The trouble is, the results are turning bad too. Even while economic science is attempting to establish hegemony over child rearing, crime and punishment, mating and dating, and the political process, it is still no closer to accurately predicting business-cycle turning points than it

*Portions of this introduction are reproduced, by permission, from our article in *The Journal of Behavioral Economics* (Winter, 1984).

was a generation ago. Economists are in danger of moving to a situation where the only people who take them seriously are other economists, and even that may be in doubt.[1] There is nothing wrong with straining reader credulity about the irrelevancy of behavioral assumptions when the results are good. However, we may not have this luxury when the public's need for results isn't being met. Faith has its bounds.

Modern behavioral economics doubtless owes its revival to the ever-growing dissatisfaction with the direction economics is taking and to the recent work that offers a viable alternative. In this volume we combine the work of some of the veterans of the behavioral wars, such as Simon, Leibenstein, Winter, and the associates of George Katona, with that of the young Turks in the field who are seizing on the insights of Amos Tversky and Daniel Kahneman and carrying the battle to all subjects in economics. The theme that ties behavioral economists together is a shared set of *objections* to the mainstream tradition of economic theorizing. Among these objections are (1) a rejection of positivism as *the* methodological foundation for economic research, (2) a refusal to accept the use of deductive reasoning as a sufficient basis for a (social) science, and (3) a marked dislike of static analysis of equilibrium *outcomes* rather than disequilibrium processes. But their most important criticism of mainstream theory is (4) an objection to the *simplistic* economic model of rational agents exhibiting optimizing behavior.

As alternate points of focus, some behavioralists seek substitutes for conscious utility maximization (e.g., satisficing, heuristics, routines);[2] some examine the difference between optimizing behavior that individual members of an organization may exhibit for their own good and the less than optimal decisions this produces for the organization they belong to (the economic unit);[3] some have no objection to the utility maximization assumption but advocate a behaviorally modified objective function that reflects dissonance and framing biases found in the laboratory.[4] All agree that the neoclassical model of perfect information availability, optimal information processing, and the utility maximization that results is in severe need of overhaul.

It is often claimed that a common cause stated in a rejectionist mode is not sufficient to define a new field. Does this apply to behavioral economics? We think not for two reasons. First, behavioral economics is not a field in economics as much as a way of looking at the traditional fields in economics. Second, while shared objections bind us together, behavioral economics is indeed defined by a *positive* common denominator.

Evidence that behavioral economics is not a field in itself is found in the diversity of the fields of specialization represented in this book. James Morgan, Thomas Juster, and their associates at the Michigan Institute of Social Research engage in behavioral macroeconomics; Harvey Leibenstein, John Tomer, and Randall Filer do behavioral microeconomics; Stanley Schachter and his team of psychologists at Columbia University study what might be termed behavioral finance; Sidney Winter offers a behavioral theory of the firm; while Amyra Grossbard-Shechtman's research is in behavioral labor economics and Howard Kunreuther and his Wharton group are interested in behavioral public finance. In our opinion the best label for behavioral economics is to call it *an approach to doing economic research*—an approach that conforms to the following broad behavioral postulates (the positive platform):[5]

1. Economic theory must be consistent with the accumulated body of knowledge in the behavioral disciplines, including psychology, sociology, anthropology, organization theory, and decision sciences. This requirement is at the root of the behavioral economics studies attempting to improve the *assumptive realism* of economic theory (e.g., Simon [1978, 1979]).
2. Economic theory should concentrate on and be able to explain real observed behavior. This shift in emphasis to what actually happens rather than the logical conditions necessary for things to happen unites behavioral economists in a quest for a stronger descriptive base to economics. The survey-based research of Katona (1980) and his successors is a manifestation of this postulate.[6]
3. Economic theory should be empirically verifiable with field, laboratory, survey, and other microdata-generating techniques being acceptable means of verification. The recent rise in the popularity of experimental economics is certainly consistent with the "behaviorification" of economics.

Given these three postulates, it is not surprising to find Keynesians, post-Keynesians, institutionalists, Austrians, and some basically neoclassical economists with open minds engaged in behavioral economics research. Some critics may view this diversity as a weakness. We believe the contrary to be the case. The underlying strength of this new approach to economic theorizing is contained in its independent flowering in various places. Baumol observed in his 1981 presidential address to the American Economic Association that: "No uprising by a tiny band of rebels can hope to change an established order, and when the time for rebellion is ripe it seems to break out simultaneously and independently in a variety of disconnected centers, each offering its own program for the future" (Baumol, 1982, p. 1).

Baumol, of course, was referring to the new industrial organization theory of contestable markets, but his definition of a revolution is certainly just as appropriate for behavioral economics. Pursuing his point

further, Baumol suggests that a true revolution should offer a novel
look at a given phenomenon, provide a unifying analytical structure,
and offer useful insights for empirical work and public policy.

Judging by the ideas presented in this book and by the work presently
being carried out in Europe and the United States, behavioral economics
fulfills all three conditions for a genuine uprising. It looks at micro and
macro behavior in a novel way through its use of new empirical techniques and findings taken from a variety of disciplines. The emerging
picture of economic man is definitely that of a less than fully rational,
organizationally rooted creature who is systematically biased, often mis-
informed, always a role player, and who frequently violates the rationality postulates of consistent ordering and transitivity. When aggregated
into groups he carries his psychology with him, making organizational
behavior no more rational than that seen among individuals. But most
important for economics, his behavior can still be modeled and these
models tested empirically. Finally, in terms of usefulness for policy formulation, once we deal with real behavior with its foundation of real
motives, real aspirations, and empirically determined dynamics, we have
a better chance of judging whether public policy achieves the positive
goals its proponents intended.

POLICY IMPLICATIONS AND NORMATIVE
BEHAVIORAL ECONOMICS

One of the issues brought to the focus of attention by several works in
this volume is the implication of behavioral research to normative economics. Several studies suggest a new rationale for government intervention in the economy, given the failure of markets to promote a
classical optimization due to individual judgment bias. The long-run
efficiency produced by the standard competitive model rests on the assumption of Pareto optimal allocation of resources, which in turn assumes agents who maximize expected utility. If maximization and full
information are questioned, the normative criterion of orthodox economics is in doubt. As Nelson and Winter (1982, p. 356) say, "The normative properties associated with competitive equilibrium become
meaningless, just as that equilibrium is meaningless as a description of
behavior." Do the advances in behavioral economics therefore open the
door for promiscuous intervention due to market failure? Not
necessarily.

As early as 1945, Hayek's famous essay, "The Use of Knowledge in
Society," contended that the most important function of the market
system is "the utilization of knowledge which is not given to anyone in

its totality." Thus the market is especially important in its function as a mechanism of coordination *because* people are imperfect, possess less than complete knowledge, and make biased choices based on unstable preferences. The assumption of full rationality, so essential to standard welfare theory, is crucial for the defense of the standard *competitive model* but not for the real world market system. Several contemporary economists have advanced the notion of markets as instruments (or processes) of economic experimentation and entrepreneurial discovery, with the related criterion of success being higher coordination (Kirzner, 1973) or Schumpeterian evolution (Nelson and Winter, 1982). As Hayek pointed out, the market in orthodox theory is just a computational device for the mathematical solution to the social allocation problem, *assuming full information* in preferences and the availability of resources to satisfy them. This is quite different from the view of markets as social instruments for "mobilizing all the bits of knowledge scattered throughout the economy" (Kirzner, 1973, p. 214). In short, conclusions regarding market failure and the need for governmental intervention are not the inevitable implication of behavioral economics research, but are the inevitable result of using the concept of market equilibrium as found in standard welfare theory.

Despite the disagreement on the implication of behavioral economics for normative economics, the usefulness of behavioral economics research to policy makers is unquestionable. There is little doubt, following the studies by Dickens, Juster, Kunreuther, Strumpel, and many others, that the *effectiveness* of public policy can be enormously enhanced by introducing behavioral considerations. The response of the constituents, as well as the effect of framing on the choice of policy options, are among the issues policy design must face. Without behavioral considerations even the best intentions underlying a policy may lead down that famous paved pathway to perdition.

With this volume we hope to provide economists with the starting steps in the long and tortuous journey to make economics more relevant and economic policy more effective. This is an ambitious—perhaps even pretentious—goal. But it is most worthwhile.

B. Gilad and S. Kaish
Newark, New Jersey, 1985

NOTES

1. See Filippello (1985) for a bleak assessment of economics from the business economist's point of view and Ulmer (1984) and Eichner (1983) for a view from within academia.

2. See Simon (1955, 1959, 1979), Kahneman and Tversky (1982, 1984), and Nelson and Winter (1982), as well as Heiner's (1983) interesting article.

3. See Leibenstein (1976).

4. See Akerlof and Dickens (1982); Gilad, Loeb, and Kaish (forthcoming); Cohen and Axelrod (1984); Spechler (1982–1983); and Kunreuther et al. (1978, 1983).

5. We are grateful to Alfred Eichner for his insights on this issue during a recent conversation.

6. As Philip Klein observed, by this postulate institutionalists such as Mitchell [were] behavioral economists long before the term was coined (see also Klein, 1983). We might add that several other schools such as post-Keynesian also have a more behaviorally oriented approach to economics.

REFERENCES

Akerlof, George A. and William T. Dickens, "The Economic Consequence of Cognitive Dissonance," *American Economic Review*, 72 (June 1982), 307-319.

Baumol, William J., "Contestable Markets: An Uprising in the Theory of Industry Structure," *American Economic Review*, 72 (March 1982), 1-13.

Cohen, Michael D. and Robert Axelrod, "Coping with Complexity: The Adaptive Value of Changing Utility," *American Economic Review*, 74 (March 1984), 30-42.

Eichner, Alfred S., "Why Economics is Not Yet a Science," *Journal of Economic Issues*, XVII (June 1983), 507-520.

Filippello, Nicholas A., "Presidential Address: Where Do Business Economists Go From Here," *Business Economics*, 20, no. 1 (January 1985).

Gilad, Benjamin, Peter D. Loeb and Stanley Kaish, "Cognitive Dissonance and Utility Maximization: A General Framework." *Journal of Economic Behavior and Organization*, forthcoming.

Hayek, Frederick A., "The Use of Knowledge in Society," *American Economic Review*, 35 (1945), 519-530.

Heiner, Ronald A., "The Origin of Predictable Behavior," *American Economic Review*, 73 (September 1983), pp. 560-595.

Kahneman, Daniel and Amos Tversky, "The Psychology of Preferences," *Scientific American*, 246 (January 1982), 162-173.

Kahneman, Daniel and Amos Tversky, "Choices, Values and Frames," *American Psychologist*, 39 (1984), 1-10.

Katona, George, *Essays on Behavioral Economics*. Ann Arbor: Survey Research Center, The University of Michigan, 1980.

Kirzner, Israel M., *Competition and Entrepreneurship*. Chicago: The University of Chicago Press, 1973.

Klein, Philip A., "The Neglected Institutionalism of Wesley Clair Mitchell: The Theoretical Basis for Business Cycle Indicators," *Journal of Economic Issues*, XVII (December 1983), 867-899.

Kunreuther, H., R. Ginsberg, L. Miller, et al., *Disaster Insurance Protection: Public Policy Lessons*. New York: Wiley and Sons, 1978.

Kunreuther, H., W. Sanderson and R. A. Vetschera, "A Behavioral Model of the Adoption of Protective Activities." Decision Sciences Department Working Paper No. 83-03-03, The Wharton School, University of Pennsylvania, 1983.

Leibenstein, Harvey, *Beyond Economic Man*. Cambridge, MA: Harvard University Press, 1976.

Nelson, Richard and Sidney Winter, *An Evolutionary Theory of Economic Change*. Cambridge, MA: Harvard University Press, 1982.

Simon, Herbert A., "A Behavioral Theory of Rational Choice," *Quarterly Journal of Economics*, 69, (February 1955), 99-118.

Simon, Herbert A., *Administrative Behavior*, 2nd ed. New York: Macmillan, 1959.

Simon, Herbert A., "Rationality as Process and as Product of Thought," *American Economic Review*, 68, (May 1978), 1-16.

Simon, Herbert A., "Rational Decision Making in Business Organizations," *American Economic Review*, 69, (September 1979), 493-513.

Spechler, Martin C., "Taste Variability is Indisputable," *Forum for Social Economics* (Fall/Winter, 1982-1983).

Ulmer, Melville J., "Economics in Decline," *Commentary* (November 1984), 42-46.

PART I

METHODS AND TOOLS

INTRODUCTION TO PART I:

METHODS AND TOOLS

One of the distinctive marks of behavioral economics and behavioral economists is the rejection of the methodology and practice of mainstream economics as too restrictive and, at times, philosophically inappropriate. Recently, voices within the profession have joined those outside in agreement.[1] In light of this growing dissent within the field of economics, we have included a separate part on methodology to make explicit the methodological foundations of behavioral economics that can be glimpsed in the research presented later in the handbook. This part includes two articles. In the first, Bruce Caldwell demonstrates that the current generation of behavioral economists is not breaking wholly new ground; rather, it is going back to the roots of marginal analysis. During the twentieth century, economics has become more austere, going from a science of behavior to an exercise in the logic of choice. We might say that from the behavioralist point of view, there was a Gresham's law at work in which bad theory drove out good. But all is not lost: as Caldwell shows, recent developments in the philosophy of science (e.g., the rise of postpositivist thinking) bring new hope for behavioral economists.

In the second article, Bob Forsythe describes the use of experimental methods in economics. The article is addressed to the uninitiated reader and attempts to persuade behavioral (and other) economists of the value of including this particular tool for data generation in their repertoire.

Despite the fact that experiment is the principal research tool in many behavioral and social sciences, to say nothing of the physical sciences that economics strives to emulate, it has never gained widespread acceptance in mainstream economics. We leave the explanation of this phenomenon to the sociologists. In behavioral economics at least, these "new" tools (including also surveys, field studies, and case studies) find a receptive audience.

One last thought regarding this part on methodology. In his paper, Caldwell argues that what behavioral economics needs most is a new Marshall to synthesize its various strands, and a Samuelson to preach it to the new generation of economics students. It is our opinion that what this handbook needed was a Caldwell to put us on the right road and give us the philosophical green light.

NOTES

1.   For example, Donald McCloskey, "The rhetoric of economics," *Journal of Economic Literature*, 20 (June, 1983), 481–517.

ECONOMIC METHODOLOGY AND BEHAVIORAL ECONOMICS:
AN INTERPRETIVE HISTORY

Bruce J. Caldwell

It is perhaps best to begin by stating that I am neither a psychologist nor a behavioral economist. I am an historian of economic thought whose primary area of research is economic methodology. In this paper I will present a historical survey of the development of certain methodological issues in economics over the last century. The interplay among the ideas of philosophers of science, economic methodologists, and economists proper will figure prominently in the survey. I will also attempt to link the discussion of methodology with the loosely grouped set of concepts and theories whose study is the purpose of this volume: the research program of behavioral economics.

I. THE PROFESSIONALIZATION OF ECONOMICS: 1880–1960

Those with an interest in methodology remember that an important debate, dubbed the *Methodenstreit* ("conflict of methods"), took place at the end of the last century. The two antagonists in the struggle were Carl Menger, father of the Austrian school, who argued for an abstract-theoretical approach to the study of economics, and Gustav Schmoller, leader of the German historical school and proponent of an historical-empirical methodology. But if one digs more deeply into the literature of that time, one will discover another, less heralded debate, in which psychologists and economists crossed swords. In some future history of our discipline, it may turn out that this second debate will be judged far more significant than the *Methodenstreit*.

Between roughly 1880 and 1920, the still emergent subjective theory of value, arguably the most important result of the marginal revolution in economics, came under sustained fire from psychologists and various heterodox sympathizers in economics. The opponents of the new theory of value were armed with the psychological theories of William James, William McDougall, and John Watson. Seeking objective and measurable behavioral and physiological determinants of human behavior, they rejected the discredited hedonistic psychology that seemed to form the motivational underpinnings of the behavior of "economic man." Members of the economics profession were divided in their responses to these charges. Some were openly hostile, others were sympathetic. Significantly, most of the major figures of the day felt compelled to take some position on the issue. In the end, the controversy died down, apparently for two reasons. First, the psychologists could not settle on any single theory of motivation, so their forces became dispersed. In the meantime, economics was being transformed into a pure logic of choice. This riposte undercut the arguments from psychology, because a pure logic of choice is independent of any motivational postulates. The new science of economics was on its way toward becoming an autonomous discipline.[1]

In 1932, Lionel Robbins defended economics as a pure logic of choice in his *An Essay on the Nature and Significance of Economic Science*. Robbins confidently proclaimed that the efforts of economists had yielded "a body of generalizations whose substantial accuracy and importance are open to question only by the ignorant or the perverse" (p. 1). The truth of these generalizations cannot be established by appeals to history or by surveying the results of controlled experiments. Rather

> the propositions of economic theory, like all scientific theory, are obviously deductions from a series of postulates. And the chief of these postulates are all assumptions involving in some way simple and indisputable facts of experience. ... These are not postulates the existence of whose counterpart in reality admits of extensive dispute once their nature is fully realized. We do not need controlled experiment to establish their validity: they are so much the stuff of our everyday experience that they have only to be stated to be recognized as obvious (pp. 78–79).

In this and other passages, Robbins argues against the claims of historicists and proponents of the experimental method. He also rejects the "behaviorist" claim that science must deal only with observable phenomena, on the grounds that explanations in economics must make reference to an individual's subjective valuation process, a process that is understandable but not observable (pp. 87–90). Finally, in defending the notion of "rational economic man," Robbins asserts that a belief in *Homo economicus* does not entail an acceptance of psychological hedonism. For Robbins, rationality implies only consistency in choice. Furthermore, he admits that under certain circumstances even such consistency may be irrational if the time and effort required for it could be better used; in his delightful prose, "the marginal utility of not bothering about marginal utility" may be a legitimate way to explain apparently inconsistent behavior (pp. 83–86, 92).

Six short years after the publication of his essay, the pure logic of choice that Lord Robbins had so eloquently defended was under attack. Psychology was not the opponent this time. Rather, it was a brash new philosophy of science, logical positivism, which had sprung up in Vienna in the 1920s and soon swept westward across Europe. A young British economist named Terence Hutchison went to Germany in the mid-1930s to study the new scientific philosophy. In 1938, Hutchison published his famous methodological treatise, *The Significance and Basic Postulates of Economic Theory*, in which the principles of logical positivism were deftly applied. The book can be read as a point-by-point empiricist assault on the ideas espoused by Robbins. As it had in so many other disciplines, positivism entered economics like a lion.

Philosophy was dominated by speculative idealism at the end of the last century, and logical positivism may be viewed as an empirical over-reaction to the excesses of idealism. One goal of the logical positivist movement was to eliminate metaphysics (the bread and butter of the idealists) from the domain of science. This could be accomplished, it was believed, by the logical analysis of scientific propositions. Two sorts of statements were to be permitted in science: analytic statements and synthetic statements. Analytic statements are true or false by definition, and hence they are empirically empty. Analytic statements nonetheless had to be permitted entry into science because many scientific theories employ analytic statements in the form of identities and definitions. Synthetic statements make empirical claims about the world; their truth or falsity is contingent. One discovers whether a synthetic statement is true or false by testing it. Scientific theories would ideally contain only analytic statements and true synthetic statements. One would discover which synthetic statements were true by testing, or verifying, them. In the real world, testing is usually difficult, and the results of tests may be ambiguous. So as a practical matter, legitimate scientific theories may be distinguished from pseudoscientific metaphysics because the former, but not the latter, contain statements that are, at minimum, *conceivably testable*. Hutchison incorporates this idea early on in his essay:

> If the finished propositions of a science, as against the accessory purely logical or mathematical propositions used in many sciences, including Economics, are to have

any empirical content, as the finished propositions of all sciences except of Logic and Mathematics must have, then these propositions must *conceivably* be capable of empirical testing *or be reducible to such propositions* by logical or mathematical deduction (p. 9, emphasis in the original).

This posed problems for Robbins' pure logic of choice, and especially for his defense of the rationality postulate. The first problem, soon to be solved by Samuelson's (1938, 1948, 1950) revealed preference gambit, was that agents' choices are based on subjective, unobservable, and hence untestable states of mind called preferences.[2] The second and far more lethal problem has to do with Robbins' definition of rationality, which is equivalent to consistency in choice. Reading Robbins carefully, it is evident that individuals may on occasion be *rationally inconsistent* in choice, especially when (in modern terms) information is costly. As Hutchison notes in his book, this difficulty is often overcome by defenders of the rationality postulate with the addition of another assumption, that of perfect knowledge. Since the perfect-knowledge assumption is demonstrably false empirically, such a tactic did not impress Hutchison. The major thrust of his criticism should by now be evident: Robbins' pure logic of choice fails because it is untestable. Robbins' position boils down to the assertion that agents are always rational in their choices, even when their choices appear inconsistent to outsiders. No observed behavior can falsify the rationality postulate, and as such, it is empirically empty. (Whether one then wishes to categorize it as a metaphysical or a tautological statement is another matter. For the record, Hutchison viewed it as a tautology.)

For the next twenty years, the status of the rationality postulate was hotly debated among economic methodologists. A priorists like Ludwig von Mises insisted that all human action is rational, in the sense of being purposeful, by definition. For von Mises and other adherents of praxeology, the basic postulates of the science of human action were apodictical. Hutchison, later labeled an "ultra-empiricist" by Fritz Machlup, continued to press for testable assumptions. For his part, Machlup took the middle road, arguing that theories may be "verified" by comparing their predictions, but not their assumptions, with phenomenal reality.[3]

Meanwhile, most of the rest of the economics profession was paying scant attention to the scribblings of the methodologists. The Keynesian revolution was in full bloom on both sides of the Atlantic. Econometrics was being born as the work of Schultz, Frisch, Koopmans, Tinbergen, Haavelmo, and Tintner became more widely known. At the hands of Hicks and Samuelson, dynamic analysis was developed to supplement static equilibrium theory. Von Neumann and Morgenstern gave us game theory and axiomatic utility theory; a long line of theorists built on the work of Walras, Pareto, and Cassel to construct general equilibrium theory. At less lofty heights, "applied" fields like labor and industrial organization were shedding the remnants of institutionalism as empirical tests of hypotheses became the *modus operandi* for publishable work. In a phrase, economics was becoming a *professional science*. Verbal exercises on the nature and significance of economics, the endless rehashing of seemingly unanswerable methodological questions, seemed to be useless wastes of time in the face of so many advances being made on so many fronts. Those familiar with the work of Thomas Kuhn recognize that a cyclical waxing and waning of interest in methodology is a common occurrence in science. When new paradigms emerge, and normal scientists busy themselves with "filling in the boxes" of their new theories, discussions of methodology are left behind. Kuhn's scenario is well illustrated by the economics profession in the 1950s and 1960s. All that was needed, in terms of methodology, was a simple statement of scientific procedure. As we will see, this was provided in economics by Milton Friedman (1953).

Before moving to Friedman, let us go back to the philosophy of science. Remember that Hutchison invoked logical positivism, a radically empirical philosophy of science, in his demands that economics become more scientific by becoming more testable. Logical positivism gradually fell out of vogue in the 1930s and 1940s, chiefly because it became evident that *no* science, including physics, could meet its strict standards of scientificity. By the 1950s, logical positivism had been replaced by a more moderate form of empirical philosophy, logical empiricism. Logical empiricists did not insist that every sentence in a scientific theory be either definitional or testable, since some statements in theoretical physics (e.g., those referring to atoms or forces) were neither. Instead, theories as a whole might be tested by comparing their implications, or predictions, with phenomenal reality.[4]

Though there are subtle differences of detail between Milton Friedman's brand of instrumentalism and logical empiricism, it should be evident that Friedman's views on methodology closely resemble those of the logical empiricists. According to Friedman, economic theories are tested by comparing their predictions with the data. The best predictors are the best theories, and if more than one give good predictions, choose the simplest theory. I find nothing wrong with this position if one is using a theory *solely* as an instrument for prediction. But Friedman's instrumentalism becomes a powerfully conservative force in economic methodology when one adds his further claim that the realism of assumptions does not matter. This is a step that Friedman takes on his own, and one that would not be acceptable to a logical empiricist philosopher of science.[5] In any case, the implications of Friedman's essay for the debate we have been following are dramatic. In one sweep, any and all attempts to come up with better descriptions of the actual choice behavior of individuals, any attempts to examine the rationality postulate in economics, are declared to be unnecessary and possibly unscientific. They are unnecessary because the "realism" of assumptions does not matter. And they are unscientific because we should always choose the simplist theory, and what could be simpler than to assume that all agents maximize?

It is paradoxical that though Friedman's views on economics were scathingly criticized during the 1950s and 1960s, during the same period his methodological views were widely accepted by most of the profession. If one were to reflect on what comprises accepted scientific procedure in economics, the following set of instructions might emerge: Find a problem, model it as a maximization problem, derive some testable hypotheses (the predictions of the model), find empirical proxies for the theoretical constructs, do the econometrics, get your results. (It might well be added: If the results agree with the model, publish them; if not, find out why, and then publish them.) This description of the practices of many economists accords very well with Friedman's methodological prescriptions, and it accounts in my mind for the success of his essay.

But there is a darker side to all of this. If Friedman's views are consistent with certain ways of "doing" economics, it is inconsistent with others. In some cases it did not matter. In the 1950s and 1960s, few macroeconomists worried about using maximization models. In their pursuit of proofs of the existence, uniqueness, and stability of equilibrium, few general equilibrium theorists were bothered that their models yielded no testable implications. Yet both macroeconomics and general equilibrium theory grew in prestige.

Yet for other research programs in economics, a failure to meet Friedman's prescriptions was devastating. The traditional triad of heterodoxy—Marxian, Austrian, and institutional economics—could now be excluded from serious consideration. (These three had always been excluded, but now it could be argued that they *should* be because they were *unscientific*.) In addition to these groups, others were shut out. In particular, those who sought to analyze the actual choice behavior of agents, those who challenged the usefulness of the maximization hypothesis for understanding the behavior of individuals and firms, were given second billing. This is not to say that the work of men like Simon, Scitovsky, Cyert, March, Leibenstein, Katona, Nelson, Winter, and Williamson went unnoticed by the profession: unlike traditional heterodoxy, these people eventually got published. But for the most part, these researchers were mentioned only in passing in undergraduate texts and (with the exception of the institutions at which they taught) not at all in graduate courses.

A final point: the methodological prescriptions embraced by most of the economics profession in the 1950s and 1960s blocked the development of interdisciplinary work in the social sciences. The only type of interdisciplinary work that existed in this period was aptly labeled (and this by its defenders!) "economic imperialism." In the behavior of political agents or the foraging behavior of forest creatures or the consumption patterns of laboratory rats, the point of "economic imperialism" is not to gain insights from fields like political science or psychology or sociobiology. The point is to show that all of God's creatures, from female psychotics to congressmen to less distinguished members of the animal kingdom, maximize subject to constraints. As long as the use of constrained maximization models is viewed as the only legitimate way to model social phenomena, interdisciplinary efforts must be viewed as just another variation on the theme of "economic imperialism."

To sum up this section: Attempts to bridge some interdisciplinary gaps early in the century failed and resulted in the severing of economic theory from any considerations of psychology as economics began to be viewed as a logic of choice. When logical positivist ideas were introduced by Terence Hutchison, a number of economists interested in methodology argued about the status and content of the rationality, or maximization, postulate. Meanwhile, economics was becoming more professional, as theories were expressed in mathematical form and econometric techniques became increasingly sophisticated. The methodological debates of old seemed dated and otiose in the face of such advances. Friedman's methodology of positive economics, on the other hand, fit the times nicely. Not all of established economics fit its mold, but enough of it did. And it instructed economists to exclude from consideration, on the grounds that they were *unscientific*, a number of alternative approaches to understanding economic reality. Thus we find that methodology, a term so often associated with the interplay of diverse approaches to a subject, became a powerfully conservative force in the 1950s and 1960s. It is no small irony that many mainstream economists of this period thought that the study of methodology was a waste of time, while at the same time they believed that alternative approaches to the study of economics should be excluded *on methodological grounds*!

II. PHILOSOPHY AND ECONOMIC METHODOLOGY IN THE POSTPOSITIVIST PERIOD

During the same time period that economic methodology was entering its conservative stage, a revolution of enormous consequence was taking place in the philosophy of science. The *ancien régime* was logical empiricism, the latest and most mature variant of positivism. The revolutionaries were neither radicals nor reactionaries. They were historians and philosophers of natural science, and some of their names have become familiar, even to economists: Karl Popper, Thomas Kuhn, Imre Lakatos, Norwood Hanson, Stephen Toulmin, Paul Feyerabend. In the course of twenty years, the revolution succeeded. Positivism was overthrown; the postpositivist era had dawned.

Little of the logical empiricist structure withstood the attack. A number of types of scientific explanation (motivational, functional, genetic, historical), which were considered legitimate explanations in their respective fields, could not be squared with the famous "covering-law" models of explanation. The hypothetico-deductive model of theory structure depended for its force on a one-to-one correspondence between, on the one hand, theoretical terms and nonobservable entities, and on the other, nontheoretical terms and observable entities. Too often the one-to-one correspondence did not exist. The "symmetry thesis," which states that all legitimate scientific explanations must be transformable into predictions, was frequently violated. Evolutionary theory cannot predict but can explain which species are selected to survive; one can explain a suicide without being able to predict it: must such explanations be deemed unscientific? Confirmationism stated that the most highly confirmed theories were the best theories. But certain "paradoxes of confirmation" showed that confirmations are easy to multiply (a non-black non-raven, e.g., a white shoe, confirms the statement, "All ravens are black"), and Popper's critique of inductivism challenged the idea that high confirmation is even desirable. Simply put, if the tenets of logical empiricism were ever taken seriously (they never were followed by scientists), most of what we call science would be deemed unscientific.[6]

More important than the details of the case against logical empiricism are the new visions of the scientific enterprise that have emerged in the last twenty-five years. I use the plural of *vision* because no unified, monolithic approach has yet arisen in response to the failures of positivism. But certain common themes are in evidence. Logical empiricists attempted to articulate universal models and procedural rules which they felt were characteristic of legitimate scientific practice. Postpositivists instead emphasize the growth of knowledge over time, the dynamics of change within individual disciplines, and the actual practice of scientists. Logical empiricists used the tools of logic in their analyses. Postpositivists attempt to interpret the development of specific research programs in specific disciplines, and often make use of tools from such disciplines as history, sociology, linguistics, and even psychology in their rational reconstructions. Logical empiricists sought a definition of scientific rationality that was absolute, universal, and immutable. Having recognized with Thomas Kuhn that "paradigm-switching" is seldom a rational affair, or with Lakatos that "instant rationality" is impossible when two research programs collide, post-positivists seek a definition of scientific rationality that is organic, contingent, and flexible. It should be evident that there are dangers of relativistic and skeptical excesses in the new environment. Most of the philosophers mentioned earlier eschew such excesses. But if the dangers are great, so are the rewards: namely, a more complete and honest understanding of the nature of science, in all its variety and complexity.

It may finally be mentioned that the revolution in philosophy is by now spreading to the special sciences. Within economics, there has been a massive increase in interest in the study of methodology. Like philosophers before them, economic methodologists are asking many more and different types of questions and are borrowing from fields like rhetoric, sociology, history, and philosophy in their attempts to formulate answers. Books on methodology have multiplied, sessions on methodological topics are being scheduled at academic conferences, articles on a wide variety of topics are appearing in journals.[7] This is not to say that a heightened methodological consciousness is sweeping the discipline. But it is a welcome change from twenty or even ten years ago, when the only topic considered worthy of discussion was Friedman's essay.

III. BEHAVIORAL ECONOMICS IN THE POSTPOSITIVIST PERIOD

What are the implications of all this for the behavioral economics research program?

First of all, at least one objection to the proliferation of alternative research programs, that provided by strict positivist restrictions on what constitutes legitimate scientific behavior, has been substantially overcome. The implication in economics is clear. One may no longer argue that the use of a maximization model that yields testable implications is the *only* permissible way to do economic science. If, instead of using the rationality assumption, an economist chooses to begin his analysis with some other assumption about an agent's decision-making process (be that satisficing, rule-of-thumb behavior, imitative behavior, routine-following, or something else), such approaches may no longer be judged a priori as being less scientific. If an economist presents a model whose virtues are to explain or describe rather than predict behavior, his opponents who insist that a model *must* have predictive content may no longer look to the philosophy of science to buttress their claims.[8]

An example will show that this claim is not as provocative as it might

at first appear. In a recent article, Paul Schoemaker (1982) notes that a
theory may be assessed according to its objectives. He shows that expected utility models have been used descriptively, predictively, postdict-
ively, and normatively, and then assesses the theory according to how
well it performs these various functions (pp. 538-541). For example, in
examining how well the expected utility model describes the actual choice
behavior of agents, he reviews a number of studies in which the axioms
of the model are frequently violated (pp. 541-548). He also notes alternatives to the model, for example, psychologists Kahneman and Tversky's prospect theory (1979), that help account for some of the anomalies.
Such work would be judged scientific by most observers. A positivist
economist, however, would insist that tests of the axioms and alternative
explanations of violations are unnecessary and unscientific. The axioms
are "unrealistic" assumptions; they should not be directly tested; their
worth may only be assessed by how well a theory employing the assumptions predicts. (As Schoemaker shows, the expected utility model
does not work well in terms of prediction either, but that is another
story.)

Another insight attributable to the new philosophy of science is the
recognition of the importance of tradition in science. The scientific enterprise is a conservative one; change does not occur quickly. Kuhn
points out that, even if a paradigm is shot through with anomalies, a
scientific revolution will not occur until an alternative paradigm emerges.
Lakatos (1970) notes that a research program may degenerate for a long
time before it is superseded. Such conservative tendencies are beneficial
in certain respects: When the best minds of a scientific community are
all focused on working within a single paradigm, great advances are
possible. But there are costs as well, and these are borne by those who
wish to change the direction of scientific research. Questions of strategy
arise, then, if proponents of behavioral economics want their approach
to be viewed as a scientific revolution. If we take to heart Kuhn's observation that theories are never successfully challenged by anomalous facts,
but only by other theories, then it is clear that a synthesis of ideas must
occur among behavioral economists. As I read some of the contributions
of behavioral economists—for example, Leibenstein's "Micro-micro Theory" paper, or Nelson and Winter's book, *An Evolutionary Theory of Economic Change* (1982), I noticed the tendency of these authors to
distinguish their own work not only from neoclassical economics but also
from other critics of the maximization model. Such distinctions are valuable and necessary for clarifying the nuances of various approaches,
but they are best left in the background if it is one's intention to construct
an alternative research program. Behavioral economics, then, may need

an Alfred Marshall—someone who can bring together a number of disparate strands of thought into a unified whole.

Given the large number of pretenders to the throne of neoclassical economics (a throne, it should be mentioned, that has yet to be vacated), the more modest strategy of aiming at a synthesis between behavioral and neoclassical economics has a certain appeal. Nelson and Winter (1982) sometimes seem to take this approach in their superlative book. Borrowing analogies from evolutionary theory and biology, they come up with theories of decision-making in the firm and of firm survivorship that are much richer than the neoclassical view. Yet they also constrain their models to yield many of the same predictions that emerge from standard analysis. At least for this reviewer, such an approach is eminently sensible: the baby has been distinguished from the bath water.

A final strategic point is to get some of these ideas into the textbooks. In an article in which he disparaged the survival of the kinked oligopoly demand curve in intermediate microeconomics texts, George Stigler wrote, "The textbooks of a discipline play a powerfully conservative role in the transmission of doctrine" (Stigler, 1978, p. 200). Stigler's point is that it is nearly impossible, once an idea gets into the textbooks of a discipline, to get it out. The converse is also true: new ideas are not easily added to textbooks. In addition to a Marshall, then, behavioral economics may need a Samuelson. I am not talking about the Samuelson of the *Foundations*, but rather the Samuelson of the *Principles*: the Samuelson who introduced the Keynesian cross to generations of introductory economics students here and around the world. If behavioral economics can find a Marshall and a Samuelson—that is to say, a synthesizer and a popularizer—the prospects for a successful interdisciplinary revolution will be improved. But again, that none of this will be easy should be understood at the outset.

Putting questions of strategy aside, I will end these musings with what I see as the ray of hope in all this. It is a ray of hope for progress in the long run and, as such, involves what is best described as a wishful prophecy. Many of the papers in this volume were presented at a conference attended primarily by psychologists and economists, though a few other disciplines were also represented. At one point in the discussion, it was noted that behavioral economics should not be considered the exclusive province of psychology and economics, and everyone present agreed. More to the point, the sort of interest in genuine intercourse across disciplines exhibited at the conference was, in my experience, both unique and refreshing. This is not to say that communication was always easy. As an economist, I found that I could usually understand the points made by economists, but that I was often confused about why the psychologists asked the questions they asked and why they chose to answer them in such curious ways. Such confusion may cause some to despair, since it is only the first obstacle in a movement toward mutual understanding.

But putting the best face on it, perhaps these and other obstacles may be overcome, so that the social science of the next century will be a truly interdisciplinary endeavor. We saw earlier in this paper that a movement toward autonomy by economics in the first part of the twentieth century was probably a necessary first step for it to become a professional discipline. That autonomy allowed economics to advance as a science. Perhaps the next stage in its advancement will be a movement toward becoming a part of a larger science of society. If such a step occurs, the place of behavioral economics in the advancement of our knowledge of society will loom larger than even its fondest proponents might now imagine.

NOTES

1. For a more detailed examination of this debate, see Coats (1976).
2. Whether Samuelson's revealed preference program actually succeeded in accomplishing its goals is contested by Wong (1978).
3. See von Mises (1949); Machlup (1955, 1956); Hutchison (1956).
4. For critical surveys of these and other issues in twentieth-century philosophy of science, see Suppe (1977), Blaug (1980), and Caldwell (1982).
5. This is why in a recent discussion, Friedman was characterized as an instrumentalist rather than as a positivist or a logical empiricist. See, for example, Boland (1979), Caldwell (1980).
6. Again, these developments are surveyed in the citations in note 4.
7. The size of the bibliography in Caldwell (1984) supports this claim.
8. Of course, this does not mean that a novel approach is necessarily better. All I am saying is that new approaches should not be judged inadequate *solely* because they are new.

REFERENCES

Blaug, Mark, *The Methodology of Economics: Or How Economists Explain*. Cambridge: Cambridge University Press, 1980.
Boland, Lawrence, "A Critique of Friedman's Critics," *Journal of Economic Literature*, 17 (June 1979), 503–522.
Caldwell, Bruce, "A Critique of Friedman's Methodological Instrumentalism," *Southern Economic Journal*, 47 (October 1980), 366–374.
Caldwell, Bruce, *Beyond Positivism: Economic Methodology in the Twentieth Century*. London: Allen and Unwin, 1982.
Caldwell, Bruce, *Appraisal and Criticism in Economics: A Book of Readings*. London: Allen and Unwin, 1984.

Coats, A.W., "Economics and Psychology: The Death and Resurrection of a Research Program," in Spiro Latsis, ed., *Method and Appraisal in Economics.* Cambridge: Cambridge University Press, 1976, pp. 43–64.

Friedman, Milton, "The Methodology of Positive Economics," in *Essays in Positive Economics.* Chicago: University of Chicago Press, 1953, pp. 3–43.

Hutchison, T.W., *The Significance and Basic Postulates of Economic Theory,* 1938; reprint ed. New York: Augustus Kelley, 1960.

Hutchison, T.W., "Professor Machlup on Verification in Economics," *Southern Economic Journal,* 22 (April 1956), 476–483.

Kahneman, Daniel and Amos Tversky, "Prospect Theory: An Analysis of Decision Under Risk," *Econometrica,* 47 (March 1979), 263–291.

Lakatos, Imre, "Falsification and the Methodology of Scientific Research Programmes," in I. Lakatos and A. Musgrave, eds. *Criticism and the Growth of Knowledge.* Cambridge: Cambridge University Press, 1970.

Machlup, Fritz, "The Problem of Verification in Economics," *Southern Economic Journal,* 22 (July 1955), 483–493.

von Mises, Ludwig, *Human Action: A Treatise on Economics.* New Haven, CT: Yale University Press, 1949.

Nelson, Richard and Sidney Winter, *An Evolutionary Theory of Economic Change.* Cambridge, MA: Harvard University Press, 1982.

Robbins, Lionel, *An Essay on the Nature and Significance of Economic Science,* 1932, 2nd ed. London: Macmillan, 1935.

Samuelson, Paul, "A Note of the Pure Theory of Consumer's Behavior," *Economica,* 5 (February 1938), 51–61.

Samuelson, Paul, "Consumption Theory in Terms of Revealed Preference," *Economica,* 15 (November 1948), 243–253.

Samuelson, Paul, "The Problem of Integrability in Utility Theory," *Economica,* 17 (November 1950), pp. 355–385.

Schoemaker, Paul, "The Expected Utility Model: Its Variants, Purposes, Evidence and Limitations," *Journal of Economic Literature,* 20 (June 1982), 529–563.

Stigler, George, "The Literature of Economics: The Case of the Kinked Oligopoly Demand Curve," *Economic Inquiry,* 16 (April 1978), 185–204.

Suppe, Frederick, ed., *The Structure of Scientific Theories,* 1973; 2nd ed. Urbana, IL: University of Illinois Press, 1977.

Wong, Stanley, *The Foundations of Paul Samuelson's Revealed Preference Theory: A Study by the Method of Rational Reconstruction.* London: Routledge and Kegan Paul, 1978.

THE APPLICATION
OF LABORATORY METHODS
TO TESTING THEORIES
OF RESOURCE ALLOCATION
UNDER UNCERTAINTY

Robert Forsythe

I. INTRODUCTION

Over the past twenty-five years, there has been a substantial increase in the use of laboratory experimental methods in economics, and a considerable body of literature has evolved. These methods have been used to study the allocation of resources that results in a variety of market and nonmarket processes, and both individual and group decision-making have been examined in these settings. The intent of this present paper is twofold—first, to provide the uninitiated reader with a brief introduction to the use of laboratory methods in economics and second, to present a survey of recent attempts to apply these methods to environments in which value uncertainty is present.

The uninitiated generally find themselves asking: Why do experimentation in economics? The recent increase in the use of these methods is due, at least in part, to the growing recognition that this methodology provides a relatively low-cost source of data for testing economic theories and for generating new hypotheses. Further, this methodology gives the experimenter a substantial degree of control over many of the environmental parameters by allowing him to specify such things as consumers' preferences, firms' production technologies, and the market institution that specifies the rules governing trade. Because of this control, labo-

ratory market data are generally superior to data from naturally occurring processes in testing a theory or distinguishing between competing
theories, since, with the latter, one can never be sure that the data were
generated in an environment that conformed to the assumptions of the
models being tested.

Once it has been decided to subject a theory to the scrutiny of the
laboratory, the next question that arises is: How is a laboratory market
created? The general rules for creating and implementing a laboratory
market will be presented in the next section of this paper. To assist with
this task, Vernon Smith (1982) has set forth a set of precepts that provide
a foundation for constructing a controlled, well-defined microeconomic
experiment. These precepts, which allow an experimenter to assign the
values market participants place on the object being transacted, will be
reviewed and illustrated. In addition, the experimenter must specify the
rules by which trade may take place. A continuum of possible trading
institutions exists, and some of the more common forms that have been
operationalized will also be discussed in Part II.

The original uses of laboratory market experimentation were restricted almost exclusively to environments in which there was no value
uncertainty. In other words, each trader in an experiment knew with
certainty his value for each item being traded. Buyers were given redemption-value schedules that told them how much they would earn
for each unit they purchased, and sellers were given cost schedules specifying how much they would have to pay for each unit sold. Thus, when
making a trade, a market participant had no uncertainty surrounding
the profitability of that trade. The buyer earned the difference between
his redemption value for the unit and the purchase price, while the
seller's profit was the difference between the price and his cost of providing the unit.

Recently, experimentalists have turned their attention to environments in which value uncertainty is present. These environments may
be characterized by exogenous uncertainty or asymmetric information
or both. In the presence of exogenous uncertainty, buyers' redemption
values and sellers' costs may be determined by the outcome of a random
occurrence that does not depend on the actions of any of the traders.
When asymmetric information exists in the market, a subset of market
participants are better informed about the outcome of some random
event. Further, the outcome may depend directly on their actions.

Recent theoretical work in both macroeconomics and microeconomics
has focused on these environments and has generated a large number
of competing theories. The differences in most of the theoretical predictions stem from behavioral assumptions regarding how economic
agents form expectations. Laboratory methods are ideally suited for

examining these environments to sort out these theories and the corresponding behavioral assumptions. Indeed, in his recent testimony before the National Science Foundation hearings of the House of Representative's Subcommittee on Science, Research, and Technology, Herbert A. Simon, in describing the diversity of views regarding macroeconomic theory and business cycle theory in general and rational expectations theory in particular, stated:[1]

> The only thing we don't know about rational expectations theory is whether or not it describes any real human behavior. Where economics and psychology need to bed down together, much more closely than they have in the past, is in finding ways to verify—by direct observation of human behavior and by human laboratory experiments of the sort that were described here—to find out which of the rather large set of theories of expectation formation that are now current really do describe how human beings go about predicting the future.

Designing laboratory experiments in which there is asymmetric information and exogenous uncertainty is not a simple matter, however. In particular, the precepts set forth by Smith are no longer sufficient to provide adequate control over these environments, since they do not specify how individuals make choices among risky prospects. Nonetheless, tests of propositions that depend on the risk attitudes of agents in the market require some knowledge of, or control over, the risk preferences of subjects in the laboratory. In section III of this paper, one additional precept will be proposed that overcomes this difficulty, and some possible extensions will be discussed. Further, some of the details necessary to extend laboratory procedures to these environments will be presented. In the remainder of the paper, some recent work that uses laboratory methods will be reviewed. Recent surveys by Charles Plott (1979, 1982) and Smith (1982) elegantly and expertly summarize the application of laboratory methods to a wide variety of problems. To avoid duplication, the reader is referred to these works and the references contained therein for a comprehensive review of this literature. Instead, this paper will focus on reviewing those recent studies that have examined environments in which value uncertainty is present. In section IV, the study of rational expectations models as applied to experimental asset markets will be analyzed. The results of laboratory market studies of environments in which agents possess asymmetric information will be reviewed in section V. While some suggestions for future research are interspersed in all sections, additional suggestions along with concluding remarks are presented in section VI.

II. LABORATORY MARKET CREATION
AND IMPLEMENTATION: THE CERTAINTY CASE

The creation of a laboratory market is quite simple. Subjects, typically students, are recruited through announcements made in class or placed on bulletin boards or in newspapers. The subjects are asked to appear at a specific location at a designated time and, upon their arrival, each subject is given a copy of a list of instructions that tells him how he will earn money based on the decisions he will be required to make. The instructions also inform each subject of the rules that govern his interaction with other subjects and, in particular, how trade may take place during the experiment. These two features, the reward structure and the trading institution, form the core of a laboratory market experiment. Since we know that market behavior crucially depends on these features, an experimenter must be extremely careful in designing and providing for the adequate control of these variables. It should always be kept in mind that if one generates new and interesting results through experimentation then other researchers will have an incentive to try to replicate these results. To allow for such replication, it is essential that an experimenter keep a complete and well-documented set of experimental procedures that describe how adequate control was maintained.

A. The Reward Structure

The reward structure is used to "induce preferences" in each experimental subject. Consider a buyer who is told that he may purchase as many units of the commodity being traded at any price that he wishes just as long as he stays within the confines of the trading rules. He is also told that the experimenter will redeem each unit he purchases according to a redemption-value schedule. For example, a buyer's redemption-value schedule might be given as follows:

Unit	Redemption Value
1	$6.00
2	5.00
3	4.50
4	4.25

This schedule informs the buyer that he will receive $6.00 for the first unit he purchases, $5.00 for the second unit he purchases, and so on.

Similarly, each seller is told that he may sell as many units of the commodity being traded at any price that he wishes just as long as he stays within the confines of the trading rules. He is given a marginal-cost schedule that specifies the amount he must pay for each unit he purchases. A sample marginal-cost schedule for a seller is as follows:

Unit	Cost
1	$4.50
2	5.00
3	5.75
4	6.75

This schedule informs the seller that he must pay $4.50 for the first unit he sells, $5.00 for the second unit he sells, and so on.

The obvious question that now arises is: when can these schedules be interpreted as the buyer's and seller's limit-price schedules? When they can, then, under competitive conditions, these schedules become the buyer's inverse-demand schedule and the seller's inverse-supply schedule, respectively. With several buyers and several sellers in a market, the market demand and supply schedules may be obtained by the usual process of horizontally summing these individual demand and supply schedules.

Smith (1982) has provided four conditions that allow this interpretation. These conditions, which extend those originally given by Louis Wilde (1980) and by Smith (1976, 1980), are sufficient for transforming a laboratory environment into a controlled, well-defined microeconomic experiment. These conditions, or precepts, as Smith calls them, are not to be regarded as self-evident truths but rather should themselves be subjected to empirical verification.

The first two precepts, *nonsatiation* and *saliency*, ensure the creation of a well-defined microeconomic experiment in which individuals have consistent preferences and act so as to maximize their well-being. Nonsatiation requires that "given a costless choice between two alternatives, identical (i.e., equivalent) except that the first yields more of a reward medium (e.g., U.S. currency) than the second, the first will always be chosen (i.e., preferred) over the second, by an *autonomous* individual." So that individual decisions will be tied to the reward structure, a *saliency* precept must also be used. This requires that individual rewards depend on the outcome of the experiment and that the institutional setting used defines how individual decisions will be translated into outcomes.

Outside the laboratory, individuals make decisions about commodities or activities that are valuable because they have utility. In the laboratory, the experimenter must be able to assign or control the individual values that each participant assigns to the abstract commodity being allocated. To test propositions about resource allocation under certainty, these first two precepts allow the experimenter to induce any arbitrary pattern of valuations among subjects in the laboratory.[2]

The other two precepts, *dominance* and *privacy*, are needed to guarantee the full control of the microeconomic experiment. In particular, dominance requires that the reward structure being used be sufficiently high so as to offset any nonmonetary subjective costs of participation in the experiment. For example, some of the activities in an experiment require subjects to expend effort in making calculations, decisions, and trades. Dominance requires that the reward structure overcome these transaction costs. As a case in point, Plott and Smith (1978) observed that market participants frequently would not exchange marginal units on which they earned only very small profits. To overcome this, they paid subjects a small (five-cent) commission for each trade that they made, and this commission was sufficient to induce marginal trades. Referring to the sample redemption value and cost schedules given above, note that if the price is $5.00, the buyer is indifferent to buying a second unit, since its monetary redemption value is exactly equal to its price. Likewise, using similar reasoning, the seller is indifferent about selling a second unit. Further, if either or both of these individuals incur some small subjective cost in transacting, then neither would want to trade their second unit. The use of a small commission will, in general, induce these marginal units to be traded.

The privacy precept requires that each subject be aware of only his own reward structure. The lack of knowledge about the reward structures of others seems to effectively control any "consumption externality" in which a subject places an additional subjective valuation on the rewards earned by others. For example, Smith (1976) demonstrates that when subjects have complete information about each other's payoff, the equilibrium tendencies of a double oral auction market are retarded. Subjects seem to modify their selfinterested choices with equity considerations.

B. The Trading Institution

Few economic theories specify the details of how contracts are made between buyers and sellers, but instead make equilibrium predictions based on the limit-price functions of each trader in the market. In order to examine any such theory within a laboratory environment, an experimenter is immediately confronted with the problem of specifying the mechanics by which trade can take place. Further, he must also specify what information each trader can observe about the trades made by other market participants. For example, in some markets the terms of all trades are publicly displayed, while in others they are not. As most experimentalists will quickly point out, even seemingly subtle changes in trading rules and/or information disclosure can often have a substantial effect on market performance. Since these effects are the major focus of the survey by Plott (1982) and can also be found in the empirical propositions stated in Smith (1982), they will not be repeated here. We will, however, discuss the details of the prominent forms of market institutions that have been examined to date. These institutions are action markets, sealed-bid (offer) markets, posted-price markets, and negotiated-price markets.

The *auction market* is the institution that has been most extensively studied, and numerous variants of this market exist. When the auction is for a single object, it can be either an English or a Dutch auction, depending on whether the price begins at a low level and is increased until only one willing buyer remains or whether the price starts high and is decreased until some buyer indicates a willingness to purchase.[3] Auctions for single or multiple objects can be either a double auction or a one-sided auction. In a double auction, buyers can publicly make bids to buy units, and sellers can publicly make offers to sell units. Buyers are free to accept any seller's terms, and sellers are free to accept any buyer's terms. In a one-sided auction,[4] only one side of the market (either the buyers' side or the sellers' side) is free to announce prices publicly in an attempt to trade units. The other side of the market may not announce prices but may accept any outstanding contract terms they observe. An auction market may also be conducted orally, where buyers and sellers make verbal bids and offers, or the auction may be computerized, where bids and offers are logged through a computer. This technological difference may have a significant impact on trading behavior. As observed by Arlington Williams (1980), computerized double auctions converge more slowly than oral double auctions, at least with inexperienced subjects.

The rules by which bids and offers may be tendered may also be varied. There is usually one outstanding bid and one outstanding offer available in the market. To tender a new bid or offer, an "improvement" rule typically is used. That is, any bid must be higher than the standing bid, and any offer must be lower than the standing offer. An acceptance may be made at any time. Alternatively, any bid (offer) may be allowed, but it can be made only if the previous bid (offer) has been standing open for acceptance for a minimum length of time. A comparison of four variations of these rules is reported in a study by Smith and Williams (1982).

In a *sealed-bid (offer) market*, two kinds of competing rules for tendering bids (offers) have been examined. In one, buyers (sellers) submit demand (supply) schedules specifying a bid (offer) price for each unit they wish to transact. In the other, buyers (sellers) submit a single price and specify the number of units they are willing to buy (sell) at that price. All traders have been informed in advance of the algorithm that will be used to determine the market-clearing quantity and the prices they will pay (receive) for units they have purchased (sold). The auction may be either competitive or discriminative. In a competitive auction, buyers pay (sellers receive) a single market-clearing price for each unit they purchase (sold). In a discriminative auction, buyers pay (sellers receive) their bid (offer) price for each unit they purchase (sold).[5]

In *posted-price markets*, either sellers post their offer prices or buyers post their bid prices at the beginning of a market period. These prices cannot be changed during the period and become take-it-or-leave-it offers (bids) to the buyers (sellers) in the market. Buyers (sellers) may then choose an offer (bid) they wish to accept along with the number of units they wish to transact. The seller (buyer) whose bid (offer) has been accepted then must decide how much of this quantity to transact, and a binding contract is made. Studies by Fred Williams (1973) and Plott and Smith (1978) have shown that prices in posted-offer (bid) markets tend to be higher (lower) than in double oral auction markets. In a study of monopoly, Smith (1981) demonstrated the importance of the trading institution for market performance. In particular, he shows that the standard monopoly model does not perform well when a monopoly seller transacts in a double oral auction market, since prices tend to erode toward the competitive equilibrium. On the other hand, monopoly theory more accurately predicts market performance when a posted-offer institution is used.

Finally, *negotiated-price markets* have received the least attention of any trading mechanism. In these markets, initiated in a study by Hong and Plott (1982) and also used by Grether and Plott (1981), traders are allowed to negotiate the terms of trade of each transaction privately. Buyers and sellers may discuss terms and agree to a contract, but the contract prices are not generally made public. To assure this, buyers are prohibited from contacting other buyers, and sellers may not contact other sellers. The competitive model seems to predict the outcomes in these markets adequately, yet prices tend to remain slightly above the competitive price.

In all forms of market organization, trade usually takes place over a sequence of market periods. Frequently, each period is a strict replication of previous periods in which all endowments are reinitialized, although this need not be the case. In other studies, endowments and/or redemption value and cost schedules have been changed from one period to the next. The set of trades that occur and, in particular, the transaction prices that are observed change from one replication to the next until the market equilibrates.

III.　LABORATORY MARKET CREATION AND IMPLEMENTATION: THE UNCERTAINTY CASE

The methods and procedures outlined in the previous section must be modified and extended when some or all of the traders in a market must engage in transactions prior to having certain knowledge about their values for the unit being traded. In particular, Smith's four precepts are no longer sufficient for creating a controlled, well-defined micro-economic experiment if value uncertainty is introduced into the environment.

The following example illustrates the difficulties that arise in the presence of value uncertainty. Suppose an experimenter wishes to create a sealed-offer market in which there are B buyers and S sellers. Each seller has two types of units for sale: "high-quality" units and "low-quality" units. In a market period, each seller is permitted to make at most one sealed offer to each buyer. An offer consists of the type of unit the seller wishes to sell and the price the seller requires to sell the unit. After all sealed offers have been submitted, each buyer may accept at most one offer. An acceptance constitutes a binding contract. The seller must deliver the type of unit he has contracted to provide, and the buyer must accept delivery of that unit and pay the seller's offer price. This consti-tutes a market period. Many such market periods are observed, where each period is a strict replication of previous periods. Major attention is paid to the time path of contract prices and the quality of all units sold.

Thus far, there is no exogenous uncertainty present in the environ-ment, and buyers and sellers possess the same information regarding the quality of the product being delivered. Using the precepts and meth-ods described in the previous section, a well-defined microeconomic experiment to study this institution may be created by specifying a re-ward structure for each trader. However, we can change the environ-ment to allow some element of uncertainty. In particular, we can assume that the difference between a high-quality and a low-quality unit is the likelihood that the latter will be defective and therefore worthless to the buyer. Further, let us examine an institution where buyers have no recourse against the seller if the item is defective. Suppose that the probability of a unit being defective, the redemption value of a unit for each buyer, and the cost of providing each unit by each seller is given in the following table:

	High-Quality Unit	Low-Quality Unit
Probability of a defective unit	.1	.55
Buyer's redemption value if a unit is not defective	$1.00	$1.00
Seller's cost per unit	$ .60	$ .10

The redemption value for each unit bought is the same for all buyers, and all sellers are assessed the same constant costs for each unit sold. Here, the supply curve is defined as in the certainty case: it is horizontal at $.60 for the high-quality good and horizontal at $.10 for the low-quality good. The demand curve is not so easily determined from the information given, since it depends on each buyer's own risk preferences. A high-quality item has a 90-percent chance of being worth $1.00 to a buyer and a 10-percent chance of being worth zero. A low-quality item has a 45-percent chance of being worth $1.00 to a buyer and a 55-percent chance of being worthless. Any theoretical prediction as to the equilibrium price and the quality of units transacted requires an assumption about buyers' risk preferences, and thus any test of that prediction requires knowledge of the subjects' risk preferences. To see this, suppose buyers are all risk-neutral. In this case, their expected redemption value is $.90 for a high-quality unit and $.45 for a low-quality unit. The demand and supply curves for each type of unit are given in Figure 1. Here, the risk-neutral competitive model predicts that only low-quality units will be sold at an equilibrium price of $.10, since buyers will, on average, earn $.35 on low-quality units as opposed to $.30 on high-quality units. Now suppose instead that all buyers are sufficiently risk-averse to the extent that the additional $.05 in expected earnings no longer offsets the increased risk of buying a defective item when a low-quality unit is purchased. In this case, the competitive model would predict that the high-quality unit will be sold at an equilibrium price of $.60. The demand curves for each type of unit shift inward from the risk-neutral case but in a way that cannot be specified without full knowledge about subjects' risk attitudes. Thus the lack of control over subjects' preferences leads to a breakdown of control over the microeconomic environment.

To overcome this difficulty, a fifth precept is required, which specifies how individuals make choices among risky prospects. This precept, called *expected utility*, is that an individual uses the expected utility model to

Figure 1.   Risk-neutral predictions.

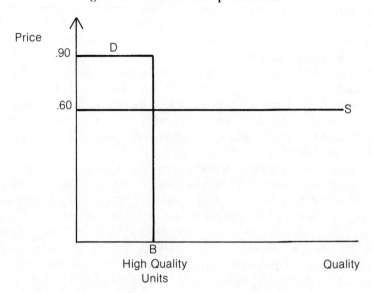

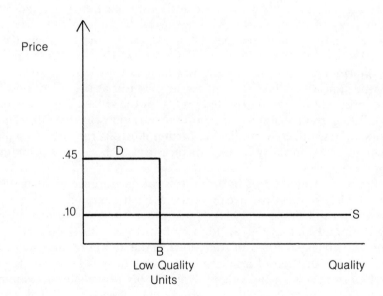

evaluate risky alternatives. This precept has been the subject of extensive laboratory investigation and is admittedly controversial. The recent survey by Schoemaker (1982) gives many instances in which individuals seem to violate some of the axioms underlying expected utility theory. All these violations arise in laboratory investigations of individual choice behavior, and it has yet to be shown that similar behavior results in the rejection of theories that predict *market* equilibrium behavior under uncertainty. To the contrary, the results that are reviewed in the subsequent sections seem remarkably consistent with the predictions of theories, which themselves rely on the expected utility model as their decision-making paradigm.

The vast bulk of experimental research on resource allocation in uncertain environments requires one further assumption beyond this fifth precept regarding each individual trader's specific attitude toward risk. The most common assumption is that all traders are risk-neutral. The validity of this assumption can often be tested directly by the experimenter, since, for example, a model with risk-averse traders will frequently predict results that differ qualitatively from the risk-neutral model. It is interesting, however, that the results of all such tests give an ambiguous body of evidence. In particular, Plott and Wilde (1982) find that "risk aversion is a very significant phenomenon"; also, in considering a large class of first-price auctions, Cox, Roberson, and Smith (1982) reject a risk-neutral bidding model in favor of one where all bidders have constant relative risk aversion. To the contrary, Palfrey and Romer (1984) and DeJong, Forsythe, and Uecker (1984) find that equilibrium models that assume risk-neutral traders outperform ones that assume risk-averse traders, to the extent that the prices observed are consistent with zero expected profits for the sellers. These seemingly conflicting results could well be due to variations in the subject pools used in these different studies but further illustrate the need for a methodology that accurately controls or measures each subject's preferences concerning risk.

Recently, a method of inducing the risk preference of each subject based solely on the above five precepts has been proposed by Berg, Daley, Dickhaut, and O'Brien (1984). Their procedure extends one adopted by Roth and Malouf (1979), Roth and Murningham (1982), and Roth and Schoumaker (1983) to study environments where individuals bargain on the division of a fixed number of lottery tickets. The fraction of lottery tickets an individual obtains is his probability of winning a prespecified prize. Since the expected utility of each individual is linear in these probabilities, and the utilities attached to winning versus not winning the prize can be treated as constants, the expected utility maximization model reduces to one in which each individual acts so as to maximize the probability of winning the prize. That is, if x_1 is the prize, p is the probability of winning the prize and $U(x_1)$ and $U(0)$ are the utilities of winning and not winning the prize, respectively, then the expected utility maximization problem faced by an individual is to choose p so as to maximize

$$U(x_1)p + U(0)(1-p) = [U(x_1) - U(0)]p + U(0)$$

Since $U(x_1) - U(0) > 0$, this is equivalent to maximizing p. With each individual's maximization problem so defined, the authors of these studies are able to make precise equilibrium predictions about the division of the lottery tickets based on alternative bargaining models.

In extending this procedure, Berg et al. (1984) allow for a two-prize lottery with prizes x_1 and x_2, where $x_1 > x_2$. Each subject is told his probability of winning each prize based on the number of "game points" he has accumulated. Let $P(x_1|q)$ and $P(x_2|q) \equiv 1 - P(x_1|q)$ be these probabilities, where $q \epsilon Q$ is the number of game points an individual may possess and Q is the set of possible game points an individual may accumulate. To earn these points, each individual must choose an action a, which determines his probability of receiving a certain number of game points, $f(q|a)$. As with the procedure used by Roth et al., each individual's expected utility maximization problem reduces to one of choosing an action so as to maximize the probability of winning the larger prize, that is, each individual is assumed to choose a so as to maximize

$$_Q\!\int U(x_1)\, P(x_1|q)\, f(q|a)\, dq \,+\, _Q\!\int U(x_2) \{1 - P(x_1|q)\}\, f(q|a)\, dq$$

$$= [U(x_1) - U(x_2)]\, _Q\!\int P(x_1|q)\, f(q|a)\, dq \,+\, U(x_2)$$

and so an individual will be choosing an expected utility maximizing action when he chooses an action, a, to maximize

$$_Q\!\int P(x_1|q)\, f(q|a)\, dq.$$

Thus the assignment of the probability function $P(x_1|q)$ to an individual is equivalent to giving him a utility function defined over points. Further, to induce a subject to act as if he has any particular utility function, $G(q)$, convert it into a legitimate probability function, $P(x_1|q)$, by taking an increasing linear combination of $G(q)$.

While this procedure ensures that it is theoretically possible to induce any risk attitude, we must await some extensive laboratory testing before we can comment on its effectiveness as a method of inducing risk preferences. Quite possibly it may fall victim to the shortcomings found in the investigations of the expected-utility model, since this procedure depends on the validity of that model. Berg et al. (1984) reported on a limited series of paired choice experiments, where subjects were asked which of two lotteries they preferred. The investigators found that 88.3 percent of the choices made correspond to the subject's most preferred lottery, given the risk preferences they induced. Berg et al. also asked subjects to report the minimum they would require to sell each lottery. While the experimenters rejected the null hypothesis of no relationship between the average observed price and the average predicted price, they found that the average price reported by a "risk-averse" trader tended to be systematically higher than the predicted price. Cox, Smith, and Walker (1984) also attempted to use this method to induce risk-neutral behavior among traders in a sealed-bid market for a single object. They also found that subjects tended to systematically bid above the predicted risk-neutral bid. The results of these initial tests are not very encouraging, but a final verdict on this procedure cannot be given until a more extensive set of tests is performed.

The previous section has provided a brief description of laboratory market procedures when there is no exogenous uncertainty. To test models that involve exogenous uncertainty, several additional procedures must be adopted. At the beginning of an experiment, most studies incorporate some form of probability training. The purpose of this is to ensure that subjects are aware of the mechanism being used to determine the outcome randomly and that they have an understanding of how the random draws are being made. To do this, subjects are first given the opportunity to observe a substantial number of draws from a random mechanism such as a bingo cage. Following this, subjects are asked to predict the outcome for some small number of draws; they are paid some small amount (such as a quarter) for guessing correctly and charged a small amount (such as a dime) for guessing incorrectly. (See Plott and Sunder [1982, 1983] for examples of instructions for such training.)

Also, in several experiments run to date, subjects are given "clues" regarding the likelihood of an uncertain outcome and are required to evaluate them (e.g., Plott and Sunder [1983] and Plott and Wilde [1982]). This "clue training" is an attempt to help subjects understand the informational content of the clues. Before beginning the experiment, subjects are told how they will receive clues and again are asked to make predictions based on sample clues they are given. As in the probability-training session, they are paid some small amount for correct predictions and charged some small amount for incorrect predictions.

Following the probability-training and, if necessary, clue-training sessions, the actual laboratory environment may be constructed; subjects then typically receive instructions that inform them of how they will be paid and are given the trading and recording rules they will use. The randomization device is not always used during the actual experiment.

Some studies use preselected random sequences that have been chosen before the experiment begins. There are both major advantages and potential drawbacks associated with the use of these preselected sequences. One advantage is that their use can decrease the time required to run an experiment, especially when a separate independent draw is required for each contract that has been made (see, e.g., DeJong, Forsythe, and Uecker [1984]). Also, a preselected random sequence provides further control over the parameters of the experiment. The sequence of random draws becomes an essential part of the parameter set. When the sequence of random draws is not "representative," control may be lost over the probabilities that subjects are using. An excellent illustration of this can be found in Plott and Aga (1983). In that study, the effect of speculation and carry forward on two sequential markets was studied. The second market was characterized by random demand, in that one of two possible demand curves could result—the "good," or high-demand, state with a two-thirds probability and a "bad," or low-demand, state with a one-third probability. In one of the experiments reported, the good state occurred in all eight market periods. Toward the end of that experiment, the market adjustment was very close to what would be expected if the bad state had a zero probability of occurring. Apparently, the subjects had chosen to ignore the bingo cage and assumed either that the draws were "rigged" or at least had arrived at a posterior distribution that gave rise to this result. There is also some limited evidence that nonrepresentative samples affected the market convergence observed in the studies by DeJong, Forsythe, and Uecker (1984) and Palfrey and Romer (1984).

One potential drawback that may occur using a preselected random sequence is that subjects may not believe the probabilities they have been told, since they do not see a randomization device being used to determine each outcome. As the Plott-Aga experiment points out, this may also result when a randomization device is used for every draw but the sample selected is not representative. If, however, the sequence is representative, subjects will at least find that their sample information is consistent with the distribution they have been told to expect. Another major difficulty will arise if subjects are able to learn that the random sequence they are observing has been preselected. If they are also able to determine the method used to preselect the sequence, they may use this information when making their decisions. For example, suppose subjects are told that there are two states of the world that may occur: state X, which will occur with probability .60, and state Y, which will occur with probability .40. To ensure that the subjects see a representative sample, the experimenter preselects a sequence in which three Xs randomly occur in each group of five outcomes. If subjects are able to

learn this preselection method, then they should learn that the probability of an X or a Y occurring will change as they observe outcomes.
That is, if they observe an X in the first outcome, then they should act
as if either state is equally likely to occur as a second outcome. Further,
after observing the first four outcomes, subjects should know the fifth
outcome with certainty. For subjects to determine the preselection
method being used would, I suspect, require them to be very sophisticated and very experienced. To date, there is no evidence that such
behavior has been observed. In the study by DeJong et al. (1984), subjects
were never shown a randomization device in the entire experiment. They
were seated at computer terminals and told that computers would make
the random selection. These random selections had also been preselected
to ensure their representativeness, and there is no evidence to suggest
that subjects acted on the basis of any probability distribution other than
the one they had been told they would be observing.

IV. EXPERIMENTAL ASSET MARKETS

Theories of asset-price behavior rely on assumptions concerning traders'
subjective beliefs about future price levels. Thus, even in the absence of
exogenous uncertainty, traders are confronted with value uncertainty,
since the value they give an asset depends on the price at which they
may be able to resell the asset in the future. The assumption about
traders' future price expectations typically varies between the two extremes of a prior-information hypothesis on the one hand and a rational-
expectations hypothesis on the other. The prior-information hypothesis
requires that agents act only on the basis of their own private information
and that their expectations are not influenced by the price-formation
process. Alternatively, the rational-expectations hypothesis asserts that
individuals condition their expectations on the prices they observe and,
in turn, these prices aggregate and disseminate the collective information
of all traders.

The expectational theories of asset price have two important dimensions: time and uncertainty. The initial laboratory studies focused on
the role of time and ignored the impact of uncertainty on asset prices.
Without uncertainty, a theory of asset prices consists of a set of difference
equations that relate asset prices and their returns at different dates. In
a finite-time problem, the asset price at each date is determined by a
backward recursion from the price of the following date. The use of this
solution technique assumes that traders correctly anticipate the market
clearing prices in all future time periods. This is the rational-expectations, or, in this case, the perfect-foresight equilibrium model. On the

other hand, the prior-information hypothesis requires that in each period, traders assume that they will be unable to trade in all future periods. Thus traders behave as if any trades they make in the current period will not be revised in future periods. The prior-information hypothesis leads to an autarchic equilibrium, since the equilibrium prices in each period are those that would prevail if the asset market never operated at any point in the future.

The use of experimental methods to study asset markets was initiated by Forsythe, Palfrey, and Plott (1982). In that study, we examined trading behavior in double oral auction markets for assets with two period lives. In these markets, trading took place in a sequence of market years, each of which had two periods, A and B. The monetary returns (dividends) received by each individual were linear in the number of units of the asset held at the end of each period. All traders who held units of the asset at the end of a period received their dividend for that period for each unit of the asset they possessed. Individuals were of different trader "types," where individuals of a given type had identical returns but the returns differed across types.

Consider the parameters given in the following table:

Investor Type	Initial Certificate Holdings	Period A Dividend Value	Period B Dividend Value	Number of Traders
I	2	300	50	3
II	2	50	300	3
III	2	150	250	3

All traders were given a sufficient amount of currency so that there were no effective wealth limitations. Short sales were not permitted. The price prediction, P_E^B, for period B is 300 and is the same for both the prior-information and the perfect-foresight models. Since each individual's wealth limitation was sufficiently large so as never to be binding, this price prediction follows from the application of a demand and supply model since this is the maximum amount any trader type should be willing to pay in period B.

The period A price predictions are more involved, however. Under the prior-information hypothesis, investors do not take any potential future capital gains into account, since they trade only on their private information. Thus, in period A, the most an individual should be willing to pay for any asset is simply the sum of his dividend values in each period. Under the prior-information hypothesis, the period A price prediction, P_N^A, is 400, since individuals of trader type III should be willing

to pay this amount. Alternatively, the perfect-foresight hypothesis requires that all individuals realize that the asset can be traded in period
B for a price of 300 and that they take this into account in their valuations
of the asset in period A. Using this approach, the period A price prediction, P_F^A, is 600. Traders of type I should be willing to pay up to this
amount, since they receive a period A dividend for 300 and correctly
anticipate a resale value of an additional 300.

A typical time path of prices for an asset-market experiment is shown
in Figure 2. In this experiment, the parameters used were those given
above, and it can be seen that with replication, the perfect-foresight
hypothesis is an excellent predictor of the asset-price behavior in these
markets. Interestingly, the prices in these markets seem to begin to
converge toward the prior-information equilibrium until investors receive sufficient information about potential capital gains in period B.
The pattern of convergence in these markets is consistent with the back-
ward-recursion principle discussed above, where the last period converges first and the convergence works back from there to earlier periods
on replication. Examining asset markets with three period market years,
Friedman, Harrison, and Salmon (1984) found that these results continued to hold.

These results show that replication is both necessary and sufficient for
the rational-expectations hypothesis to hold. Because of this, it was natural to ask what institutions might develop to eliminate this need for
replication. An obvious candidate seemed to be a futures market that
could allow information about future prices to be conveyed in the current
period. As hypothesized by Grossman (1978), futures markets can pub-
licize the private information that exists in the economy. In our (Forsythe, Palfrey, and Plott) 1982 study, we examined a single futures
market and found that it did indeed increase the speed at which information about future (period-B) prices was made public and seemed to
eliminate the need for replication.

In Forsythe, Palfrey, and Plott (1984) we turned our attention to a
systematic study of the role of a futures market in environments where
the induced preferences of each trader were nonlinear for the number
of units of the asset held at the end of each period. The preference
structure was changed in order to examine the effect of time-interdependent preferences on the convergence pattern of asset prices. The
linear, or time-independent, preferences used in the previous study give
rise to equilibrium prices in period B that are independent of the trades
that individuals have made in period A. With time-interdependent preferences, period-B equilibrium prices do depend on the individual's final
asset position at the end of period A. Thus individuals who revise their
period-A trading strategies with the expectation that a previously ob-

Figure 2. Experiment 1.

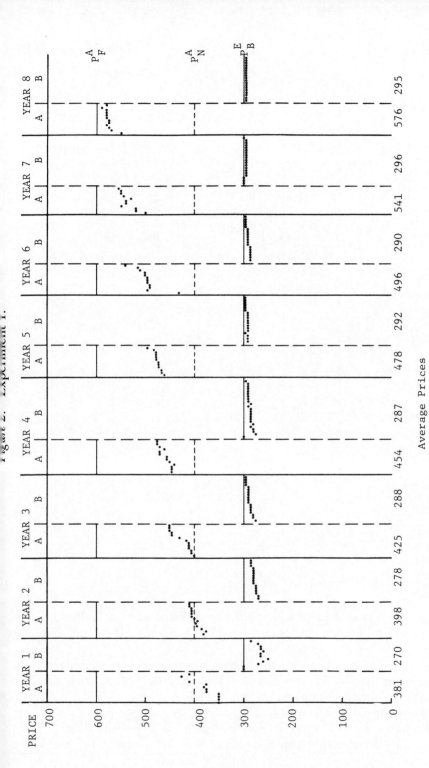

Source: Forsythe, Palfrey and Plott (1982, p. 550).

37

Figure 3.   Experiment 3.

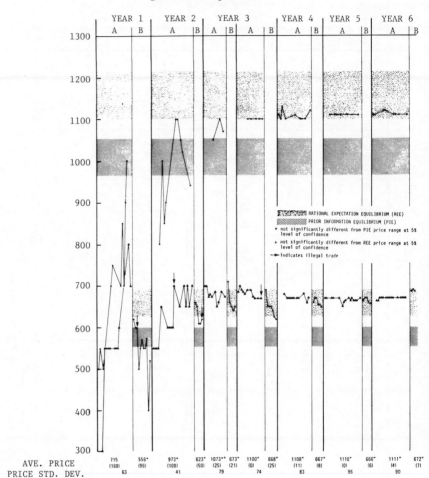

Source: Forsythe, Palfrey and Plott (1984, p. 965).

served period-B price will remain unchanged will generally find that these expectations are not correct unless a rational-expectations equilibrium has already been achieved.

The time paths of asset prices over a sequence of seven market years are displayed in Figures 3 and 4 for one environment with and one without a futures market, respectively. As can be seen in these figures, the existence of a futures market affects spot market prices in general. In particular, a futures market increases the speed with which information about future prices is reflected in spot market prices and, in

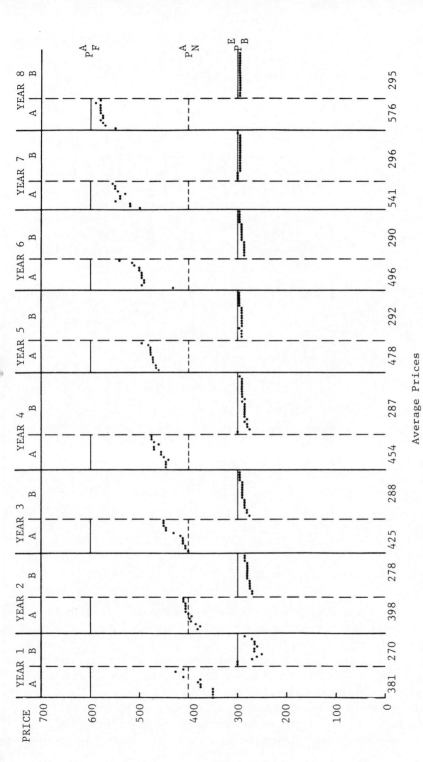

Source: **Forsythe, Palfrey and Plott (1982, p. 550).**

Figure 3.   Experiment 3.

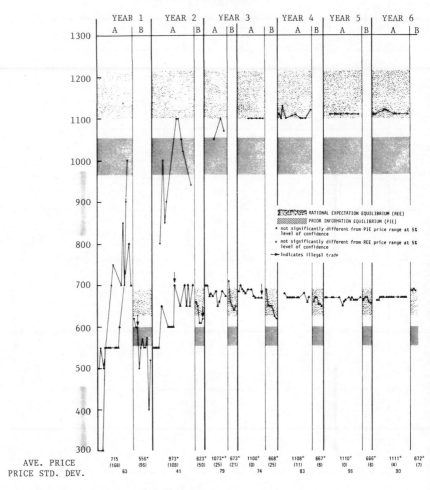

AVE. PRICE
PRICE STD. DEV.

Source: Forsythe, Palfrey and Plott (1984, p. 965).

served period-B price will remain unchanged will generally find that these expectations are not correct unless a rational-expectations equilibrium has already been achieved.

The time paths of asset prices over a sequence of seven market years are displayed in Figures 3 and 4 for one environment with and one without a futures market, respectively. As can be seen in these figures, the existence of a futures market affects spot market prices in general. In particular, a futures market increases the speed with which information about future prices is reflected in spot market prices and, in

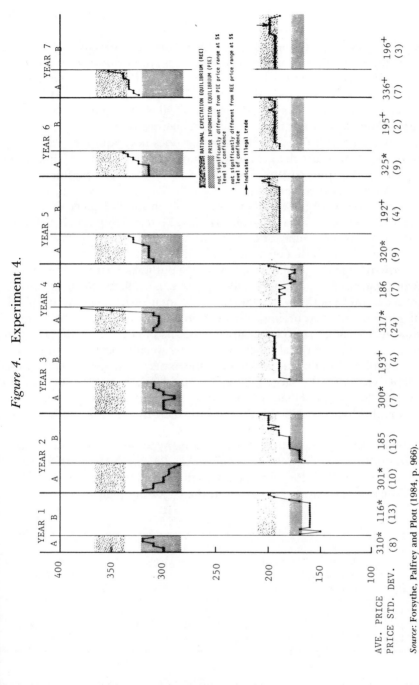

Figure 4. Experiment 4.

Source: Forsythe, Palfrey and Plott (1984, p. 966).

39

doing so, increases the speed with which a perfect-foresight equilibrium is achieved. As in our previous (1982) study, the prior-information hypothesis is accurate in the early market years of the experiment, before individuals have acquired information about period-B prices. As for our previous conjecture that futures markets will eliminate the necessity for replication, such is not the case here. As before, a strict rational-expectations (or perfect-foresight) theory that does not require replication is inconsistent with the data. This is evident from Figure 3, which is quite typical of the time path of asset prices in all of our experiments that incorporate futures markets.

We turn next to the other important dimension in expectational theories of asset-price behavior—uncertainty. Plott and Sunder (1982) studied the asset-price behavior of a one-period lived security whose returns or dividends depended on a randomly drawn state of nature. The prior-information and rational-expectations hypotheses again represent the two polar cases regarding traders' price expectations. With the prior-information hypothesis, traders use only their own subjective probabilities of each state occurring, and assuming they are risk-neutral, a trader should be willing to purchase the asset for any price less than his expected dividend value. In the absence of a binding wealth constraint, the prior-information equilibrium price equals the expected dividend value of the agent type with the largest expected dividend. Even if some traders possess "inside information" and know with certainty which state will occur, this hypothesis states that uninformed traders will not learn this information from either the prices or the quantities traded in the market. To the contrary, the rational-expectations hypothesis states that traders will condition their expectations on market data; in this way, uninformed traders learn the information possessed by insiders.

Consider the parameters given in the following table:

Investor Type	Initial Certificate Holdings	Dividends		Prior Probabilities		Expected Dividends	Number of Traders
		State X	State Y	State X	State Y		
I	2	400	100	.4	.6	220	4
II	2	300	150	.4	.6	210	4
III	2	125	175	.4	.6	155	4

For this example, also assume that one half of each type of investor know with certainty which state will occur. Uninformed traders know that some investors possess information but are not aware of their identities. The fully revealing rational-expectations equilibrium prices are computed on the basis that all investors know (or come to learn) that information, so the rational-expectations hypothesis predicts equilibrium prices of 400 in state X and 175 in state Y. Under the prior-information hypothesis, the demand price for one half of each investor type (the informed traders) will be the actual dividends, and the demand price for the other half (the uninformed traders) will be the expected dividends, computed using the prior probabilities. Using these demand prices, the prior-information hypothesis predicts that in state X, the equilibrium price is 400 and all units of the asset will be purchased by informed type I traders, while in state Y, the equilibrium price is 220 and all units of the asset will be purchased by uninformed type I traders.

The time path of asset prices for a sequence of market prices in an environment using the above parameters is given in Figure 5. In the first two replications of this market, none of the traders was informed and prices were at or near the risk-neutral equilibrium price. In subsequent periods, at least one half of the market received information. It can be seen that with replication, the fully revealing rational-expectations model gives relatively accurate predictions.[6] In these environments, informed traders are told which state will occur or which state will not occur; they are not simply given sample information with which to revise their prior probabilities.[7] As discussed in the previous section, this is due to the inability to control or measure risk preferences and also to the fact that individuals seem to violate systematically Bayes' law when updating their priors (see Grether [1980]).

In two-state environments, the revelation of which state will not occur is equivalent to providing complete information about which state will occur. In light of this, Plott and Sunder (1983) examined three-state environments in which investors received information about which state would not occur. In these situations, no individual was told which state would occur, but one half of each investor type were informed of one of the states that would not occur, while the other half were told of the other state that would not occur. Thus the information present in these markets is sufficient for complete state revelation if the market can aggregate this information and disseminate it across traders.

Under these conditions, the results reported in Plott and Sunder (1983) are a bit perplexing, to say the least. In environments with a complete set of contingent claims[8] or in those in which dividends varied across states but were uniform across all investors, a fully revealing rational-expectations model was again the most accurate. In all other environments, rational-expectations equilibria were not attained.

The time path of prices for a typical experiment is given in Figure 6. Here there is not a complete set of contingent claims, and dividends

Figure 5.

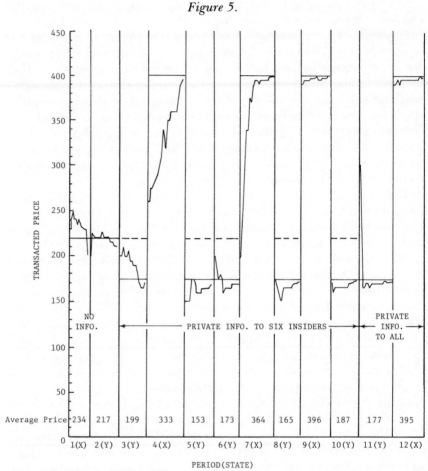

Source: Plott and Sunder (1982, p. 680).

vary across investors. Besides the rational-expectations (RE) and prior-information (PI) equilibrium predictions, a maximin (MM) prediction is also given. The maximin hypothesis states that a trader will not purchase the asset unless its price is less than the smallest possible dividend value that trader would receive given his prior information. Most astonishingly, both the MM and PI predictions outperform the RE prediction on the basis of the mean absolute deviation of the actual prices from the predicted price for most of these environments, including the one demonstrated in the figure.

The obvious open question that remains here is: Why does the rational-expectations hypothesis fare so badly in this class of environments? One explanation is that these markets are very slow to adjust and that, given

Figure 6. Market 10 transaction prices.

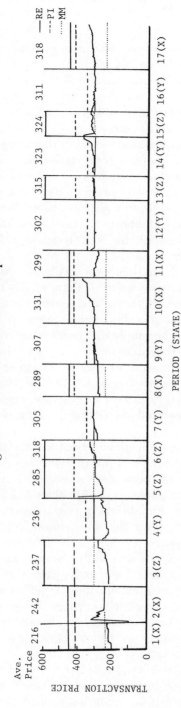

Source: Plott and Sunder (1983).

43

more replications, the prices would converge in the rational-expectations predictions. This may indeed occur, but in some of the price data, such as those presented in Figure 6, there are no signs of such movement and, in this particular market, the prices seem to have converged to a single price that is independent of the information present in the market.

Alternatively, it seems that the ability of traders to infer the true state based on the data is at least hampered in these single security markets. In environments with complete contingent claim trading this inference is made relatively easy, since traders, who are aware that a particular state will not occur, drive the price of the corresponding contingent claim to zero by their aggressive attempts to sell that security. Similarly, when all traders receive identical returns, if their initial belief is that the returns are, in fact, identical, that belief is quickly substantiated. Further, they then can learn the rational-expectations equilibrium price-state correspondence directly from their own dividend valuations.

In all other environments investors seem unable to learn how to infer the true state from the sequence of transaction prices they observe and arrive at the corresponding rational-expectations price for that state. On the other hand, it may be simply that individuals are slow to disentangle these two processes; they may need to observe the equilibrium price-state correspondence in order to learn how to infer the true state, while at the same time they must correctly infer the true state if the market is to reveal the equilibrium price-state correspondence. To help in disentangling these processes and to facilitate learning, these security markets could be analyzed in the context of two-period markets. In the first period, traders receive information about which state will not occur and can make trades on the basis of this information. At the end of the first period, the true state of the world is announced, the security market is reopened, and traders can again adjust their holdings. In this way, individuals can learn the equilibrium price-state correspondence from this second-period market. Given this information, individuals, who are able to infer the true state from prices in the first period, can pursue any arbitrage opportunities that arise in that period. This procedure permits a direct test of the market's ability to aggregate and disseminate information when the rational-expectations equilibrium price-state correspondence is common knowledge. Further, this procedure also gives the rational-expectations hypothesis its best chance. If the hypothesis fails to work in this environment, its relevancy in more complex environments can certainly be challenged.

In a recent paper, Sunder (1984) has returned to examine two-state environments in which information about which state will occur is not costlessly given to some individuals, but instead, traders have an opportunity to purchase information. He examined two different types of markets for information. In the first, there was a fixed supply of information. At the beginning of each market period, traders were asked to submit sealed bids for the information about which state would occur. The four (out of twelve) highest bidders received the information and paid the fifth highest price. As the rational-expectations hypothesis would predict, the price of information converged toward zero as asset prices converged toward the fully revealing rational-expectations price.

Sunder also examined an information market where the price of information was held fixed. Initially, a number of traders purchased the information, but, after they learned to infer the state from market prices, most traders no longer purchased. At that point, a state-price indeterminacy was observed.[9] In particular, when too few traders purchased information, the observed asset prices moved toward the rational-expectations price for the wrong state.

Two other recent studies have begun to examine asset-price behavior in markets where uncertainty is present and no trader has any "inside" information about which future states will occur. Coursey and Dyl (1984) constructed laboratory asset markets in which the asset traded earned an uncertain "dividend" at the end of each trading period. Within each market they examine, the life of the asset varied from one to two periods. In the one-period case, the dividend received by traders who hold the asset at the end of the period was determined by a single random draw. In the two-period case, the market was not reopened in the second period. Traders who held units of the asset at the end of the first period simply continued to hold those units in the second period. These traders received dividends in both periods based on the outcome of two independent and identically distributed random draws from the same probability distribution that was used in the one-period case. In three of the four markets they examined, Coursey and Dyl observed that the price for a two-period lived asset was significantly greater than twice the price of the one-period lived asset. In the fourth market, the reverse was true— the price of the two-period lived asset was significantly less than twice the price of the one-period lived asset. They conclude that these observations may be related to the so-called weekend effect that is observed in empirical studies of daily common stock returns. The empirical result is that the returns on a common stock on the last trading day of a week are significantly higher than the average daily returns.

In a preliminary report, Smith, Suchanek, and Williams (1984) reopened the question of the role of replication in a model of asset-price behavior. They examined computerized auction markets that were open for 15 periods each; in each period, traders could exchange rights to an asset that would yield them a random return according to a known, fixed distribution. Using inexperienced traders, the investigators observed price bubbles sometime during the first 10 market periods. In this study, a bubble was said to occur whenever the asset sold for a price in excess of its market value. This is consistent with risk-seeking behavior on the part of the traders. In the markets examined, the bubble burst between periods 10 and 15, resulting in a price crash or steady price decline to or below the asset's expected value. Further, when experienced traders were used in similar markets, the size and duration of the bubbles observed declined. These results again suggest that replication is necessary for the rational-expectations hypothesis to hold. As opposed to the findings of Forsythe, Palfrey and Plott (1982, 1984), where asset-price behavior was initially consistent with the prior-information hypothesis, the results of Smith, Suchanek, and Williams' study appear to be consistent with the "castles-in-the-air" description first introduced by Keynes (1936).

In summary, the laboratory provides a rich and promising environment for examining the behavior of asset prices. Such examinations in turn allow us to test the various expectational hypotheses found in the literature regarding how individuals use information in forming expectations and also their ability to acquire information by observing market data. The studies reviewed here consider only a number of highly stylized situations. Some extensions should be relatively straightforward. For example, one might wish to examine how the above results change when trades must be made through a system of specialists or market-makers (as utilized by most organized security exchanges) rather than in a double oral auction market. In particular, one might ask whether specialists impede or enhance the information aggregation and dissemination process. Other questions, such as those involving individuals' use of probabilistic signals or clues regarding which state will occur, may have to wait until a technique for adequately controlling and/or measuring risk attitudes is developed.

V. EXPERIMENTAL MARKETS WITH ASYMMETRIC INFORMATION

Much attention has recently been focused on markets in which there are informational asymmetries where, for example, the seller knows the quality of his product but the buyer does not. The nature of equilibrium in these models depends on buyers' expectations about the quality of the product they are purchasing. In this regard, the rational-expectations hypothesis plays a critical role in many of these models, since buyers are assumed to know the frequency with which sellers deliver different quality levels. Further, as Wilson (1980) has shown, the equilibrium predictions in this class of models are very sensitive to the price-setting convention adopted by the agents in the market. Because of this sensitivity, the laboratory provides an ideal environment for distinguishing between competing equilibrium predictions in alternative institutional settings, based on competing behavioral or expectational assumptions.

Many of the existing theories show that informational asymmetries can lead to certain types of market failure. Beginning with the seminal study by George Akerlof (1970) of the used-car, or "lemons," market, economic theories have been constructed showing that buyers' inability to observe quality prior to purchase would cause all high-quality items to be driven from the market and would lead to only the lowest-quality items being traded. It was also thought that this result stemmed from the inability of price alone to reflect quality and serve a market-clearing function simultaneously. While these types of models based on informational asymmetries have remained popular with theorists, what empirical evidence exists to demonstrate the existence of lemons? In many of the theoretical models, including Akerlof's, the quality of the product is given to each seller, so even if he so desired, a seller cannot offer a higher-quality item. Will sellers continue to provide low-quality items when they can choose which quality level to produce, or will a concern for their reputation eliminate the lemons phenomenon? Second, these models assume that buyers know the quality of an item immediately after purchase. Will these results change if the goods being transacted possess hidden characteristics?

One remedy to the informational inefficiencies that arise in these markets is product-quality signaling, as first suggested by Spence (1974). Here a signal is some characteristic other than price, which sellers can select and buyers can observe prior to purchasing the good. In this setting, a signaling equilibrium is a situation in which buyers' beliefs about the relationship between product quality and the signal are confirmed by the buyer's purchases in the market. In markets in which signaling possibilities are present, there is not only the opportunity for multiple Nash equilibria to occur, but there have also been several definitions of equilibrium proposed (see Riley [1979] and Wilson [1977]). These possibilities make this a ripe area for laboratory study, and such an initial examination was undertaken by Miller and Plott (1985).

In their study of eleven double oral auction markets in which signaling opportunities existed, Miller and Plott observed a variety of outcomes and were unable to find a single model that accounted for the behavior in all markets. In particular, they did observe signaling equilibria in which the signals effectively separated the different quality types. However, pooling equilibria also occurred. In this type of equilibrium, the sellers' signals do not identify quality, so buyers must treat any purchase as a lottery.[10] In an attempt to suggest which environmental or institutional characteristics influenced the type of equilibrium that was observed, Miller and Plott (1985) found that the occurrence of signaling equilibria increased as they lowered the cost of signaling a high-quality unit relative to that of signaling a low-quality unit. They also found that signaling equilibria occurred more often after they adopted procedures for recording the data during the experiment in such a way as to call attention to the relationship between quality and the signal. This suggests that institutions that affect the public nature of the signal will have an impact on which type of equilibrium occurs. Clearly, further studies are needed in order to identify systematically those characteristics of a market environment that have significant impacts on the nature of the equilibrium that results.

In the Miller and Plott (1985) study, sellers were randomly endowed at the beginning of each period with units of a given quality. Sellers could not choose their own quality level, nor did they necessarily have any incentive to take repeat sales into account and attempt to gain a reputation. In markets in which a seller can choose the quality level of the good he is producing, the lemons phenomenon may be partially mitigated or even eliminated. This would result either if sellers find it profitable to maintain a reputation for honesty or if they develop some instrument, such as warranties, with which to signal the quality of their product. Should reputation effects fail to develop or warranties not be offered, alternative forms of market intervention might be considered in order to eliminate the informational inefficiency.

Environments in which the possibility of lemons existed were the object of two separate and independent investigations by Lynch et al. (1984) and DeJong et al. (1984). Lynch et al. examined double oral auction markets in which the quality of a product offered by the seller is not observable by the buyer prior to purchase but is completely revealed to the buyer after the purchase. Alternatively, in DeJong et al., products were sold via a computerized sealed-offer auction and possessed "credence" qualities of the sort first identified by Darby and Karni (1973). Such types of commodity or service arise naturally in the course of a principal-agent relationship of the form we have considered. In particular, if the principal is unable to monitor the agent's action and cannot observe the actual state of nature that occurs, he can never be sure that his receipt of a low return is the result of the agent's shirking (i.e., his delivery of a lemon) or is in fact due to an unfortunate occurrence of a state of nature. As Darby and Karni argued, market failure appears to be more likely in these situations.

Both studies conclude that the lemons phenomenon can indeed occur. In particular, when buyers are unaware of which seller they are pur-

Figure 7. Lemon market 1.

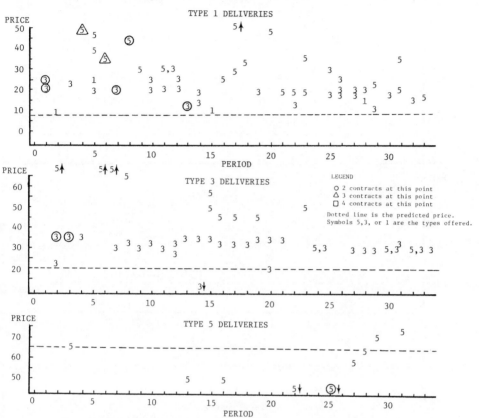

Source: DeJong, Forsythe, Lundholm and Uecker (1984).

chasing from, the lemons phenomenon occurred in 96 percent of all sales in the markets studied by Lynch et al. Interestingly, both studies found that when buyers know the identity of the seller they purchase from, the lemons phenomenon still occurs but less frequently. When specific information about seller performance is publicly announced (either costlessly as in Lynch et al. or at a cost to a buyer as in DeJong et al.), the frequency of lemons is further reduced. These results suggest that sellers are attempting to form reputations (or are at least concerned about them). While this seems to mitigate partially the informational inefficiency that results in a market for lemons, it does not totally eliminate the inefficiency.

To illustrate these effects, two of the markets we studied in DeJong et al. are presented in Figures 7 and 8. In these markets, each principal (buyer) was given $1.30 at the beginning of each market period but knew

Figure 8. Reputation market 1.

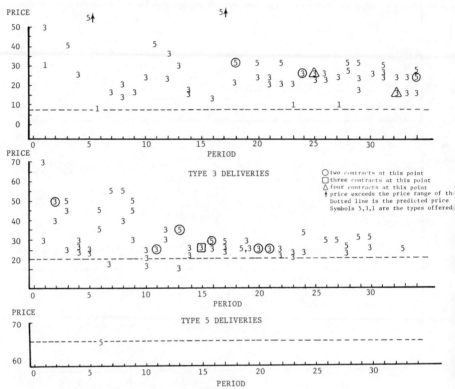

TYPE 1 DELIVERIES

Source: DeJong, Forsythe, Lundholm and Uecker (1984).

that if he did not hire an agent (seller) during the period he would lose $.80 with certainty. If he did hire an agent, he might still incur an $.80 loss, but the probability of that loss occurring depended on the quality of service provided by the agent. The probability of loss associated with each quality level and each agent's cost of providing each level of service are given in the following table:

Level of Quality	Probability of Loss	Expected Loss	Cost of Service
No purchase	1.0	80¢	—
1	.8	64¢	8¢
3	.5	40¢	20¢
5	.1	8¢	65¢

In the markets illustrated in Figures 7 and 8, there were four principals and three agents. These individuals participated in a sealed-offer auction in which each agent could offer a particular quality of service to each principal at a specified price. After each principal decided which agent, if any, was to be hired, agents were paid their offer price and then asked what quality of service they were actually going to provide. This decision determined the agent's cost of providing this level of service and the probability of the $.80 loss occurring to the principal.

For the parameters given above, the efficient quality level of service is quality level 3 if all principals are risk-neutral, since each risk-neutral principal should be willing to pay $.80 less the expected loss for each level of service. The expected surplus for each level of service is computed by subtracting the agent's cost of providing this level of service from the principal's willingness to pay. This gives an expected surplus of $.08, $.20 and $.07 for quality levels 1, 3, and 5, respectively. Thus level 3 is the efficient level of service, since it yields the largest surplus.

In Figures 7 and 8, the entire time series of transacted prices and quality levels (both offered and delivered) are presented. Each figure is organized into three panels, with each panel displaying the time series of deliveries of each particular quality type; that is, type 1, type 3, or type 5. The symbols (1, 3, and 5) on each panel correspond to the quality types that were offered. Principals could only observe whether or not a loss occurred and not what quality level of service had been delivered in the market presented in Figure 7. Here the lemons phenomenon also occurs, but only in 52 percent of all sales. The fact that this frequency is significantly less than 100 percent is consistent with the hypothesis that agents are concerned about their reputations. To further examine this hypothesis, the data presented in Figure 8 concern a market in which principals had an opportunity to investigate an agent, whenever a loss occurred, to learn the actual level of service provided. To do this, a principal had to agree to pay an investigation cost (32 cents), and the outcome of the investigation was made public to all market participants. A visual examination of the markets presented in the two figures clearly indicates the decrease in the number of lemons delivered when public information about the quality of service provided is publicly announced. Second, the fact that the principals investigated over 10 percent of the losses is evidence of their concern about the agents' reputations and also seems to serve to reinforce each agent's awareness.

In the first market, one principal-agent pair repeatedly contracted with each other in periods 7 through 21, 24, and 27 through 32. In each of these instances, the agent offered and delivered a type 3 quality product at a price between 28 and 35 cents. This price exceeded the competitive price prediction by 8 to 15 cents and seems consistent with the notion of a quality-assuring price as presented by Klein and Leffler (1981). This notion is that reputable sellers will receive a premium for their sales. This premium, the authors argue, is not driven to zero as other reputable sellers enter the market. Instead, sellers perceive that they must incur reputation-building costs in order to earn this premium. These costs result from the requirement that they can build a reputation for quality only by offering high-quality products at low-quality prices. In equilibrium, the present value of this reputation-building strategy must be zero. Further evidence in support of the theory offered by Klein and Leffler can be seen in the market for type 5s in Figure 7. All sales and deliveries of items with this quality level from period 22 onward are made by the same agent. This agent seems to be pursuing a reputation-building strategy, since the initial sales are well below the agent's cost of providing that level of service. Eventually, the agent is able to sell at a premium over cost in an attempt to recoup some of his earlier losses.

The difficulty of applying the reputation models of Klein and Leffler and others that exist in the literature is that they all rely on an infinite horizon, whereas all subjects know that a laboratory market will last only for a short, finite time, although they are unaware of the stopping rule. The hypothesized inability to generate a reputation effect in a finite-time model relies on a backward induction argument. That is, in the final period, profit-maximizing sellers will deliver only lemons. Buyers are assumed to be aware of this and thus do not use sellers' performance in the next-to-last period as an indicator of what they will deliver in the final period. Sellers are aware that their deliveries in the next-to-last period have no effect on their reputation and thus deliver lemons in that period also. This argument is then used to demonstrate that sellers will deliver lemons two periods from the end, and so forth, until it is argued that an equilibrium requires that lemons be delivered in all periods by all sellers.

The fact that reputation effects were observed in both of the above studies indicates that this backward induction model is not applicable to the laboratory environments that have been examined. The backward induction model is somewhat reminiscent of Grossman's (1978) argument, discussed in the previous section—that replication is necessary for the attainment of a rational-expectations equilibrium. In particular, it seems likely that three or more replications of a three-period lived economy would be necessary before all sellers would deliver lemons in every period. Just as in the asset-market environments previously discussed, where final-year prices had to be observed before being incorporated into subjects' decision rules in earlier periods, buyers may well have to observe that sellers deliver only lemons in the final period before they cease using observations about sellers' performances in the next-to-last period to infer what those sellers are likely to do in the last period. Further, sellers would then have to become aware that their behavior in this period will not affect their reputation in the final period before beginning to deliver lemons in this earlier period. Thus replications of finite-lived economies may be necessary to yield a pattern of convergence consistent with the backward induction argument discussed above, where the last period converges first and the convergence works back from there. The accuracy of this conjecture will have to await further laboratory analysis.

In addition, the theory proposed by Kreps et al. (1982) is applicable here. They consider a repeated version of a prisoners' dilemma game and show that if a prisoner believes there is some positive probability that his opponent may cooperate, he should play a tit-for-tat strategy. Using this strategy, a prisoner should cooperate until he observes his opponent not cooperating and then retaliate by not cooperating. Similar strategies seem to be employed here, where sellers do not deliver lemons (i.e., they cooperate) to the extent that buyers take the sellers' past performance into account when deciding on repeat purchases. The experiments run to date are not amenable to providing a direct test of the theory proposed by Kreps et al but the results seem to be consistent with it. Hopefully, further tests will be provided at some later date.

Since reputation effects fail to eliminate lemons completely, both studies consider alternative remedies. Lynch et al (1984) examine the effect of warranties that are perfectly and costlessly enforceable. These warranties eliminate the occurrence of lemons and serve as a very effective remedy.

Also, in the DeJong et al. study we imposed a negligence liability rule on the environment discussed earlier in this section. In particular, agents (sellers) were prohibited from offering service of quality level 1, but they could deliver this level of service. If they did deliver a type-1 level of service and a loss occurred and if the principal (buyer) investigated the agent's performance and discovered this, the agent was ruled negligent and forced to reimburse the buyer for the loss. As before, the principal had to pay an investigation cost to discover the actual quality delivered by the agent, and the outcomes of all investigations were made public to all market participants. In these markets, less than 5 percent of all sales were lemons. The number of investigations observed in these markets was remarkably high, especially given that agents were delivering very few lemons. These investigations seemed to reinforce the sellers' concern for their reputations and almost completely eliminated the occurrence of lemons. The effect of the public announcement of the outcome in the presence of a negligence liability rule was also examined. When the outcome of the investigation was revealed only to the principal who initiated the investigation, the frequency of lemons delivered increased to almost 20 percent.

Two recent studies by Plott and Wilde (1982) and Pitchik and Schotter (1984) examine seller-diagnostic markets. In these markets, as in the markets for automobile repairs or physicians' services, a prospective buyer could request a diagnosis from the seller, who would receive information about the buyer's condition and then could make a recommendation about the type of repair the buyer should purchase. As in all of the above studies, the Akerlof model gives rise to the "big lie" hypothesis, which predicts that dishonest opinions will drive out honest ones. In these studies there were two possible repair recommendations—major and minor. Sellers' costs were such that they had an incentive to "push" major repairs. Thus, given the differential profits on the two types of repairs, the Akerlof model predicts that only major repairs will be recommended.

In the Plott and Wilde experiments, transactions were made via a semiposted price institution. Prior to providing a customer with a diagnostic recommendation, each seller posted prices for both types of repair; if the customer made a purchase, it was at the posted price. Sellers were free to change prices among customers. When a buyer requested a recommendation, the seller received uncertain information in the form of a clue about the buyer's need for a repair. Buyers could either purchase a repair (of either type) from the seller or choose to visit another seller. Plott and Wilde found no evidence in support of the big lie hypothesis. Sellers' advice was definitely related to the clues and did not change even after the supply curve for major repairs was shifted so as to decrease the price for major repairs.

Pitchik and Schotter examined the big lie hypothesis in a different environment. Both competent and incompetent sellers were present in their markets. A competent seller received perfect information all the time about the type of repair needed by a buyer, while an incompetent seller received perfect information some predetermined percentage of the time. At the beginning of each period, sellers were asked to select the fraction of the time they wished to provide honest recommendations based on their information about buyer's conditions. Since their markets were computerized, the computer used this fraction along with information on a buyer's condition to generate each seller's recommendations to a buyer who requested a diagnosis during the period. As before, a recommendation was limited to two possible repair types—major and minor. Buyers were charged a search cost for each diagnosis they requested, and prices for both types of repair were fixed by the experimenters. The use of fixed prices here is troublesome, since no evidence can be gathered regarding sellers' incentive to lie as these markets converge to an equilibrium. If sellers' profits converge to zero in equilibrium, they may well decide to recommend only major repairs. Pitchik and Schotter also found no evidence in support of the big lie hypothesis, although some sizable levels of dishonesty were observed. Further, no significant differences in honesty levels existed between competent and incompetent sellers.

In summary, a great many questions remain about the occurrence of the lemons phenomena. Why does it occur in the markets studied by Lynch et al. and DeJong et al. but not in those studied by Plott and Wilde and Pitchik and Schotter? Is it because of the differences in market organization and trading rules used in the various studies? Insofar as a sellers' concern about his reputation may inhibit him from supplying lemons, what forms of market organization will enhance this reputation effect? What alternative institutions will lessen or eliminate the number of lemons in the market? Do these institutions actually increase market efficiency in addition to preventing good products from driving out bad? How do these results change when the commodities being transacted have credence qualities or hidden characteristics that buyers may not observe even after purchase?

VI. CONCLUDING REMARKS

Laboratory methods have been used to examine two other environments in which asymmetric information and uncertainty are present. The first examines the theory and behavior of single-object auctions and has been included in Smith's (1982) survey. Uncertainty enters each bidder's problem, since he is unaware of the values all other bidders place on the object for sale. The works of Coppinger, Smith, and Titus (1980); Cox, Roberson, and Smith (1982); and Cox, Smith, and Walker (1983) represent a fairly extensive set of studies on common forms of oral and sealed-bid auctions.

The other environment examines many of the hypotheses that exist in the literature on equilibrium-search models. This work, begun by Schotter and Braunstein (1981) and Grether, Schwartz, and Wilde (1984), examines how buyers and sellers behave in the presence of costly information. In particular, the latter study finds that the equilibrium price dispersion that a number of theoretical models predict seems to occur in the laboratory markets examined. This research has demonstrated a methodology for constructing laboratory markets for examining search behavior, and future studies in this area should be able to examine the robustness of a number of competing models that appear in the literature.

In summary, theories based on the rational-expectations hypothesis have exhibited a considerable amount of success when value uncertainty is present. This hypothesis is not without its difficulties, however. In particular, it seems to require replication; because of this it may apply only to environments that exhibit some amount of stationarity. Further, the study by Plott and Sunder (1983) casts more doubt on the robustness of the rational-expectations model even in the presence of replication. At this point in time, it is appropriate to design a set of boundary experiments to establish the limits on the generality of this hypothesis.

When asymmetric information is present in markets, the lemons phenomenon, as hypothesized by Akerlof (1970), can and does occur. This phenomenon is at least partially mitigated when buyers can acquire information about the reliability of individual sellers. Even in the finite-horizon environment of the laboratory, traders are concerned with their reputations. Additional work is necessary to understand how different market institutions (e.g., trading rules, warranty provisions, liability rules) assist in enhancing the reputation-formation process to the extent that the lemons phenomenon is eliminated.

Finally, the use of laboratory markets to study environments characterized by value uncertainty seems quite promising. This methodology appears to provide a fruitful means for collecting evidence with which to test competing theories of expectation formation. There is also a growing body of evidence that market institutions can effect this expectation formation process. To capture these elements, current theories will have to be restructured and subjected to further laboratory testing.

ACKNOWLEDGMENT

I would like to thank Elizabeth Hoffman, Darryl Jenkins, Russell Lundholm, Ross Miller, Vernon Smith, and Matthew Spitzer for their many helpful comments on an earlier draft of this paper.

NOTES

1. Social Science Research Council, *Items*, 34 (March 1980), pp. 6–7.
2. For several examples of this, see Smith (1982), pp. 932–933.
3. See the studies by Coppinger, Smith, and Titus (1980) and Cox, Roberson, and Smith (1982) for complete details on English, Dutch, and sealed-bid auctions.
4. One-sided auctions were first studied by Smith (1964), who found that the path of convergence to equilibrium was from above (below) in a one-sided bid (offer) auction. Thus the side of the market that articulates terms receives an unfavorable distribution of income.

5. See the studies by Smith (1967), Belovicz (1979); Gary Miller and Plott (1985); and Smith, Williams, Bratton, and Vannoni (1982) for further details about different forms of sealed-bid (offer) auctions.

6. Plott and Sunder (1982) held the set of informed traders constant throughout the life of the market. Banks (1984) replicated these results when the set of informed traders was varied from period to period.

7. An exception to this is the first experiment reported in Plott and Sunder (1982). There, certain traders were given less than certain information about which state would occur, and the market failed to converge to a risk-neutral rational expectations equilibrium.

8. A contingent claim is a security that returns a positive amount if a certain state occurs; otherwise it earns zero. A complete set of contingent claims is present when there is a contingent claim corresponding to each state that might occur.

9. Grossman (1976), Beja (1976), and Milgrom (1981) have all pointed out the potential for this state-price indeterminacy. Once individuals learn that price is a sufficient statistic for the state of nature, they either ignore or do not purchase any private information. Without this information, any of the previously fully revealing rational-expectations prices are possible and the equilibrium price no longer reveals the state.

10. These equilibria also require that buyers have rational expectations insofar as the probabilities they use to value the lottery are equal to the proportions of quality types delivered by sellers.

REFERENCES

Akerlof, George A., "The Market for 'Lemons': Quality Uncertainty and the Market Mechanism," *Quarterly Journal of Economics*, 84 (August 1970), 488–500.

Banks, Jeffrey S., "Price-Conveyed Information vs. Observed Insider Behavior: A Note on Rational Expectations Convergence," *Journal of Political Economy*, 93 (August 1985), 807–815.

Beja, Avraham, "The Limited Information Efficiency of Market Processes." Working Paper 43, University of California, Berkeley, 1976.

Belovicz, Meyer W., "Sealed-Bid Auctions: Experimental Results and Applications," in Vernon L. Smith, ed., *Research in Experimental Economics*, Vol. 1. Greenwich, CT: JAI Press, 1979, 279–338.

Berg, Joyce E., Lane A. Daley, John W. Dickhaut, and John R. O'Brien, "Controlling Preferences for Lotteries on Units of Experimental Exchange." Working Paper 1983-5, School of Management, University of Minnesota, February 1984.

Coppinger, Vickie M., Vernon L. Smith, and Jon A. Titus, "Incentives and Behavior in English, Dutch and Sealed-Bid Auctions," *Economic Inquiry*, 18 (January 1980), 1–22.

Coursey, Don L., and Edward A. Dyl, "Price Effects of Trading Interruptions in an Experimental Market." Mimeo, University of Wyoming, September 1984.

Cox, James C., Bruce Roberson, and Vernon L. Smith, "Theory and Behavior of Single Object Auctions," in Vernon L. Smith, ed., *Research in Experimental Economics*, Vol. 2. Greenwich, CT: JAI Press, 1982, pp. 1–44.

Cox, James C., Vernon L. Smith, and James M. Walker, "A Test that Discriminates between Two Models of the Dutch-First Auction Non-Isomorphism," *Journal of Economic Behavior and Organization*, 4 (September 1983), 205–219.

———. "Experimental Development of Sealed Bid Auction Theory; Calibrating Controls for Risk Aversion." Mimeo, University of Arizona, 1984.

Darby, Michael and Edi Karni, "Free Competition and the Optimal Amount of Fraud," *Journal of Law and Economics*, 16 (April 1973), 67–88.

DeJong, Douglas V., Robert Forsythe, Russell J. Lundholm, and Wilfred C. Uecker, "A Laboratory Investigation of the Moral Hazard Problem in Agency Relationships." Mimeo, University of Iowa, November 1984.

DeJong, Douglas V., Robert Forsythe, and Wilfred C. Uecker, "The Methodology of Laboratory Markets and its Implications for Agency Research in Accounting and Auditing." Working Paper 84-4A, University of Iowa, July 1984 (*Journal of Accounting Research*, forthcoming).

Forsythe, Robert, Thomas R. Palfrey, and Charles R. Plott, "Asset Valuation in an Experimental Market," *Econometrica*, 50 (May 1982), 537–567.

Forsythe, Robert, Thomas R. Palfrey, and Charles R. Plott, "Futures Markets and Informational Efficiency: A Laboratory Examination," *Journal of Finance*, 39 (September 1984), 955–981.

Friedman, Daniel, Glenn W. Harrison, and Jon W. Salmon, "The Informational Efficiency of Experimental Asset Markets," *Journal of Political Economy*, 92 (June 1984), 349–408.

Grether, David M., "Bayes Rule as a Descriptive Model: The Representativeness Heuristic," *Quarterly Journal of Economics*, 95 (November 1980), 537–557.

Grether, David M. and Charles R. Plott, "The Effects of Market Practices in Oligopolistic Markets: An Experimental Examination of the Ethyl Case." Working Paper 404, California Institute of Technology, October 1981.

Grether, David M., Alan Schwartz, and Louis L. Wilde, "Uncertainty and Shopping Behavior: An Experimental Analysis." Working Paper 511, California Institute of Technology, March 1984.

Grossman, Sanford J., "On the Efficiency of Competitive Stock Markets Where Traders Have Diverse Information," *Journal of Finance*, 31 (May 1976), 573–585.

Grossman, Sanford J., "Further Results on the Informational Efficiency of Competitive Stock Markets," *Journal of Economic Theory*, 18 (June 1978), 81–101.

Hong, James T. and Charles R. Plott, "Rate Filing Policies for Inland Water Transportation: An Experimental Approach," *Bell Journal of Economics*, 13 (Spring 1982), 1–19.

Keynes, John M., *The General Theory of Employment, Interest and Money*. New York: Harcourt Brace, 1936.

Klein, Benjamin and Keith B. Leffler, "Non-Governmental Enforcement of Contracts: The Role of Market Forces in Guaranteeing Quality," *Journal of Political Economy*, 89 (August 1981), 615–641.

Kreps, David M., Paul Milgrom, John Roberts, and Robert Wilson, "Rational Cooperation in the Finitely Repeated Prisoners' Dilemma," *Journal of Economic Theory*, 27 (August 1982), 245–252.

Lynch, Michael, Ross M. Miller, Charles R. Plott, and Russell Porter, "Product Quality, Informational Efficiency, and Regulations in Experimental Markets." Working Paper 518, California Institute of Technology, March 1984.

Milgrom, Paul, "Rational Expectations, Information Acquisition and Competitive Bidding," *Econometrica*, 49 (July 1981), 921–944.

Miller, Gary J., and Charles R. Plott, "Revenue Generating Properties of Sealed-Bid Auctions: An Experimental Analysis of One-Price and Discriminative Processes," in Vernon L. Smith, ed., *Research in Experimental Economics*, Vol. 3, Greenwich, CT: JAI Press, 1985.

Miller, Ross M. and Charles R. Plott, "Product Quality Signalling in Experimental Markets," *Econometrica*, 53 (July 1985), 837–872.

Palfrey, Thomas R. and Thomas Romer, "An Experimental Study of Warranty Coverage and Dispute Resolution in Competitive Markets." Working Paper 34-83-84, Carnegie-Mellon University, April 1984.

Pitchik, Carolyn and Andrew Schotter, "The 'Big Lie' Hypothesis in Markets With Asymmetric Information: An Experimental Study." Working Paper 83–29, New York University, November 1983.

Plott, Charles R., "The Application of Laboratory Experimental Methods to Public Choice," in C. S. Russell, ed., *Collective Decision Making: Applications from Public Choice Theory.* Baltimore: Resources for the Future, 1979, pp. 137–169.

Plott, Charles R., "Industrial Organization Theory and Experimental Economics," *Journal of Economic Literature*, 20 (December 1982), 1485–1527.

Plott, Charles R. and Gul Aga, "Intertemporal Speculation With a Random Demand in an Experimental Market," in Reinhard Tietz, ed., *Aspiration Levels in Bargaining and Economic Decision Making.* Berlin, Germany: Springer-Verlag, 1983.

Plott, Charles R. and Vernon L. Smith, "An Experimental Examination of Two Exchange Institutions," *Review of Economic Studies*, 45 (February 1978), 133-153.

Plott, Charles R. and Shyam Sunder, "Efficiency of Experimental Security Markets with Insider Information: An Application of Rational Expectations Models," *Journal of Political Economy*, 90 (August 1982), 663–698.

Plott, Charles R. and Shyam Sunder, "Rational Expectations and the Aggregation of Diverse Information in Laboratory Security Markets." Working Paper 463, California Institute of Technology, January 1983.

Plott, Charles R. and Louis L. Wilde, "Professional Diagnosis vs. Self-Diagnosis: An Experimental Examination of Some Special Features of Markets With Uncertainty," in Vernon L. Smith, ed., *Research in Experimental Economics*, Vol. 2, Greenwich, CT: JAI Press, 1982, pp. 63–112.

Riley, John G., "Informational Equilibrium," *Econometrica*, 47 (March 1979), 331–359.

Roth, Alvin E. and Michael W. K. Malouf, "Game-Theoretic Models and the Role of Information in Bargaining," *Psychological Review*, 86 (November 1979), 574–594.

Roth, Alvin E. and J. Keith Murningham, "The Role of Information in Bargaining: An Experimental Study," *Econometrica*, 50 (September 1982), 1123–1142.

Roth, Alvin E. and Francoise Schoumaker, "Expectations and Reputations in Bargaining: An Experimental Study," *American Economic Review*, 73 (June 1983), 362–372.

Schoemaker, Paul J. H., "The Expected Utility Model: Its Variants, Purposes, Evidence and Limitations," *Journal of Economic Literature*, 20 (June 1982), 529–563.

Schotter, Andrew and Yale M. Braunstein, "Economic Search: An Experimental Study," *Economic Inquiry*, 19 (January 1981), 1–25.

Smith, Vernon L., "Effect of Market Organization on Competitive Equilibrium," *Quarterly Journal of Economics*, 78 (May 1964), 181–201.

Smith, Vernon L., "Experimental Studies of Discrimination Versus Competition in Sealed-Bid Auction Markets," *Journal of Business*, 40 (January 1967), 56–84.

Smith, Vernon L., "Experimental Economics: Induced Value Theory," *American Economic Review*, 66 (May 1976), 274–279.

Smith, Vernon L., "Relevance of Laboratory Experiments to Testing Resource Allocation Theory," in Jan Kmenta and James B. Ramsey, eds., *Evaluation of Econometric Models.* New York: 1980, pp. 345–377.

Smith, Vernon L., "An Empirical Study of Decentralized Institutions of Monopoly Restraint," in George Horowich and James P. Quirk, eds., *Essays in Contemporary Fields of Economics.* West Lafayette: 1981.

Smith, Vernon L., "Microeconomic Systems as an Experimental Science," *American Economic Review*, 72 (December 1982), 923–955.

Smith, Vernon L., Gerry L. Suchanek, and Arlington W. Williams, "Rational Expectations Risk Aversion and Asset Markets." Mimeo, University of Arizona, 1984.

Smith, Vernon L., and Arlington W. Williams, "An Experimental Examination of Alternative Rules for Competitive Market Exchange," in Martin Shubik, ed., *Auctions, Bidding and Contracting: Uses and Theory.* New York: 1982.

Smith, Vernon, L., Arlington W. Williams, W. Kenneth Bratton, and Michael G. Vannoni, "Competitive Market Institutions: Double Auctions vs. Sealed Bid-Offer Auctions," *American Economic Review,* 72 (March 1982), 58–77.

Social Science Research Council, *Items,* 34, March 1980.

Spence, A. Michael, *Market Signaling: Informational Transfer in Hiring and Screening Processes.* Cambridge, MA: Harvard University Press, 1974.

Sunder, Shyam, "Rational Expectations Equilibrium in Asset Markets with Costly Information: Experimental Evidence." Working Paper 1984–3, University of Minnesota, February 1984.

Wilde, Louis L., "On the Use of Laboratory Experiments in Economics," in Joseph Pitt, ed., *The Philosophy of Economics.* Dordrecht: Reidel, 1980.

Williams, Arlington W., "Computerized Double-Auction Markets: Some Initial Experimental Results," *Journal of Business,* 53 (July 1980), 235–258.

Williams, Fred E., "The Effect of Market Organization on Competitive Equilibrium: The Multiunit Case," *Review of Economic Studies,* 40 (January 1973), 97–113.

Wilson, Charles, "A Model of Insurance Markets with Incomplete Information," *Journal of Economic Theory,* 16 (December 1977), 167–207.

Wilson, Charles, "The Nature of Equilibrium in Models with Adverse Selection," *Bell Journal of Economics,* 11 (Spring 1980), 108–130.

PART II

CONSUMER BEHAVIOR

INTRODUCTION TO PART II:
CONSUMER BEHAVIOR

This part comprises papers by Van Raaij and Morgan on consumer behavior and by Wärneryd on advertising. All three are notable in that they deal with the most common economic topic, consumption, in manners that will likely seem quite novel to readers who have restricted their economic reading to mainstream neoclassical authors.

Van Raaij's major purpose is to show some of the heuristics we use in making choices. The framework is that of an economist: Lancaster's view of commodities as bundles of attributes. From this can be constructed a decision matrix with columns and rows of attributes and alternatives. Given the variety of alternatives, attributes of each, the choice situation, and the personality of the consumer, it would appear that the rational selection would be long and complex. However, as a visit to the closest shopping center during the week before Christmas will indicate, purchases are made at a dazzling rate. Van Raaij points out that cognitive simplification quickly sets in to the decision process and takes us through a flow chart of mental processes that sequentially filter information until a choice is made. The result is a process of choice making that is rational, all right. However, given the rapid reduction of information taken into consideration as a result of emotional reaction, it clearly isn't the economist's rationality.

Wärneryd is concerned with the interplay of advertising and these same cognitive simplification processes. As a result of the heuristics we employ, some of the distinctions economists conventionally make about advertising, such as whether it is informational or persuasive, lose their significance. Choice depends as heavily on emotion as on facts. In addition to the cognitive simplification heuristics, Wärneryd acquaints us with processes such as latent learning, adaptation level, generalization gradient, and memory search. Again, psychological decision-making is shown to have little to do with the economists' notion of rationality.

The impact of advertising on competition, its effect on price and quality elasticity, and the propensity to consume are standard topics in economic writing. Wärneryd takes up these questions too, but once again, they take on a different coloration in the context of the theory of choice that psychologists employ. This paper will not answer all the questions economists want answered about advertising. It will, however, give them some dandy new ones to consider.

Morgan's paper might well be titled *Back to Basics*. In questioning the rationality postulates of mainstream economics, Morgan casts doubt not only on whether people process all the information available to them but also on whether they know how to do it, whether they understand the information they need in order to do it, and, indeed, whether they would find it worthwhile to do even if someone took them aside and explained to them the methods and benefits of economic analysis. In order to use cost-benefit analysis to determine internal rates of return so a choice can be made among a narrow selection of alternatives, Morgan points out, people must understand the concepts of present value, expected utility, and real versus nominal values, and they must be able to convert before-tax to after-tax returns. Both survey data and introspection suggest that most citizens neither know nor want to know any of it.

Morgan here proposes a research agenda of the most basic sort aimed at determining how people decide. He suggests that the ingredients of one's decision are rooted in what amounts to a stream-of-consciousness series of associations going back to the earliest socialization and decision-making experiences. While the analyst's couch may seem like the appropriate research instrument for the program proposed, this is not what Morgan has in mind. Rather, drawing on his Survey Research Center experience, he proposes a carefully crafted series of surveys in which the interviewer would explore with the subject the associations that enter into the subject's decisions.

Positivist economists claim that it does not matter whether people know or follow consciously the principles of economic theory. What matters is that their behavior or decisions can be shown to be consistent with the prediction of the economic model. These papers take the opposite approach: let us first understand how people really make decisions before attempting to model behavior. This is a classic behavioral scientists' approach that hopefully will rescue economics from the grip of theorists who are oblivious to the real world and its insistence on refuting their predictions.

DEVELOPMENTS IN CONSUMER BEHAVIOR RESEARCH

W. Fred van Raaij

ABSTRACT

Consumer behavior research develops along two lines, at the aggregate (macro) level and at the individual (micro) level. At the macro level, consumption functions are estimated and the contribution of consumer confidence and expectations is discussed. At the micro level, consumer decision-making among multiattribute alternatives is the central focus. Nonlinear combination rules and the importance of affective factors are discussed.

I. INTRODUCTION

Consumer behavior is the study of purchasing, using, and disposing of products and the determinants and consequences of purchasing, using, and disposition. In macroeconomics the emphasis is on the aggregate consumption, saving, and credit. In microeconomics, decision processes, how consumers select products, are of central importance.

This chapter on consumer behavior starts from general consumption functions of the relationship between income, spending, and saving (Section II). These consumption functions provide explanations and pre-

67

dictions of consumption and saving quotes at an aggregate level. The first contribution of psychology is related to this aggregate approach. In Section III, the contribution of consumer confidence and expectations to the explanation and prediction of spending and saving is discussed.

Utility theory in economics and attitude theory in social psychology have strong similarities and constitute the base for research on consumer decision and choice processes (Sections IV and V). A general combination rule model is proposed as a sequential number of steps in the evaluation choice of multiattribute alternatives (Section VI). One should distinguish decision processes with high and low involvement, both starting from a primary affective reaction, which triggers and partly directs the cognitive elaboration and choice (Section VII). Affective (emotional) and cognitive (knowledge) factors both affect consumer decision-making. The impact of affective factors is generally underestimated. A primary affective reaction and a secondary affective reaction (attitude, utility) are parts of the decision and choice process.

II. CONSUMPTION FUNCTIONS

Keynes (1936) asserted that aggregate demand influences employment. Unemployment results from a deficiency of total demand. Effective demand manifests itself in the spending of income. A fundamental principle is that as real income increases, consumption will also increase but by less than income. An increase in real investment equal to the difference between real income and the consumption demand out of that income creates sufficient demand to sustain an increase in employment. Keynes assumed a stable relationship between the size of the national income and the amount spent by the public for consumption. The propensity to consume, that is, the actual consumption that takes place, follows the rule that when income rises, consumption also rises, but proportionally less than income.

> The psychology of the community is such that when aggregate real income is increased, aggregate consumption is increased, but not so much as income. . . . Unless the psychological propensities of the public are different from what we are supposing, we have here established the law that increased employment for investment must necessarily stimulate the industries producing for consumption and thus lead to a total increase of employment which is a multiple of the primary employment required by the investment itself (Keynes, 1936, pp. 27,118).

Figure 1 indicates the above relationship. CC' is the propensity to consume for different levels of income. For the income level at B, AB is the amount of consumption and AE is the amount of saving. For low-

Figure 1.   Income determined by the propensity to consume and the
amount of investment (Samuelson, 1967, Chapter 11).
AB: consumption.
AE: saving.

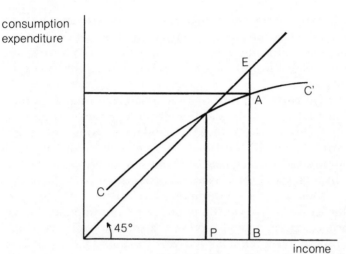

income levels (left of P), consumption exceeds actual income; that is,
there is dissaving of income. Note that wealthy people tend to save more
of their income than do poor people. If Y is income and C is consumption, the average propensity to consume is C/Y and the average propensity to save is S/Y.

$$\frac{C}{Y} + \frac{S}{Y} = 1. \tag{1}$$

The marginal propensity to consume, dC/dY, is less than the average
propensity to consume at any given income level.

$$0 < \frac{dC}{dY} < 1. \tag{2}$$

This became known later as the *absolute-income hypothesis.* Keynes's absolute income hypothesis inspired many studies to find the "consumption
function," the relationship between aggregate income and aggregate
consumption, holding other relevant variables constant. Other variables,
however, such as prices, expectations, past income, and income of and
consumption by reference persons, tend to influence the consumption
function.

Brady and Friedman (1947) were the first to suggest that the saving rate, and consequently consumption, of individuals depend not on their present income but rather on their relative position on the income scale:

$$\frac{S}{Y} = a + b\frac{Y}{\bar{Y}} \tag{3}$$

S is saving and $\bar{Y}$ represents average income. The *relative-income hypothesis* states that the level of consumption expenditure depends on the relative income; that is, income related to a prior standard in the case of time series or relative to income of a reference group in the case of cross-sectional data.

Duesenberry (1949) favored the relative-income hypothesis. Consumer behavior, according to Duesenberry, is the outcome of a conflict between the desire to improve the standard of living (consumption) and the desire to obtain future welfare (saving). The actual consumption level is a compromise between increased consumption and saving. Consumers learn through social contacts about goods superior to the ones they use. Comparisons with the consumption level of the reference group tend to influence one's own consumption level. Consumption also has a social significance. Occupational success and social mobility are expressed in the consumption level. This is a reaffirmation of the emphasis placed by Veblen (1899) on the competitive aspects of consumption.

Duesenberry's theory of saving, and thus of consumption, is primarily based on the assumptions that consumer preferences are interdependent and irreversible. Interdependence means that the savings ratio is dependent on the income distribution of the reference group, rather than on the absolute income of the individual. Irreversibility reflects the tendency to increase both consumption and saving with rising income, and to maintain this consumption level with a decreasing income at the expense of saving. It means that the consumption at a given income level depends on past income, but only if past income levels were higher than the current income (ratchet effect). This is exemplified by the hardship consumers experience of reducing their consumption level with declining income (e.g., as an effect of unemployment). Dissaving is possible only down to a certain point.

Social comparisons with reference persons (reference group) is mainly possible through the visible and conspicuous class of goods that are accepted as a basis for social comparisons. People tend to compare themselves with persons of somewhat higher status and try to become similar to these higher-status persons (Rijsman, 1974). After having made oneself similar, another reference person will be selected. It is probable that some consumption goods, such as house, automobile, and furniture, are the basis for social comparison and thus have a special significance for the relative-income hypothesis (Veblen, 1899).

In the 1950s, two separate *permanent-income hypotheses* were independently developed by Modigliani (1949) and by Friedman (1957). The underlying assumption in both hypotheses is that the individual consumer or household plans its expenditure based not on the income received currently but on what it is expected to be in the long run. Thus long-term or lifetime income expectation is considered to be important. Consumers plan their expenditure for a given period of time, based on their expectations of future income receipts.

In these hypotheses, both income and consumption are divided into a permanent (Y_p, C_p) and a transitory (Y_t, C_t) component:

$$Y = Y_p + Y_t. \tag{4}$$

$$C = C_p + C_t. \tag{5}$$

$$C_p = k. Y_p. \tag{6}$$

Permanent consumption is a function of permanent income. The multiple k is a function of time, the age of the consumer unit, and the rate of return at which it is discounted, in particular the net worth (Ferber, 1973).

It is difficult, in practice, to separate the permanent and transitory components of both income and consumption. Transitory income should not have an effect on transitory consumption. However, Katona and Mueller (1968) found that transitory ("windfall") income (Y_t) was more important in explaining expenditure on durables than was permanent income. On the positive side, the permanent-income hypothesis provides a good starting point as far as model building is concerned. The concept is comparable to the "true score" approach in psychological test theory. The actual score is considered to be a random deviation from the "true" score.

Modigliani (1949) and Duesenberry (1949) proposed that through habit formation a link is formed between past and present expenditures. Habits and tastes account for autocorrelation in the time series. The habit of cigarette smoking, for instance, tends to link past and present purchases of cigarettes (a positive autocorrelation). The purchase of a refrigerator, however, is not likely to be followed by another purchase of the same product (a negative autocorrelation). Houthakker and Taylor (1970) combined both views in the *stock-adjustment hypothesis*:

$$C_t = \alpha + \beta.S_t + \gamma.Y_t. \tag{7}$$

C_t is current consumption, S_t is the stock, and Y_t is the present (transitory) income. α, β and γ are parameters. β is the stock adjustment parameter. If β is positive, the consumption is said to be influenced by habit formation, so that an increase in stock leads to more consumption (addiction). If β is negative, an increase in stock tends to inhibit new consumption.

III. CONSUMER CONFIDENCE

The relative- and permanent-income hypotheses suggest that not only the current income but also past and future levels of income determine consumption, as do a comparison with reference persons and habit formation. The extrapolation of future income depends on one's income expectations and thus on employment and career expectations.

In consumption, contractual and discretionary components are distinguished. Contractual spending is the necessary expenditure on rent, mortgage, energy, insurance premiums, and basic food and clothing. Contractual spending cannot be changed overnight and limits the discretionary spending of income. Discretionary expenditures have a large degree of freedom (discretion) regarding the timing and the degree of spending. Consumers are "powerful" at the aggregate level, able to delay and to forgo discretionary purchases. In the same way, one can distinguish between contractual and discretionary saving (Katona, 1975) (Figure 2).

Discretionary spending is not only a matter of sufficient income but also of consumer confidence in future developments. When optimism prevails, consumers are willing to spend their discretionary income on durable luxury goods and on vacation and recreation. Buying on credit is also stimulated by an optimistic outlook. When pessimism prevails in times of economic recession, consumers are by and large unwilling to spend their discretionary income, and thus they save more. The demand for consumer credit shows a downward trend in these pessimistic days.

It is not only the ability to buy (income to be spent on discretionary expenditure) but also the willingness to buy that determines the economic behavior of discretionary spending, saving, and borrowing (Figure

Figure 2.   Contractual/discretionary consumption and saving.

	Contractual	Discretionary
Consumption	Rent, mortgage, energy, insurance premiums	Luxury goods
Saving	Pension premiums, saving plans, habitual saving	"Free" saving

Figure 3. Economic and psychological determinants
of economic behavior.

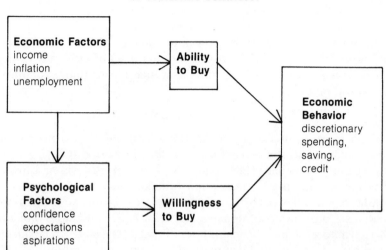

3). Psychological factors become important in an economy in which a large number of households have discretionary spending power— whether to spend or to save, on what to spend, how much to spend, and how to save. There is no need to make these expenditures at a given time. Replacement often takes place before the old product becomes unusable. Discretionary spending is often not governed by habit. And discretionary spending is mainly done after considerable deliberation and discussion among household members. The planning and orientation period before purchase may be as short as one week (for a vacuum cleaner) but is usually one month or longer.

Which factors determine the willingness to buy or save? First, personal financial expectations and the changes one expects in personal finances may affect discretionary spending. Second, expectations of business-cycle developments and changes in economic trends (recession or prosperous times) may be clues to consumer confidence (or lack of confidence). A third area concerns perceived market conditions ("a good time to buy") as an indicator of consumer confidence. In 1952, Katona (1975) constructed an Index of Consumer Sentiment (ICS), which contributed to the prediction of consumption expenditures.

Consumer confidence, and thus willingness to buy, either is a consequence of economic developments of the business cycle, personal finances, and market conditions or is an independent, autonomous force in the economy. In the first case, measures of consumer confidence serve to explain how consumers evaluate the economic conditions and extrapolate expectations. In the second case, economic and political news in the mass media affects consumer confidence and, consequently, consumer spending and saving. In most studies, income *and* consumer confidence are used as predictors of consumption expenditure in general, on durables, on cars, and for consumer saving. Mueller (1963) shows that the addition of consumer confidence to the set of predictor variables increases the proportion of explained variance in consumer expenditure. The typical model is:

$$C_t = \alpha + \beta.Y_t + \gamma.(ICS)_t + \delta.C_{t-1}. \tag{8}$$

in which consumption (C_t) is a function of income (Y_t), consumer confidence $(ICS)_t$, and the consumption in the last period (C_{t-1}).

Praet and Vuchelen (1984) conclude from an analysis of European consumer surveys that consumption functions incorporating consumer confidence variables perform surprisingly well, given the measurement problems. Consumer confidence measures are helpful guides only in the short-term forecasting of consumption. Praet (1985) states that consumer confidence cannot easily be explained by economic variables only. Consumer confidence surveys contain original information useful in explaining and in forecasting consumption, credit, and saving levels.

IV.   UTILITY AND ATTITUDE

Consumption functions, including the ones with consumer confidence, give relationships between income and consumption at the aggregate level or at the level of a product category (automobiles, houses, household durables). Consumption functions do not explain how the consumption "package" is constituted and how consumers evaluate and select the products that are offered. The second part of this chapter is necessarily on micro choice and decision processes of consumers. Two concepts are central: utility, as defined in economics, and attitude, as defined in social psychology.

Utility, according to Bentham (1789) is derived from the pleasure or pain associated with commodities and is thus related to emotion and affect. Although early researchers tried to define and measure utility or marginal utility, the order-preserving function of utility is considered sufficient to explain behavior. Utility was considered to be associated with commodities, as such (Stigler,1950).

Lancaster (1966) and Ironmonger (1972) were the first to think of commodities as "bundles of characteristics." Characteristics are objective, universal properties and attributes of commodities. Lancaster views goods as inputs and characteristics as outputs. However, consumers do not want characteristics; they want product benefits or services. "Product characteristics are of interest to the consumer only in that they combine to produce the consumption services, from which consumers obtain utility" (Cude, 1980). Characteristics are no longer considered to be outputs but rather technical product specifications, such as the amount of sugar or protein in a food product.

Attitude is a constellation of cognitive (beliefs), affective (emotions), and conative (behavioral intentions) components. Attitude, in its pure sense, is the affective reaction (evaluation) to beliefs about product characteristics. Take, for instance, a pair of jogging shoes. A consumer may believe that the shoes are shock-absorbing. This belief is usually measured as the probability that the jogging shoes are shock-absorbing. The affective reaction is how good or bad, how favorable or unfavorable, a consumer considers shock absorption to be in jogging shoes.

One observes the similarity with the utility concept. Consumers derive utility from product characteristics. In an analogous manner, affect is the favorability of product characteristics. The utility and affect toward product characteristics are combined in a linear way into an overall utility on attitude toward the product:

$$U_o = \Sigma\, p_i.u_i, \tag{9}$$

$$A_o = \Sigma\, b_i.e_i. \tag{10}$$

The overall utility toward a product (U_o) is the summated multiplication of the probability that a product characteristic is present (p_i) times the utility of that product characteristic (u_i). The overall attitude toward a product (A_o) is the summated multiplication of the belief (probability) that a product characteristic is present times the evaluation (favorability) of this belief. In later research, Fishbein and Azjen (1975) define attitude toward the act (A_{act}). It is not the product and its characteristics that are most important; rather it is the consequences of purchasing and using the product. It is not jogging shoes as such, but purchasing and using jogging shoes are the relevant attitude objects. Thus one observes the development from product to product characteristics (Lancaster, 1966), from product characteristics to product benefits (Haley, 1968; Cude, 1980), and last, from product benefits to the consequences of behavior (purchase, usage) with regard to the product.

Utility and attitude models belong to the general class of expectancy-value models, in which an expectancy (probability) and a value (evaluation) are combined (Van Raaij, 1977). Antonides (1984) states that both utility and attitude refer to want- or need-satisfying properties of products, and both are supposed to represent preference and influence behavior. Both involve cognitive and affective components, knowledge and emotion, respectively.

Most utility and attitude models combine cognitive and affective information in a "linear compensatory" way. Whereas this may be effective in the prediction of decision outcomes, it does not necessarily describe the consumer decision process and the way consumers use and combine information to reach a decision.

V. CONSUMER DECISION-MAKING

From cognitive psychology, the information-processing approach to consumer decision-making became very popular in consumer research. It is essentially based on a "hierarchy" of sequential steps: awareness, search for alternatives, acquisition of information, deliberation, and choice. Especially for nonroutine and risky decisions, one might assume that consumers are willing to go through this process. However, substantial evidence has accumulated to indicate that many consumer purchases, notably routine- and low-involvement purchases, are unplanned; that is, they are undertaken without much information search and deliberation. It may be true that the decision process has been performed on an earlier occasion or that a shopper uses the supermarket as his or her shopping list; nevertheless, these findings challenge the "rational" sequence of steps that underlies the cognitive model. Another observation (Katona and Mueller, 1954) is that deliberate decision-making is more likely to take place in better educated, middle-income, professional households.

The combination of attribute information and evaluation in the expectancy-value class of models may be performed in a number of ways (Van Raaij, 1977).

1. The combination rule often used in the above-mentioned choice models is the linear-additive rule, in which the two components are multiplied for each attribute and summed over all attributes. A low value on one attribute may be compensated by a higher value on another attribute. The linear-additive combination is also called the *compensatory rule*.

Nonlinear combination rules are:

2. *Conjunctive rule:* A cutoff value on each attribute eliminates products that have values outside the acceptable range for that attribute. Unacceptability on one attribute cannot be compensated for by a high value on another attribute. Westwood, Lunn, and Beaz-

ley's (1974) threshold model falls into this category. Lehtinen's (1974) choice limitation mechanism operates according to this rule.

3. *Disjunctive rule:* A product with a superior score on one attribute is chosen regardless of its value on other attributes. If this superior score represents a unique product property, low values on other attributes are accepted. The best attribute of a product is vital.

4. *Lexicographic rule:* A hierarchical ordering of the product attributes is assumed. The products are first compared on the most important attributes. If two products are the same or nearly the same on the first attribute, the second attribute enters the picture, and the remaining products are compared on that attribute. Sometimes only differences beyond a certain standard are considered: this is lexicographic semiorder.

5. *Sequential elimination rule,* or choice by elimination as defined by Tversky (1972). According to this rule, the choice alternatives that do not include a certain attribute are eliminated: *choice by elimination.* This evaluation-process model is related to the lexicographic model, although Tversky's model does not assume a fixed prior ordering of the attributes. Complex alternatives tend to be evaluated in terms of their attributes, and an alternative that does not meet a certain a priori standard value on one of its attributes is discarded. The process goes on until only one alternative is left. This sequential elimination process is certainly not a rational choice process, because an alternative is eliminated based on its value on one attribute, while the values on the other attributes may be sufficiently high that they compensate for the low value. In a choice situation with a large number of alternatives, and where the negative attributes of the alternatives are more easily perceived, choice by elimination may become the only way to reach a decision.

6. *Trade-off:* A special case of the compensatory combination rule is the trade-off model proposed by Westwood, Lunn, and Beazley (1974) and Johnson (1974). This model is related to the statistical conjoint analysis technique. The trade-off model assumes that the consumer's purchase intention toward a brand can be regarded as the sum of the values (utilities) he associates with its perceived attributes. The utility of the various attribute levels is determined such that by recombining these utilities, the original purchase intentions can be reproduced. The trade-offs between combinations of levels of any number of attributes can be studied, and this will prove important in the evaluation process. The analysis assumes that attributes neither correlate nor interact. Only discrete levels

of each attribute are studied, so that realistic attribute values or
levels must be specified.

Trade-off models can handle discrete and dichotomous attributes but are normally confined to "objective" and "subjective"
attributes. Perceived product attributes are more difficult to specify. Not only trade-offs between levels of attributes but also trade-
offs between dichotomous attributes can be studied. The presence
of a feature of one brand is weighed against the presence of another feature of a second brand.

A number of factors affect consumer choice behavior:

1. *Acceptability of alternatives*
   The decision-maker defines a set of acceptable alternatives, com-
   parable to Howard and Sheth's (1969) "evoked set." Pras and
   Summers (1975) define acceptable brands in two ways:

   a. They pass the minimum acceptable criteria: that is, they are
       acceptable on all attributes (cf. conjunctive rule).
   b. They have a nonzero probability of being purchased.

   Pras and Summers (1975) found that different choice rules are
   used for a set of acceptable brands and for a set consisting of
   acceptable and unacceptable brands. However, the selection of
   acceptable brands may be considered the first stage in the consumer choice process, and not only as a boundary condition.

2. *Number of attributes*
   Many studies show that only the salient or dominant product attributes are considered in the evaluation process. Raju, Bhagat,
   and Sheth (1974) use factor analysis to extract the three major
   components in the evaluative and normative beliefs included in
   the Sheth model.

   Much disagreement exists among researchers concerning the
   number of attributes considered by the decision-maker. Katona
   and Mueller (1954) found that in major-appliance purchase decisions an average of less than three attributes are considered. In
   the multidimensional scaling approach, only two or three attributes (dimensions) are sufficient to distinguish among brands. The
   number of attributes is probably related to the acceptability of the
   brands. In the selection of brands according to their acceptability,
   all attributes are used to eliminate an unacceptable brand. The
   acceptable brands ("evoked set") are evaluated on the basis of the
   most important attributes only.

   There is a need for a systematic investigation of the interaction of brand acceptability and the number of attributes. The measurement method (recall versus recognition) also influences the number of attributes found in the research.

3. *Confidence*

Howard and Sheth (1969) define confidence as "the extent to which the buyer believes that he can estimate the net payoff, the reward from buying a given brand." A consumer may lack confidence in the rating of a brand and/or in the rating of the attribute. Cox (1967) already postulated that available information is not used when confidence value is low. Pras and Summers (1975) hypothesized that the decision-maker does not tolerate uncertainty (low confidence) concerning (a) the values of the most important attributes or (b) a possible brand unacceptability on any relevant attribute. Predictions of brand choice for consumers who are uncertain or unstable in their judgements are expected to be poor.

4. *Situational factors*

Wright (1974) found that in a situation of time pressure and distraction, judges tend to place greater weight on negative evidence to eliminate alternatives (conjunctive model). Under stressful conditions a situation of information overload is reached earlier—that is, with a smaller number of alternatives or attributes—than in a "normal" situation. It may be hypothesized that under these stressful conditions, more alternatives are downgraded as unacceptable and a smaller number of attributes is considered in selecting the "best" alternative.

In general, an individual faced with a choice task of challenging complexity tries to restructure that task into a simpler one. Several simplifying strategies may be used. A negative bias—focus on negative evidence—occurs when the consumer wants to avoid choosing an alternative with an undesirable attribute. That is what most consumers do in a complex situation (conjunctive rule). A positive bias—focus on positive evidence—occurs when the consumer wants to choose an alternative with at least one desirable attribute. This situation is found when we choose an alternative from a set of acceptable alternatives and if one alternative has an outstanding value on one or more attributes (disjunctive rule).

Choice behavior is partly dependent on the choice environment or contingency.

5. *Personality factors*

The decision maker's personality may influence the evaluation strategy: venturesomeness versus cautiousness may correspond to a disjunctive versus conjunctive evaluation strategy. A risk-taking propensity seems to be a critical personality factor in consumer choice. However, intertask consistency of individual differences in risk-taking behavior is low. Risk-taking behavior is contingent on the choice environment and response mode (Slovic, 1972). Kernan (1968) investigated the decision behavior of groups and related their choice model to personality characteristics. Verbal, intellectual, and social abilities also determine the evaluation process. Verhallen (1975) found that higher-educated persons consider more alternatives, use more neutral information sources (consumers' guides), and have a longer deliberation time compared with persons with a lower education.

VI. A GENERAL COMBINATION RULE MODEL

In the foregoing, a number of choice-process models and some phenomena in the choice process were reviewed. The use of a model by the decision maker depends on the choice situation or task environment, the number of alternatives and attributes, the acceptability of the alternatives, the certainty of the consumer, and the experience and personality of the decision maker. At first glance, the conclusion of a researcher is that a classification of choice situations, a classification of consumer cognitive styles, and a classification of products and services are necessary to predict which model is used by a certain consumer in a certain situation for a certain product.

Nevertheless, it is reasonable to expect that in most consumer evaluation processes, especially those for initial purchases and purchases involving large expenditures, the following strategy is adopted. (A *strategy* means a sequence of combination rules.)

A. Conjunctive model

↓

B. Disjunctive model

↓

C. Compensatory model

↓

D. Choice rule

The only shortcuts in the general sequence ABCD are A, AB, or AC. The general combination rule model is given in Figure 4.

Figure 4. Sequential usage of combination rules.

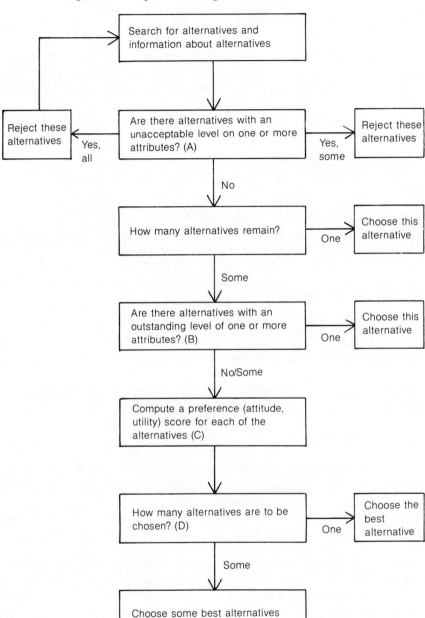

Notes: A. Conjunctive rule
B. Disjunctive rule
C. Compensatory rule
D. Choice rule

A. Conjunctive Model

In this first stage in the choice process, the known alternatives (brands) are examined and judged on their acceptability. Alternatives that do not meet the standards of the consumer on one or more attributes are rejected. Lehtinen (1974) calls the selection of alternatives "choice limitation." From the larger set of all alternatives, a smaller set of acceptable alternatives ("evoked set") remains.

If only one acceptable alternative remains, this alternative is taken and the evaluation process is finished.

B. Disjunctive Model

If one alternative from the acceptable set has an outstanding value on one of its attributes (and the values on the other attributes are acceptable, as we have seen), this alternative is chosen and the evaluation process is completed. If more than one, or no alternative shows any outstanding attribute values, the next stage is C.

C. Compensatory Model

The set of acceptable alternatives is evaluated by the consumer. Attribute evaluations are given to the alternatives, and the relevance of each attribute is rated. A linear combination of the expectancy X value score for each attribute gives an overall preference score for each alternative. The tradeoff model also depicts a compensatory evaluation process and is applicable in some cases.

D. Choice Rule

The alternative with the highest preference score is generally chosen. If more than one alternative can be chosen, as in the case of graduate-school admissions or applicant selection for more than one job, the alternatives (students, applicants) with the highest preference score are chosen. In consumer choice only one best alternative is generally selected.

The combination rule model (Figure 4) leads to the "best alternative." This suggests that even small product differences are considered and that utility is maximized. The choice rule could be related to "an alternative that satisfies certain criteria." This is in fact the conjunctive rule. If product differences are small and if the benefits of utility maximization are small relative to the information-processing costs, consumers may use a "satisficing rule;" that is, they may select the first alternative that is satisfactory according to certain criteria. Simon and Stedry (1969) state that in this "satisficing" theory of behavior, the individual examines the alternatives available to him, and if a subset of these alternatives is perceived as satisfactory (conjunctive rule), he selects one of them (presumably the best of the subset) and proceeds to act. The definition of *satisfactory* determines the aspiration level. If search does not produce better alternatives, the aspiration level will decline, so that some alternative, possibly a previously rejected one, will now be "satisfactory" and will be selected (Simon and Stedry, 1969, p. 279).

VII. HIGH- AND LOW-INVOLVEMENT CHOICE

The proposed general choice-process model assumes a high involvement on the part of the consumer. The consumer must be willing to expend time and effort to come to *a* or *the* best decision. Consumers are willing to expend the costs of time and effort only if they expect the benefits of a good choice to be higher than the costs.

The cognitive models, mentioned above, including the Fishbein and Ajzen (1975) attitude model, assume that consumers start with information acquisition from a neutral position. Only after information has been collected, the information (attributes) are evaluated and a decision will be reached. One may conclude that the cognitive models are largely concerned with the comparison of alternatives and the cognitive elaboration of the information about the alternatives.

Evidence from psychological research shows that an affective reaction often precedes a cognitive reaction and elaboration. After that, an elaborated affective reaction may follow. In the primary affective reaction, the object is evaluated and a (subconscious) decision is made concerning whether it is necessary, useful, or interesting to collect and process more information about the object. The cognitive elaboration is not neutral but serves to support and justify the primary affective reaction. The secondary, more elaborated affective reaction attitude is often no different from the primary affective reaction. It is only more detailed and supported by cognitive elements.

Van Raaij (1984) applies this model (Figure 5) to the perception of advertising and the use of advertising information. A primary affective reaction may be triggered when a consumer is confronted with a familiar product, brand, situation, or advertisement or with a new product, brand, situation, or advertisement that elicits interest through novelty, humor, or ambiguity.

The primary affective reaction is both a selection filter to further cognitive elaboration and a first reaction to the object stimulus. Cognitive

Figure 5. A general information-processing model.

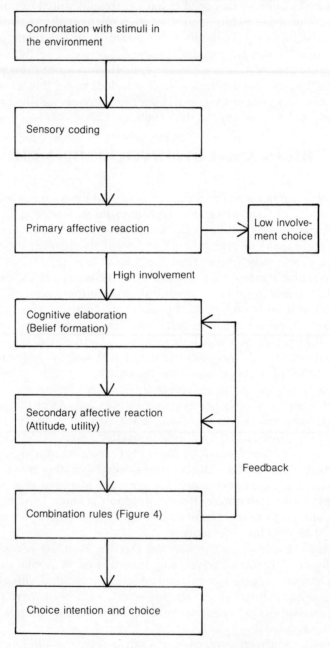

elaboration leads to the formation of beliefs and knowledge about the choice alternatives. The secondary affective reaction is the combination of beliefs and evaluation of beliefs leading to a decision.

Primary affective reactions are difficult to assess because they are overruled by the cognitive elaboration that follows directly afterward. Consumers tend to rationalize and justify their decisions with cognitive arguments, nor or only vaguely conscious of the emotional reaction that preceded the cognitive elaboration.

The first impression of an advertisement, product, package, magazine, or salesperson may be crucial. In the later cognitive elaboration, this impression may be refined or altered, although probably not too much. The cognitive elaboration serves as a justification of the primary affective reaction.

It is not true that we collect "cool" information and evaluate it afterward. Most information is "hot," that is, emotional. We don't see "a house"—we see a nice or an ugly house. We see a "home" and refer to ourselves: "Would I like to live there?" Much information processing is a justification of our subjective preferences. Wright (1975) calls this decision style "affect referral" but does not develop the concept any further.

In a low-involvement situation (low-risk or inexpensive products), a primary affective reaction may be the only reaction of the consumer that triggers a purchase. Consumers tend to select familiar and/or attractive alternatives (e.g., soft drinks, cigarettes). In a high-involvement situation (high physical, financial, or social risk), a primary affective reaction is the "gatekeeper" of cognitive elaboration. It creates enough arousal to support the combining and trading off of attribute information. Risk aversion might become manifest in the use of the conjunctive rule.

Keenan and Bailett (1979) conclude that "the crucial dimension underlying memory is not what the subject knows or the amount of knowledge that is used in encoding the item, but rather what the subject feels about what he knows" (p. 25). A person's self-concept is loaded with affect, and in perception an affective or emotional matching of object and self-concept can be performed quickly. The primary affective reaction is quick and global, and faster than the cognitive elaboration of the discrimination and combination of attribute information.

Products that create a favorable primary affective reaction are more likely to be considered. More cognitive elaboration will take place, and probably a more positive attitude toward these products will be developed. The use of a disjunctive combination rule and a disproportionate weighting of the attributes on which the product scores well are probable. This means that the cognitive elaboration and decision-making is biased toward a positive outcome for the products with a favorable primary affective reaction.

Products that create an unfavorable primary affective reaction are less likely to be considered, except if one wants to find supportive information for the unfavorable reaction. Less cognitive elaboration will take place and probably a negative attitude toward these products will be developed. The use of a conjunctive combination rule and a disproportionate weighting of the attributes on which the products score badly is probable. This means that the cognitive elaboration and decision making are biased toward a negative outcome for the products with an unfavorable primary affective reaction.

VIII. CONCLUSIONS

Consumer behavior research is related to both macroeconomics and microeconomics. Its relationship with macroeconomics can be seen as a development of the consumption functions, which explain spending, saving, and credit at the aggregate level with a number of predictors. Not only income (absolute, relative, or permanent) but also consumer confidence and expectation contribute to the explanation of consumption levels. Consumers are restricted by their budgets, but within their budgets they have discretionary spending (or saving) power. Katona (1975) has helped stress the important role of consumers in the economy.

Consumer behavior research, in its relationship to microeconomics, can be seen as a development of utility theory (and its counterpart in social psychology, attitude theory). The information-processing approach shows that consumers employ simplifying (nonlinear) combination rules in order to find a satisficing or the best alternative. Information processing will be relatively simple in cases of low-involvement, routine products but may become more complex in cases of high involvement and high perceived risk. It is argued that consumers form a primary affective reaction that influences the "objectivity" of the decision process.

REFERENCES

Antonides, G., "An Attempt at Integration of Economic and Psychological Theories in Consumption Problems." Papers on Economic Psychology, No. 31, Erasmus University, Rotterdam, 1984.

Bentham, J., *Introduction to the Principles of Morals and Legislation*, 1789 (*Works of Jeremy Bentham*. Edinburgh: Tait, 1843).

Brady, D.S. and R. Friedman, "Savings and the Income Distribution," in *Studies in Income and Wealth*, Vol. 10. New York: National Bureau of Economic Research, 1947, pp. 247–265.

Cox. D.F., "The Sorting Rule Model of the Consumer Product Evaluation Process," in

D.F. Cox, ed., *Risk Taking and Information Handling in Consumer Behavior*. Boston, MA: Harvard Graduate School of Management, 1967.

Cude, B.J., "An Objective Method of Determining the Relevancy of Product Characteristics," in *Proceedings of the American Council of Consumer Interests*, 1980, pp. 111–116.

Duesenberry, J.S., *Income, Saving, and the Theory of Consumer Behavior*. Cambridge, MA: Harvard University Press, 1949.

Ferber, R., "Consumer Economics: A Survey," *Journal of Economic Literature*, 11 (1973), 1303–1342.

Fishbein, M., and I. Ajzen, *Belief, Attitude, Intention and Behavior*. Reading, MA: Addison-Wesley, 1975.

Friedman, M., *A Theory of the Consumption Function*. Princeton, NJ: Princeton University Press, 1957.

Haley, R.I., "Benefit Segmentation," *Journal of Marketing*, 32 (1968), 30–35.

Houthakker, H.S. and L.D. Taylor, *Consumer Demand in the United States*. Cambridge, MA: Harvard University Press, 1970 (2nd edition).

Howard, J.A. and J.N. Sheth, *The Theory of Buyer Behavior*. New York: Wiley, 1969.

Ironmonger, D.S., *New Commodities and Consumer Behavior*. Cambridge, MA: University Press, 1972.

Johnson, R.M., "Trade-off Analysis of Consumer Values," *Journal of Marketing Research*, 11 (1974), 121–127.

Katona, G., *Psychological Economics*. New York: Elsevier, 1975.

Katona, G. and E. Mueller, "A Study of Purchase Decision," in L.H. Clark, ed., *Consumer Behavior*. New York: New York University Press, 1954, pp. 30–87.

Katona, G. and E. Mueller, *Consumer Response to Income Increases*. Washington, DC: Brookings Institution, 1968.

Keenan, J.M. and S.D. Bailett, "Memory of Personally and Socially Significant Events," in R.S. Nickerson, ed., *Attention and Performance VIII*, Hillsdale, NJ: Erlbaum, 1979.

Kernan, J.B., "Choice Criteria, Decision Behavior, and Personality," *Journal of Marketing Research*, 5 (1968), 155–164.

Keynes, J.M., *The General Theory of Employment, Interest, and Money*. New York: Harcourt, Brace & Co., 1936.

Lancaster, K.J., "A New Approach to Consumer Theory," *Journal of Political Economy*, 74 (1966), 132–157.

Lehtinen, U., "A Brand Choice Model—Theoretical Framework and Empirical Results," *European Research* (ESOMAR), 2 (1974), 51–68, 83.

Modigliani, F., "Fluctuations in the Saving-Income Ration: A Problem in Economic Forecasting," in *Studies in Income and Wealth*, Vol. 11. New York: National Bureau of Economic Research, 1949, pp. 371–443.

Mueller, E., "Ten Years of Consumer Attitude Surveys: Their Forecasting Record," *Journal of the American Statistical Association*, 58 (1963), 899–917.

Praet, P., "Endogenizing Consumers' Expectations in Four Major EC Countries," *Journal of Economic Psychology*, 6 (1985), 255–269.

Praet, P. and J. Vuchelen, "The Contribution of E.C. Consumer Surveys in Forecasting Consumer Expenditures: An Econometric Analysis for Four Major Countries," *Journal of Economic Psychology*, 5 (1984), 101–124.

Pras, B. and J. Summers, "A Comparison of Linear and Nonlinear Evaluation Process Models," *Journal of Marketing Research*, 12 (1975), 276–281.

Raju, P.S., R.S. Bhagat, and J.N. Sheth, "Predictive Validation and Cross-Validation of the Fishbein, Rosenberg, and Sheth Models of Attitudes," *Advances in Consumer Research*, 2 (1975), 405–425.

Rijsman, J.B., "Factors in Social Comparison of Performance Influencing Actual Performance," *European Journal of Social Psychology*, 4 (1974), 279–311.

Samuelson, P.A., *Economics*. New York: McGraw-Hill, 1967.

Simon, H.A. and A.C. Stedry, "Psychology and Economics," in G. Lindzey and E. Aronson, eds., *Handbook of Social Psychology*, Vol. 5. Reading, MA: Addison-Wesley, 1968.

Slovic, P., "Information Processing, Situation Specificity, and the Generality of Risk-Taking Behavior," *Journal of Personality and Social Psychology*, 22 (1972), 128–134.

Stigler, G.J., "The Development of Utility Theory," *Journal of Political Economy*, 58 (1950), 307–327, 373–396.

Tversky, A., "Elimination By Aspects: A Theory of Choice," *Psychological Review*, 79 (1972), 281–299.

Van Raaij, W.F., *Consumer Choice Behavior: An Information-Processing Approach*. Tilburg: Tilburg University, 1977.

Van Raaij, W.F., "Affective and Cognitive Reactions to Advertising." Report No. 84–111, Cambridge, MA: Marketing Science Institute, 1984.

Veblen, T., *The Theory of the Leisure Class*. New York: Macmillan, 1899.

Verhallen, T.M.M., "Het Beslissingsproces bij Laagstbetaalden," *Gedrag*, 3 (1975), 362–383.

Westwood, R.A., A. Lunn, and D. Beazley, "Models and Modelling, I. New Approaches to Belief Importance, II. Modelling and Structures," *European Research* (ESOMAR), 2 (1974), 95–104, 152–158.

Wright, P.L., "The Harassed Decision Maker: Time Pressures, Distractions, and the Use of Evidence," *Journal of Applied Psychology*, 59 (1974), 555–561.

Wright, P.L., "Consumer Choice Strategies: Simplifying vs. Optimizing," *Journal of Marketing Research*, 12 (1975), 60–67.

ADVERTISING AND CONSUMER BEHAVIOR

Karl-Erik Wärneryd

I. ADVERTISING AND ECONOMIC THEORY

A. Economic Rationality and Imperfect Markets

According to economic theory, advertising belongs to markets characterized by imperfect competition. Imperfections in market information, that is, deficient market transparency, are characteristic features of such markets. If consumers by definition are assumed to behave rationally, advertising can do nothing (Chiplin and Sturgess, 1982). It is true that the postulate of consumer rationality, when accompanied by an assumption of perfectly competitive markets, does not admit any explicit role for advertising unless advertising costs are seen as part of production costs. This implies that the manufacture of a product is not finished until the potential consumers know about it. If, on the other hand, the assumption of consumer rationality can be coupled with the assumption that there are markets with less than perfect competition, further aspects of advertising can be discussed. Economic rationality in the strictest sense seems to presuppose the existence of perfect markets. Otherwise it cannot obtain. If, however, economic rationality only means optimization under given circumstances, there may be a different role for advertising. The main question then becomes: Does advertising serve to reduce imperfections, or does it increase imperfections? A preliminary answer to this question is that both alternatives seem to be true depending on the circumstances. The task of advertising research is to separate out the circumstances when one type of effects obtains and when the other type of effects obtains.

Attempts to assess the economic role of advertising are based on the assumption that there are two major kinds of advertising, with respect to how advertising is purposely used or to how it functions in reality: through providing information or through suggestion and persuasion. While the former function may promote market transparency and can be taken to be part of the process of producing goods so that they come within the reach of prospective buyers, the latter function may be seen as a disturbing factor creating monopolistic tendencies, that is, it accomplishes unilateral changes in power relations (Farris and Albion, 1980). The net economic value of advertising seen from a societal vantage point is a matter of debate, depending on how much of advertising is judged to be information and how much is judged to be persuasion. The conclusion is sometimes heard that the effects of advertising, whether positive or negative, cannot be too dramatic, since advertising is not very important in quantitative terms, amounting to an average of 1 per cent of the gross national product (GNP) (in Great Britain; see *The Economics of Advertising*, 1967; Scitovsky, 1976).

In practice, advertising is a multifaceted phenomenon that develops rather independently of macroeconomic advertising theory, in spite of the fact that the theory has often been used as an argument for government regulation of advertising. Both advertising practice and the theory that comes closest to advertising practice are influenced by the behavioral sciences. While economic theory favors the view that advertising is a unitary phenomenon with regular effects of a preponderant type, practitioners make a number of distinctions among types of advertising, conditions for effects, and kinds of effects. Distinctions are made, for example, between industrial and consumer advertising; advertising for different products, such as high- and low-involvement products; products at different stages in the life cycle; and various communication effects, such as effects on awareness, knowledge, and attitudes. Hardly ever is a distinction made between information and persuasion: The purpose of advertising is to persuade for commercial objectives, and information, in the sense of factual data, is used to varying degrees as a means of persuasion.

B. Contributions from the Behavioral Sciences

Many discussions of economic issues in advertising contain assumptions about consumer behavior that elaborate the economic-rationality concept. Consumer behavior has in the last twenty years become an area of increasing interest to behavioral scientists. The potential role of insights based on behavioral-science findings, notably in psychology, can be taken as highly varying:

1. The behavioral sciences can be expected to provide useful concepts and empirical research results for extending the theory of consumer choice and elaborating or enriching the postulate of rationality.
2. The behavioral sciences can be expected to shed new light on well-known economic issues pertaining to advertising: advertising and competition; advertising effects on prices, propensity to consume, and consumer-demand curves; and advertising as related to new entries in markets and to innovation and new product development. This may be achieved partly through an extended consumer-choice theory and partly through the study of noneconomic factors, a study in which behavioral-science thinking is adopted.
3. The behavioral sciences can be expected to contribute methods that make it possible to measure certain noneconomic factors that are usually not considered to be amenable to measurement by economists or have not earlier entered into discussions of economic problems. A difficulty is that even though similar-sounding concepts are used in economics and psychology, their operational meanings may differ considerably.

C. The Main Focus of the Chapter

The main focus of this paper will be on the theory of consumer choice and the possibilities of shedding new light on selected macroeconomic issues in advertising by means of behavioral science. The actual use of the behavioral sciences in advertising practice will hardly be covered at all. Textbooks on marketing and advertising management tend to give very full coverage of the manifold uses of the behavioral sciences for marketing purposes, and some of this stock of knowledge will be utilized (see, e.g., Aaker and Myers, 1975).

Ideally, the role of the behavioral scientist in a context like this would be to take up an issue where the economist must leave it unresolved, without recourse to noneconomic thinking, and provide insights that could contribute toward resolution of the controversies. An example may be the role of advertising in prices. An important question is whether advertising affects price elasticity, either increasing or decreasing it. There is as yet no firm basis in economic theory or in empirical findings for giving a definitive answer to this question. Various contingencies have been suggested, but too little is known about the actual explanatory value of these contingencies (Farris and Albion, 1980, 1982; Ferguson, 1982). Unfortunately, the behavioral scientist, as will be shown later, can hardly improve directly on the knowledge of the suggested contingencies; rather, he can add a few new ones for exploration.

Generally speaking, the role of the behavioral scientist with regard to economic issues and demands for explanation remains one of adding contingencies to relations that the economists want to be simple. There is, for the behavioral scientist with a background in psychology, always a temptation to add a large number of contingencies that economists may believe to be unnecessary, since the differences are expected or assumed to cancel out in a large population. In this article I shall introduce a few new contingencies, but I shall try to make a number of psychological negligibility assumptions to make the treatment more general and more abstract (see Musgrave, 1981; and Epstein, 1980).

II. SOME CHARACTERISTICS OF ADVERTISING

A. Definition of Advertising

The definition of advertising that is prevalent in marketing contexts encompasses five major features. Advertising is

1. a paid presentation of messages
2. via the mass media, such as the press, broadcasting, movies, direct mail, and posters,
3. by an identifiable sender
4. with the goal of promoting sales of a good (product, service, or idea)
5. in a profitable way.

As seen by an advertiser, the effects of advertising derive from:

- How much money is spent on advertising (the advertising appropriation).
- What media are used for transmitting the advertising messages (media selection).
- What format and contents are given to the advertising messages (advertising creativity).

Advertising costs are to a very large extent media costs. Estimates of the media cost share of total advertising costs vary somewhat from country to country and over time, but generally over 75 percent of advertising costs are media costs.

In the present context there is no need for a more precise definition or of a more detailed discussion of advertising characteristics. I shall deal only with aspects relating to consumer behavior. There are possible direct effects on consumer demand, and there are possible indirect effects such as effects on prices, quality levels, concentration of firms within an industry, and new product development.

B. Advertising and Consumer Welfare

The ultimate criterion for assessing the value of advertising is consumer welfare, which, interpreted in terms of the behavioral sciences, is tantamount to consumer well-being. Direct measurements of consumer well-being are sometimes carried out but hardly ever cover directly the effects of advertising on this criterion. Although some attempts at rough assessments using surveys have been made (Bauer and Greyser, 1968; Treasure, 1970), a discussion of the value of advertising for consumer welfare must rely primarily on piecemeal evidence and indirect assessment and reasoning.

There may be several reasons for wanting to establish whether advertising is good or bad or to what extent advertising is good or bad for consumer welfare. Advertising costs may go up in a country, and the question arises whether this increases or decreases consumer welfare. The established level of advertising may also seem too high even though it does not change. As a matter of fact, advertising costs as a percentage of GNP or private consumption tend to be fairly stable over long periods of time in industrialized countries. The question is usually whether a decrease in the level of advertising expenditure through a lowering of consumer prices will increase consumer welfare or at least not affect it in any bad way. Advertising regulation through the imposition of taxes seems to aim at reducing the volume of advertising, because the level of advertising is held to be exceedingly high in some industries. (Boddewyn, 1983). If it cannot be specifically stated that advertising contributes to or decreases consumer welfare, it is again desirable to be able to specify under what circumstances one type of effect or another obtains and, moreover, to make some estimate of the frequency of both types of occurrences.

III. ADVERTISING AND CONSUMER CHOICE

A. Advertising and Economic Rationality

The basic assumption in economic theory is that consumer behavior is rational, in the sense that it involves maximization of utility for given financial resources. Rationality in the basic sense is possible only when markets are perfect, involving complete information about alternatives and, if Lancaster's (1979) view is adopted, the relevant characteristics pertaining to each alternative expenditure. There are two major reasons for imperfections, from this point of view. One has to do with the time aspect. It is logically not possible to know in advance what utility can be had from the consumption of a certain amount or of a certain object. This can be remedied in theory by introducing the concept of expectation and, further, by postulating that expectations are exclusively based on previous experience; no heed is paid to the difficulty of explaining the first consumption. The second source of imperfection is in a sense spatial and refers to the fact that knowledge is somehow unavailable to the consumer in its fullest extent.

A first attempt to describe the role of advertising can be made using the simple fundamental model of consumer behavior of microeconomic theory. The next step is to see what new developments in behavioral consumer choice theory can do to elaborate and clarify the role of advertising.

The rationality model for consumer choice postulates that the consumer maximizes his utility when using his purchasing power. Essentially this involves following the preference scale and observing the budget limit when he allocates money to different expenditures. If the assumption is made that the consumer should be fully informed about his preferences and the alternatives available on the market, advertising can, logically, have the following potential effects:

    a. It can contribute to the fact that the consumer is fully informed about the alternatives, including prices and other attributes of alternatives.
    b. It can contribute to the fact that the consumer knows his preferences.
    c. It can serve as a source for building up realistic expectations about the utility to be derived from the consumption of different alternatives.

These are advertising's potentially good effects, which facilitate rationality. The potentially negative effects are:

    a. Advertising can obfuscate the consumer's preferences and cause temporary deviations from the prevailing preference scale (short-term versus long-term need satisfaction or utility).
    b. It can enhance certain alternatives or features of alternatives in an inappropriate way.

c. It can inspire disregard of the budget limit and encourage over-spending or dissaving.

If the criterion that a notion should be amenable to empirical assessment is applied to the above model, it appears that some concepts are hardly amenable to empirical testing, except perhaps in strict laboratory experiments with control-group designs. Full information and stable or true preference scales are concepts that are difficult to give operational meaning. The concepts can still provide some ideas for economic research related to advertising.

B. *Information in Advertising*

In general, economic discussions of advertising assume that informative advertising may serve the three rationality-promoting functions, whereas suggestive or persuasive advertising may be accompanied by the three adverse effects. Following this line of reasoning, some attempts have been made to measure the informative contents of consumer advertising. Content analytical studies tend to be critical of the informative contents of advertising; this is particularly true for television advertising (Resnick and Stern, 1977; Andrén et al., 1978; Möller, 1970). Difficulties in interpreting results arise because there is necessarily some arbitrariness in the operational definition of information, which easily creates disagreement among judges and provokes criticisms of the research. Independent of any research, there is fairly general agreement among observers and advertising practitioners that there is very little information, in the sense of factual statements, in the advertising for certain types of goods that are fairly homogeneous and carry brand names and, furthermore, are heavily advertised. To a cognitive psychologist the value of content analysis remains limited, since he distinguishes between availability of certain information in a medium, actual consumer exposure, and further reception and storage of the information. Advertising contents and effects often may not correspond.

Theoretically there are at least four information concepts to take into account (Wärneryd, 1978):

1. The universal set of all facts about a product X.
2. The factual information given by advertisers about product X.
3. The information needed by the consumer about product X.
4. The information actually used by the consumer about product X.

The third information category can refer to the subjective judgment of the consumer or—and this is usually foreign to psychological thinking—

be defined by outsiders, such as consumer advisers. I shall not go into the difficulties of investigating the consumer need for information and the actual consumer use of information. Suffice to say there are some possibilities to do studies retrospectively and find evidence of differences between the need for and the use of information. Most often the two seem to coincide, if no new information is given to the consumer.

What has been said so far indicates that content analysis of advertising can at best give only part of the story. The role of the consumer himself must also be elaborated if the effects of different types of advertising are to be properly understood.

In the next section we will look at some new developments in the consumer behavior area and pay special attention to the consumer choice theories, which inform much of present consumer behavior research. The theories reflect the general progress in cognitive psychology and the increased acceptance of it. There are actually several trends behind these phenomena: the development of decision theory (see Slovic et al., 1977; Einhorn and Hogarth, 1981), of problem-solving theory (Simon, 1979), and of the study of cognitive processes such as information processing and memory (Bettman, 1979).

C. Elaboration of the Consumer Choice Process

1. The Broadened Concept of Rationality. The discussion here will focus on a broadened concept of rationality, which tries to incorporate ideas and results from psychological studies of judgment and choice. The tenor of the reasoning is that:

1. Decision making is a process, the end results of which cannot be understood without recourse to knowledge about the process.
2. Being fully informed about all available alternatives and equally informed about their characteristics are impossibilities. The consumer faces limited sets of alternatives and has limited cognitive capacity for receiving and handling information.
3. External search of information may occur, involving behavioral (time and effort) and possibly monetary costs.
4. The handling of information requires skills and abilities that are not freely available and equally distributed among consumers. Man is generally a poor decision maker, partly because he is a poor intuitive statistician and calculator (Bettman, 1979).
5. Subjective rationality is attained through the use of heuristics, i.e., through simplified rules of thumb of which the consumer himself may not always be conscious.

The potential role of advertising naturally becomes more complex with this approach than with the economic-rationality model. Among other things, the distinction that is commonly made by economists between informative and suggestive advertising, or rational and emotional advertising, loses some of its meaning, since exposure, attention, interpretation, storage, and use related to information are important factors in determining the consequences for consumer welfare. Persuasion may yield increased consumer welfare.

2. Consumer Information Processing. The consumer-choice situation can be depicted as a situation in which the consumer becomes aware of a need that demands satisfaction. The need arousal may vary from the registration of a minor problem like becoming aware of the necessity for replenishing some storage of convenience goods (food items, toiletries, detergents, etc.) to the demanding and acute feeling of high tension. The common factor is that there is a problem calling for a solution. The next stage in the process, following the awareness of the problem, is the construction of an information matrix containing, say, rows of alternatives (objects) and columns of characteristics (attributes). An internal search in the consumer's own memory may be enough for him to construct an information matrix that he finds satisfactory. If it is not satisfactory, an external search may start in order to improve the matrix. An information matrix may be highly incomplete in comparison with what the market has to offer and still be regarded as satisfactory by the decision-maker.

If there is an information matrix comprising more than one alternative, the question is how the consumer goes about reducing the matrix to one alternative; that is, how he makes his choice. Behavioral-choice theory distinguishes between three types of processes representing varying degrees of complexity and earlier experience:

1. extended problem-solving with considerable external search,
2. limited problem-solving with some internal and external search,
3. routinized purchasing behavior with internal search, if any.

The consumer may continue the search after the initial awareness of the problem; that is, he may search for more alternatives when earlier experience is felt to be insufficient, or he may search for information on one or more attributes for one or more alternatives. Or he can decide that he has enough information to make a final evaluation and choice. It is also likely that the consumer, in the process of collecting information, makes partial or total evaluations of objects and attributes.

In summary, when the information matrix concept is used to describe a consumer-choice situation, the consumer is assumed to have several options during the process. He can:

1. Stop the search and apply a decision heuristic.
2. Continue the search for information, being open to external information to a varying extent: the consumer may be open only to surprising information, he may be a passive learner, or he may be an active searcher for information.
3. Continue the search for information and, during the process, make value judgments involving the use of heuristics for rejecting objects and attributes as not acceptable.

The term *information* is used here in the general sense that the symbols used convey some meaning to the receiver. The information is not necessarily factual, objective, relevant, or even true, but it makes sense to the receiver.

D. Advertising and Consumer Information Processing

Seen in relation to the consumer's information matrix, advertising—whether referring to the totality of advertising or to the advertising of a single seller—may fulfill the following functions:

1. Furnish information about alternatives and attributes of alternatives.
2. Furnish information about the relevance and importance of attributes.
3. Suggest heuristics ("Choose only brands with attribute X").
4. Speed up the process ("Buy now").

Since emotions are not explicitly handled in the model, the emotion-stirring effect of advertising is covered only through evaluation heuristics, which are usually believed to have some consistency over time. The more persuasive aspects of the impact of advertising are thus not well taken care of by the information-processing models. Consumer information-processing theory implicitly utilizes a kind of subjective relevance criterion for advertising. If the information, given exposure, is judged to be relevant by the consumer who wants to move from an initial, unsatisfactory state to a desired state, it will be used independently of its degree of bias or emotionality. The emphasis is on cognitive rather than emotional or noncognitive motivational factors. The subjective criterion involves a cognitive fit with the consumer's goal hierarchy, which is a means-ends hierarchy perceived as leading to the desired state. If advertising is perceived as not fitting, it will be disregarded. If it is considered and then contributes to a wrong choice, the consumer will make some change in the heuristics used the next time.

If advertising is taken as the joint output of competing advertisers, a possible advertising affect may be to stop a certain process because a more attractive alternative belonging to a different object class catches the consumer's attention and serves as an interrupt in Simon's terms (Bettman, 1979). Recent developments in the study of memory have influenced the development of advertising theory and advertising practice (see Bettman, 1979; van Raaij, 1983; Lynch and Srull, 1982; Singh and Rothschild, 1983; and Hansen, 1984). More will be said about this in the next section.

Many studies of consumer information processing have indicated that consumers use very little of the available information, even in situations where the information is conveniently at hand (Beales et al., 1981). Consumer information-processing theory is based on a large number of laboratory experiments that, to some extent at least, are corroborated by survey research results. The typical laboratory experiment uses an information display with a number of small boxes arrayed in matrix form, with brands as rows and attributes as columns. Each box contains information cards about the brand indicated by the row regarding the attribute indicated by the column. The subject, who is instructed to make a choice among brands, is free to use as many of the information cards as he chooses. There are a large number of variations on this basic design for process tracing that can make the task more similar to reality. The most important feature is that the information-processing behavior of the subject can be observed, often through the additional experimental demand that the subject should "think aloud" while making the choice (Svensson, 1979).

Studies of consumer information processing can elucidate some aspects relating to consumer use of advertising as well as to the use of other information. Advertising is seen as part of the information environment of the consumer. When results from laboratory studies are combined with results from consumer surveys, they give rise to hypotheses about how mass media advertising affects consumer choice. A point of particular interest is how advertising that reaches the consumer at home works together with advertising and product stimuli in the place of purchase (see, e.g., Bettman, 1979, Chapter 11).

Consumer information-processing theory shows many similarities to the microeconomic theory of choice. A major difference is that rationality is taken to be subjective, meaning that different consumers may reach different decisions on the basis of the same objective information. While the theory improves the understanding of how advertising works, it misses certain aspects that are of interest when the economic role of advertising is being assessed.

IV. SOME ADDITIONAL USEFUL PSYCHOLOGICAL CONCEPTS

Consumer information-processing theory is based on cognitive psychology. It is becoming more and more clear that *cognitive* and *conscious* are not synonomous concepts. Doubts have arisen as to how well subjects can report on cognitions (Nisbett and Wilson, 1977; Ericsson and Simon, 1980). Furthermore, the role of emotional reactions is underestimated by the theory (Zajonc, 1980; Zajonc and Markus, 1982). Despite good attempts to enrich the theory with findings and hypotheses from many other areas of consumer research, there are still rather serious lacunae in the systematic knowledge about the effects of advertising on individual consumer behavior. Bettman's attempt at integration of different strands is still the most comprehensive and successful one (Bettman, 1979).

A few concepts in addition to those already mentioned will now be briefly introduced and applied in the discussion of some advertising issues. Obvious candidates for consideration are:

preferences, attitudes, and values
learning
  latent learning
  memory
  stimulus generalization
  adaptation level
  adoption of innovation
social comparisons

A. Preferences, Attitudes, and Values

Decision heuristics are assumed to reflect the underlying values of the decision-maker. While the concept of preference, which is less often used in psychology than in economics, refers to direct comparisons among concrete choice alternatives, attitudes and values refer to more complex patterns of responses. *Value* is the most comprehensive and most abstract of the concepts. Value studies usually concentrate on a few selected values, such as the 18 terminal values of the Rokeach value scale, which also comprises 18 instrumental values (Rokeach, 1973).

Becker's (1979) definition of preferences reminds one of Rokeach's terminal values. Becker argues that "the preferences that are assumed to be stable do not refer to market goods and services. . . . These underlying preferences are defined over fundamental aspects of life—such as health, prestige, sensual pleasure, benevolence, or envy—that do not always bear a stable relation to market goods and services." Obviously, an advertising campaign or even the total amount of advertising at a certain point in time does not affect terminal values in Rokeach's sense or preferences in Becker's sense. Evaluations of specific goods and less comprehensive groups of goods may, of course, be affected by advertising. Attitudes that are more specifically related to objects than are values are, as a matter of fact, a popular dependent variable in many advertising effect studies. It is an open, much debated question whether advertising in the long run contributes to changing basic values in society or, on a more behavioral level, to changing life-styles.

Content analyses of advertising over long periods of time have attempted to provide at least partial answers to this question. A major difficulty is in deciding whether advertising actually conserves prevailing norms, actively inspires changes, or is a mere reflection of what stronger societal forces achieve. Sociological content analyses of advertising seem to reach the conclusion that, on the whole, advertising has a conserving influence and that there are lags before advertising, which is mass appeal, picks up new trends (Möller, 1970). It is significant that studies of gender in advertising conclude that there has been less change in sex roles in advertisements than in reality (Nowak and Andrén, 1982; Courtney and Lockeretz, 1971). Advertising tends to reflect majority opinions, with some exceptions. Exceptions occur when the target groups of advertising campaigns are population segments that differ from the majority. Laboratory studies indicate that advertising can influence children's values (see Roberts and Bachen, 1981, for a review).

B. *Learning*

Learning implies that behavior is changed as a consequence of experience. When there is learning, a consumer may, over time, develop from a badly informed first-time buyer into a well-informed, advice-giving, full-fledged consumer. This assumption implies that a market may differ in terms of imperfection from time to time. In a market where few new consumers are added, imperfect information may become less serious over time because of increasing consumer experience. A fairly well-informed market may—independently of the informative and persuasive efforts of sellers—lose in information when a new generation of buyers emerges on the market.

In a stable market where the addition of new buyers occurs slowly, the learning concept may be tied to the product life cycle. When a really new product is launched on the market, there is little or no experience of it. When the product has been on the market for some time, there are experienced buyers. Advertising theory incorporates the idea that advertising media, format, and contents should vary with the stage in the product life cycle, which reflects consumers' knowledge about the product.

1. Latent Learning. Economic search is based on the notion that the consumer weighs the value of each additional piece of information against the costs of acquiring the information (Stigler, 1961). Psychological learning theory offers the concept of latent learning, or incidental learning, to indicate that (some) learning may occur passively and without conscious registration or motivation to learn. In consumer behavior theory, more and more attention is given to the fact that consumer reception of information may be primarily passive and occur when the consumer is doing something else (see, e.g., Beales et al., 1981). The latent learning is then put to use in the internal search that starts when the purchasing problem arises. The low degree of information-seeking that is usually found in consumer surveys of specific purchasing processes may be explainable by such circumstances.

2. Stimulus Generalization. A special kind of learning involves the acquisition of a certain response to a certain stimulus. Classical Pavlovian conditioning establishes a conditioned response to a stimulus that does not originally elicit this response. In Pavlov's experiments, a bell could be rung to elicit salivation in dogs by being associated with the serving of food; the salivation triggered by the bell is a conditioned response. Advertising of a type that is common in the convenience goods area functions much the same as a conditioning situation. In this kind of advertisement, something pleasant is coupled with a product or a brand. A particularly interesting feature is that a conditioned response may also be elicited by stimuli other than the conditioned one. The fact that one brand prompts a conditioned response in consumers, so that it receives favorable treatment from them, spreads to other brands. The probability of such spreading depends on the degree of similarity between the conditioning stimulus and the new stimulus. Discrimination among stimuli is a matter of learning. The generalization gradient is flat; that is, there is a lot of generalization and little discrimination at the beginning of the learning process. The gradient becomes steeper as learning proceeds. This phenomenon is called stimulus generalization and is particularly interesting in a discussion of brand loyalty as a consequence of advertising. In more general terms, the fact that a stimulus has been reinforced tends to have effects for similar stimuli. High arousal (activation level) leads, as a rule, to less discrimination and more generalization among stimuli.

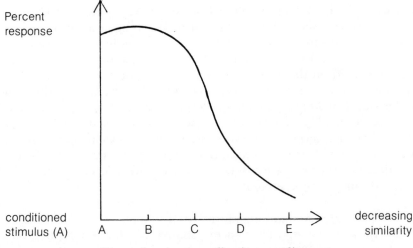

Percent
response

conditioned
stimulus (A)   A   B   C   D   E   decreasing
                                                similarity

Figure 1. A generalization gradient.

Stimulus generalization means that there is no perfect brand loyalty. Even if a consumer is brand loyal, he may not be willing to "walk a mile for a Camel" (cigarette), as the Broadway advertising sign pretended. If similar brands are available, some generalization of the buying response will occur. Barriers of entry based on brand loyalty instigated by advertising may then not be insurmountable. The degree of generalization among the available brands in a product class can be studied through market research (see Figure 1).

3. Recognition and Recall. A distinction is often made between two ways of retrieving stored material from memory. The simplest type of retrieval is when some stimulus information that has been presented earlier is again presented and is recognized. The other retrieval occurs in the absence of the original or similar information and requires more of an effort—this is called recall. The ability to recognize is much better than the ability to recall. Transfer to storage for recognition takes place much more rapidly than storage for recall. Recognition is facilitated at higher levels of arousal, while recall easily becomes impaired. There seems to be a tendency in modern advertising, especially for convenience goods that are commonly referred to as low-involvement goods, to aim at the recognition part of the memory. Advertising may, according to some studies and to practical experience, have effects that are the result of recognition without recourse to recall. If a consumer is exposed to advertising stimuli that may not register consciously, he may still recognize the advertised product or brand in the store and choose among the alternatives on the basis of recognition alone.

4. Adaptation Level. The concept of level of adaptation originated in psychophysics. When stimuli such as weights were judged, it was noted that the subjects seemed to use anchoring points against which comparisons were made to decide whether a particular weight was light or heavy. The measure of the adaptation level was defined as that stimulus weight that is judged on the average as being neither heavy nor light. Above the adaptation level weights tend to be judged heavy; below it they tend to be judged light. The adaptation level corresponds to a psychological zero point on a bipolar scale of quantitative meanings (Guilford, 1954). The adaptation level was shown to shift when special anchor stimuli of varying weights were introduced. Long experience with a particular type of stimulus decreased such shifts. The adaptation level is determined through three sets of stimuli:

1. The set of stimuli judged (the focal stimuli).
2. Background stimuli or anchor stimuli, which are not judged (the contextual stimuli).
3. Stimuli judged earlier: the residual effect of all pertinent, previous experiences (the residual stimuli).

The adaptation level is defined as the weighted geometric mean of all stimuli affecting the organism (Helson, 1964). The general equation for adaptation level is found in psychophysics (Guilford, 1954, p. 330).

$$A_e = A_p^m \cdot A_c^n \cdot \bar{S}_i^e$$

where

A_e is the adaptation level resulting from all three sources of determination, including the stimuli being judged,

A_p is the adaptation level at the time the experiment begins,

A_c is the adaptation level that would be given by the contextual stimuli only,

S_i is a stimulus being judged,

$\bar{S}_i$ is the geometric mean of S_i; it is the adaptation level that would be determined by the experimental stimuli alone, and

m, n, and e are weights summing to unity.

In the more convenient logarithmic form the equation reads

$$\log A_e = m \log A_p + n \log A_c + e \log \bar{S}_i$$

From its origin in psychophysics, adaptation-level theory has spread into many other areas (Insko, 1967; Emery, 1969; Appley, 1971; Stroebe and Frey, 1980). At first there were great hopes that the theory would have wide application to all sorts of judgments of social phenomena, but because of the complexity of the dimensions in such cases, the studies have not added significantly to knowledge about social phenomena (Insko, 1967). Some interesting applications have been made in the area of prices and pricing (see section on advertising and price sensitivity).

5. Adoption of Innovation. When a consumer is confronted with an innovation, he passes through a sequence of stages—from first awareness to decision—according to diffusion of innovation theory (see Rogers, 1983). It is a learning process that can assume various forms and have different durations depending on the characteristics of the innovation, the degree of innovativeness of the potential adopter, the adopter's belongingness and degree of integration in the social system, and how far the diffusion has spread. The role of advertising is often one of spreading awareness of the existence of an innovation, notably a new product. The influence of the social system serves to convince the adopter so that he can decide whether to adopt or reject the new product. If experience can be gained easily at low cost, the adopter may make the process short and try the innovation himself, with little or no social support. According to this theory, advertising serves, in the first place, to draw attention to the existence of the new product. Personal influence is assumed to be more important than advertising at the conviction and decision stage.

C. Social Comparisons

People live in social systems that affect their values and their behavior. This fundamental fact is often neglected in much of economic theory. Consumers are not independent of one another but are characterized by social interaction and interdependencies. When yielding to their drive toward social comparisons, human beings receive information and learn norms that influence their behavior. The interactions and comparisons give rise to similarities in values and behavior among the members of each social system. If the influences are concentrated in small groups, similarities in one set of groups may cancel out the effects of similarities in another direction in another set of groups. If, for example, certain groups are optimistic and other groups of similar total size are pessimistic, the influence on behavior at the aggregate level may be negligible. If either the pessimistic or the optimistic groups constitute a majority of the population, optimism-pessimism measures may serve explanatory and predictive purposes. Optimism or pessimism sometimes seem to spread very quickly through social networks with the synergic effects of mass media and social groups (Katona, 1975). At the macro level there may be interaction between such consumer sentiment and advertising.

The effects of advertising are mixed with group influences, mediated through personal contacts and through the mass media. There is no space here to discuss this complex question. It should be enough to stress the importance of social processes, point out that advertising tries to utilize the existence of groups, and that advertising effects can be strengthened or diminished as a result of social processes.

V. ADVERTISING AND THE PROPENSITY TO CONSUME

Advertising critics maintain that advertising increases the propensity to consume. The important question is whether there is less household saving because of advertising. One of the arguments is that advertising has effects on spending behavior and that there is no advertising for nonconsumption alternatives. In rebuttal, it can be asserted that there is certainly advertising and propaganda for saving, especially saving in real terms (for example, real estate) and second, that empirical studies indicate that advertising has effects on the way income is spent but not on how much is spent. It has been suggested that advertising may increase the number of hours people are willing to work (Chiplin and Sturgess, 1982, p. 89). This would affect the propensity to consume. Advertising is not commonly used as an explanatory variable in econometric studies of, for example, private consumption. This can be taken as a sign that the role of advertising in the propensity to consume is insignificant, since there is no lack of advertising data that could be used (see Scitovsky, 1976, p. 205).

A related question is whether advertising influences propensity to consume in certain population groups about which it might be interesting to gain some knowledge; for example, low-income consumers. While advertising may stimulate some people to increase their consumption, it may stimulate others to postpone consumption, work longer, and save, for example, in order to buy expensive durables at a later date. The average effects may be zero, but the effects in a certain population group may be significant. Advertising of credit cards and other forms of consumer credit may stimulate consumption, but it also leads to corresponding contractual saving when the debts are paid back. It is difficult and not always sufficient to assess only the net effects of advertising.

Simon (1970) concludes that the "spread-it-around" hypothesis, which means that advertising influences the way income is used on expenditures but does not influence the level of expenses, is compatible with the psychological evidence. And so is the hypothesis that demand is influenced by advertising. If there is an unsatisfied need for something, money available, and advertising promoting the satisfaction of the need, total demand may increase. Psychological evidence does not help to discriminate between the hypotheses, according to Simon.

The two most important reasons for saving money seem to be postponed consumption, which requires some sort of cash management as long as the money is not spent, and the need for a buffer, which enables the saver to maintain some control if he is hit by mishaps (Katona, 1975). From a psychological point of view it is conceivable that the weight a household gives these reasons could be changed by advertising influence. Yielding to the urge to buy earlier would mean changes in the use of cash management. It is more difficult to see how the need for buffer capital could be affected by product advertising in such a way that this type of saving behavior is negatively affected.

VI. ADVERTISING AND CONSUMER SENSITIVITY TO PRODUCT QUALITY AND PRICES

A. Advertising and Product Quality

It is somewhat surprising to a behavioral scientist that economists classify as imperfect product markets where there are different product alternatives and quality differences. If there are real differences and these are appreciated by consumers, there is no imperfection, in a behavioral sense. Even if the products from different manufacturers are homogeneous but are perceived as different by consumers as a consequence of advertising and other marketing activities, there may be no cause for alarm; there may still be very flat generalization gradients and little discrimination, that is, a high level of substitutability.

The demand for differences in product quality is generally called a matter of taste in economics, which hints that such differences are only superficial. From a psychological point of view, there is no doubt that quality differences can be very important and that they may correspond to considerable differences in needs. So-called image differences often encompass differences in aesthetic quality where taste differences exist and matter. Lancaster's (1979) conceptualization of goods as bundles of characteristics is therefore much more acceptable to behavioral scientists than is the neoclassical consumer choice theory, especially since Lancaster's conceptualization is commensurate with multidimensional scaling methods in psychology. The existence of products with varying quality and varying sets of characteristics makes additional demands on consumer knowledge. It increases the likelihood that the consumer will be to some extent ignorant. From a cognitive point of view, the market can then be said to be characterized by imperfect information. Economists, on the other hand, tend to see a lack of homogeneity in products as the primary phenomenon.

1. Types of Goods. Nelson (1970, 1974) has suggested that a consumer may proceed in two ways to gain information about product qualities: search and experience. Search means that the consumer inspects the options prior to making a purchase decision. By experience is meant the fact that the consumer gains information through buying the product and trying it. Goods are divided into search goods, which are generally durable goods, and experience goods, which correspond more or less to what marketers call convenience goods. Only clothing and clothing-related products in the nondurable group of goods are search goods, according to Nelson's classification (1970). Durables with relatively high repair costs, such as automobiles, radios, television sets, and household appliances are classified as experience goods. China, glassware, furniture, floor coverings, and cameras are examples of search goods. Since many goods have both experience and search qualities, I prefer the distinction made in marketing theory between convenience goods and shopping goods (see also Porter,1974).

Search goods are held to be relatively unaffected by advertising. If they are advertised, retail advertising, which tries to attract customers to the store, prevails over manufacturer advertising. Related to the idea of search and experience behavior is the hypothesis that advertised goods are of a higher quality than nonadvertised goods (Nelson, 1974; Klein and Leffler, 1981).

2. Consumer Reactions to Product Quality. There has been much debate about whether advertising promotes consumer sensitivity to differences in product quality. Nelson's argument that higher quality means more repeat purchases implies a high sensitivity. Producers of high-quality brands will, according to this reasoning, have more incentive to advertise than producers of low-quality brands. The consumer expects that more heavily advertised brands will exhibit a better relation between price and quality than will unadvertised or less heavily advertised brands (Wilde, 1980). The price per unit quality is also, by some other authors, assumed to be more favorable for advertised than for nonadvertised brands because advertising helps higher-quality brands proliferate and because it increases price elasticity and forces sellers of nonadvertised brands to lower their prices per unit of quality (Ferguson, 1982).

Comanor and Wilson (1974), in a study of thirty-eight consumer-goods industries, reached the conclusion that advertising decreased price sensitivity (at the factory level); the same authors (1979) suggest that highly advertised products tend to have high prices and low quality. If both Nelson's and Comanor and Wilson's suggestions are true, the question arises under what circumstances one or the other is true. According to Archibald et al. (1983), Schmalensee (1978) points out an intervening variable that can resolve the controversy. Schmalensee demonstrates that if advertising is assumed to be highly effective or if there are large cost advantages involved in producing low-quality goods, the advertising levels and quality will be negatively related. This is not tantamount to an assumption that low-quality products can survive for long periods of time if they are backed by heavy advertising, which is denied by most practitioners. The term *low quality* actually is used in a relative sense and means lower quality than that of nonadvertised products in the same class. Products of this kind of low quality can thus be perfectly satisfactory from the consumer's point of view.

When it is difficult to judge and grade product quality and there are frequent introductions of new product variants, launched with heavy advertising, the situation described above is more likely to occur. The argument is sometimes referred to as the quality-erosion hypothesis (see, e.g., Kwoka, 1984).

Differentiated products carry with them uncertainty, which can be reduced through search and experience. Wiggins and Lane (1983) extend Nelson's notion about advertising as a signal of product quality. They note that imperfect information may generate risk, which will affect the decisions of risk-averse consumers. They develop a model that incorporates risk and two sources of information about product quality, namely, advertising and search. Advertising is assumed to convey only the fact that a product is advertised but carries no direct information about product quality. Search is the consumer's attempt to supply himself with direct quality information. One source may be substituted for the other. The model is then used to show how firms may use advertising as a sign that advertised products are less risky than unadvertised products. In a numerical example, the authors show that consumers who buy few units and are quite risk-averse tend to purchase advertised products, mainly because there is lower variation in product quality among the advertised brands. The result of this analysis is similar to Telser's (1964) conclusion, based on his studies of toiletries, cosmetics, and foods, that advertised goods may have the same average quality as nonadvertised goods but vary less in quality.

It seems unlikely that a general assessment of advertising's role in product quality, or even consumers' perceptions of product quality, can ever be made. There are many dimensions that have to be considered in the treatment of this problem. The economists have touched on some of them, for instance, the nature of the goods (search or experience), ways of consumer information acquisition, consumer use of advertising, and consumer risk-aversion. In studies of industrial organization, other variables such as the relations between manufacturers and retailers are dealt with (Porter, 1974, 1976). Behavioral considerations can suggest some other factors using the consumer as a starting point.

3. Advertising Content. Nelson and his followers avoid assumptions about the content of advertising and consider only the fact that a product is advertised. This implies that advertising content is uninteresting, except perhaps to the extent that the content influences consumer attention and awareness of the product. For so-called low-involvement goods, which the consumer tends to buy after very simple decision processes, the assumption may be true (Olshavsky and Granbois, 1979). For high-involvement purchases, the assumption does not agree with advertising practice or consumer choice theory. A behavioral question is: What does advertising tell the consumer about product quality, or, more appropriately, How is the consumer's perception of product quality affected? At the base of this question is how well the consumer, using different sources of information, is able to judge product quality when such judgments are relevant. For example, seeking information with a view to judging the quality of gasoline for automobiles when the brands are perfectly similar (unless gas-station attributes are defined as dimensions of the brand) is a complete waste of time for the individual.

Discussions about the flow of commercial advertising have stressed the fact that consumer information from impartial, noncommercial sources is an essential complement to advertising. Product ratings published by consumer agencies are a source of information about product quality. The direct influence of published ratings on consumers is usually, judging from consumer surveys, not very impressive. There may still be effects on the market behavior of sellers if the information is used by certain elite consumers, the so-called information seekers (Thorelli et al., 1975). One study approaches the issue of the relation between advertising and product quality by stating that published ratings for a product class should strengthen the relationships between advertising levels and quality, be followed by a drop in overall advertising levels, and strengthen the relationships between price and quality (Archibald et al., 1983).

These hypotheses were borne out for running shoes—an experience product for which ratings were published in the leading magazine for runners. The results on the whole agree with Nelson's position. Nelson maintains that advertising for search goods has to be close to the facts, since product quality can be ascertained before the purchase. For experience goods there may be seller incentives for dishonest or misleading advertising. Exaggerated claims may stimulate trial purchases by consumers, since the claims cannot be verified prior to actual consumption of the goods (Wilde, 1980). Archibald et al. (1983) conclude that the publication of ratings had such an impact on firms that misleading advertising was made much less likely.

Even if considerable weakness in advertising information exists—despite advertising self-regulation and government regulations—the consumer can usually get some information about product quality from advertising. The name of the manufacturer or the retailer may, for example, hold important information that will influence the consumer's perception of product quality—not only is the product advertised, but it is advertised by a firm that is well-known, has an assortment of products some of which have been tried earlier by the consumer or recommended to him by trustworthy persons, and has appeared in advertisements many times before. Company reputation, which is at least partly built up by advertising, is an important means of making product-quality judgments.

It is not possible to determine empirically either the extent to which homogeneous products can be differentiated through advertising or, in a related issue, the extent to which products are specially equipped with attributes that are planned to furnish arguments for advertising. Simon (1970) declares that homogeneous package goods are characterized by such attempts and that attempts to make a consumer buy an image rather than a product are often successful. Weighing the positive and negative consequences of such advertising, Simon (pp. 284–285) concludes; "those branches of advertising which are most in dispute—advertising for such products as beer, autos, soap and aspirin—do not seem to have much effect upon the economy in any way, direct or indirect, and hence from an economic point of view it is immaterial whether they are present or absent."

4. Psychological Judgments of Product Quality. Consumer information-processing theory, which was briefly presented earlier, gives a framework for describing quality judgments and some hypotheses about how judgments are actually made in situations of uncertainly (Bettman, 1979). Product quality is seen as comprising a number of dimensions that are usually referred to as attributes. In market research, a simple linear-compensatory model of the following type has often been applied (Bettman, 1979):

$$E = \sum_{i=1}^{n} W_i v_i$$

where E is the evaluation of an alternative, v_i is the evaluation of the ith attribute of n attributes, and W_i is the weight attached to the ith attribute. This model has been extensively used in attitude research and is often associated with the psychologist Martin Fishbein (Fishbein and Ajzen, 1975), who has been a protagonist in this area. The basic idea in Fishbein's model is that an attitude toward an object consists of a cognitive component, which reflects the subject's belief about how much of a certain attribute an object has (v_i) and an affective component, which expresses the importance attached to a particular attribute (W_i).

This model makes it possible to further describe advertising's potential role for perceptions of product quality. The linear-compensatory model may contain price as one of the attributes, which distinguishes it from economic utility models. A question to be answered empirically concerns what attributes make up product quality. Market research on attitudes usually starts with attempts to find out which are the relevant attributes. The main focus here is on what the model can contribute to the discussion of advertising and product quality.

Consumer perception and evaluation of product quality can be expressed in terms of the described model. Advertising can affect perception and evaluation in the following manner:

Change the belief about attribute i.
Change the importance weight given to attribute i.
Change the number of attributes (n) considered.

Advertising strategy obviously often works with one or more of these possibilities. Brand advertising for a convenience good—say, a food item or a cosmetic product—may, for example, try to hammer in that the brand is well equipped with a certain attribute that is highly valued by the consumer (the meat of the hamburger!). Or, in another situation, the advertising might aim at changing the importance attached to a certain attribute.

The model is compensatory, which means that low values for one attribute may be compensated for by high values on other attributes. There is a tendency in some advertising to stress certain attributes and to encourage the consumer to stop considering alternative brands that do not have high values on these attributes. If such emphasis is put on certain attributes, the linear-compensatory model is no longer an appropriate description. There are a number of noncompensatory models, but they usually do not give the simple choice rules that the linear-compensatory model does.

Empirical studies of consumer decision-making processes indicate that the processes often can be seen as sequences where first a noncompensatory heuristic is used to arrive at a tractable number of alternatives and then a compensatory heuristic is applied to the remaining alternatives (van Raaij, 1976; Bettman, 1979). The conjunctive model describes behavior where there is a cutoff point for each relevant attribute and elimination of alternatives that do not lie above the cutoff point on all attributes. Even in the absence of appropriate content analyses of brand advertising, it can hardly be rash to state that the arguments of some advertising obviously follow this pattern. This is simply the idea of using product differentiation to advantage in advertising.

A decision process that involves a choice among many alternatives can be made more or less efficient through the choice of heuristics. A principle that rejects a larger number of alternatives in the process is more efficient when it is used early in the process than when it is used later (Wilde, 1980; Bettman, 1979, p. 255). If advertising operates in such a way that the most important, relevant attributes are judged and evaluated early in the process, it can save time and search costs for the consumer. Again, there is the question of whether advertising as a rule actually stresses the attributes that are most important to the consumer. Advertising may increase quality sensitivity, emphasizing irrelevant attributes in such a way that consumer welfare is not furthered. Such an effect presupposes that all brand advertisers act the same way, which is usually not the case. The consumer may get important information about relevant attributes from comparing the advertising of several brands.

B. Advertising and Price Sensitivity

1. Manufacturers' Advertising. "Does advertising increase prices?" is a common question in advertising debates. Critics of advertising say yes and defenders say no. Using the simple argument that advertising has to be paid for, many economists also agree on yes as an answer to this question. In industrial organization studies many attempts have been made to answer the question on both theoretical and empirical grounds. A review (Farris and Albion, 1980) of the empirical evidence related to the question shows that there is conflicting evidence. There are cases where manufacturers' advertising seems to decrease price sensitivity (Comanor and Wilson, 1974; Lambin, 1976), and there are cases where advertising seems to increase price sensitivity (see, e.g., Backman, 1967; Benham 1972; Kwoka, 1984). The authors try to reconcile the apparently conflicting results through introducing a third factor, namely, retail competition. The idea is that manufacturer advertising may decrease price sensitivity at the factory level but increase it at the retail level. The assumption is that the more manufacturer advertising there is, the more interest there will be among retailers to stock and promote the product. Retail competition can thus be encouraged through manufacturer advertising and may involve lower retail prices.

The following implications of the review of the evidence are stated "with some degree of confidence" by the authors (Farris and Albion, 1980, p. 33).

1. High relative manufacturer advertising is associated with high relative manufacturer factory prices.
2. High relative manufacturer advertising is associated with low relative retail margins.
3. High relative retail advertising is associated with low relative consumer brand price.
4. High relative manufacturer advertising is associated with high relative consumer brand price, but not as strongly as in 1.
5. High manufacturer advertising can be associated with high or low absolute consumer price levels.

The issue is thus on the whole left unresolved. The authors have been criticized for their attempt to use retail competition as an explanatory factor. This use goes against the theory of derived demand, which tends to see retailers' demand for manufacturers' brands as derived demand with manufacturer advertising as an influence (Ferguson, 1982). This means that the more elastic consumer demand is at the retail level, the more elastic will be the retailers' demand for goods from the manufacturers. The authors' reply to the criticism is that their reasoning is based on observations of reality, not on theory and that the theory, rather than reality, may be wrong (Farris and Albion, 1982).

Manufacturers' advertising may, for several reasons, be lacking in price information. Resale price maintenance is forbidden in many countries; manufacturers are restricted to suggested retail prices and can thus mention only these prices in their advertisements. Such price information may irritate retailers who want to maintain price policies of their own, and this may be a reason for manufacturers to be reluctant to include price information in their advertising. Advertising by retailers is typically informative about prices. Big-scale retail outlets generally operate with low margins, low relative prices, and heavy advertising.

2. Retail Advertising. One American study found that eyeglasses were cheaper in states where advertising for eyeglasses was permitted than in states where such advertising was prohibited (Benham, 1972). The findings can be explained in several ways. It has been suggested that consumer loyalty or attachment to the products of individual firms is limited when there is advertising and the product is a shopping good. Advertising in such cases promotes more elastic demand by providing information about alternatives. If eyeglasses are not advertised, the consumer costs for external search become higher, since buyers have to substitute window-shopping and store visits for advertising. It may be argued that the scope and quality of the information consumers can get from such activities far surpass what they get from advertising, but a reasonable assumption is that availability and price are very important dimensions in consumer choice heuristics and that consumers in general hesitate to incur search costs when their behavioral cost budget is limited (see Verhallen and Pieters, 1984). In a later study of optometric services the hypothesis was again confirmed. "The evidence reveals that advertisers' prices and quality are indeed lower, and while nonadvertisers' prices fall, their quality actually is greater. Furthermore, nonadvertisers remain in sufficient numbers in the market so that average market quality is not lower, but indeed greater" (Kwoka, 1984, p. 216). The hypothesis that advertising leads to quality erosion was thus rejected.

3. Factors Influencing Price Sensitivity. Nelson (1974) has argued that consumers, independently of learning any specific product information, may get the conviction that the product is good for its price. While Nelson points to frequent exposure to a seller's advertising as an important persuasive factor irrespective of advertising contents, Klein and Leffler (1981) assume that the fact that an advertiser spends a lot of money on advertising make consumers believe that the firm has great confidence in its own products and that they can rely on their quality. Recent studies of reactions to quantitative information in persuasive messages give some indirect support to these ideas (Yalch and Elmore-Yalch, 1984).

Price sensitivity at the household level is usually assumed to presuppose knowledge about prices. When consumers are asked about the prices of different products, they often display ignorance, even of the prices of frequently bought grocery items. Studies indicate that consumers may remember price relations rather than absolute prices and that they rely on price information in the store for making price comparisons (Zeithaml, 1982).

A consumer may very well remember that a product is cheap in relation to something else without remembering its absolute price. This can be explained by adaptation-level theory. Conversely, a consumer may gain the impression that something is relatively cheap without any price information at all. A typical phenomenon, which has been verified through market research, is that the consumer in a grocery store or supermarket consistently looks for item labels—often in attention-getting colors—which indicate special prices. Advertising may use more or less subtle hints or downright statements that a product is cheap to convey an image of cheapness both in an absolute sense and in the sense of quality for the price. There is no way of telling exactly how long such effects can last if the impression of cheapness is not corroborated in its essentials by reality. A general surmise is that the effects cannot last very long even though the consumers may not know the absolute price differences.

Retail stores may be anxious to create the image of being cheap. Low prices for a few products may contribute efficiently to creating such an image through the phenomenon of stimulus generalization, which was mentioned earlier (Nyström, 1970). The idea that prices are low is generalized from the products for which this is true to products where it is not true. Obviously, advertising can be used for such purposes. Price reductions may even be so considerable on some products that they become what is known in marketing as loss leaders.

4. Price as an Indicator of Product Quality. Price and quality are generally believed by consumers to be positively correlated. This does not necessarily imply that a consumer is therefore willing to pay more for higher quality. There is a budgetary limit, if nothing else, and in many cases also an adaptation level for prices relating to a product class. Adaptation-level theory, which was briefly presented earlier, has some interesting implications for consumer price sensitivity (see Emery, 1969). In the first place, products are hypothesized to be judged in relative terms—such as cheap or expensive—depending on an internal standard, in other terminology often called fair price, rather than in any absolute way (Kamen and Toman, 1970). Second, the internal standard tends to shift systematically on the basis of new experience. If a consumer has negligible earlier experience of prices in a product class, his judgments are affected by contextual stimuli and by the prices of competing products. Contextual stimuli are, for example, consumer information from commercial or noncommercial sources. Advertising can furnish contextual stimuli that can raise or lower the adaptation level. If an extremely high price is presented as a contextual stimulus and the consumer has little previous price experience, the adaptation level is raised and other prices are judged as lower. Similarly, if an extremely low price is shown, other prices will be judged to be higher and the products thus more expensive. This coincides with techniques used by skilled hagglers.

Many studies, comprising both field surveys and laboratory and field experiments, show that there is a lower price limit below which a consumer does not want to buy a product because he does not believe it can have sufficient quality at that lower price (Gabor, 1977). There is an upper price limit above which a product is seen as too expensive. The upper limit is not expressed in quality terms—the price is too high independently of the quality offered. These studies and many others bear out perceptions of positive correlation between price and quality (see Monroe, 1973, for a review). It is generally concluded that in the absence of other informational cues about product quality and for lack of product experience, the consumer tends to use price as an indicator of product quality; if quality but not price is known, the consumer will infer a higher price for a higher quality.

Advertising can use this perception of positive correlation between price and quality; for example, by implicitly and explicitly connecting brand price and brand quality. If an advertisement for a brand is pervaded by cues of high product quality and the price is not mentioned, the consumer is likely to infer a high price. The consequence of such an inference may be that his interest in the product is lessened. Or a lower actual price than expected may be a pleasant surprise with persuasive effects. Few studies have so far been carried out of how consumers make trade-offs between price and quality when they choose among products. Conjoint analysis and similar techniques are becoming common in market research for proprietary purposes, but few results have been published about quality-price trade-offs. In a recent experimental study, it was found that consumers use simple heuristics such as comparing arithmetic differences in price with perceived differences in quality when they make their purchasing decisions (Levin and Johnson, 1984). This may be true if there is a very simple scale of quality differences, but it may become too complicated when quality is a more complex phenomenon.

VII. ADVERTISING AND COMPETITION

A. *Firm Concentration, Barriers to Entry, and Brand Loyalty*

Advertising's effect on competition is one of the major controversies in the macroeconomic discussion of advertising. Some problem areas can be distinguished.

Does advertising lead to the concentration of firms?
Does advertising serve as a barrier to entry?
Does advertising stimulate new product development?

It is commonly assumed that advertising promotes concentration tendencies, that it serves as a barrier to entry for new competitors, and that it may promote new product development but may thereby spur product differentiation that is not equivalent to improved products. The theoretical analyses have been criticized by economists, and the empirical studies have often found little evidence for the assumed negative effects (Lambin, 1976). In a review of theoretical and empirical studies related to advertising and competition, Comanor and Wilson (1979) arrive at the following conclusion: "The weight of available evidence is consistent with the hypothesis that heavy advertising can have substantial anticompetitive consequences. However, because the distribution of advertising intensities is highly skewed, there is no indication that these effects are pervasive throughout the economy or even within the manufacturing sector. Rather, they appear to be concentrated in a small number of industries with high advertising-sales ratios and/or high absolute levels of advertising per firm" (p. 470). The authors agree with Kaldor (1950) in noting that retail advertising disseminates market information, which tends to reduce market imperfection. They seem to find industries that are characterized by what Simon (1970) calls "homogeneous package goods" guilty of creating anticompetitive tendencies through advertising.

Concentration is usually operationally defined as the share of the market held by the four largest firms in a product class. The phenomenon can be further studied by finding out whether the same companies appear among the four dominant firms over long periods of time. In the consumer goods area, the discussion primarily concerns the effects of advertising of convenience goods.

The questions of the concentration tendencies of manufacturers of convenience goods as a consequence of advertising and of advertising serving as a barrier to entry are closely related, especially when the time dimension is taken into account. From a behavioral point of view the question is, in both cases, whether advertising can contribute to buying behavior so that the consumers make clear and consistent discriminations among brands and, through favoring a brand, can give monopolistic power to that brand.

The existence of and the reasons for brand loyalty thus become crucial issues in the discussion of advertising effects (Schmalensee, 1974). Brand loyalty in the sense of a stable consumer habit of buying only or predominantly one brand is not a necessary prerequisite for oligopolistic market concentration. The idea of concentration is compatible with the idea that at some stage in the decision process, the consumer limits the number of alternatives for further consideration through, for example, a noncompensatory heuristic. If consideration is restricted to three or four alternatives at most (in marketing referred to as the evoked set), through the influence of advertising, and these are the most advertised brands, the dominance effect may arise. A less contrived idea is that advertising and brand availability in retail outlets are highly correlated and that availability is most important for consumer choice. The latter has been indicated by many studies (see, e.g., Buzzell, 1964, for an early field experiment). The relative amount of advertising of a brand may influence both retailer and consumer demand so that availability becomes proportionate to the advertising.

Buying a brand regularly, so that whenever the need for the product arises a certain brand is most likely to be chosen, is usually a mixture of several factors. The most important may be the reinforcement the consumer has received from earlier purchases. Ehrenberg (1974) maintains that reinforcement is the conviction that the brand is at least as good as any other brand. This assumption means that the generalization gradient is rather flat and that catching the attention of the consumer is a significant factor in one brand winning over competing brands. The share of total industry advertising and the share of the market for the brands will then tend to coincide.

Store loyalty, which may exclude some otherwise possible alternative brands from the evoked set, is another important factor. Brand loyalty and store loyalty are often mixed, which may give an exaggerated impression of brand loyalty. Prices and search costs are not the only things considered by the consumer when selecting a store. Rather than search costs in a strict sense there may often be other behavioral costs related to availability, consumer knowledge about availability, and store image (Verhallen and de Nooij, 1982).

There are distributions of brand loyalty; relatively few consumers are highly loyal even for a well-established brand. There is some evidence (Raj, 1982) that advertising for brand A has more effect on highly loyal buyers than on buyers with low loyalty toward brand A. Raj's study concerned a convenience good for which an increase in consumption was possible through market growth.

Advertising of a brand also affects the sales of other brands through the phenomenon of generalization. This is true in particular at the earlier stages in the product life cycle, when consumers are ignorant of product attributes and learn about them from brand advertising. The degree of generalization depends on how similar the brands are perceived to be. If the brands are similar and this can be established with some ease, brand loyalty will become rather frail and can easily break down. Advertising can apparently increase cross elasticities among brands, in some cases.

From a behavioral point of view, advertising does not appear to be a barrier to entry in principle. Buying habits or routines for convenience goods are never completely established and are changeable, although there may be difficulties if they are old. New stimuli are, other things being equal, more likely to arouse interest than are familiar stimuli. If consumers are confronted with new products in a store, in other people's homes, and in the advertising media, these new items are more likely to arouse attention than are old products. The cost of media space may seem prohibitive to some product innovators who want to launch a new product on a market in which a few brands dominate, their dominance

supported by heavy advertising, but creative uses of media have overcome such difficulties. Acquiring the new product may involve too much
effort—too great a behavioral cost—for the consumer to be willing to
make a change in purchasing habits, but that is a question of availability
rather than of advertising.

B. Advertising and New Products

Studies of influences at different stages of the individual adoption
process show that after the first stage of awareness of the innovation
there follows a stage of consideration and deliberation. If the adopter
has little earlier experience with the product and there is some amount
of risk involved in acquiring the innovation, the consumer tends to look
for support from a trusted source ("legitimation"). This would tend to
reduce the persuasive effect of advertising on consumer durables and
favor personal influence.

Convenience goods (nondurables) are characterized by low risk, in the
sense that they are mostly cheap to purchase and try out. In buying a
food item, there may be some social risk involved if all the members of
a household reject a new brand or new product variant that the housewife
has bought for the purpose of trying it. The arguments for a product
provided by advertising may help the housewife cope with such social
risks ("They [the advertisement] said it tasted so good"). It is the role of
advertising first to make the consumer try the product, which means the
consumer must attend to it in the store and make a trial purchase. It is
important for the effect that the store arrangements facilitate the trial.
For repeat purchases, the consumer's evaluation after the trial is decisive.
There must be the reinforcement that the product or brand was worth
trying and is worthy of further consideration (Ehrenberg, 1974). Advertising may contribute to the reinforcement by giving the consumer
a pat on the back for having made a good choice.

The consumer's willingness to take risks and the perception of risk
may be affected by advertising. Some risk-taking is necessary to produce
consumer welfare and, as in other areas of risk-taking, there may be a
need for persuasion to make people take the jump and engage in a risky
act. There are practical limits to persuasion; that is, short of coercion,
persuasion is not always effective. There are obvious ethical restraints,
implying that the consumer's personal integrity must not be violated
through the persuasive attempts.

The role of advertising when new products are introduced is one of
creating awareness of the existence of the new product and of building
up interest in it. Theories of diffusion and adoption of new products
stress the importance of the social systems where the introductions occur

(Rogers, 1983). If a new product deviates from the prevailing norms, for example, because of unexpected attributes, the diffusion is likely to be a slow process and the product may be totally rejected despite heavy advertising. The majority of new convenience goods or, rather, product variants launched on the market are complete market failures. It takes something more than the sheer amount of advertising for a new product to succeed.

Advertising is no doubt an important technique for promoting new products. The alternative to advertising is usually other selling efforts involving communication. Whether the effect of advertising is economically sound or unsound ultimately becomes a question of how the new product is valued. In certain product areas, it seems possible that advertising can promote product differentiation that, from an economic point of view, has little value to the consumer (see Simon, 1970). Advertising research using the behavioral sciences tends to show that there are consumers who appreciate such product differences, especially when they derive from aesthetic properties.

VIII. CONCLUDING REMARKS

In this chapter, I have treated advertising and consumer behavior in a perspective provided by some macroeconomic issues related to advertising effects. Theoretical and empirical analyses of these issues have usually been inconclusive, in the sense that no simple relationships between advertising and such phenomena as consumer choice, propensity to consume, price sensitivity, and competition have been found. This means that it is desirable to investigate under which circumstances advertising has specific types of effect. Many attempts to throw light on the intervening factors involve assumptions about consumer behavior (Porter, 1974, 1976; Comanor and Wilson, 1979). The behavioral sciences may thus be able to furnish some insights which might make it possible to differentiate better among the hypotheses.

In many discussions of advertising effects, attempts are made to derive conclusions about the different types of possible effects on the basis of assumptions about consumer behavior. Typically, consumers are assumed to be alike: The models specify one type of behavior that is expected from every consumer or the average consumer. With the possible exception of psychophysics, psychological research does not primarily focus on finding general laws of behavior or on average behavior. On the contrary, it is, to a large extent, differential psychology that tries to bring forth and explain individual differences. Economists tend to be interested in the average consumer, with as little dispersion as possible around the average. The effects of many individual differences are assumed to cancel out in a large population. Being based on psychology, consumer behavior theory is poor in broad generalizations and rich in details. For the discussion of advertising effects, it would probably be good if behavioral scientists could be induced to make more negligibility assumptions and become more inclined to accept averages over large populations (Epstein, 1980; Katona, 1975). Economists could perhaps discard a few canceling-out assumptions and open up new domains of study guided by behavioral science knowledge.

I have wanted to draw attention to some psychological concepts and variables of potential explanatory value in the analysis of advertising effects. First, I pointed to the extended concept of rationality as it is displayed in consumer information-processing theory. The potential role of advertising appears complex and somewhat different from its role when economic rationality is used as a framework for describing individual advertising effects. External and internal search for information in combination with surprising information and passive information reception (latent or incidental learning) are important concepts for explaining advertising effects at the micro level.

Learning comprises a series of phenomena that all hold potential interest for explaining advertising effects. Memory research has found that recognition memory has certain characteristics that favor the use of certain types of mass-media advertising—especially pictorial advertising such as television commercials—in combination with point-of-sale advertising. Advertising of many convenience goods that are typically characterized by low-involvement purchasing processes tends to function differently from advertising of shopping goods. Since advertising effects are generalized from one brand to another depending on their perceived similarity, brand loyalty based on advertising tends to be limited. Price sensitivity can be discussed in terms of adaptation level—a kind of anchoring point that can be affected positively or negatively by advertising.

The adoption of an innovation like a new product can be seen as learning over time. In this perspective, advertising appears to be important in creating awareness of the new product, while personal influence must supplement it at the persuasive stage. This relates potential advertising effects to the product life cycle, which is a very important concept in marketing but is rarely mentioned in macroeconomic discussions of advertising.

Finally, the effects of advertising are mingled with social influences that are enmeshed in social networks of differing complexity and strength. The effects of advertising are, in some cases at least, indirect— through social contacts—rather than direct and impersonal. Direct effects seem to prevail when acquiring the product means little risk, which facilitates trial.

My discussion is not intended to be conclusive; it is meant to suggest new research possibilities. The purpose has been to illustrate the use of theoretical and empirical concepts, including their manifold marketing applications, to the discussion of advertising issues. As a final point, it should be said that there has been considerable research on advertising and consumer behavior that uses behavioral sciences and that is apart from immediate commercial interests. Since the available data on consumer behavior often come from commercial sources that have practical purposes, and since analyses have focused on developing marketing theory, there is too seldom direct relevance with macroeconomic issues. Still, macroeconomists working with advertising problems can certainly find worthwhile results in the type of studies mentioned.

REFERENCES

Aaker, D.A. and J.G. Myers, *Advertising Management*. Englewood Cliffs, NJ: Prentice-Hall, 1975.

Andrén, G., L.O. Ericsson, R. Ohlsson, and T. Tännsjö, *Rhetoric and Ideology in Advertising: A Content Analytical Study of American Advertising*. Stockholm: Liber Förlag, 1978.

Appley, M.H., ed., *Adaptation-Level Theory: A Symposium*. New York: Academic Press, 1971.

Archibald, R.B., C.A. Haulman, and C.E. Moody Jr., "Quality, Price, Advertising and Published Quality Ratings," *Journal of Consumer Research* 9 (1983), 347–356.

Arndt, J. and J.L. Simon, "Advertising and Economics of Scale: Critical Comments on the Evidence," *Journal of Industrial Economics* 32 (1983), 229–240.

Backman, J., *Advertising and Competition*. New York: New York University Press, 1967.

Bauer, R.A. and S.A. Greyser, *Advertising in America: The Consumer View*. Boston, MA: Harvard School of Business, 1968.

Beales, H., M.B. Mazis, S.C. Salop, and R. Staelin, "Consumer Search and Public Policy," *Journal of Consumer Research* 8 (1981), 11–22.

Becker, G., "Economic Analysis and Human Behavior," in L. Levy-Garbona, ed., *Sociological Economics*. London: Sage Publications, 1979, pp. 7–24.

Benham, L., "The Effect of Advertising on the Price of Eyeglasses," *Journal of Law and Economics*, 15 (October 1972), 337–352.

Bettman, J., *An Information Processing Theory of Consumer Choice*. Reading, MA: Addison-Wesley, 1979.

Boddewyn, J.J., "Advertising Taxation is Here to Stay—and Fight," *International Journal of Advertising*, 2 (1983), 291–300.

Buzzell, R.D., *Mathematical Models and Marketing Management*. Boston: Graduate School of Business Administration, Harvard University, 1964.

Chiplin, B., and B. Sturgess, *Economics of Advertising*, 2nd ed. London: Holt Rinehart and Winston, with the Advertising Association, 1982.

Comanor, W.S., and T.A. Wilson, "The Effect of Advertising on Competition: A Survey," *Journal of Economic Literature*, 17 (1979), 453–476.

Comanor, W.S., and T.A. Wilson, *Advertising and Market Power*. Cambridge, MA: Harvard University Press, 1974.

Courtney, A.E., and S.W. Lockeretz, "A Woman's Place: An Analysis of the Roles Portrayed by Women in Magazine Advertisements," *Journal of Marketing Research*, 8 (1971), 92–96.

The Economics of Advertising. A study prepared by the Economists Advisory Group. London: The Advertising Association, 1967.

Ehrenberg, A.S.C., "Repetitive Advertising and the Consumer," *Journal of Advertising Research*, 14 (1974), No. 2, 25–34.

Einhorn, H.J., and R.M. Hogarth, "Behavioral Decision Theory: Processes of Judgment and Choice," *Annual Review of Psychology*, 32 (1981), 53–88.

Emery, F., "Some Psychological Aspects of Price," in B. Taylor and G. Wills, eds., *Pricing Strategy*. London: Staples, 1969, pp. 98–111.

Epstein, S., "The Stability of Behavior, II. Implications for Psychological Research," *American Psychologist*, 35 (1980), 790–806.

Ericsson, K.A. and H.A. Simon, "Verbal Reports as Data," *Psychological Review*, 87 (1980), 215–251.

Farris, P.W., and M.S. Albion, "Reply to 'Comments on "The Impact of Advertising on the Price of Consumer Products,"' " *Journal of Marketing*, 46 (Winter, 1982), 106–107.

Farris, P.W., and M.S. Albion, "The Impact of Advertising on the Price of Consumer Products," *Journal of Marketing*, 44 (Summer 1980), 17–35.

Ferguson, J.M., "Comments on 'The Impact of Advertising on the Price of Consumer Products,' " *Journal of Marketing*, 46 (Winter 1982), 102–105.

Fishbein, M., and I. Ajzen, *Belief, Attitude, Intention and Behavior: An Introduction to Theory and Research*. Reading, MA: Addison-Wesley, 1975.

Gabor, A., *Pricing: Principles and Practices*. London: Heinemann Educational Books, 1977.

Guilford, J.P., *Psychometric Methods*, 2nd ed. New York: McGraw-Hill, 1954.

Hansen, F., "Towards an Alternative Theory of the Advertising Communication Process?" *International Journal of Research in Marketing*, 1 (1984), 69–80.

Helson, H., *Adaptation-Level Theory*. New York: Harper and Row, 1964.

Insko, C.A., *Theories of Attitude Change*. New York: Appleton-Century-Crofts, 1967.

Jacobson, R., and F.M. Nicosia, "Advertising and Public Policy: The Macro-Economic Effects of Advertising," *Journal of Marketing Research*, 18 (1981), 29–38.

Jacoby, J., and J.C. Olson, "Consumer Response to Price: An Attitudinal Information Processing Perspective," in Y. Wind and M. Greenberg, eds., *Moving Ahead in Attitude Research*. Chicago: American Marketing Association, 1977.

Kaldor, N., "The Economic Aspects of Advertising," *Review of Economic Studies*, 18, (1950), 1–27.

Katona, G., *Psychological Economics*. New York: Elsevier, 1975.

Klein, B., and K. Leffler, "The Role of Market Forces in Assuring Contractual Performance," *Journal of Political Economy*, 89, (1981), no. 4, 615–641.

Kwoka, J.R., "Advertising and the Price and Quality of Optometric Services," *American Economic Review*, 74, (March 1984), 211–216.

Lambin, J.J., *Advertising, Competition and Market Conduct in Oligopoly Over Time: An Econometric Investigation in Western European Countries*. Amsterdam: North-Holland Publishing Company, 1976.

Lancaster, K., *Variety Equity and Efficiency: Product Variety in an Industrial Society*. New York: Columbia University Press, 1979.

Levin, I.P., and R.D. Johnson, "Estimating Price-Quality Tradeoffs Using Comparative Judgments," *Journal of Consumer Research*, 11 (1984), 593–600.

Lynch, J.G., and T.K. Srull, "Memory and Attentional Factors in Consumer Choice: Concepts and Research Methods," *Journal of Consumer Research*, 9 (1982), 18–37.

Möller, C., *Gesellschaftliche Funktionen der Konsumwerbung*. Stuttgart: C.E. Poeschel Verlag, 1970.

Monroe, K.B., "Buyer's Subjective Perceptions of Price," *Journal of Marketing Research*, 10 (1973), 70–80.

Musgrave, A., "Unreal Assumptions in Economic Theory: The F-Twist Untwisted," *Kyklos*, 34 (1981), 377–387.

Nelson, P., "Advertising as Information," *Journal of Political Economy*, 82 (July-August 1974), 729–754.

Nelson, P., "Information and Consumer Behavior," *Journal of Political Economy*, 78 (March/April 1970), 311–329.

Nisbett, R.E., and T.D. Wilson, "Telling More Than We Can Know: Verbal Reports on Mental Processes," *Psychological Review*, 84 (1977), 231–259.

Nowak, K., and G. Andrén, *Reklam och samhällsförändring: Variation och konstans i svenska populärpressannonser 1950–1975* (Advertising and Social Change: Variation and Constancy in Swedish Magazine Advertisements 1950–1975). Lund: Studentlitteratur, 1982.

Nyström, H., *Retail Pricing: An Integrated Economic and Psychological Approach*. Stockholm: The Economic Research Institute at the Stockholm Schoool of Economics, 1970.

Olshavsky, R.W., and D.H. Granbois, "Consumer Decision Making—Fact or Fiction?" *Journal of Consumer Research*, 6 (1979), 93–100.

Porter, M.E., "Interbrand Choice, Media Mix and Market Performance," *American Economic Review*, 66, (1976), no. 2, 398–406.

Porter, M.E., "Consumer Behavior, Retailer Power and Market Performance in Consumer Goods Industries," *Review of Economics and Statistics*, 56 (1974), no. 4, 419–436.

Punj, G.W., and R.A. Staelin, "A Model of Consumer Information Search Behavior for New Automobiles," *Journal of Consumer Research*, 9 (1983), 336–380.

Raj, S.P., "The Effects of Advertising on High and Low Loyalty Consumer Segments," *Journal of Consumer Research*, 9 (1982), 77–89.

Resnick, A., and B.L. Stern, "An Analysis of Information Content in Television Advertising," *Journal of Marketing*, 41 (1977), 50–53.

Roberts, D.F., and C.M. Bachen, "Mass Communication Effects," *Annual Review of Psychology*, 32 (1981), 307–356.

Rogers, E., *Diffusion of Innovations*, 3rd ed. New York: Free Press, 1983.

Rokeach, M., *The Nature of Human Values*. New York: Free Press, 1973.

Schmalensee, R., "A Model of Advertising and Product Quality," *Journal of Political Economy*, 86 (1978), 485–503.

Schmalensee, R., "Brand Loyalty and Barriers to Entry," *Southern Economic Journal*, 40, (1974), no. 4, 579–588.

Scitovsky, T., *The Joyless Economy*. New York: Oxford University Press, 1976.

Simon, H.A., "Information Processing Models of Cognition," *Annual Review of Psychology*, 30 (1979) 363–396.

Simon, J.L., *Issues in the Economics of Advertising*. Urbana, IL: University of Illinois Press, 1970.

Singh, S.N., and M.L. Rothschild, "Recognition as a Measure of Learning from Television Commercials," *Journal of Marketing Research*, 20 (1983), 235–248.

Slovic, P., B. Fischhoff, and S. Lichtenstein, "Behavioral Decision Theory," *Annual Review of Psychology*, 28 (1977), 1–39.

Stigler, G., "The Economics of Information," *Journal of Political Economy*, 69 (1961), 213–235.

Stroebe, W., and B.S. Frey, "In Defense of Economic Man: Towards an Integration of Economics and Psychology," *Schweizerische Zeitschrift für Volkswirtschaft und Statistik*, 116 (June 1980), 119–148.

Svensson, O., "Process Description of Decision Making," *Organizational Behavior and Human Performance*, 23 (1979), 86–112.

Telser, L.G., "Advertising and Competition," *Journal of Political Economy*, 72 (December 1964), 537–562.

Thorelli, M.B., H. Becker, and J. Engledow, *The Information Seekers—An International Study of Consumer Information and Advertising Image*. Cambridge, MA: Ballinger, 1975.

Treasure, J., *Advertising and the Public*. London: Institute of Practitioners in Advertising, IPA Forum, January 1970.

Van Raaij, W.F., "Affective and Cognitive Reactions to Advertising." Papers on Economic Psychology, No. 26, Erasmus University, Rotterdam, 1983.

Van Raaij, W.F., "Consumer Choice Behavior: An Information-Processing Approach." Doctoral Dissertation, Tilburg University, the Netherlands, 1976.

Verhallen, T., and G. de Nooij, "Retail Attribute Sensitivity and Shopping Patronage," *Journal of Economic Psychology*, (1982), 39–55.

Verhallen, T. and R. Pieters, "Attitude Theory and Behavioral Costs," *Journal of Economic Psychology*, 5 (1984).

Wärneryd, K-E, "Emerging Concepts of Consumer Interest in Marketing Communication," in G. Fisk, J. Arndt and K. Grønhaug, eds., *Future Directions for Marketing*. Cambridge, MA: Marketing Science Institute, 1978, pp. 96–110.

Wiggins, S.N., and W.J. Lane, "Quality, Uncertainty, Search and Advertising," *American Economic Review*, 73 (1983), 881–894.

Wilde, L., "The Economics of Consumer Information Acquisition" *The Journal of Business*, 53 (1980), 143–148.

Yalch, R.F., and R. Elmore-Yalch, "The Effect of Numbers on the Route to Persuasion," *Journal of Consumer Research*, 11 (1984), 522–527.

Zajonc, R.B., "Feeling and Thinking: Preferences Need No Inferences," *American Psychologist*, 35 (1980), 151–175.

Zajonc, R.B., and H. Markus, "Affective and Cognitive Factors in Preferences," *Journal of Consumer Research*, 9 (1982), 123–131.

Zeithaml, V.A., "Consumer Response to In-store Price Information Environments," *Journal of Consumer Research*, 8 (1982), 357–369.

RESEARCH ON CHOICES WITH ALTERNATIVES, RELATED CHOICES, RELATED CHOOSERS, AND USE OF ECONOMIC INSIGHTS

James N. Morgan

We address the question of the relation of the theory of rational choice to the understanding and prediction of actual behavior. This in turn can be broken down into several questions:

1. How common is actual choice, whether or not an action is involved; in other words, how often are people actually at the margin where the theory applies?
2. How many of those choices have involved the use of an informed, sophisticated, cost-benefit analysis that estimates internal rates of return.
3. Are the other choices mostly random and ignorable, or are they subject to systematic biases?
4. What are the reasons some people do not make rational informed choices? Is it the inability to understand economic insights, the difficulty and cost of the calculations involved, the noneconomic concerns, or other factors?

We can think of an individual during any short time period as potentially having a choice to make and as taking some action or not. Reports on actions tend to include those in which no real choice is possible, while discussions of choice frequently exclude mention of people who did not take action, such as studies of car buyers or people who have gone bankrupt. Hence we shall be forced to discuss the need for better data.

I. OTHER APPROACHES

Developing an economic theory of consumer behavior has meant a search for simple models of utility maximization, and economic research has used existing data to see whether the theoretical models fit those data. Two main problems arose in this search: the aggregation problem, when one uses data from many individuals with persistent interpersonal differences; and the independence problem, when one wishes to think of separable additive utilities from each good or service, or at least from each class of good or service. The first problem involved omitted variables (or "specification errors") or spurious correlation, hopefully randomized out by the use of representative probability samples, differenced out by the use of dynamic data on change from panel studies, or controlled for by the introduction of other variables in multivariate analyses. The second problem raised more difficult issues of substitutability among commodities. A third problem arose with the data categories, that of quality differences within categories. There have been attempts to derive measures of quality differences (hedonic prices) from data, assuming, of course, stable and uniform preferences.

There had also been a long discussion about the problem of integrability of the indifference surface until Paul Samuelson showed that transitivity of preferences and integrability were one and the same problem. There have been attempts to derive price and income elasticities from consumption data by imposing various constraints, such as homothetic utility functions; examples have been given by Biorn and Jansen (1982) and Deaton and Muellbauer (1980). And there have been iterations back and forth between labor supply on the one hand and utility functions for leisure and money on the other. Some utility functions imply nonsense labor supply functions (perfectly inelastic, for example). More recently, Betson and van der Gaag (1983) have estimated labor-supply models, derived the implied utility functions, and then inferred from them the costs of an added child. Of course, the model selected determines whether there will also be a time-cost of children and whether costs will vary with income levels.

Our purpose is not to criticize or try to summarize that large body of sophisticated and often excellent work but to ask whether we might, without getting too complicated, start with a more realistic theory of human behavior and then move to the question of what kinds of data and analysis would comprise efficient ways of selecting among competing theories or assessing the relative importance of competing elements of those theories.

II. THE ECONOMIC THEORY OF CHOICE

The economic theory of choice can be summarized before we put it into a broader behavioral context: Choices involve comparisons of alternatives, with the focus, for efficiency, on a few of the more likely ones, and the use of a cost-benefit analysis to estimate an implied internal rate of return. In order for costs and benefits to be compared, they must be converted into comparable units, which means:

- present (discounting future amounts by some interest rate),
- expected (multiplying uncertain amounts by some probability),
- real (converting to current price levels),
- money (imputing on the basis of opportunity cost, e.g., foregone earnings on money tied up),
- after taxes (multiplying taxable benefits or deductible costs by one minus the marginal income tax rate).

For choices involving the distant future in a world of uncertain future inflation the adjustments for interest and price changes can be simplified by adding one further assumption: that the relevant real interest rate is about 2 to 3 percent, so one can use that figure for discounting, do all calculations in current dollars, strive to earn 2 to 3 percent plus the rate of inflation on any invested funds, and it will all work out right.

Since the present value of net benefits is in dollars, comparing alternatives of different size is difficult, and the final estimate of a rate of discount that makes the present value of that alternative zero, the so-called internal rate of return, provides a single number representing the value of each alternative. It is a very useful number because it can be compared directly with the rate of interest on one's savings account or current yield of any stocks or bonds. For steady net flows, some pocket calculators can estimate the rate, but for more complex alternatives, an iterative computer program is required. For details, see any recent consumer economics text (e.g., Morgan and Duncan, 1981).

And after all that, one must relate differences in the rate of return for what can be measured with unmeasurable other differences among the alternatives—style, color, location, uncertainty about the probability—which cannot be handled by simple expected values.

III. RELEVANCE FOR ECONOMIC ANALYSIS

Of course, not all choices involve the distant future or all the various translations, and some approximations may be possible. Clearly, the complex insights and calculations required would only be worth the effort for major, salient decisions, even if one were capable of them.

From the beginning, discussions about the relevance of economic theory to behavior have concluded that for purposes of economic analysis and even prediction at the market level, all that was necessary was for some small set of choosers at the margin to be responding rationally to economic forces such as prices and incomes. There was even empirical evidence, such as an early study of the corn-hog cycle, that showed that the rational-supply responses were the result of the actions of a very few large, sophisticated farmers, while most farmers continued an unchanged pattern of production of hogs and/or corn no matter what the relative prices were.

But it is an empirical question whether there is a sufficient set of people with choices (neither constrained or impelled to act or not act nor far from the margin) who are informed about the facts, capable of dealing with uncertainty, and able to use the insights of economics to compare the rates of return of alternatives.

People are often ignorant of what alternatives exist or of the facts about them. They may also be uncertain about what the outcomes of alternative choices are likely to be, simply because the world is full of risk and uncertainty. More important, they may be confused about what questions to ask about the alternatives. Many choices, even simple ones such as whether to keep on shopping, require solving complex functions if one is to optimize, much less maximize, some utility function.

Take the apparently simple decision of whether to continue shopping or to purchase the best buy among the alternatives already located. The variance of the quality-adjusted prices already known allows an estimate of the expected value of the lowest price in a set that contains one more element with the same overall variance. The difference between that and the lowest price in the present set of prices is the expected payoff from shopping at one more place, which can be compared with the cost in time and travel of that action. So far, the pocket-computer people have not programmed them to make these estimates. After each new price one must reestimate the potential gain from one more search, since the one new price may change the estimated variance of prices, and the number of cases is larger by one. Also, with each additional alternative, the likelihood of having to return to a store visited earlier increases. (Though the probabilities are not equal among the stores, the very decision to visit one more implies that the probability that it will have the lowest price is greater than 1/n, where n is the number of stores.) In reality, of course, there are quality differences, even with brand goods, because of service, delivery, credit, and the like, and perhaps increasing costs of travel and time as the remaining possibilities are found farther afield. It is interesting that the early articles on optimal search did not even deal with the potential change in knowledge about the distribution of prices that comes from shopping itself. Does anyone really think ordinary consumers would bother to do the calculations involved in deciding whether to continue shopping, even if they understood the logic? Probably not; at the same time, consumers' decisions might be moved in the direction of optimality if they intuitively keep shopping when they discover a large variety of prices, or if they stop shopping when prices seem to be uniform.

The fact that net benefit must also be estimated after taxes means that the benefit varies among individuals according to their tax status—marginal tax rates and for some things whether they itemize deductions. In a 1980 article, Greg Duncan and this author estimated that U.S. tax law, combined with inflation and high interest rates, made the same home cost some people four times as much as it cost others, and we noted that half of all the benefits from these "tax expenditures" go to those in the top one seventh of the income distribution.

It is an empirical question whether people know how to estimate the tax effects of alternative decisions. A study in the mid-1960s that focused on the affluent found that most of them claimed not to know what their own marginal tax rates were, that is, how much an extra $100 in earnings would raise their taxes (Barlow, Brazer and Morgan, 1965). But there may have been social learning since then. Certainly we are frequently instructed in this by those urging us to contribute to charity and by those selling some kinds of investments, often in misleading ways. For example, some vendors of tax-free bonds compare the after-tax yield of taxable investments with the imaginary pretax yield that would give, after taxes, the same yield as their nontaxable investments! These vendors must assume that readers of their ads do not realize that comparisons must all be made either before taxes or after taxes.

Relatively recent experience with the very high interest rates a large majority of people have had to face may well have changed people's sensitivity to the difference between money now and money later, and to the costs of letting someone else use their money or having it tied up in a home. And the experience of having interest earnings limited to 5 percent when the inflation rate was 10 percent perhaps alerted some people to the declining real value of their savings and the need to protect themselves. On the other hand, they may well have concluded from the experience of the past twenty years that the only protection was owning a home, ignoring the demographic and market facts that make it unlikely that homes will rise in value faster than inflation in the future and make it likely that more liquid investments will pay a reasonable real (inflation-adjusted) return. Perhaps the classic example of the ignoring of opportunity costs, so familiar to economists, is the ignoring of the real costs of owning a large home: the depreciation and the foregone interest on the owners equity (not on his original investment but on current sale value minus remaining debt). It is also possible that people exaggerate the value of certain tax advantages like the deductibility of property taxes and mortgage interest, in their delight in getting back at the government. However, there is no empirical evidence to support any of these possibilities.

There are two more levels of complexity we must at least consider before we ask what kind of research is needed. They are the issues of related choices and related choosers. By related choices we mean that commonly a decision in one area is related to (depends on, affects, or is really made jointly with) a decision in another area. Where one chooses to live may be affected by choices of jobs. By related choosers we mean that most people live in families and their choices affect the whole family. These days people seldom think of decisions about careers and marriage as separate and independent. We can think of related choices and related choosers as constraints on the choices of an individual, and they might well be systematic rather than random.

IV. IMPLICATIONS FOR RESEARCH

The potential disparity between theory and reality strongly suggests that we should design some research to explore the circumstances people report under which they have made past decisions and the (perhaps distorted) explanations they give. To improve theory we must also know whether people understand the economic insights our theories give about how they should choose and perhaps whether they could learn these insights easily or why they resist using them. With such data we should then be able to justify a more realistic theory, and with such a theory we should then be able to design a research model, select its most important variables, and measure them.

Such a program should focus on large, salient decisions or areas where even doing nothing might imply conscious decisions to do nothing. One attractive set of such decisions is that involved in the process of economic socialization. We would ask people about leaving school, leaving home, first job, first marriage, and first independent dwelling and how each such action was related to decisions to act or not to act in each of the other areas. And of course we would ask what the next best alternative would have been in each case (see example in the Appendix).

In a national sample of people of all ages, some will report events that occurred many years ago; others, events for which the process is still going on. It is not obvious that recency implies greater accuracy—people's explanations of decisions about marriage and divorce may well be far more distorted by emotion and selection to present a favorable picture shortly after the event than later on. In any case, the differences between reports by those of different ages may well indicate social trends that are large enough to show up above all the measurement error and bias—for example, younger women generally report that they decided first about careers and afterward about spouses, while older women report marriage first, then career decisions. Of course, the data confound birth-cohort differences with differences between the particular historical periods when the respective decisions were being made, with each period having different levels of unemployment or inflation.

A second set of potential choices would be investigated. These would focus on the recent past; people would be asked about actions or their choosing not to act in each of the areas in the last five years and, for the most recent of each, about its relation to each of the other choice-areas. Again, we could inquire about what was seen as the next-best alternative in each choice—for those who changed jobs or residences this alternate choice might not have been keeping the old job or residence. These data would confound the effects of age and birth cohort, but they would be specific for one historical environment.

The structure of questions would be similar whether we were asking about the first or the most recent choices people had faced. There would be sequences of questions centered around each major choice area, its alternatives, and its relations to the other areas. People would report how considerations of marriage were related to concurrent considerations about leaving home, quitting school, finding a job, or deciding where to live, while elsewhere they would report how considerations of leaving home were related to considerations of marriage, school, job. So each pair of choice areas would have information about how each of the pair was related to the other.

We would ask about how considerations (not decisions) in each area were related to (not caused by) considerations (not decisions) in the other areas. We do not want selection bias that would come from talking only about decisions to act or "decisions" not to act, nor do we wish to suggest causal direction when it might be in either direction or be a genuine joint decision, working with some complex utility function. We would also ask whether things were going on in the other areas, which is probably less subject to distortion or memory error than interpretations about what caused what. Note that the relationship between each pair is asked in two contexts, once when talking about everything related to one of the choices, and again when talking about everything related to the other choice. This might seem redundant but is actually likely to provide a more realistic picture.

We might also ask, in the case of some choices, whether there was a search for alternatives and whether any really competitive alternatives existed, and if so, what the characteristics of the two best alternatives were, as well as an explanation of the reasons for the choice. Once again, we could probably put more trust in statements whether there had been another job available at the time than in the characteristics of the two alternatives, and more trust in reports of the characteristics of the alternatives than in explanations for the choice that was made. (See the Appendix for an example.) There have been studies of information seeking, levels of information, and even of the effects of information, for example, in energy conservation, but none that we know of on the use of economic insights in processing or interpreting information, or even in selecting it.

We think there is reason to combine statistical inferences about how choices are made with this richer set of information, to see whether they confirm one another and provide a plausible picture. Some of those who, like Herbert Simon, have been active in modeling thinking and problem-solving processes on the computer are now talking about using more introspection in order to be more selective about the possible processes to model on the computer.

What we propose would be not only to model these processes, and perhaps simulate them on a computer, but ultimately to see whether it would be possible to specify a set of experiments or pieces of survey research that would estimate and test the most plausible of the models.

For example, the final, more realistic testing of models might well also have to deal with choices related to the choices of significant others, mostly spouses, and might also have procedures for selecting from among large representative samples those who were sufficiently unconstrained, sufficiently aware of alternatives, and sufficiently informed and sophisticated about the nature of their problems to be able to reveal real problem-solving choices. It takes only a small group like this at the margin to make the aggregate theories of economics work, particularly if those decisions are least likely to be regretted and offset by later decisions.

V. IGNORANCE, UNCERTAINTY, AND CONFUSION

An important complementary investigation to a history of major and salient choices would be an exploration of the present state of people's decision-making capabilities and habits and their receptivity to some of the insights that economists think make decisions less subject to future regret. Notice that we avoid using the term *rational* here, since people can have perfectly rational reasons for doing things differently from the way the paradigms of economic theory suggest.

Even for those not dominated by constraints or pressures, there are three further sources of departure from "optimal": ignorance of the facts or of available alternatives, risk and uncertainty and the feelings people have about risk, and finally, confusion about the meaning of the facts and how to compare alternative options. One of the easiest ways to improve our realism in consumer behavior is to discover that people are unaware of things we had been assuming were determining their choices, such as the interest they can earn on their savings or their own marginal tax rates. A more sophisticated approach, however, asks whether, in situations where it is relevant, they could acquire the information.

The usual rule for uncertainty is to hope it is an estimable risk and suggest using expected values (probability times value). Whether people's distorted treatment of risky decisions, well documented in experiments by Tversky and Kahneman, makes it impossible to talk about any simple utility-disutility of risk transformation, much less the still simpler expected-value norm (value times its probability), is uncertain and calls for further investigation.

But it is the third issue, the ability of people to use economic insights in processing information when making economic choices, that is crucial and most difficult to investigate empirically. An individual must structure a choice before it is clear what information is needed, or even whether it is worth getting. And the formal "expected value" approach to risk, combined with the other insights of cost-benefit analysis, provides at least a norm from which people could depart if they understood it. Hence the most important and potentially researchable issue in choice behavior is how much economic insight is available to the chooser.

It may be useful to explain in some detail what kind of research would be required here. One might conduct tests of economic understanding, concentrated in the areas relevant to personal choices, but that is both difficult and dismal for respondents, as well as insufficient. How the respondents would respond when these insights were presented to them is clearly a more important question. The respondents could treat the insights as obvious and not see their relevance to their own choices; they could refuse to accept the insights; or they could introduce other (noneconomic?) considerations. One could do this in the context of talking about some major decision like buying a car or owning a home. The interview becomes a kind of Socratic dialogue, with insights introduced systematically. Additional examples would be introduced to see whether the insights could be translated and used in new situations. The Appendix provides some illustrations of the approach, but they are necessarily wordy and inadequate. A great deal of pretesting would be required.

VI. SUMMARY

An approach has been presented that, amplified and worked out, would, we think, tell us a great deal about how the adult population thinks about its economic choices, whether it will accept the logical insights of the economists, and what other considerations or constraints are involved. Additionally, this approach might well reveal differences among subgroups of the population according to age, education, and so on. The results would be of use in developing and testing better theories of behavior and of learning and cognition. What people understand is less crucial than what they would rapidly come to understand if salience (motivation) and availability were combined. And basic to all of this is why the insights that economists think would reduce later regret over decisions appear to be so little used.

APPENDIX:
OUTLINE AND ILLUSTRATIVE SECTIONS
OF THE INTERVIEW

First Choices
Quitting school
Setting up own household
First full-time regular job
First marriage
Spouse's first job while a spouse

For each of these: Next-best alternative
                      Relation to each of the other choices
                      Main reasons for choice

Recent Choices—Most Recent in Last Five Years
Changing residence
Changing job
Getting married or divorced
Change of spouse's job

For each of these: Next-best alternative
                      Relation to each of the other choices
                      Main reasons for choice

Considerations involved in deciding to buy a new car or keep an old one:
    Depreciation and interest costs
    Tax considerations
    Inflation
Application to owning or renting a home
Adjusting for uncertainty—insurance example
Acceptance of principles:
    Choice means giving up the second best
    Past is irrelevant except as it affects our expectations for the future
    Benefits-costs of any alternative must be in comparable units, namely:
        Present (not future)
        Expected (discounted for uncertainty by multiplying by probability)
        After tax (net of any tax savings)
        Money (imputed, using opportunity cost)
        Real (adjusted to today's prices)
Acceptance of one generalization:
    Interest rates, paid or foregone, tend to reflect inflation, so depreciation and interest costs are affected in exactly offsetting ways by inflation, and their sum remains stable. So we need not foresee future inflation to estimate future costs of owning depreciating assets like houses or cars.
    Finally, response to the idea of the implied (internal) rate of return, for easy comparison with the interest on savings or with other alternatives.

Some Illustrative Sections for an Experimental Interview

First Choices
We are interested in how people make choices where the future is involved, such as whether to keep the old car or buy a new one or to

become a home-owner or to move or change jobs. Let's start with the first regular full-time job you ever had.

How old were you when you got your first job?
What kind of job was it?
What would you have done if you had not taken that job: was there another possible job, or would you have stayed in school, or did you have another option?
Was your choice related in any way to decisions about quitting school? In what way? Did one affect the other, did they affect each other, or was there a third interaction?
Was your choice of job related in any way to considerations about getting married? In what way? Did one affect the other, did they affect each other, or was there another set of relationships?
Was your choice of job related in any way to deciding where to live? In what way?
Was it related in any way to job choices of a spouse? In what way?
Tell me about the first residence you had that was your own household, not your parents' home or a school or dormitory. How old where you when you first had your own place?
What would you have done if you had not moved there? Was there some second-best place, would you have stayed home, or did you have other options?
Was your choice of residence related in any way to your job? In what way did your job choice affect your choice of residence? Did they affect each other? Or was there another relationship between the two?
Was your choice of residence related in any way to your getting married? In what way?
Was the choice of residence related to job choices of your spouse? In what way?

(Use similar sequences for first marriage and spouse's first job after marriage.)
Now all that was a while ago, at least for many of us. What about more recent choices of that same type—when was the last time you changed jobs?

Less than six years	More than five years ago
How many times have you changed jobs in the last five years?	Have you considered taking another job any time in the last five years?
_____	Yes No (skip out)

What was the best alternative to your present job at the time you took it?

What was the best other job that you didn't take?

Was that job choice related in any way to choices about where to live? In what way did one choice affect the other, did they affect each other, or was there another relationship between the two?
Was your job choice related to choices about your spouse's job? In what way?

Recent Choices
(Similar sequences on recent changes in residence, spouse's job, and marital status).

Reactions to Presentation of Economic Insights
(Spelled out in more preliminary but illustrative detail because this area is newer and more difficult, and will require more development and pretesting).

Now we're interested in people's decisions about investing in things that involve the future, like buying cars or houses or insurance, or investing savings. Let's talk about cars. Suppose you were thinking of buying a new car and trading in an older one; how would you compare the costs to see whether the advantages of the new car were worth the cost? Suppose you have a five-year-old car you could sell for $2,000 and were thinking of buying a new one for $10,000. What would it cost to keep the old car another year? Let's assume that either there is 10 percent inflation, interest rates are 13 percent, and the car depreciates 15 percent in sale value; or that there is no inflation, interest rates are 3 percent, and the car's sale value drops 25 percent. In either case, the interest plus the depreciation is 28 percent of the $2,000 it is worth now, or $560. What about the cost of a new one?

One problem is that the new car will last a lot longer than the old one, and another problem is that we cannot just take next year's costs, because a new car always costs a lot the first year because of the dealer's margin and sales tax and depreciation. If we consider only the first year's cost, a new car would always seem too expensive.

If we decided to estimate the average cost per year of the new car, how many years would we use? Suppose your old car is five years old; then, if you are thinking of trading it in now, you would not be likely to keep the next one more than five years, would you? So perhaps we should compare the cost of one more year's use of the old car with a fifth of the five-year cost of a new car. Then the next year we could make another calculation and another decision. Does that seem reasonable to you?

Now how could we estimate the five-year cost of a new car? It will still be worth something at the end of that time; should we deduct that? Well, we must pay the $10,000 now, but we must wait five years for the $2,000 on the trade-in. Therefore, we should deduct the present value of $2,000 that is available only after five years—that is, we should ask what amount now would accumulate enough interest to total $2,000 in five years. Does that make sense?

We can rely on a rule that whenever interest rates are above 3 percent, there is inflation that raises prices, including the price of trade-ins, so we can use 3 percent to discount that $2,000 to a present value using the argument that if interest rates were higher, the trade-in value would be too. At 3 percent, $2,000 in five years is worth $1,725. If we then subtract that from the $10,000 and divide by 5, we have a yearly cost of $1,655, compared with $560 for the old car.

But what about interest lost because that money is tied up? We have implicitly taken account of that by not discounting the depreciation costs. In fact, we could make the calculation another way by thinking of buying an $8,000 asset that will be worth nothing in five years and tying up $2,000 for five years in the replacement-asset. There is a little-known fact that for an asset that depreciates to zero, the sum of the present values of all the annual depreciations and foregone interest amounts is exactly equal to the initial price, whatever the interest rate or the life of the asset! So another estimate is $8,000 plus the present value of $60 a year in foregone interest on the $2,000, which is $275. Divided by 5, this is again $1,655 per year. Have you ever done such calculations?

You will notice that the rule says that the present value of the total future interest and depreciation cost of an asset is equal to its present price, regardless of actual interest or depreciation rates or how long it will last. That means that the cost per year of assets that cost the same to buy is proportionately less the longer they last. However, a muffler that cost twice as much and lasts twice as long is not a better or worse bargain. But there is something else. Do you itemize deductions from your income when you pay your federal income taxes?

Yes (skip to A)   No, or Don't Know (continue)

Well, those who do itemize deductions can deduct any interest they pay, and it will reduce their taxes by the amount deducted times their tax rate on their last dollar of income.

(A)   Will the cost depend on your tax bracket only if you borrowed money? No, because even if you used your own money, the interest you lost would not be the interest you would have earned but what you could have kept after income taxes. So you can think of yourself as earning tax-free interest on your investment in your car, even if you don't itemize.

But this also means that the real cost depends on your tax bracket, which means that cars cost high-income people less (after taxes) than they cost low-income people. Does that seem true to you? If you buy a car, you are competing with people for whom that same car really costs less after their taxes. Of course, this is even more so with houses.

Of course there may be higher repair bills on the old car, and you might spend more of your time taking it in for repairs. How would you value the extra time it might take you? And how would you account for the replacement of things like tires or battery or brakes, which should not have to be done again for another five years?

We have actually be using a number of principles or ideas from economics:

The cost of keeping something includes giving up what you could earn on the money you would get if you sold it, and that depends on what it would sell for, not what you paid for it. So if you had bought a house for $20,000 and it is now worth $100,000, part of its cost is the foregone interest, not on the $20,000 you invested but on the $100,000 you could invest if you sold it. In other words, the past doesn't matter; only the present and the future do.

Another principle is that money you must wait for—for example, money from a future trade-in—is worth less now because if you had the money now you could earn interest on it—so we "discount" back to the present.

Still another idea is that you can estimate costs even when there is no out-of-pocket payment, as when you ask what the money you have tied up could be earning elsewhere.

And there is a rule, rather than a principle, that real interest rates are about 3 percent and anything else is inflation, so that the sum of interest lost on money tied up in your car or house and the depreciation on it tend to be constant. This means that you don't have to forecast future inflation rates to make decisions. For a car, you would lose 3 percent in interest and 25 percent in depreciation if there were no inflation, or 13 percent in interest and 15 percent in depreciation with a 10 percent inflation—a total of 28 percent in either case. For a house, there would be 3 percent interest plus 2 percent depreciation if there were no inflation, or 13 percent interest minus 8 percent appreciation with 10 percent inflation; the sum of interest lost is always 5%.

We notice that we have to calculate costs after taxes. The interest you forego is what you could earn and keep after taxes, just as your paid interest costs, if you itemize them, should be reduced by the amount of income tax you save.

There is one other idea from economics that concerns the way to treat outcomes of which you are not sure. What is it worth to have a very small chance of winning a lottery or of collecting on your insurance? Life insurance pays off if you die, and you are in a sense betting with the insurance company, because you want to offset the risk you already run of leaving dependents without support. The value of any right to collect is called an expected value and is equal to the amount times the probability of collecting. If there is one chance in a hundred that you will collect, then a bet or an insurance policy that will pay $1,000 is worth $10.

Now, with all these translations, we can estimate the present net value of the benefits minus the costs of any alternative, but alternatives are of different sizes, so economists suggest that wherever we have investments with net positive benefits, instead of assuming a real interest rate, we should estimate the interest rate at which the present value of an alternative is zero—the rate of return on the investment. This is comparable across all alternatives and is directly comparable with the interest you could earn on your savings. Do you think you would find it useful if you were able to get such estimated rates of return? Does all this seem reasonable to you?

Do you think that, keeping all the preceding in mind, you would have changed any of your choices in recent years?

How do you feel about this systematic approach to choices? Do you think it would reduce the chance of doing things that would be regretted later?

REFERENCES

Barlow, Robin, Harvey Brazer, and James Morgan, *The Economic Behavior of the Affluent.* Washington D.C.: The Brookings Institution, 1965.

Betson, David, and Jacques van der Gaag, "A Note on an Alternative Strategy for the Estimation of Equivalent Scales." Draft, May, 1983 (Notre Dame University and World Bank).

Biorn, Eric, and Eilev S. Jansen, *Econometrics of Incomplete Cross-Section/Time-Series Data: Consumer Demand in Norwegian Households.* Oslo, Norway: Central Bureau of Statistics, 1982.

Deaton, A., and J. Muellbauer, *Economics and Consumer Behavior.* Cambridge: Cambridge University Press, 1980.

Duncan, Greg, and James Morgan, "The Effects of Inflation and Taxes on the Costs of Home Ownership," *Journal of Consumer Affairs,* (Winter 1980), 383–393.

Merz, Joachim, "The Functionalized Extended Linear Expenditure System." FELES. Working Paper 19, Sonderforschungsbereich 3, J.W. Goethe Universitaet Frankfurt, und Universitaet Mannheim, February, 1980.

Morgan, James, and Greg Duncan, *The Economics of Personal Choice*, Ann Arbor: University of Michigan Press, 1981.

PART III

THE THEORY OF THE FIRM

Section A

Entrepreneurial and Managerial Behavior

INTRODUCTION TO SECTION A:
ENTREPRENEURIAL AND MANAGERIAL
BEHAVIOR

One of the areas in which behavioral economics has made considerable progress is that of the behavior of the firm. As a matter of historical fact, this is where behavioral economics began its journey, with the works of Herbert Simon, which incorporated economics, management theory, and psychology. This is also one of the areas of inquiry where economists may find an already well-developed and relevant body of accumulated research in the neighboring behavioral disciplines just waiting to be applied to economic theory. For example, one may easily apply the label *behavioral economics* to much of the contemporary work of management scholars. It is also revealing that several of the current leading researchers in behavioral economics come from management schools rather than traditional economics departments. It is thus not surprising that the topic of business behavior received close attention from behavioral economists.

In the following section we include two essays on the subject. In the first, Sidney Winter presents a broad agenda for behavioral research in the theory of the firm. As an early advocate of an evolutionary theory in economics, Winter experienced a wide spectrum of orthodox criticism. In the current paper he analyzes the various claims raised over the years against a behavioral approach to economics and their relative merits. He then concentrates on the most important one, the claim that the patterns discovered by behavioral research are transitory and epiphenomenal. Acknowledging the validity of such a claim in regard to *both*

149

traditional and behavioral research findings, Winter proposes a behavioral research program aimed at discovering the relatively fundamental and durable patterns of behavior (or routines) of real organizations.

While Winter's paper concentrates on the firm as an organization, Gilad's paper attacks the topic of entrepreneurship. The two papers are not as different as their different emphases might suggest. Gilad investigates the factors affecting entrepreneurial behavior, which is, by definition, that aspect of decision making that is not *routine*. Thus the two papers complement each other. Both authors reject the restrictive rhetoric of neoclassical economics and point to the benefits derived from investigating processes rather than (equilibrium) outcomes. They also share the indifference to the question of whether actual behavior displays the orthodox form of rationality. In that respect, at least, the two papers continue the journey started by Simon 30 years ago.

THE RESEARCH PROGRAM
OF THE BEHAVIORAL THEORY
OF THE FIRM:
ORTHODOX CRITIQUE AND
EVOLUTIONARY PERSPECTIVE

Sidney G. Winter

I. INTRODUCTION

The contents of this volume amply demonstrate that behavioral economics is a highly diversified portfolio of intellectual undertakings. A number of schools of thought are involved, distinguished by differences in several dimensions.

There are, for example, differences with respect to key sources of intellectual inspiration beyond the boundaries of economics and with respect to the candidates that different schools would nominate for a "Behavioral Economics Hall of Fame." There are also quite marked differences with respect to the focal concerns to which inquiry is directed. The spectrum includes, *inter alia*, the development and testing of general laws of individual human behavior; the explanation of individual "outcomes" such as a bankruptcy or an innovation by a particular firm; the measurement, explanation, and prediction of various aspects of consumer behavior; detailed mapping of particular organizational practices; and efforts to explain market-level statistical evidence with modeling approaches that depart in some way from conventional economic rationality assumptions. Related to, but not coextensive with, these differences in focal concerns are differences among the schools in terms of characteristic methods of empirical observation. There are laboratory experiments; large-scale surveys; interview and direct observation studies that may emphasize depth or breadth; and the expedient use of evidence generated for other purposes by government agencies, courts, trade associations, journalists and others.

The variety of behavioral economics discussed in this paper has as its focal concern the description and explanation of "how things are done" in business firms and in organizations more generally. The subject embraces both technological and organizational aspects of how things are done, and under the organizational heading includes matters of detailed routine, decision-making, and overall structure. This sort of inquiry is distinguished from orthodox economics,[1] and is properly labeled behavioral, by virtue of a number of characteristics; in particular, by the emphasis on "how"—the characterization of process—and by comparative indifference to the question of whether actual behavior displays the narrow form of rationality—"rationality as consistency"—so emphasized in formal orthodoxy. In one way or another, all the empirical methods listed in the preceding paragraph can enhance understanding of how things are done. However, the method that is probably most characteristic of this area of inquiry is "asking businessmen what they do," that is, finding out how things are done by asking those who are closely involved in doing it.[2] This method of empirical observation is central to the area of inquiry both because it is often the only feasible method for obtaining evidence on how things are done and because the methodological and theoretical issues that it raises have been so prominent in the protracted discussion of this branch of behavioral economics.

In the title of this paper, the area of inquiry under discussion is identified by the phrase "behavioral theory of the firm." This phrase evokes in particular the research effort that was begun at Carnegie-Mellon University[3] in the 1950s and that culminated in the publication of the Cyert and March volume, *A Behavioral Theory of the Firm*, in 1963. Although the historical sources of this behavioral approach go back a long way, and although additional important work has been done in the past two decades, I believe that the achievements of the Carnegie group do represent the high-water mark thus far for this type of economic research.

In conformity with this judgment, my first nominations for the "Behavioral Economics Hall of Fame" would be Herbert Simon, Richard Cyert, and James March. I further nominate, as the paradigmatic example of detailed empirical research on how things are done, the markup pricing study by Cyert, March, and Chadwick Moore that is reported in Chapter 7 of the Cyert and March book. The replication of that study by Baumol and Stewart (1971) is, as I shall argue below, an impressive and important testimonial to the basic validity of the Carnegie approach.

I do not, however, mean to identify the whole field of inquiry with what was done at Carnegie. Rather, I would point to that work as the most prominent single source of "exemplars" for the broader field.

A similar interpretive comment should be offered for the term *research program*. This term evokes the contributions of Imre Lakatos to the philosophy of science, particularly Lakatos, 1970. While I will make no effort to operate strictly within the Lakatos scheme, it would be appropriate to characterize the thrust of this paper as an attempt to argue that there is a possible scientific research program in the area of firm behavior that is at least potentially "progressive" in Lakatos's sense, and to contribute to the definition of that program.

As a first step toward this end, the following section reviews the critique by orthodox economists[4] of the behavioral research program and, more specifically, of the observation method of "asking businessmen what they do." It is concluded that the most subtle and important element of the critique is the claim that the patterns discerned by behavioral research are epiphenomena—superficial and transitory consequences of underlying economic mechanisms. Section III examines the behavioral theory of the firm from the perspective of the evolutionary theory put forward by Richard Nelson and myself (Nelson and Winter, 1982). It identifies a need for a theory of the persistence of routines and proposes some elements for such a theory. Section IV is a concluding comment on the viability of the behavioral research program.

II. ORTHODOX CRITIQUE

About as often as economists of the behavioral persuasion have ventured into business firms in an attempt to find out how things are "really" done, approximately that often have orthodox economists rejected their conclusions as unfounded and their efforts as a waste of time. No attempt will be made here at documentation of that history. Rather, the attempt is to distill the orthodox side of the published literature—and also the similar orthodox views reflected in seminar and lunch-table discussions and in referee reports on journal submissions and grant applications— into a short list of recurrent claims and propositions. Of course, there are many degrees and shades of orthodoxy; not every orthodox commentator would subscribe to all the propositions set forth here, and many other individual points have been made at one time or another. Certainly no single orthodox contribution states all these propositions or consistently uses language similar to that used here. Milton Friedman's famous methodological essay (Friedman, 1953) does stand out, however, as a key statement of many of the orthodox propositions. Its centrality to the orthodox appraisal of behavioralism becomes even more apparent if one appends to that complex and sophisticated essay all the interpretations, amplifications, popularizations, and simplifications provided for it by sympathetic orthodox commentators.

The primary focus in the following account of the orthodox critique is on the matter of direct empirical observation of business behavior at the individual firm level. Although there is an orthodox canard to the contrary, such observation is not, and cannot be, an atheoretical undertaking. At a minimum there is always a structure of guiding ideas that identifies the sorts of questions that need answers and the ways in which answers might be found—and also determines the limits of the set of unanticipated observations that might succeed in capturing the investigator's attention. In many cases, and certainly in the Carnegie work, behavioral studies have been guided by explicit and elaborate theoretical structures, derived in part from psychology and organization theory. This paper itself is centrally concerned with the relationships between theory and observation in the behavioral economics of the firm, and it amply illustrates the inevitable intimacy of that relationship. This said, it should nevertheless be acknowledged that there is an important issue between orthodoxy and behavioralism concerning the degree to which empirical inquiry should be narrowly constrained by definite theoretical commitments, and by orthodox commitments in particular. Behavioralists tend to believe that economic science needs more investigators modeled on the historical patterns of Tycho Brahe and Johannes Kepler, whereas orthodox theorists aspire to the role of Isaac Newton, and orthodox empiricism is sharply focused on estimation and testing of extant orthodox models. The orthodox critique falls under four main headings, described below.

1. *Events "inside" individual business firms are not part of the subject matter of economics.*

There is an interesting paradox here: whereas in psychology "behaviorism" stands for the methodological dictum, "Don't look inside the black box," in economics the behavioral approach to the firm is concerned precisely with what goes on inside the black box. Aside from the terminological inversion, there is a strong parallelism between the methodological arguments in the two contexts. The "Don't look inside" viewpoint both affirms the strength of a scientific program based on external observation only and alleges that the internal events are very unpromising territory for the scientific method. (Such territory, it is suggested, should be freely ceded to those with a taste for subjectivism and vagueness.)

In economics, there are related normative and positive strands in the wire that carries the "off-limits" sign. The normative strand denies the direct usefulness of economic theory in business management, whereas the positive strand denies that economic theories are properly testable by reference to events within firms. A. C. Pigou's famous statement (1922) that "it is not the business of the economists to teach woolen manufacturers how to make and sell wool, or brewers how to make and sell beer, or any other business men (*sic*) how to do their job" encapsulates the normative aspect. Fritz Machlup reiterated the point on the positive side in his many writings on methodology and firm behavior; a relatively late statement is the following:

> We [economists] are not primarily interested in businessmen, business decisions, business routine and business reactions; we are interested in firms only because of the effects of their actions and reactions upon production, resource use, incomes, and prices. Our main purpose is to explain and predict changes in these variables, and we must look into the actions and reactions of firms only to the extent necessary for this purpose. Often this "look" will be merely one at a mental construct (ideal type) of a firm rather than at a collection of real people in a corporate organization (Machlup, 1974, p. 277).

Although Machlup did not underscore the word *changes* in the above quotation, it would have been quite consistent with his position to have done so. His conception of the predictions made possible by neoclassical economic theory seems to have been dominated by qualitative comparative statics results virtually to the exclusion of other sorts of prediction.

It augurs well for behavioral economics that item one of the orthodox critique has declined further in credibility with each passing decade since 1950, and at present its weight as a debating point is probably negligible. Whatever its abstract merit as a stipulation of what economics *should* be about, it bears very little relation to what contemporary economics actually *is* about. Since 1950, economics has become strongly linked to the normative subject of management science through the shared interest in optimization methods; regardless of whether MR = MC provides useful normative guidance at the individual firm level, linear programming clearly does. More recently, a strong link has been forged between the field of industrial organization and the normative subject of corporate strategy (see Porter, 1980, and Caves, 1980). (Many an economist is now pulling down handsome consulting fees telling "businessmen how to do their job." For a similar observation, see Samuelson, 1972, p. 249.)

On the positive economics side, it has never been the case that the interest in actual prediction was centered on qualitative predictions for the quite hypothetical context of a comparative statics exercise; rather, the interest was and is in quantitative predictions for the dynamic real-world context that gives rise to actual economic data. As economics has

developed, a more and more sophisticated apparatus has been developed
to respond to this demand for quantitative prediction—but the theoretical basis of this apparatus is very much the same neoclassical theory
that Machlup said was not intended for this purpose. In such areas as
antitrust and regulation, it is obvious that the actions and reactions of
large, identifiable individual enterprises are of central concern, and that
a theory whose claim to attention is founded on its account of results
under anonymous, atomistic competition is a theory with a small claim
indeed.[5] Finally, in the writings of Machlup and others, one sometimes
senses the presence of an implicit assumption that the main problem
under discussion is what to tell the students in the classroom. Happily,
however, under contemporary conditions, the occasions are not infrequent when intellectual resources much larger than those that go into
a typical course are available for the study of economic questions involving particular enterprises, industries, or policy choices. For these
high-budget situations, the narrow scope of orthodox theory is not a
virtue reflected in definiteness of prediction but a weakness reflected in
a poverty of guidance for the interpretation and predictive use of available data.

The most fundamental rebuttal to point one of the orthodox critique
of behavioralism is, I believe, gradually emerging as a long-run consequence of Ronald Coase's classic paper "The Nature of the Firm" (Coase,
1937). By posing the problem of the economic determination of the
boundaries of the enterprise, Coase called into question the basic premise
of the view that the theoretical firm is a simple "mental construct," introduced to facilitate market analysis, "an individual decision unit that
has nothing to do but adjust the output and the prices of one or two
imaginary products to very simple imagined changes" (Machlup, 1967,
p. 10). The discipline is visibly drifting away from the long-standing
textbook view of economic organization as firms (and consumers) *in*
markets to seeing firms *as* markets, or to posing the question, "Firms *or*
markets?" and seeing a variety of types of firms and types of market
relations as constituting alternative responses to underlying conditions
affecting economic organization. In the extended "Coasean tradition"
that embraces such authors as Alchian and Demsetz (1972), Williamson
(1975, 1979, and 1985), Fama and Jensen (1983a, b), Jensen and Meckling (1976), and Teece (1980, 1982), it is the pattern of economic organization itself that is to be explained, rather than the response of a
given system to various changes in its data. It seems clear that this promising line of inquiry is quite incompatible with the view that while markets
and their workings are appropriate objects for study by economists, firms
and their workings are not.

There are other important factors pushing the discipline in the same direction. The "stagflation" of the 1970s posed a challenge to macroeconomics which, among other things, promoted interest in a more detailed analysis of the varieties of exchange relations that coexist in the modern economy and the roles of the different types in the inflationary mechanism (see, e.g., Okun, 1981). The rising technical prowess of practitioners of game theory, decision analysis, and information economics has brought a variety of interesting "inside-the-firm" problems within technical range—leading, *ex post*, to the thought that perhaps these problems were formerly "off limits" because they were hard. These developments converge in the modern formal analysis of contracting practices and "agency" relations; see, for example, Diamond and Maskin (1979), Geanakoplos and Milgrom (1984), Holmstrom (1982), and Radner (1981).

2. *Evidence obtained for individual firm behavior by interview or survey methods is of dubious validity.*

In some absolute sense, this proposition is no doubt true as stated— but it does not provide a criterion to distinguish modes of empirical inquiry that are approved by orthodoxy from those that are disapproved. If reasonable doubts about the quality of the empirical evidence are sufficient grounds to terminate lines of inquiry, virtually all of empirical economics (excluding perhaps experimental economics) should be terminated. Assuming that this is not the right answer, it becomes clear that the only interesting assessments of the quality of evidence are *comparative* assessments. To the best of my knowledge, no one has attempted a comparative assessment of the quality of, say, interview or survey data gathered by the individual investigator versus "official" data gathered by government agencies. It does appear, however, that when it comes to data, most economists display an uncharacteristic prejudice in favor of the efforts of government agencies as compared with those of small-scale private enterprise. (On these points, see Morgenstern [1963] and Leontief [1971, 1982].)

There are two more specific issues that require some discussion. The first is the fact that respondents to interviews or survey inquiries are not necessarily motivated to respond truthfully and accurately. They may dissemble or distort their responses in a self-interested or self-justifying way, or they may respond in whatever manner seems likely to minimize the duration of the interruption of their normal work. The second issue concerns whether respondents actually have the ability to answer the posed questions in a scientifically helpful way, even assuming the best of intentions on their part. Both of these are serious concerns, but in my view they are part of the theoretical framework that guides the effort to gather good empirical data, rather than reasons to abstain from gathering the data at all.[6]

That people do not always answer questions truthfully is not an insight that is unique to orthodox economists. A pragmatic ability to deal with this fact is a condition of moderate competence in everyday life, to say nothing of more specific contexts such as legal proceedings and political choices, or research in the other social sciences or in history. This pragmatic ability involves an effort to avoid being misled through some combination of the following measures: (1) alertness to the motivational situation of the respondent at the time, that is, to the possible incentives to depart from the truth; (2) alertness to cues arising from the manner in which the response was given, including signs of stress, haste or hesitation; (3) scrutiny of the responses themselves to assess internal consistency and to determine whether simple hypotheses involving dissembling or distortion explain patterns in the responses; and (4) the attempt to obtain corroborative evidence from independent sources.

The effectiveness of these measures varies tremendously depending on the questions asked, and this fact is certainly fundamental to the design, conduct, and critical scrutiny of empirical investigations. In particular, efforts to probe the basic *motivations* of the respondent may produce results that are sufficiently vague to be highly resistant to consistency checks and corroboration, while inducing motivations in which questions of self-presentation or "public relations" are fundamental. For this and other good reasons,[7] answers to questions about basic motivations are of little value except as evidence of the social or personality forces bearing on the answering of such questions.

The second issue, whether people are actually able to answer the questions posed, is a very subtle one. It is useful to begin with Michael Polanyi's statement that it is a "well known fact that the aim of a skillful performance is achieved by the observance of a set of rules which are not known as such to the person following them" (Polanyi, 1964, p. 49). Polanyi's discussion makes this statement quite compelling on the basis of introspective evidence available to anyone. It is a direct implication of this statement that if a researcher is attempting to discover the rules governing a skilled performance *merely* by asking the performer, his effort is doomed to fail.[8]

In our book (Nelson and Winter, 1982), Richard Nelson and I have made extensive use of Polanyi's analysis of skills and of tacit knowledge generally. In particular, we note that there is an important element in the methodological writings of Friedman and Machlup that is plausibly interpreted as affirming the same points about business decision-making that Polanyi makes about skills in general. In Friedman's use of the billiard player analogy (1953, p. 22) or Machlup's discussion of overtaking a truck (1946, pp. 534–535), the key point is that the businessman's actual performance may be a great deal more sophisticated than the answers to the questions, and that the performance may display the working of underlying economic "rules" or principles even when the answers do not obviously do so. As Nelson and I say, there is "no reason to expect that the language chosen by the businessman to articulate his skill would be the language of economics theory. There is, after all, no reason to expect a bicyclist to be able to explain in the language of physics how he remains upright, but this does not imply that he usually falls over" (1982, p. 92). Our discussion emphasizes that viewing business decision-making as a skill does not entail buying into the whole orthodox apparatus of optimization and equilibrium. On the contrary, if its full implications are accepted, it drives one to the evolutionary view.

There is, however, a useful warning sign to be posted here, analogous to the earlier warning about inquiring into basic motivations. The subtlety of commonplace skilled performances of human beings severely challenges present-day methods of scientific description and analysis.[9] Economic life, and firm behavior in particular, involves a multitude of both commonplace and exemplary skilled performances. To determine "how things are done" at the *intra*personal level by survey, interview, or direct observation methods is thus a complex and challenging undertaking. This does not mean that simpler and more superficial probes are of no value, but it does imply a need for great caution in interpretation of the results—especially in assessing the "quality" of the performance or its conformity to a particular conceptual model of the situation (such as MR = MC). These concerns are significantly alleviated when the attempted description of how things are done is primarily at the interpersonal level, where articulation of procedures naturally plays a larger role. For this reason, organizations of moderate to large size may be better targets for this type of behavioral research than are small organizations. The small businessman who "keeps it all in his head" may be the most difficult target of all.

In general, it seems reasonable to concede that in research on firm behavior, as elsewhere, gullibility and naivete are to be avoided if possible.

3. *Even if behavioral research correctly describes patterns of behavior at a particular time and place, such patterns are merely epiphenomena—transitory reflections of the workings of underlying economic mechanisms in that particular context.*

Whereas the preceding point of the orthodox critique is often encountered as a general charge, rather than in the more constructive form of specific criticisms directed at the validity of particular data, this one is commonly encountered in the form of a specific objection to a purported finding or tentative assumption about behavior. What the critic does is to posit an environmental condition that is different from, or perhaps an extreme case of, the situation apparently envisaged by the proponent of the finding or assumption. The question is then raised as to whether the behavioral pattern alleged is plausible, or even well defined, in the alternative circumstances. The critic's claim or implication is that the answer is in the negative, and that this demonstrates that there is something superficial and untrustworthy about the pattern described. It is further implied that there is some alternative (orthodox) characterization of the situation that is not flawed by the same sort of superficiality.

Consider, for example, the previously mentioned markup-pricing study of Cyert, March, and Moore. Central to the computer model that describes pricing behavior in the department store studied is a specific quantitative value of the conventional standard markup: "Divide each cost by .6 . . . and move the result to the nearest $.95" (Cyert and March, 1963, p. 138). It goes against the grain of the most basic kind of economic understanding to suppose that the figure .6 in that rule is some sort of natural behavioral constant. Surely, it must in some way reflect the relative levels of wholesale prices of department store goods on the one hand and the costs of providing department store retailing services on the other. For, depending on the ratio of those values, a given conventional markup on invoice may be, on the one hand, insufficient to cover the full costs of retailing services or, on the other, the source of an enormous rate of return on invested capital (assuming full utilization). The Carnegie authors acknowledged this point.

Indeed, when Baumol and Stewart (1971) replicated the study years later in a different department store in a different city, they found a different value of the key markup parameter—.55 instead of .6. Resist, but only for the moment, the obvious temptation to be impressed by the success of the replication across years, miles, and organizational boundaries, and focus on the epiphenomenal nature of the original .6 figure. Note also that the change is in the direction that an orthodox critic might predict, assuming he is aware of the broad historical tendency for labor-intensive services to rise in price relative to manufactured goods. Note finally that while the original authors were alert to the issue, and while the notion that there are higher-level adaptation processes adjusting the parameters of lower-level routines is an important part of the behavioral theory of the firm (as is discussed further below), the markup model itself was not supplemented by an explicit adaptive model for adjustment of the key markup parameter.

Within the logical structure of formal orthodoxy, the notion that a decision rule might depend on the state of the environment in ways that are not explicitly specified is anathema. The general plan of formal orthodoxy is to proceed from "given" data on opportunities and objectives, through optimization, to decision rules characterizing behavior in every possible environment and thence, through equilibrium calculation, to the determination of the environment (or distribution or time sequence of environments) that is actually realized. The decision rules as functions are logically prior to the determination of the actual environment, which will bring forth particular equilibrium decisions. One does not "know" what the actual environment will be until "after" one "knows" the rules. There is no question but that the sort of situation illustrated in the markup pricing example is a fundamental obstacle to the pursuit of this orthodox analytical path.

Here, as in the discussion of the data validity point, the first question is whether orthodoxy can validly claim to be exempt from the difficulties it sees in behavioralism. It is true that there is no such problem in the *logical* structure of particular orthodox models—but then, the objection to the notion of .6 as a natural constant in a markup formula is not one that points to a logical flaw. Rather, it points to a likely source of predictive error and views the authors' warning on this point as a confession that their approach is inadequate. The question is whether the logical foundations of orthodoxy are not subject to analogous empirical weakness, though perhaps less well posted with warnings. There are as many aspects to this question as there are features of the logical foundations of orthodoxy. The focus here will be on production sets.

In our joint work (see especially Nelson and Winter, 1982, pp. 59–65) and in independent writings (Nelson, 1980; Winter, 1982), Nelson and I have pointed out that the production set/function concept is fundamentally implicated in the failure of orthodox economics to deal satisfactorily with technological change. The concept presumes that there are sharply defined limits to "given" technological knowledge. This is no more the case in reality than that there are given values for behavioral markup factors. What *is* the case is that both ongoing production activities and plans for prospective activities are based on knowledge that is of less than perfect clarity and certainty, and is imperfect in variable degree in a number of different dimensions. For example, there is the problem of limited "causal depth": the specifications of the range of environmental conditions under which a particular productive performance can be continued, or successfully undertaken, are never perfectly known—and, of course, some degree of change in the actual environment is taking place all the time. What is also the case is that, however one might choose to define the limits of productive knowledge for the purposes of a particular inquiry, those limits are subject to change under the pressure of sufficiently strong economic forces. To be sure, the second law of thermodynamics will not be repealed by a change in relative price ratios. But the production functions of orthodoxy are supposed to characterize the limits of available knowledge, not the limits of physical feasibility. The limits of available knowledge, like markup factors, move in response to economic pressure.

To the extent that orthodoxy aspires to being a successful empirical science, its practitioners find themselves in the same box as the behavioralists. The constants and "given data" that they choose to introduce in the construction of their models are not "given" to them with an ontological warranty that something like that really exists. From an empirical, as opposed to a doctrinal or aesthetic, point of view, these assumptions are mere expedient choices, affirming propositions often known to be false, perhaps adequate for the purpose at hand, perhaps not. Nor is there a comprehensive rule that says that behavioral and organizational change is always faster than technological change—compare the relative constancy found for the department-store markup factor with the remarkable pace of change in semiconductor or computer technology.[10] In addition, the notion of a *generalized* comparison between rates of technological change and rates of behavioral/organizational change implicitly assumes that there is a reasonably well-demarcated boundary between the two realms—another idea that will not withstand careful scrutiny and in fact is increasingly undermined by the results of work in the orthodox tradition itself.

That the problem afflicts orthodoxy as well as behavioralism does not mean that it is a small problem. On the contrary, it is an enormous problem. There is a need to learn to distinguish that which is relatively durable and fundamental in economic patterns from that which is relatively transitory and epiphenomenal, and beyond that to identify the kinds and levels of economic pressure that produce change in particular patterns. This problem is considered further in the "evolutionary perspective" below.

4. *Behavioral research on individual firms is too expensive, at least relative to the benefits it produces, to be justified.*

A crude kind of cost-benefit approach to the philosophy of science crops up in much orthodox discussion of methodology in general and behavioralism in particular. In the "realism-of-assumptions" discussion, it has been suggested that realism is a matter of degree and that just as the optimal amount of crime in a society is not zero, so the optimal amount of realism in a scientific theory is not 100 percent realism. Friedman wrote in his classic essay (1953) that:

> complete "realism" is clearly unattainable, and the question of whether a theory is realistic "enough" can be settled only by seeing whether it yields predictions good enough for the purpose in hand, or that are better than alternative theories (p. 41).

In his discussions of behavioralism, Machlup emphasized the requirements of the behavioral theory for detailed information on each individual firm, and stressed that such detailed treatment could be justified (if at all) only in cases where detailed predictions of the behavior of particular firms were clearly required. For example, in Machlup (1974) we find:

> It would be a strange methodological principle indeed that were to command us to seek the heaps of information that may be required in some cases also for problems where they are not needed (p. 276).

It is probably the case that the philosophy of science could benefit from a substantial infusion of economic reasoning. The advance of science is, after all, resource constrained, and it is hard to see how useful normative guidance to promote that advance can be formulated in disregard of the principles of efficient resource allocation. Thus far, however, there does not seem to be any real progress along this line; such arguments as those just cited are almost embarrassingly casual. In his forceful defense of Friedman's methodology as "instrumentalist" philosophy of science, Lawrence Boland (1979) writes:

> *Finally, and most importantly, I think it is essential to realize that instrumentalism is solely concerned with [immediate] practical success.* In this light, one should ask, "What are the criteria of success? Who decides what they are?" Questions of this type, I think, must also be dealt with before one can ever begin—constructively or destructively— to criticize effectively the instrumentalism that constitutes the foundation of Friedman's methodology (p. 521; emphasis in original).

Indeed, a philosophy that is solely concerned with success but as yet offers no notion of what success *is* would seem to be an intellectual project that has not yet started. (One hopes that, when the work begins, the above-stated commitment to total myopia will be reconsidered.)

As I have argued elsewhere, the reference to "predictions good enough for the purpose in hand" introduces to Friedman's methodology considerations that seem more appropriate to the discussion of approximation schemes, or "engineering calculations," than to the discussion of scientific theories and the testing thereof (Winter, 1975, pp. 94–95). There is ordinarily no specific "purpose in hand" for a theory, because the range of actual application may be large and the range of potential application is indeterminate. Machlup, too, seems to have misunderstood the relationship between theories and approximation schemes, in a manner more or less symmetric with Friedman's. When there *is* a definite purpose in hand, the cost-accuracy trade-offs characteristic of that purpose legitimately shape the "engineering" application of the theory in that particular context. Certainly, the use of "heaps of information" is not compelled when it is not necessary (or economically efficient), but this has little to do with the relative merits of different theories.

Regarding the relative merits of orthodoxy and behavioralism, note that it is not as if there were a unique orthodox (or "marginalist") way to approach a given problem and a unique behavioralist way to approach the same problem. Both theories have, to their credit, the capacity to adjust to the research resources actually available; they provide useful guidance over a range of research budgets. Simple versions of either theory can be subsumed as approximation schemes within the other; for example, behavioralism offers an unapologetic rationale for the use of the lagged dependent variable when theoretically appropriate dynamic optimization models cannot be operationalized; orthodoxy offers simple comparative statics models to assess the qualitative results of a more complex behavioral process.

Overall, however, it does seem correct to say that behavioralism generates a larger appetite for information than orthodoxy does, for there are few, if any, facts of interest to orthodoxy that are not of interest to behavioralism, but there are many facts of interest to behavioralism that orthodoxy deems irrelevant. Thus the issue of whether the costs of gathering the additional facts are justified by the benefits does have a certain amount of substance to it. The relative strength of the behavioralist approach is probably greatest at high research budget levels, both in the case of individual projects and of the overall level of effort on issues involving business behavior.

I would argue that economists have a tendency to think too small on these matters. The stakes involved in major economic policy questions, even those affecting single industries, are typically orders of magnitude larger than the total expenditure on economic research. A tiny relative improvement in economic performance would, accordingly, cover very large percentage increases in economic research costs. The main thing that is needed to shift out the overall budget constraint for economics is greater credibility, derived from greater predictive accuracy. It is not our high unit cost that limits the growth of our scholarly industry, it is the low quality of our output. Hence, if behavioralism offers a way to a stronger predictive theory, the additional expense probably does not matter very much.

III. EVOLUTIONARY PERSPECTIVE

The central task of evolutionary economics is to understand the changing prevalence of various ways of doing things. Or, as Thorstein Veblen (1898) put it:

> For the purpose of economic science the process of cumulative change that is to be accounted for is the sequence of change in the methods of doing things,—the methods of dealing with the material means of life (pp. 70–71).

Nelson and I use the word *routine* as the generic term for a way of doing things. It is simultaneously the counterpart of a wide range of terms employed in everyday life and in various theoretical languages, including those of orthodox and behavioral economic theory; among these terms are *decision rule, technique, skill, standard operating procedure, management practice, policy, strategy, information system, information structure, program, script,* and *organization form.* Of course, these terms are sometimes used in ways that do not correspond to our understanding of *routine,* and they typically carry specific connotations related to the contexts in which they are used. However, to the extent that reference is made to a relatively complex pattern of behavior (or the theoretical representation of such a pattern) triggered by a relatively small number of initiating signals or choices and functioning as a recognizable unit in a relatively automatic fashion, to that extent reference is made to something called a routine in evolutionary theory.

For the purposes of empirical inquiry, the term *routine* may be operationalized in a variety of ways. At one extreme, approached by the Carnegie markup pricing model, the characterization of the pattern of behavior in question may be highly specific and detailed. For some theoretical purposes, exhaustive description is the conceptual ideal, just as the terms *state of the world* and *commodity* in orthodox economics are properly understood to subsume all differentiating characteristics relevant to the problem at hand. At the other extreme, the characterization may not go beyond the information ordinarily conveyed by a commonly used name for a way of doing things—*double-entry bookkeeping, oxygen-process steel, markup pricing.* In between these extremes, there are various intermediate levels of detail, embracing, for example, taxonomic structures and the device of appending a short list of categorical and quantitative descriptor variables to a name.

In attempting to understand the changing prevalence of various ways of doing things, one major subtask is to understand the persistence of routines within a single business firm, or still more specifically, within a single establishment. It is, of course, a fundamental commitment of evolutionary theory that routines do tend to persist. "The essential continuity underlying the process of evolutionary change is the continuity of routinized behavior" (Winter, 1975, p. 101). "As a first approximation . . . firms may be expected to behave in the future according to the routines they have employed in the past" (Nelson and Winter, 1982, p. 134).

To proceed to the second approximation, it is necessary to recognize that routines do change, but typically in relatively incremental ways. The patterns of change reflect both the character of environmental pressures and the characteristics of the organizations and the routines on which those pressures impinge; the problem is to explain and predict the extent and direction of change under various alternative assumptions regarding the pressures, the organizations, and the routines in place. To proceed *beyond* the second approximation it would be necessary to achieve some degree of predictive power regarding the incidence and effects of more discontinuous, innovative change. Although this is clearly a tall order, useful predictive power may be attainable, at least for that portion of innovative change that is "induced" in the sense that it is an intelligent response to new and intense environmental pressure, or regarding only gross characterizations of the new routines.

In the context of evolutionary economics, it is important to determine how good the "first approximation" really is and how far it is the case that the pursuit of predictive success with first-approximation methods provides the basis for success at the levels of the second and third approximations. This question will be the focus of the discussion that follows. It is essentially a constructive rephrasing of the issue raised in point three of the orthodox critique of behavioralism: rather than proposing a sweeping conclusion to the effect that observed behavioral regularities are necessarily epiphenomenal and hence not worth investigating, it asks for a discriminating analysis of the circumstances under which various degrees of persistence in behavioral routines is to be expected. Or, assuming one can learn what is going on, how does one ascertain whether it is likely to *continue* to go on?

Before proposing an approach and some tentative answers to this question, I must take note of some limitations on the scope of the inquiry. First, I set aside the many interesting questions involving changes in routine that occur in the absence of efforts to produce such change, or even in spite of efforts to avoid it. Such changes often occur because of variation in input mix or environmental conditions, or because of the failure of organizational memory or information transmission mechanisms.[11] Second, I give scant attention to a conceptual point that is of central importance to the operational interpretation of the term *routine*: there is an intimate connection between the degree of detail with which a routine is specified and the degree of persistence of the routine thus specified. Organizational routines, like everything else in the world, are simultaneously the subject of the wisdom of *Ecclesiastes* ("There is no new thing under the sun") and of Heraclitus ("You could not step into the same river twice"). For example, if the quantitative parameter in the Carnegie study referred to above is considered integral to the description of the routine, then Baumol and Stewart did not observe the same routine in their later study—but on a more flexible definition of the routine, they did. The question of whether the Baumol and Stewart replication counts as a success for "first-approximation" methods or "second-approximation" methods is correspondingly sensitive to the specificity with which the routine is characterized. Similarly, a routine characterized only as a very high level heuristic description of an organization's sphere of competence may persist through generations of change in its particular product line. The discussion that follows should be interpreted as "holding constant" the degree of specificity of the description of routines.

Finally, and most importantly, I also regard as held constant in the discussion the underlying conditions that create opportunities for technological and organizational change and determine the appropriability of the gains from seizing such opportunities. These "Schumpeterian" aspects of the problem are obviously fundamental, particularly if it is the pattern of interindustry differences in the pace of change that one is attempting to understand (see Levin et al., 1984).

In short, my subject here is the persistence of routines within individual business organizations, in the face of changing environmental pressures that might be expected to give rise to deliberate efforts to modify or replace such routines. It should be clear, on the one hand, that persistence of routines is no great puzzle in a completely static environment, and certainly orthodoxy and behavioralism concur in predicting no change in that case. On the other hand, sufficiently drastic environmental change will render any routine infeasible, and less drastic change can create enormously powerful incentives for efforts at adaptation. Once again, behavioral, evolutionary, and orthodox viewpoints converge on the prediction that drastic pressure is likely to produce substantial change, and they would often agree on the direction of the change.[12] The interesting cases, where predictions may differ, arise in the wide interval between the two extremes.

Some elements for a theory of the persistence of routines in these cases will now be set forth. The discussion begins with considerations that are clearly compatible with the high-level commitments of orthodox theory, however neglected they may be in actual orthodox modeling. It then proceeds to considerations that are increasingly suspect or mistaken, from the orthodox viewpoint.

Routine-specific Assets

A succinct way of expressing one major difference between orthodoxy and evolutionary theory is to say that, in the analysis of the short run, evolutionary theory classifies routines with the "fixed factors" (Winter, 1984). Since orthodoxy does not seriously maintain that commitments to "fixed factors" are typically made under conditions of perfect foresight, it has no difficulty in acknowledging that firm performance is frequently "suboptimal" in the limited sense that a superior result could be achieved if only a different set of durable commitments had been made in the past. It strongly resists, however, the claim of behavioral and evolutionary theory that behavioral patterns can be similarly inappropriate and give rise to suboptimality in the same sense. For example, it treats with skepticism or ridicule the notion that, in an environment of newly accelerated inflation, firms might not smoothly accomplish the conversion of all their calculations and contracts to appropriate real terms.

The establishment of organizational routines involves investment in physical and human capital; frequently, such investments are of a highly specific and irreversible nature. The logic of sunk costs thus operates with the same force in the area of behavioral routines as it does in the case of other forms of capital. Past irreversible investments yield continuing benefits that sustain old methods when, in an unconstrained "long-run" choice context, new methods would be adopted as economically superior. Or, to phrase it the other way, the switch to a new way of doing things incurs incremental costs whose counterparts in the case of the old ways are sunk and hence irrelevant to forward-looking calculation. These considerations may provide a fully rational basis for the persistence of superficially irrational organizational routines. Of course, they also provide a handy *rationale* for inaction, based on a myopic overemphasis on control of near-term outlays and a reluctance to confront the complex information-processing task of producing a more substantial basis for a decision on the matter. Orthodoxy is committed to exclusive reliance on the former interpretation, whereas behavioral economics sees two competing hypotheses whose validity can be assessed (in principle and often in practice) by direct observation of the decision process.[13]

Consider, for example, a firm whose management is thinking of adopting a new, more "people-oriented" approach to the supervision of its production workers.[14] Management is likely to confront the problem that the firm's existing foremen are in diverse ways unsuited and unprepared for the new approach. Management may further observe that this is not an accident but a reflection of the coherence of the firm's established routines. Perhaps a differently organized personnel department, operating according to different criteria, would have selected different supervisory personnel who, after appropriate training, could effectively implement the proposed new supervision policy—but the new set-up costs that would be incurred in such a sweeping reform of the personnel system might outweigh the gains achieved relative to the system currently in place. On the other hand, an attempt to change the policy alone, ignoring the complementarities with personnel selection and training, might well backfire.

Or consider that, in a newly inflationary environment, a firm might recognize that its counsel's office might benefit from expertise on the interpretation of price indexes and on the types of price information available from various sources—but in the open market for legal talent, it is not likely that one will find such expertise effectively packaged with the detailed knowledge of the company's business that the existing personnel of the office already possess. Perhaps, therefore, it would actually be better to pretend that the inflation doesn't exist or will soon go away. (In all such cases the speculation that the world may soon change back to its previous, more comfortable state is another readily available and superficially rational excuse for not incurring the various costs of adjustment to change.)

An increasingly important class of routine-specific assets is business computer systems and their associated software. In recent years, such systems have increased very substantially the short-run flexibility manifested in a spectrum of organizational routines ranging from design through production activities to inventory control, billing, and related bookkeeping functions. On the other hand, the complex organizational routines founded on these systems have much more sharply defined limits than the older ones that relied on human beings for a much larger share of the information processing. The "first approximation" characterization of routines becomes "the scope of possible action as defined by the existing software," while a switch to a computer system incompatible with the old one is an organizational change with the costs and indeterminate consequences of a major innovation. And it is a matter of common frustrating experience that contemporary organizations often display spectacular ineptitude when confronted with situations that their existing software cannot "understand."

The concept of asset specificity plays, of course, a prominent role in contemporary transaction cost economics. In that context, the emphasis is on *transaction*-specific assets, that is, on irreversible investment commitments undertaken in anticipation of quasi-rents realizable only in some particular economic exchange relationship. According to Williamson (1985) and others, the existence of asset specificity implies that situations that may be competitive *ex ante* (precommitment) are transformed *ex post* into bilateral monopoly; this transformation has important implications for the vulnerability of each party to the opportunism of the other and hence for the relative performance of alternative governance structures within which the transaction might be conducted. Many otherwise mysterious phenomena of economic organization thus become explicable as a result of a close look at the concrete nature of the investment commitments involved in actually getting the business done.

This observation applies equally well to routine-specific assets; indeed, in the important case of recurring transactions between two firms, the terms may have the same referent. The relationship may continue in part because it is routinized by supporting investments; the routine may continue because it is incidental to valued continuing relationships and is, implicitly or explicitly, a part of the governance structure of that relationship and hence cannot be revised unilaterally. Indeed, even a unilateral proposal to jointly *consider* revision of the routine may be forestalled, either because it might be thought to signal that the proposer was considering defecting from the relationship or because the gains realizable from the adjustment could easily be overwhelmed by the costs of renewed conflict over those parameters of the relationship that are essentially "zero sum."[15]

Routine-related Intraorganizational Conflict

Of course, the same considerations often operate *within* organizations. "Prevailing routines define a truce, and attempts to change routines often provoke a renewal of conflict which is destructive to the participants and to the organization as a whole" (Nelson and Winter, 1982, p. 134).

This is a major reason why an external observer may go badly wrong in interpreting the behavior of a large organization as that of a unitary rational actor.[16] Such an observer, perceiving that the organization's routines are in minor ways poorly adapted to its environment, may attribute the maladaptation to recent environmental change and anticipate a timely adaptive response. This prediction may well go wrong, for even minor changes require an advocate or "entrepreneur" who, presumably, must believe that the promotion of the change is in his personal interest.[17] If the potential advocate is at a low level in the organization, the benefits of change to the organization as a whole are likely to translate very imperfectly into benefits for the advocate (who, if the change occurs and is successful, may even have difficulty remaining identified as its sponsor). On the other hand, promotion of the change is likely to entail very real and visible costs of friction with superiors and associates whose behavior would have to be modified to effect the change, and many of these costs are likely to be incurred whether the change effort goes forward or not. The balance of expected costs and benefits is unlikely to look promising: "Don't rock the boat" is the equilibrium strategy in this game.

A high-level executive is in a different position, of course. His or her prospects may be much better for deriving personal benefits from promoting change that benefits the organization. But, at high levels, the agenda of possible change options is likely to be crowded. A change that promises a definite but minor improvement for the organization may not cover its personal costs to the executive, since those costs include the opportunity cost of other initiatives foregone.

Things are different, but not necessarily promotive of smooth adaptation, when the stakes are high. If environmental pressures on existing routines are severe, perhaps even threatening the survival of the organization, the problem will likely receive the attention of top management. These executives are likely to see their personal interests as very much at stake in the situation. However, this does not mean that those interests need be compatible with each other or with the "interest" of the "organization as a whole"—which may be a particularly problematic concept under the prevailing circumstances. The menu of changes under consideration may well include drastic adjustments in the scope of the organization's activities or the responsibilities of individual executives. Discussion of these changes may include evaluations of managerial performance that blend objective assessment with elements of recrimination, scapegoating, and self-serving propaganda. From the economist's perspective, what is at stake in such a conflict is the level of future returns to the human capital, including firm-specific capital, possessed by different members of the managerial group. The nature and intensity of the interactions is perhaps better understood by noting that the "value of human capital" may be related to the subjective appraisal of "self-worth." The prospect of such conflict is among the factors contributing to belated organizational response to developing crises. When the need for action is finally acknowledged, the eruption of conflict may delay the formulation of an adaptive plan and degrade the plan arrived at—or hasten the demise of the organization.[18]

The appraisal of these considerations offered by orthodox economic thinking is somewhat ambiguous. It is clear enough that there is no room for them in the standard textbook model of the firm as a production function with a profit goal attached. Certainly the school of thought that considers the "Coase theorem" as broadly relevant to real economic situations is unlikely to acknowledge the existence of significant obstacles to joint maximization in the context of the business firm. On the other hand, there is no direct contradiction between the existence of intraorganizational conflict and individual rationality. And in recent years, a number of theorists working with orthodox tools have turned their attention to the consequences of intraorganizational conflicts of interest, particularly under the heading of agency theory.[19] It is at least conceivable that the assumption that organizations are unitary rational actors will ultimately be rejected, even in the textbooks, as inconsistent with the orthodox paradigm.

To make operational use of the notion that the persistence of routines is systematically related to intraorganizational conflict, it is necessary to follow the behavioralist program of seeking out "inside information" on the firm. The relationship between the activities of those involved in the routine and the structure of the organization is a key consideration. The prototypical "routine as truce" situation is one in which an important routine involves coordinated, complementary activities that are nominally subject to several different, roughly coequal authorities. In such a case, the task of getting agreement on change may be sufficiently demanding so that ultimately the routine controls the authorities rather than the other way around. But, anticipating such a result, a corporate leader may create an organizational structure, or "culture," that avoids it. Organizations clearly differ dramatically in their receptivity to change, and it appears that such differences are substantially affected by differences in the management of conflict.

Absence of Superordinate Adaptation Routines

Organizational routines form quasi-hierarchical structures. Parameters specifying the particular performance expected of many individual members and small subunits are routinely provided by authoritative communications from other individuals and units in the organization.[20] Such parameters may include, for example, the starting and ending times of particular activities, the specifications and amounts of products or components to be produced, the numbers upon which planning documents are to be based, the allocation of sales effort among regions, customers, and products—and, of course, the economist's focal variables: the quantities of particular items to be bought or sold and the price and other conditions of such transactions. Even in the simplest cases, the role of the superordinate routines is in one sense unimportant: vastly more information processing attends the actual performance of the subordinate routine than is contained in the parameters communicated. This is the essence of what routines and skills are all about. On the other hand, since the parameters do affect the particular performance that occurs, they are relevant (or essential) to accurate prediction of the behavior of the organization. To study the subordinate routine over a particular time span, ignoring the existence of the superordinate routine(s), and then to attempt prediction on the "first-approximation" assumption that the routine will persist as observed, is obviously to risk serious error. Success—even very precise success—may be achieved, but only with the aid of good luck in the specific form that there is no actual change in the routine's parameters between the observation period and the forecast period. In econometric jargon, the problem is that the observed values of the parameters are not "structural coefficients."

As Cyert and March (1963) observed, the problem posed here is not necessarily solvable simply by expanding the behavioral inquiry to include the superordinate routine(s) and in a sense it may not be solvable at all.

> Any organization as complex as a firm adapts to its environment at many different (but interrelated) levels. It changes its behavior in response to short-run feedback from the environment according to some fairly well-defined rules. It changes rules in response to longer-run feedback according to some more general rules, and so on. At some point in this hierarchy of rule change, we describe the rules involved as "learning rules." By this we mean (in effect) that we will not examine the hierarchy further, although it is clear that wherever we stop we can still imagine higher-level rules by which the lower-level learning rules are modified (pp. 101–102).

Disregarding the suggestion that the scope of the inquiry ought to have some definite limit, conventionally labeled "learning rules," let us consider some of the significant things that happen as we move the focus of inquiry up the hierarchy. First, the subtlety and complexity of the individual skills being exercised typically rises. The way the output signals of the human "black boxes" relate to the input signals becomes more and more inscrutable and probably also more consequential for organizational outcomes. This may be fine for the organization, but it is bad news for the aspiring observer/predictor of its behavior. Second, the routines being exercised tend to contain a larger and larger component of search activities guided by heuristics of an increasingly imprecise and/ or subtle nature. Third, the frequency with which the routines are evoked is declining: "long-run" learning is sporadic, not continuous. This means that there is increasing scope for lapses of individual and organizational memory and other "mutagenic" events to affect the routine in unintended ways.[21] Last, related to the sporadic nature of high-level change but deserving of special emphasis, the external environment changes in between evocations of the high-level routines. It comes to contain new solutions (or fragments of solutions) to the problems arising in the organization's lower-level routines and perhaps also new opportunities and hazards for the organization as a whole. In a changing world, reasonably adaptive high-level learning rules for an organization are linked to the ongoing change processes of the wider arena. All these considerations make it apparent that the use of terms like *rule* and *routine* involves increasing strain of ordinary usage as we move up the hierarchy.

Some further complications are introduced by the fact that the hierarchy of routines generally parallels the hierarchy of authority in the organization. In an organization's formal system of authority, the power to authorize departures from existing routines, as well as the responsibility for investigating and implementing changes in routine, typically resides in individuals of higher rank than those responsible for the execution of routines. This common pattern is concisely summarized by the phrase "management by exception" that is found in the management literature. A significant implication of this pattern is that the operation of routines at high levels in the hierarchy is complexly intertwined with the power relations among the executives at that level. In Allison's (1971) terminology, outcomes are at least partially determined by processes of "bureaucratic politics." In the game of bureaucratic politics, the interests of individual players, their personal relationships, the informational advantages and cognitive orientations specific to their roles, and the competencies of the organizational units under their supervision all combine in a complex and highly contingent fashion to determine the behavior of the organization as a whole.

It would be easy to conclude that the outlook for achieving successful prediction by way of behavioral studies is bleak. While it may be possible, in some cases, to observe and precisely describe ongoing routines at low levels in the hierarchy, and while routines at that level are frequently highly deterministic, it seems unlikely that the same approach would prove equally successful—or even successful at all—at higher levels. This pessimistic conclusion has, I fear, considerable validity in the case of highly innovative business firms. Indeed, the notion that the course of innovative effort could be predicted in detail, by *any* method, seems self-contradictory. This emphatically does not imply, however, that there is no substantial or important arena in which the methods of behavioral economics can be successful. Continuing innovation is the fundamental and pervasive phenomenon of the modern world, but it does not proceed so rapidly as to overthrow, in the span of a few years, all the behavioral regularities that we can observe today. The important task, to which the present discussion seeks to contribute, is to develop the ability to discriminate between those regularities that are subject to rapid overthrow and those that are not.

Evolutionary theory emphasizes, in this connection, the importance of organizational boundaries as impediments to information flow. As noted above, the quest for solutions to an organization's problems often leads to information sources that lie in the organization's external environment. This is especially characteristic of business firms that can function effectively in product markets where technologies are developing rapidly. But the search for information from external sources does not proceed with the same ease as for internal sources. The idiosyncratic characteristics of the individual firm shape its capabilities in the search for new routines just as they do the performance of its prevailing routines. The fact that there exists, somewhere in the world, knowledge that would be highly helpful to a particular firm in a particular situation does not imply that that firm will successfully locate and absorb that knowledge. There may, for example, be a great number of sources of advice in the world that could effectively help a department store to achieve a more profitable pricing procedure than the one originally described in the Cyert and March book. But if we are interested in the persistence of that particular routine, in a particular store, it is important to investigate whether the store has within itself the capability for systematic review and analysis of its pricing policies. If it does, one is led to expect relatively prompt response to changes in market circumstances that create strong incentives for the modification of prevailing routines. But the required capability for review and analysis is not costless, and once this obvious fact is allowed to intrude, even orthodox economic theory does not produce a prediction that a department store necessarily should contain such a capability.

Suppose, then, that it does not. The change in its circumstances might lead it to try to improvise such a capability, or the firm may have recourse to external "markets for information." The posited limitations on the firm's capabilities in its initial condition are obviously relevant to the prospects for success in the first sort of effort. Those same limitations, and the well-known transactional difficulties affecting markets for information (Arrow, 1962), both combine to limit the prospects for success of the second sort of effort. Above all, the store must rely upon its own resources in locating the sort of expertise that it requires and in evaluating whether such expertise is worth the price asked for it—and this in a world in which hucksters and mere pretenders to expertise strive mightily to masquerade as the real thing. As in the case of routine-specific assets, there is thus some rational basis for resistance to change—the resistance taking the form, in this case, of disregard of opportunities for obtaining assistance from outside the firm. For the observer of the firm's behavior, it may be difficult to distinguish between this rational basis and more straightforward affronts to the rationality assumptions of orthodox theory.

Not infrequently, the answer to the question of whether a firm contains within itself the capabilities for smooth modification of some particular routine will have a clear answer in the negative. In such cases, the probability that the routine will persist in the future is substantially increased. It is increased further if the hierarchy of routines contains strong *control* mechanisms intended to prevent or suppress deviations from the routine in question. As noted in Nelson and Winter (1982, pp. 116–117) such mechanisms are generally a necessary component of complex organizational systems, but often have the unintended consequence of preventing desirable adaptations.

David Teece (1982) has followed a line of reasoning similar to the above in his discussion of the basis of the multiproduct firm. As Teece points out, following Penrose (1959),

> The final product produced by a firm in any given time merely represents one of several ways in which the organization could be using its internal resources. As wartime experience demonstrated, automobile manufacturers suddenly began making tanks, chemical companies began making explosives, and radio manufacturers began making radar. In short, a firm's capability lies upstream from the end product—it lies in a generalizable capability which might find a variety of final product applications (p. 45).

For the observer seeking a basis for prediction, it is significant that it was not the automobile companies that began to make explosives, nor the chemical companies that began to make radar. Identifiable limits on the scope of a firm's existing capabilities are a significant indicator of its likely behavior in the future.

The attempt to assess the place of these considerations in orthodox economic theory encounters once again some ambiguities. On the one hand, the great weight of textbook orthodoxy, and of most of general equilibrium theory as well, is unquestionably thrown behind the proposition that the limits to the capabilities of business firms are at once sharply defined and permanent, and are adequately represented for theoretical purposes by production sets or production functions. This position may be regarded as an extreme form of the assumption that there are no adaptation routines superordinate to those whose structure is captured by the production set or function; it emphatically denies the existence or importance of information flows between the firm and its environment that affect the scope of its capabilities. On the other hand, in much of industrial organization, in the literature of technological change specifically, and in the modern economics of information, a good deal is said about markets for information and their imperfect workings. These discussions have, for the most part, a highly selective character. They examine the role of information market failure in particular situations and circumstances; they do not address the place that these same considerations might occupy in the fundamental conceptualization of the business firm. As Nelson and I have discussed, the tension between the textbook and general equilibrium theory literature on the one hand and the industrial organization, technological change, and economics of information literature on the other, is one of the more important symptoms of the need for basic theoretical reform (Nelson and Winter, 1982, pp. 24–30).

Routine-related Cognitive Structures

Business decision-making, like economic research and other human mental activities, is carried on within a context of belief. To a substantial extent, the content of this system of belief is not a matter of conscious awareness. Elements of the system are frequently evoked and exploited in the interpretation of events without the thinker being aware that any such process is taking place. Perceptions of phenomena in the external world, interpreted by the perceiver as perceptions of "facts," are actually fundamentally (but unconsciously) shaped by the perceiver's own beliefs and expectations. In general, phenomena that are highly incongruent with the perceiver's belief system are treated by the perceiver in a manner that is minimally disruptive of that system. Such treatment may involve outright failure to observe the phenomenon, in spite of objectively favorable conditions for doing so, or it may include a retroactive editing of what the sense organs themselves received so as to eliminate the incongruity with the belief system.

Support for these propositions and explorations of their implications for the understanding of human behavior may be found in the copious literature spanning cognitive psychology, organization theory, and the philosophy of science. They are well illustrated by the anomalous playing-card experiment and the use made of that experiment by Thomas Kuhn in his widely renowned book, *The Structure of Scientific Revolutions* (1964). The experiment, originally performed by Bruner and Postman (1949), consists of exposing playing cards to experimental subjects in a series of gradually increased exposures. Although many of the cards are of the ordinary sort, some are anomalous, such as a red seven of spades. The phenomenon observed is that on short exposures subjects "correct" their perception of anomalous cards and identify, for example, the red seven of spades as a seven of hearts, disregarding the shape of the symbols on the card. Kuhn remarks as follows:

> Either as a metaphor or because it reflects the nature of the mind, that psychological experiment provides a wonderfully simple and cogent schema for the process of scientific discovery. In science, as in the playing card experiment, novelty emerges only with difficulty, manifested by resistance, against a background provided by expectation. Initially, only the anticipated and usual are experienced even under circumstances where anomaly is later to be observed (p. 64).

Steinbruner (1974), in a pioneering work relating cognitive psychology and organization theory, writes in a similar vein:

> The principle of stability asserts that cognitive inference mechanisms resist change in the core structure of beliefs. Because of extensive lateral and hierarchical relationships within a system of beliefs—each of which must be held to some level of consistency—a major restructuring of beliefs is likely to set off a chain reaction, imposing severe burdens upon the information processing system. Economy thus requires a bias against change in major components of belief structure once they have been established (p. 102).

Not all organizational routines are tightly linked to basic belief systems of key organizational actors. In some cases, an organization may choose the routine it will follow in a particular matter with something like the casual deliberation of a person choosing the clothing he or she will wear on a particular day. In other cases, however, the scope for considering change of routine is more akin to the scope for deciding to go out into the world naked. The value-infused belief system that rules this alternative out of consideration is not normally a matter of conscious awareness, yet its effect and effectiveness as a restraint on behavior are readily observable. Organizations are similarly unconsciously circumscribed in their choice among alternatives, and not exclusively in cases where substantial external validation exists for the restraint. The learning process that matures into an established routine often contains elements of false or superstitious learning, that is, supposed requirements for successful performance that actually reflect nothing more than chance contingencies encountered in the learning process.

Another important mechanism by which such unconscious belief constraints arise and are sustained is that the organization's information system systematically provides certain kinds of information and interpretations of the world and equally systematically excludes other observations and interpretations. A particularly striking example of this phenomenon is presented in Starbuck's (1983) account of the crisis that developed at the Facit AB calculator company in Sweden.

Although some lower-level managers and engineers were acutely aware of the electronic revolution in the world at large, this awareness did not penetrate upward, and the advent of electronic calculators took Facit's top managers by surprise. Relying on the company's information-gathering programs, the top managers surmised that Facit's mechanical-calculator customers would switch to electronics very slowly because they liked mechanical calculators. Of course, Facit had no programs for gathering information from people who were buying electronic calculators.

Actual demand for mechanical calculators dropped precipitously, and Facit went through two years of loss, turmoil, and contraction (p. 92).

In the literature of management and business behavior, the sorts of considerations sketched here are often treated under the headings of "strategy" or "organizational culture." Often, a rather brief conversation with a long-time member of a particular organization suffices to acquire significant information about the nature of the belief system that constrains that organization's behavior. More systematic inquiry into such belief systems is a prominent feature of contemporary management consulting practice, and "organizational culture" is often treated as an important strategic variable that is subject to some degree of manipulation. Peters and Waterman (1982) emphasize the importance of a strong culture as a factor in the performance of the excellent companies they observed. They concede, however, that such cultural strength may bring with it some disadvantages, the first among them the possibility "that the companies might be blindsided by dramatic environmental change" (p. 77). This, of course, is exactly the phenomenon observed by Starbuck.

The possibility that information on organizational belief systems might be useful for prediction purposes is unmapped territory so far as economics is concerned. It stands as an inviting area for behavioral economics research.

In their own research, orthodox economists have no difficulty in recognizing the role of simplifying assumptions and "identifying restrictions" in making the observed world understandable. They seem to neglect, however, the fact that economic actors in general make use of analogous cognitive tools. Such neglect entails a more specific oversight, namely, the possibility that economic actors interpret their problems and environments in terms quite different from those in which a trained economist would see them. For example, it seems to be fairly commonplace that companies institute unofficial rationing systems to allocate products among their customers, when supply disruptions or sudden cost increases make it impossible to meet their customers' needs at something approaching the usual prices. Asked why the company does not simply allocate the product on the basis of willingness to pay, a businessman may reply, "That is not the way this company does business." It is the fundamental premise of behavioral economics that it is important to investigate how companies in *fact* do business. When that inquiry is much further advanced than it is at present, it will become possible to have a truly significant scientific discussion of *why* they do it that way.

Only Weak Alternatives to Prevailing Routines Are Available

The world seen by the orthodox economist is populated with economic actors and their opportunity sets; the opportunity sets in turn are populated by diverse sorts of opportunities or "alternatives"—consumption bundles, production possibilities, actions, strategies, policies. Within the opportunity sets, economic actors adjust their behavior with absolute freedom in response to changing incentives. There may, of course, be information imperfections or adjustment costs that in a larger sense produce a mismatch between the behavior actually chosen and the choices that would be made by an omnisciently rational actor unimpeded by those imperfections and costs. But strictly speaking, in the orthodox view those information imperfections and adjustment costs are not impediments to a choice among alternatives, but rather are aspects of the alternatives themselves. Nothing characteristic of the actor *as such* constitutes an impediment to perfect optimization over the opportunity set. In particular, no special status is accorded the alternative actually chosen at a particular point in time; such a choice is simply the implication, possibly evanescent, of the incentives determined by the current state of the environment.

Of all the perceptual shifts that distinguish the behavioral/evolutionary viewpoint from the orthodox one, perhaps the most fundamental is the shift that gives rise to a suspicion that these fundamental entities seen by orthodox theorists are not really there. As Quine (1963) argued, there is an intimate connection between philosophical disputes regarding what exists—the problem of ontology—and disputes regarding which scientific theory or conceptual scheme to adopt in interpreting the world. Theories, so to speak, bring their ontologies with them. As Quine illustrates, "When we say that some zoological species are cross-fertile, we are committing ourselves to recognizing as entities the several species themselves, abstract though they are" (p. 13). Where orthodox economics sees "opportunities" and "choices," evolutionary economics sees "routines" and "searches." The two ontologies suggest quite different approaches to the problem of determining the conditions under which behavioral patterns persist. Evolutionary economics accords a special status to the prevailing routine, however complex a pattern of behavior it may be. And the alternatives to prevailing routine are a variegated lot, differing greatly in availability, specificity, and concreteness.

Given an ongoing course of action by an individual or an organization, let us call an alternative course a *strong alternative* if it has much the same status that an orthodox economist would accord to a different element in the same opportunity set. A *weak alternative*, on the other hand, is more in the nature of a plan for a course of inquiry. In other words, a weak alternative is a plan for a search that may be directed, with greater or lesser precision, toward development of a strong alternative. Of course, *strong* and *weak* are here used simply to provide orientation on a continuum. There are alternatives of varying degrees of strength or weakness.

In the everyday life of an individual, strong alternatives are commonplace. There are even many situations of the sort envisaged in orthodox theory, where a range of strong alternatives are confronted simultaneously, with none having the special position of the status quo: we may choose to make dinner and eat at home, buy take-out food from the restaurant and eat at home, or go out and eat at the restaurant. On the other hand, there are aspects of individual life that are rarely, if ever, the objects of choice among strong alternatives. A significant case is one's choice of residence. The major consequences of electing to buy a particular house or rent a particular apartment are not even readily estimated without substantial costly investigation. In the absence of an event or higher-level choice that makes the current residence unavailable or unacceptable, the weakness of the alternatives to one's current residence implies a high level of inertia in the choice. Only a protracted search process can even begin to identify the possibilities with sufficient clarity such that the choice appears to be between two things roughly equally known, rather than between a known status quo and an unknown.

In large and complex organizations, significant changes in the behavior of the organization as a whole rarely take the form of a discrete choice of a strong alternative to the prevailing routine. Considerations previously discussed as contributing to the persistence of routines all play a role in making strong alternatives unavailable in the typical case. Innumerable weak alternatives may, of course, be available. Under close examination by an orthodox theoretical eye, the situation appears as a highly complex structure of sequential decision-making, involving the simultaneous pursuit of an interrelated set of information-gathering activities and actions. A fundamental requirement of this orthodox conceptualization is that there be no fundamental surprises encountered in the course of this pursuit; that is, all the possible outcomes of the process can be envisaged from the start. In addition, of course, the human actors in this orthodox description are infinitely rational in the specific sense that their information-processing capabilities are unlimited and costless. If real cost or scarcity attends such activities as identifying possible outcomes, conceptualizing the alternative choices, and doing the arithmetic (or programming the computer to do so), then no organization can reasonably be advised to attempt to analyze its problems by processes modeled on the normative principles of orthodoxy. Least of all would it be reasonable to urge such an attempt in the analysis of a particular *aspect* of the organization's activities, in disregard of the foregone alternative uses of the organization's limited cognitive capacities. Needless to say, individuals and organizations are, in fact, boundedly rational, rather than infinitely so.

Strong alternatives to prevailing routines are particularly rare at high levels in the routine hierarchy. If some of the many weak alternatives are to be explored, strengthened, and analyzed, then high-level executives will have to devote their time and energy to doing so. They have, of course, other things to do, many of which may be essential to the successful continuation of the existing routine performance. It is therefore not obvious that failure to explore weak alternatives is an example of an "*ex ante* mistake." The reason it is not an *ex ante* mistake is not to be found in orthodox theory but in the reality of bounded rationality. We have come once again to the conclusion that persistence in prevailing routine may not be "irrational," provided that word is understood in its everyday sense and not in contradistinction to the narrow rationality explored in orthodox theory.

To become operationally useful for prediction purposes, the notion of strength of an alternative must be endowed with some observable content. Perhaps the simplest approach to this complex issue is to note that routines recently employed by an organization are much more likely to constitute strong alternatives to those currently employed than are ones that have never been employed at all or were once used in the distant past. Of course, considering the ambiguity and strain affecting the use of the term *routine* at high levels in the hierarchy, this amounts to little more than the observation that routines may constitute strong alternatives to each other if the choice between them has been recently (and perhaps routinely) made.

IV. SUMMARY AND CONCLUSION

In this essay I have reviewed the orthodox critique of the research program of the behavioral theory of the firm and attempted to address its most compelling point: the problem of determining whether an observed behavioral pattern is likely to prove durable or to yield under moderate environmental pressure. Five criteria, or "tests," have been proposed for assessing the likely persistence of a particular routine under circumstances in which orthodox analysis would predict its disappearance: the existence of routine-specific assets; high levels of conflict among organization members involved with the routine; the absence of superordinate adaptation routines and competence within the organization; existence of basic belief structures that are closely linked to the routine; and the unavailability of "strong" (i.e., specific and familiar) alternatives to the prevailing routine. The more any one of these conditions obtains, the more likely it is that the routine will persist.

The obvious and important question is how these criteria might be operationalized. A few suggestions have been offered by way of tentative answers to this question, but obviously these provide only a loose sort of guidance for empirical inquiry. The best and most basic answer is, however, the same for all five criteria: they can be operationalized by behavioral research on business firms. Alternative measurement methods for the five criteria can be tried and various approaches to the problem of weighting them explored. The success of this effort can be assessed, initially, in the obvious way—by determining whether the results relate to the observed persistence of routines in the theoretically expected way. In the case of the behavioral theory of the firm, as is true for every other theory, there is an element of tautology in the operationalizing process. Good operational interpretation is the kind that makes the theory work.

Some scholars favor the rugged falsificationist definition of *theory*; according to them, the behavioral theory of the firm does not now qualify as a theory, and my own efforts may remedy that situation in only a very modest degree. In this assessment I would have to concur, although I would add that only in small subsectors of orthodox theory is the situation any different. I think it is clear, however, that the behavioral approach does constitute a research program, and one that can potentially supply the strong foundation of "organizational genetics" required for the successful development of an empirical evolutionary economics. Strong predictive theories relating to complex phenomena do not spring full-blown from the Olympian theorist's brow but are developed through protracted investment and sustained interaction between theory and empirical inquiry. As Latsis (1972, 1976) has argued, it is too early to judge the behavioral research program—the more so since, in comparison with orthodoxy, the investment in it has been negligible.[22]

Although the behavioral/evolutionary program and the orthodox program are in direct conflict with each other in significant respects, I propose that the rejuvenation of the behavioral research program is important for the pursuit of the orthodox one. The development of orthodoxy has itself undercut the old methodological dogma that economics should not inquire into what goes on inside the business firm. If such inquiry is to yield something more than mental exercise for orthodox theorists, it will need to address facts of the sort that only behavioral research can provide.

ACKNOWLEDGMENTS

I am indebted to C. Camerer, B.J. Loasby and B. Saffran for comments on an earlier draft, and to the Sloan Foundation for research support.

NOTES

1. The short form of the definition of orthodox economics is "the view of economics that dominates the textbooks of intermediate microeconomics, together with the extensions of that basic approach in advanced work." See Nelson and Winter (1982, pp. 6–9) for a discussion that attends to more of the difficulties and ambiguities.

2. I include under the "asking" rubric such activities as direct observation inside the firm and the use of internal documents, along with survey research and intensive interview studies.

3. The university was then known as the Carnegie Institute of Technology.

4. Obviously, all the difficulties of the term *orthodox* carry over to *orthodox economists*. In addition, individual economists are often orthodox on some issues and quite unorthodox on others.

5. In his retrospective discussion of the marginalist controversy, Machlup (1967) acknowledged the possible usefulness of nonorthodox models of the firm in cases of oligopoly or monopoly.

6. Once again, empirically oriented economists seem to have no difficulty adopting this view when using data the government has gathered.

7. In particular, it is difficult to frame questions that illuminate the trade-offs the respondent would be willing to make among competing objectives, and the more so if the circumstances referred to are merely hypothetical.

8. This, of course, is not the same thing as saying that the information provided by the performer is useless but only that it needs to be used in conjunction with other observational data.

9. See Salthouse (1984) for an interesting discussion of the continuing quest for an explanation that reconciles the observed skills of an expert typist with known facts of human neurophysiology.

10. See, for example, the account of technical advance in semiconductors in Levin (1982). In particular, "While the price of a digital circuit appears only (*sic*) to fall by a factor of two from 1968 to 1972, it should be noted that this period witnessed both a sixteenfold increase in the storage capacity of the best available random-access memory chips and the introduction of a revolutionary new (and initially high-priced) product, the microprocessor" (p. 34).

11. For example, yields in semiconductor production processes often vary over time and from place to place for undetermined reasons (see Robinson, 1980, p. 1019).

12. There is, however, a strong disagreement over whether the destination of the change process should be considered predetermined (by an unchanging opportunity set) or not (i.e., the result of a highly contingent and uncertain search process.)

13.   It should be emphasized that this process evidence relates to the basis of the decision, not to the separate question of whether the decision was correct, in either an *ex ante* or an *ex post* sense. In an uncertain world, *ex post* correctness is not really meaningful as a measure of the quality of the decision, whereas *ex ante* correctness is ordinarily very difficult to determine.

14.   The scenario sketched here corresponds closely to actual events in some sectors of U.S. industry (e.g., automobiles). In recent years, attention to personnel policy has been stimulated partly as a result of Japanese competition and the resulting focus on Japanese management practices.

15.   This point is akin to that made by Wachter and Williamson (1978, especially p. 555) regarding the different relational implications of price and quantity adjustments in the context of idiosyncratic exchange.

16.   The term *unitary rational actor* is Allison's (1971) title for one of his three models of organizational decision.

17.   This observation is somewhat qualified by the possibility that the advocate is a "product champion" or "zealot" who considers his interests promoted by activities others would prefer to avoid. Such individuals are an important source of change in organizations (see Downs, 1967, p. 109; Peters and Waterman, 1982, pp. 202–207).

18.   For a vivid and entertaining account of one such debacle, see Daughen and Binzen (1971) on the Penn Central bankruptcy. Nelson's study of bankruptcy (Nelson, 1981) provides a more general discussion of this process. For a related perspective on the consequences of intraorganizational conflict, see Crozier (1967), especially Chapter 5.

19.   A particularly relevant example here is Holmstrom and Ricart i Costa (1984).

20.   See Simon's (1965, Chapter 7) classic discussion of the nature of authority in organizations in his book *Administrative Behavior*.

21.   For a discussion of the peculiarities of organizational learning, see March and Olson (1975).

22.   For a summary and critique of the Latsis argument, as well as a provocative general discussion of the methodological issues relating to the theory of the firm, see Blaug (1980, Chapter 7). For a perspective on behavioral research akin to that adopted here, see Simon (1984).

REFERENCES

Allison, Graham, *Essence of Decision: Explaining the Cuban Missile Crisis.* Boston: Little, Brown, 1971.

Alchian, Armen A. and Harold Demsetz, "Production, Information Costs, and Economic Organization," *American Economic Review*, 62 (December 1972), 777–795.

Arrow, Kenneth J., "Economic Welfare and the Allocation of Resources for Invention," in Richard Nelson, ed., *The Rate and Direction of Inventive Activity*. Princeton: Princeton University Press, 1962.

Baumol, William J., and Maco Stewart, "On the Behavioral Theory of the Firm," in Robin Marris and Adrian Wood, eds., *The Corporate Economy: Growth, Competition and Innovative Potential*. Cambridge, MA: Harvard University Press, 1971, pp. 118–143.

Blaug, Mark, *The Methodology of Economics*. New York: Cambridge University Press, 1980.

Boland, Lawrence A., "A Critique of Friedman's Critics," *Journal of Economic Literature*, 17 (June 1979), 503–522.

Bruner, Jerome S., and Leo Postman, "On the Perception of Incongruity: A Paradigm," *Journal of Personality*, 18 (1949), 206–223.

Caves, Richard, "Corporate Strategy and Structure," *Journal of Economic Literature*, 18 (March 1980), 64–92.

Coase, Ronald, "The Nature of the Firm," *Economica*, 4 (1937), 386–405.

Crozier, Michel, *The Bureaucratic Phenomenon*. Chicago: Phoenix Books, 1967.

Cyert, Richard M., and James G. March, *A Behavioral Theory of the Firm*. Englewood Cliffs, NJ: Prentice Hall, 1963.

Daughen, Joseph R., and Peter Binzen, *The Wreck of the Penn Central*. Boston: Little, Brown, 1971.

Diamond, Peter A., and Eric Maskin, "An Equilibrium Analysis of Search and Breach of Contract, I: Steady States," *Bell Journal of Economics*, 10 (Spring 1979), 282–316.

Downs, Anthony, *Inside Bureaucracy*. Boston: Little, Brown, 1967.

Fama, Eugene F., and Michael C. Jensen, "Separation of Ownership and Control," *Journal of Law and Economics*, 26 (June 1983a), 301–325.

Fama, Eugene F., and Michael C. Jensen, "Agency Problems and Residual Claims," *Journal of Law and Economics*, (June 1983b), 327–349.

Friedman, Milton, "The Methodology of Positive Economics," in *Essays in Positive Economics*. Chicago: The University of Chicago Press, 1953, chapter 1.

Geanakoplos, John, and Paul Milgrom, "Information, Planning and Control in Hierarchies." Working Paper, Yale University, 1984.

Holmstrom, Bengt, "Moral Hazard in Teams," *Bell Journal of Economics*, 13 (Autumn 1982), 324–340.

Holmstrom, Bengt and Joan E. Ricart i Costa, "Managerial Incentives and Capital Management." Cowles Foundation Discussion Paper No. 729, November 1984.

Jensen, Michael and William H. Meckling, "Theory of the Firm: Managerial Behavior, Agency Costs and Ownership Structure," *Journal of Financial Economics*, 3 (1976), 305–360.

Kuhn, Thomas S., *The Structure of Scientific Revolutions*. Chicago: Phoenix Books, 1964.

Lakatos, Imre, "Falsification and the Methodology of Scientific Research Programmes," in Lakatos and Musgrave, eds., *Criticism and the Growth of Knowledge*. Cambridge: Cambridge University Press, 1970.

Latsis, Spiro J., "Situational Determinism in Economics," *The British Journal for the Philosophy of Science*, 25 (1972), 207–45.

Latsis, Spiro J., "A Research Programme in Economics," in S. J. Latsis, ed., *Method and Appraisal in Economics*. Cambridge: Cambridge University Press, 1976.

Leontief, Wassily, "Theoretical Assumptions and Nonobserved Facts," *American Economic Review*, 61 (March 1971), 1–7.

Leontief, Wassily, "Academic Economics," (letter), *Science*, 217 (July 9, 1982), 104–107.

Levin, Richard C., "The Semiconductor Industry," in Richard R. Nelson, ed., *Government and Technical Progress: A Cross-industry Analysis*. New York: Pergamon Press, 1982.

Levin, Richard C., Alvin K. Klevorick, Richard R. Nelson, and Sidney G. Winter, "Survey Research on R&D Appropriability and Technological Opportunity, Part I: Appropriability." Yale University Working Paper, July 1984.

Machlup, Fritz, "Marginal Analysis and Empirical Research," *American Economic Review*, 36 (September 1946), 519–554.

Machlup, Fritz, "Theories of the Firm: Marginalist, Behavioral, Managerial," *American Economic Review*, 57 (March 1967), 1–33.

Machlup, Fritz, "Situational Determinism in Economics," *The British Journal for the Philosophy of Science*, 25 (September 1974), 271–284.

March, James G., and J. P. Olson, "The Uncertainty of the Past: Organizational Learning Under Ambiguity," *European Journal of Political Research*, 3 (1975), 147–171.

Morgenstern, Oskar, *On the Accuracy of Economic Observations*, 2nd ed. Princeton: Princeton University Press, 1963.

Nelson, Philip B., *Corporations in Crisis: Behavioral Observations for Bankruptcy Policy*. New York: Praeger, 1981.

Nelson, Richard R., "Production Sets, Technological Knowledge and R and D: Fragile and Overworked Constructs for Analysis of Productivity Growth?" *American Economic Review*, 70 (May 1980), 62–67.

Nelson, Richard R., and Sidney G. Winter, *An Evolutionary Theory of Economic Change*. Cambridge, MA: Belknap Press of Harvard University Press, 1982.

Okun, Arthur, *Prices and Quantities: A Macroeconomic Analysis*. Washington, D.C.: Brookings Institution, 1981.

Penrose, Edith T., *The Theory of the Growth of the Firm*. New York: Wiley, 1959.

Peters, Thomas J. and Robert H. Waterman, Jr., *In Search of Excellence: Lessons from America's Best-Run Companies*. New York: Warner Books, 1982.

Pigou, A. C., "Empty Economic Boxes: A Reply," *Economic Journal*, 32 (1922), 458–465; reprinted in G. Stigler and K. Boulding, eds., *A. E. A. Readings in Price Theory*, Homewood, IL: Irwin, 1952.

Polanyi, Michael, *Personal Knowledge: Towards a Post-Critical Philosophy*. New York: Harper Torchbooks, 1964.

Porter, Michael E., *Competitive Strategy*. New York: Free Press, 1980.

Quine, Willard V. O., *From a Logical Point of View*. New York: Harper and Row, 1963.

Radner, Roy, "Monitoring Cooperative Agreements in a Repeated Principle-Agent Relationship," *Econometrica*, 49 (September 1981), 1127–1148.

Robinson, Arthur L., "New Ways to Make Microcircuits Smaller," *Science*, 208 (May 30, 1980), 1019–1022.

Salthouse, Timothy A., "The Skill of Typing," *Scientific American*, 250 (February 1984), 128–135.

Samuelson, Paul A., "Maximum Principles in Analytical Economics," *American Economic Review*, 62 (June 1972), 249–262.

Simon, Herbert A., *Administrative Behavior*, 2nd ed. New York: The Free Press, 1965.

Simon, Herbert A., "On the Behavioral and Rational Foundations of Economic Dynamics," *Journal of Economic Behavior and Organization*, 5 (March 1984), 35–55.

Starbuck, William H., "Organizations as Action Generators," *American Sociological Review*, 48 (February 1983), 91–102.

Steinbruner, John D., *The Cybernetic Theory of Decision*. Princeton: Princeton University Press, 1974.

Teece, David J., "Economics of Scope and the Scope of the Enterprise," *Journal of Economic Behavior and Organization*, 1 (September 1980), 223–247.

Teece, David J., "Towards an Economic Theory of the Multiproduct Firm," *Journal of Economic Behavior and Organization*, 3 (March 1982), 39–63.

Veblen, Thorstein, "Why is Economics Not an Evolutionary Science?" in *The Place of Science in Modern Civilization and Other Essays*. New York: Russell and Russell, 1961 (orig. pub. 1898).

Wachter, Michael L. and Oliver E. Williamson, "Obligational Markets and the Mechanics of Inflation," *Bell Journal of Economics*, 9 (Autumn 1978), 549–571.

Williamson, Oliver E., *Markets and Hierarchies: Analysis and Antitrust Implications*. New York: The Free Press, 1975.

Williamson, Oliver E., "Transaction-Cost Economics: The Governance of Contractual Relations," *The Journal of Law and Economics*, 22 (October 1979), 233–261.

Williamson, Oliver E., *The Economic Institutions of Capitalism: Firms, Markets and Relational Contracting*. New York: The Free Press, 1985.

Winter, Sidney G., "Optimization and Evolution in the Theory of the Firm," in Richard H. Day and Theodore Groves, eds., *Adaptive Economic Models*. New York: Academic Press, 1975.

Winter, Sidney G., "An Essay on the Theory of Production," in Saul H. Hymans, ed., *Economics and the World Around It*. Ann Arbor: The University of Michigan Press, 1982.

Winter, Sidney G., "Schumpeterian Competition in Alternative Technological Regimes," *Journal of Economic Behavior and Organization*, 5 (September-December, 1984), 287–320.

ENTREPRENEURIAL DECISION MAKING:

SOME BEHAVIORAL CONSIDERATIONS

Benjamin Gilad

"The subject of entrepreneurship looms as a continuing reproach to the theory of the firm and to the formal analysis of economic growth. In each of these areas, the entrepreneur is universally acknowledged to play a leading role; yet, he seems always to remain invisible in the models used to analyze them." This quote is taken from an essay by William Baumol. However, this is not an excerpt from his classic note of 1968; these lines are from his 1983 contribution to J. Ronen's book *Entrepreneurship*. To Baumol's fans (myself included), the similarity between the two reproaches to economic theory is immediately apparent. (Others are advised to go back to the 1968 article for comparison.) The striking implication is that in the last 15 years, economic theory has not made any progress in the area of entrepreneurial behavior.

Explanations abound. Baumol (1968, 1983), Kirzner (1973, 1979) and Casson (1982), to name only a few, contend that the essence of entrepreneurship is simply incompatible with the basic framework of contemporary (neoclassical) economics. On the other side of the discussion, Demsetz (in Ronen, 1983) claims that the current economic framework for analysis *does not need* to pay attention to entrepreneurship as a distinct function. The reasons given by Demsetz range from the claim that using the term *entrepreneur* does not add "new economic agent or variable to the study of competition under condition of imperfect knowledge" (Demsetz, p. 278) to the argument that pure entrepreneurship is simply luck, which is surely not the domain of science. Both Demsetz's arguments, however, remain largely unsubstantiated.[1]

The approach taken by Demsetz is probably not unique among the champions of neoclassical economics. Most attacks on economic theory regarding the neglect of the entrepreneur come from unconventional economists. The core of neoclassicists continues to accept the firm-theoretic framework as appropriate for analysis of the relevant issues, increasing evidence to the contrary notwithstanding. The recent rise in interest in research on entrepreneurship, however, might perhaps be the best sign that significant segments of the profession are at last moving away from blind adherence to the neoclassical core and are coming to grips with the subject of entrepreneurship instead of ignoring it.

The inability of neoclassical economics to account for entrepreneurship makes it a relatively easy target for criticism. The more constructive task, though, is to show the potential contribution of behavioral research on entrepreneurship to economics (if not to neoclassical theory). Such research has grown tremendously in the last 15 years, especially in the area of the psychology of the entrepreneur. The proliferation of this research should not surprise economists, since, as Casson (1982, p. 9) observed succinctly, "The subject area has been surrendered by economists to sociologists, psychologists, and political scientists. Indeed, almost all the social sciences have a theory of the entrepreneur, except economists."

This paper is divided into three sections. Section I examines the relation of neoclassical theory and entrepreneurship and the problems associated with defining entrepreneurship. Section II surveys the findings, spawned by the research carried on by behavioral scientists regarding entrepreneurial behavior and their implications to economics. Section III summarizes the argument and offers some conclusions.

I. NEOCLASSICAL ECONOMICS AND ENTREPRENEURSHIP

Why has neoclassical economics failed to recognize the figure of the entrepreneur despite its obvious prominence in the real world? Demsetz (1983, pp. 276–277) claims that the problem in analyzing entrepreneurial behavior is that "it is not easily distinguished from the economic behavior of all economic actors," and that entrepreneurship is "little more than profit maximization in a context in which knowledge is costly and imitation is not instantaneous." This is clearly in contrast to the commonsense observation of entrepreneurs as distinct from other "economic actors." Furthermore, this view underscores the explanations provided by Baumol, Kirzner, and other economists, who showed that the major cause for the neoclassical theory's failure *is* the assumption of maximization. With the growing evidence against the maximization assumption, neoclassical explanations lose much of their power.

Baumol (1968) argues that the main reason entrepreneurial activity has "generally eluded" economic theory is that by its very nature, entrepreneurship cannot be standardized. Because entrepreneurship involves exercise of imagination and departure from routine, it can be defined as those economic acts that obey no systematic principles (i.e., cannot fit the maximization and equilibrium frameworks).

Kirzner's explanation goes even further into the heart of the problem. For Kirzner, the maximization assumption precludes the exercise of entrepreneurship completely, as all that is left to the actor is the mechanical computation of the optimal allocation of *given* means to the satisfaction of *given* wants. By definition, entrepreneurship á là Kirzner is based on the act of discovering what ends are worth pursuing and what means are available for that pursuit (see Kirzner, 1979, especially Chapter 10). Seeing entrepreneurship as just "profit maximization" is clearly missing the essence of that activity.

The maximization assumption in economics is accompanied by a postulate about the amount of information possessed by the economic agent. Whether the level of information is assumed to be complete (perfect knowledge) or incomplete but always optimal (even ignorance is equated at the margin), neoclassical theorists assume an objective set of data "equally and fully perceived by all entrepreneurs" (Kirzner, 1983, p. 285).

In his book on entrepreneurship, Casson (1982) argues that the assumption of free access to all the information required for decision making reduces decision making to the "mechanical application of mathematical rules for optimization. It trivializes decision making, and makes it impossible to analyze the role of entrepreneurs in making decisions of a particular kind." Thus it is exactly the inability to separate entrepreneurial decisions from automatic maximization that prevented neoclassical economists from analyzing entrepreneurship.

Another, and related, explanation for the neoclassical neglect is its emphasis on equilibrium analysis. "Because equilibrium analysis occupies such a dominant position within received theory and because change is so often modeled as a movement from one equilibrium condition to another, the role of entrepreneurship tends to be downplayed, if not outright suppressed" (Teece and Winter, 1984, p. 119). In equilibrium, there is no scope for entrepreneurship, as all opportunities for profit are eliminated and change is delegated to exogenous shocks. The entire competitive process is excluded from analysis, and what is analyzed is only the structure of relations among the optimizing survivors of the competitive game. It is little wonder that in a scenario where competition essentially refers to a state characterized by a lack of competitive moves (in pricing, marketing, or innovations), the entrepreneur will be invisible. It is not surprising that those theorists who advanced our knowledge of entrepreneurship emphasized competition as rivalry rather than perfectly elastic demand curves, and stressed disequilibrium dynamics over static equilibrium (examples: Kirzner, 1973; Nelson and Winter, 1982, Schultz, 1975, and Rosen, 1983).

To summarize the main argument regarding the neglect of entrepreneurship in mainstream economics, it is best to refer back to Baumol's words of 1968 (p. 68): "In all these [maximizing models,] automaton maximizers the businessmen are and automaton maximizers they remain. And this shows why our body of theory, as it has developed, offers us no promise of being able to deal effectively with the description and analysis of the entrepreneurial function. For maximization and minimization have constituted the foundation of our theory; as a result of this very fact the theory is deprived of the ability to provide an analysis of entrepreneurship."

It is useful to make a distinction at this stage between the inherent inability of neoclassical economics to deal with entrepreneurship and its ability to get away with ignoring the subject for so long. The latter is probably explained by the analytical (as opposed to the practical) difficulties in defining entrepreneurship. The practical approach can be summed up in the statement, "You know it when you see it." Entrepreneurship is associated with bold, daring, imaginative, innovative, visionary business decisions, and these are easy to recognize. No one will question the labeling of Steve Jobs and Steve Wozniak, the founders of Apple Computers, entrepreneurs. But is John Doe, the owner of the corner hardware store, an entrepreneur? And was Thomas Watson, the former top executive at IBM, an entrepreneur?

The answers to these questions depend on the theoretical framework employed. Empirical researchers of entrepreneurship, such as McClelland, choose to bypass the issue by not using an explicit definition at all. Thus, McClelland's famous empirical studies on entrepreneurship and economic development (McClelland, 1961; McClelland and Winter, 1969) employed a diverse group of small businessmen, business managers, and even salespeople. On the other hand, Ronen (1983) restricted his sample to a group of owner-managers of successful firms whose companies were notable for being growth-oriented and innovative.

The different approaches of the empirical studies reflect a deeper theoretical debate. Harvard University's economic historian Arthur Cole (1959) used the narrow and descriptive definition of an entrepreneur as an individual who undertakes to "initiate, maintain, and aggrandize a profit oriented unit for the production or distribution of economic goods and services." More recently, and on the other end of the definition's continuum, Mark Casson (1982) defined the entrepreneur as "someone who specializes in taking judgmental decisions about the coordination of scarce resources." The emphasis on specialization prevents this definition from including all economic agents but greatly expands the scope of the term *entrepreneur* to include business executives, nonprofit decision-makers, and even planners in a socialistic economy.

The importance of the analytical debate goes beyond mere abstractions. The problem of identifying the entrepreneur is relevant for policy questions, welfare statements, and research into the determinants of entrepreneurial supply. It also carries implications for our concern with identifying potentially relevant findings from the behavioral research.

The definition of entrepreneurship adopted in this paper is based on the works of Kirzner (1973, 1979) and Rosen (1983). The essence of the Kirzner-Rosen approach is the association of entrepreneurial activities with disequilibrium. In equilibrium all opportunities for profit are eliminated by definition, since full coordination between the plans of all market participants prevails. A disequilibrium state, on the other hand, is characterized by the lack of perfect coordination and therefore by the possibility for improvement. Lack of perfect coordination includes, among other things, unsatisfied demand by consumers or the existence of yet untapped consumers' needs; the existence of yet unrecognized, superior means to satisfy already known ends; the possibility of producing output that can command a price higher than the cost of the inputs required to produce it; and the existence of supply in one place and demand in another where the parties are ignorant about the availability of each other. All these examples imply opportunities for profit for the person who discovers these conditions in the market and exploits them. They also imply that entrepreneurial profit is inherently derived from social profit, being the result of improvement in the state of resource coordination.

Viewing entrepreneurship as the closing of gaps associated with disequilibrium does not necessarily imply the total rejection of the Schumpeterian view of entrepreneurship as the departure from existing equilibrium. As Rosen (1983, p. 307) states: "In another sense—the sense of random stochastic process—entrepreneurship might be described as an organic equilibrium process with random elements in which available opportunities are being continually exploited . . . ." In other words, seeing the entrepreneur as the arbitrager who brings together buyers and sellers (including input sellers and output buyers), and therefore serves as an equilibrating agent, is not contrary to seeing him as the creator of new markets, that is, the mover of the economy to a higher equilibrium state, away from existing local "equilibrium."

Defining entrepreneurship as the creation of opportunities or the discovery of existing, yet overlooked, ones also draws a clear distinction between entrepreneurial and managerial decisions. Rosen distinguishes between maximizing decisions, equating marginal costs to marginal benefits in a routine (though not necessarily static) manner, and the creation of new markets, new goods, and new ways of doing things, which takes place outside the existing markets. The former are managerial decisions; the latter, entrepreneurial.

It is now clear that entrepreneurship, as defined, is not confined to commercial ventures. The small-business person who opens a new store on the corner has discovered an unsatisfied demand for a particular location, that is, a disequilibrium in distribution. The executive who stirs his company to a new market has spotted a gap in the existing supply of goods in that market. Similarly, a planner who discovers an opportunity for improvement in the existing structure of the economy is also an entrepreneur, spotting an avenue for better coordination. Though specialization in decision-making is not adopted here as the hallmark of entrepreneurship, the discovery of opportunities for better coordination is, and it enables us to include a variety of creative individuals in our hall of fame.

It is worthwhile, at this stage, to examine closely the Kirzner-Rosen definition of entrepreneurship for its implication regarding the characteristics of the entrepreneur. It is also worthwhile to clarify what this definition does not imply. First, the essence of entrepreneurship is not risk-bearing. Risk is inherent in exploiting uncertain opportunities, but it is the discovery (or creation) of these opportunities that is the crux of entrepreneurship. Therefore, one should not expect entrepreneurs to exhibit special risk-taking properties. Second, entrepreneurial activity is not to be equated with innovative or inventive activity. Entrepreneurship is "exploiting the new opportunities that inventions provide, more in the form of marketing and developing them for widespread use in the economy than developing the knowledge itself" (Rosen, p. 307). Third, the definition provides a conceptual framework for sifting through the accumulated findings regarding flesh-and-blood entrepreneurs that are found in the behavioral sciences.

The necessary and sufficient requirement to being an entrepreneur is the ability to notice opportunities for profit, overlooked or not yet imagined by the market. Kirzner terms this quality *alertness*. Alertness in the Kirznerian sense is a formal term. It renders the entrepreneurial act different from sheer luck, yet it is not a resource to be deliberately deployed, or recognized as such, by the market (Kirzner, 1979, pp. 179–

181). It is a necessary condition to becoming an entrepreneur, since underlying all entrepreneurial activities is the discovery of opportunities; it is a sufficient condition, since an opportunity for profit, by definition, is the net of all personal costs: emotional, monetary, time, and effort. Once an opportunity is discovered, one cannot "refuse the offer." In other words, if a person discovers an "opportunity" but does not take advantage of it, it wasn't an opportunity for him in the first place. A better description of the discovery is a "possibility," rather than an opportunity, for profit. Thus, if a person notices a possibility for better coordination that may yield monetary gains but the person lacks capital to pursue it, he has not discovered an opportunity for himself. On the other hand, if the discovery reflects alertness to sources of financing (and assuming *all* other costs are considerd), then the person cannot logically refuse such an opportunity for pure profit.

Though entrepreneurial alertness is not a resource that can be acquired deliberately like other aspects of human capital, it should still be possible to study its determinants and the ways its existence is encouraged or discouraged. The possibility of breathing life into the formal term is noted by Kirzner himself (p. 285): "The theorist would seek theories that explain where [entrepreneurs'] spring of activity comes from and under what circumstances they will assume Knightian uncertainty, or what makes them notice opportunities overlooked by others."

A fully developed theory that traces the determinants of alertness to opportunities is not yet available. However, a multitude of psychological studies that may shed some light on the issue already exist. Analyzing the findings from these studies can help economists understand how economic variables affect entrepreneurship. The next section is devoted to this end. The reader is warned, though, that the formal rhetoric of economics (see McCloskey, 1983) is not adopted in this section. Rather, the section freely employs speculations, intuition, and inductive/analogous reasoning. It is still hoped that the ideas will spur further research into this interface of behavioral sciences and economics.

II. ENTREPRENEURIAL TRAITS: FINDINGS FROM BEHAVIORAL RESEARCH

Given that alertness to opportunities is the essence of entrepreneurial discovery, behavioral factors may exert influence on two fronts. On the one hand, factors affecting the "cost" side of an opportunity will either increase or decrease the profit one may perceive in a given situation. For example, factors that affect the ability of the individual to handle the stress of uncertainty associated with ownership of a business will, ceteris paribus, make it easier for that individual to see an *opportunity* where others, without the appropriate "personality," may not. For the others, after taking into account the mental cost of sacrificing a secure employment, there is no profit in the particular possibility. I will term such factors affecting the cost of opportunities *motivational variables*.

On the other hand, factors related to the degree of alertness of the individual will affect the ability of the individual to notice or create opportunities. I will term these factors *cognitive variables*, in line with my treatment of alertness as a cognitive ability. And then there are those factors that may affect both components of the act of discovery simultaneously. I will term these factors *social variables*.

A. Motivational Variables

The most famous individual characteristic to be causally associated with *successful* entrepreneurial behavior is the need for achievement (*n* Ach). The construct was first introduced in 1961 by Harvard psychologist David McClelland and has gone through several testings since then (see McClelland, 1965, 1971; McClelland and Winter, 1969; Miron and McClelland, 1979; Komives, 1972; Hornaday and Aboud, 1971). McClelland (1961) defined *n* Ach as "the desire to do something better, faster, more efficiently, with less effort."

Need for achievement is attended by achievement thinking. McClelland et al. (1953) describe ten subcategories of achivement-motivation thought, of which the first category, achievement goal, is particularly relevant to the present discussion. People with high *n* Ach think about four kinds of achievement goals (the particulars of the goals will, of course, change with changing levels of aspiration):

1. Outperforming someone else.
2. Meeting or surpassing some self-imposed standard of excellence.
3. Doing something unique.
4. Career advancement.

Contrary to the popular conception of *n* Ach, it is clear from the description of *n* Ach and achievement thinking that *n* Ach is *not* a generalized desire to succeed. Rather, it is a drive to be better than others, to do something no one else has done, to beat oneself and the competition.

It is easy to see how having a high *n* Ach, ceteris paribus, lowers the cost side of an opportunity. Thus for two people with, for example, similar levels of fear of failure but varying degrees of *n* Ach, the higher-motivated person will find the possibility for a new venture more rewarding. In general, it can be claimed that the need to outperform others or one's own standards will counter the effects of some of the objective obstacles to the entrepreneurial act, increasing the probability that a possibility will be deemed an opportunity and thereby creating an apparent disposition toward entrepreneurial behavior.

According to McClelland, the antecedents of high n Ach are two: (1) training, and (2) social-cultural. Miron and McClelland (1979) summarize a decade of experience with training for achievement, concluding that n Ach can be developed deliberately in individuals. If that is indeed the case, n Ach (and entrepreneurship) should become an integral part of the theory of human capital, and it is worthwhile for economists to apply their analytical and empirical techniques to analyzing the "optimal level" of investment in the acquisition of the trait.

Though experts still disagree about the effectiveness of individual training in n Ach and subsequent entrepreneurial behavior (see Brockhaus, 1982, p. 42), few will disagree about the effect of the social and cultural environment on the development of n Ach. The seminal study by McClelland (1961) on n Ach and economic growth showed the differential effect of achievement-oriented environment on the development of n Ach in the population (and, by inference, on growth). Sociological theories of entrepreneurship (Weber, 1930; Hagen, 1962; Cochran, 1964) emphasize the role of particular ethnic and religious groups in fostering entrepreneurship by social sanctioning of creative achievements. It is therefore plausible to assume that the economic environment too may be (somehow) related to the need for achievement in society.

A case in point might be the extent of competition in the economy. Given that the essence of n Ach is the desire to outperform others—to do things better, faster, more effectively than others—competition is a necessary condition for the *expression* of that need. Individuals with high n Ach would be attracted to situations where they could prove their excellence against others. Moreover, a society built on a competitive principle, such as our capitalistic system, will clearly be a more fertile ground for the *development* of n Ach as well, compared with a soceity where obedience and conformity are encouraged (such as the socialistic system).[2]

It is also plausible to assume (and to investigate further) that different incentive systems will correlate differently with n Ach. McClelland emphasizes the role of feedback in developing high n Ach, and the desire of individuals with high n Ach to get such feedback. In a market society where individuals' efforts are quickly and unequivocally rewarded (with profit) or punished (with losses), one would expect a higher proportion of the population to possess high n Ach (further reinforced through

selective immigration). In a collective-oriented society, where emphasis
is placed on group rewards and/or service to the state and where the
relation of one's efforts to rewards is more arbitrary (e.g., is dependent
on committee decisions) one would expect a lower incidence of high n
Ach.

Other speculations follow. It is plausible, for instance, to hypothesize
that attitudes toward work and productivity, for example, the pressure
not to exceed a particular rate of production, exerted especially in un-
ionized environments, is detrimental to the expression of n Ach. Furthermore, the prevalence of this norm of mediocrity may suggest a
potential reduction in the development of high n Ach in the next generation, to which the role model turns out to be a live antithesis of the
drive to outperform others. At the least, workplaces where unions exert
strong influence and inhibit excellence will simply be unattractive to high
achievers and therefore, will be low on entrepreneurial properties.

Another implication of the relation between high n Ach and *successful*
entrepreneurship is a new perspective on Baumol's thesis of the "runner-
up" (Baumol, 1983, pp. 34–36). Baumol suggests that less successful
runner-up entrepreneurs will often push for anticompetitive regulations. If one views these acts of the runner-up as the behavioral response
of lower n Ach individuals who do not desire challenges, one can offer
some support for Baumol's claim that constraints on entrepreneurship
are not a matter of "happenstance." If entrepreneurial *success* is a function of the degree of n Ach, then less successful firms will be headed by
lower n Ach entrepreneurs. These entrepreneurs, not driven by the need
to be better, to outperform the competition, and so on, will more easily
resort to political means to limit competition. If the political system
obliges, these tactics will be used whenever competition leaves the less
alert entrepreneurs behind.

Furthermore, in an economic system where failing firms can expect
to be saved, where successful firms can expect an antitrust attack, the
value of being better than others is diminished as a societal norm. Under
such conditions, should we not anticipate a rise in lower n Ach executives
who will push for even more anticompetitive measures? Political protection of industry may well breed next generation's decision-makers
who will desire even more protection as a way to avoid challenges.

The acceptance of the above speculations depends to a large degree
on the reader's need for rigor (n Rig?). The next statement, in contrast,
will probably meet with no resistance: The neoclassical conception of
competition, epitomized by the model of perfect competition, bears very
little resemblance to the real-world competitive environment. In itself,
that is not a problem. Most economists admit the unrealistic nature of
the model but claim its usefulness as an ideal state—a benchmark against

which all other institutional arrangements should be judged. But should perfect competition really be considered the ideal state? Consider a perfectly competitive industry with instantaneous equilibrating adjustments. In such an industry, "being better" is meaningless. Unique achievements do not only go unrewarded but are also impossible, with complete information shared equally by all participants. An environment characterized by powerless agents is definitely not conducive to the development or attraction of individuals with high need for achievement. If all industries are made to approach the state of perfect competition, what will generate the move to a higher equilibrium? In other words, who will discover or create new opportunities? In the name of production and distribution efficiency, neoclassical economists ignore or sacrifice the force behind a dynamic economy.[3]

If *n* Ach is the clearest indication of the influence of intrinsic forces on entrepreneurship, displacement is the most commonly mentioned external event to influence entrepreneurship. The two influences are also termed the *push-pull hypothesis* of entrepreneurial motivation (see Brockhaus, 1980a and b; Powell and Bimmerle, 1980.) The push theory claims that people are pushed into entrepreneurship by negative situational factors, for example, loss of employment, dissatisfaction with existing careers, or, in general, factors causing a feeling of displacement (see Shapero, 1975). In a recent study, Gilad and Levine (1984) found various measures of unemployment to be positively and significantly related to entrepreneurial activity, as measured by corporate formation. Within the current classification scheme, this feeling of displacement can be seen as lowering the (opportunity) cost side for someone going into entrepreneurial venture, thereby raising the probability that an opportunity will be deemed an opportunity. It is definitely an interesting finding regarding unemployment, and the "equilibrating" power of unrestricted market environment, which is able to create new jobs despite, or more curiously, *because* of unemployment. The finding also raises new questions regarding the old issue of lifetime employment and job security. The famous proverb "Necessity is the mother of invention" seems to be especially applicable to the case at hand.

The list of other psychological variables affecting the cost side of opportunities is as long as the list of the research studies that subjected entrepreneurs to personality tests. Their relevance to economists, however, is not as apparent as that of *n* Ach and they will therefore receive only scant attention here, in the hope that behavioral economists may find them useful in future research. Table 1 summarizes the most frequently mentioned characteristics associated with entrepreneurship.

All of the personality qualities in Table 1 can be easily tied to the hypothesis that for entrepreneurs, opportunities are more abundant,

Table 1.   Entrepreneurial Characteristics

1. Self-confidence
2. Perseverance
3. Energy, diligence
4. Resourcefulness
5. Ability to take calculated risks
6. Intuition
7. Positive response to challenges
8. Independence
9. Dynamism, leadership
10. Versatility; knowledge of product, market, etc.
11. Ability to get along with people
12. Responsiveness to suggestions and criticism
13. Profit orientation
14. Optimism

Source: Adopted from J.A. Hornaday: Research about living entrepreneurs. In C.A. Kent, D.L. Sexton, and K.H. Vesper (eds): *Encyclopedia of Entrepreneurship*, Englewood Cliff, N.J.: Prentice-Hall, 1982, p. 28.

given the nature of the concept of opportunity. Each of these characteristics can be shown to reduce the subjective cost of embarking on a venture with uncertain outcomes. Still left to investigate are those factors that can directly affect the ability to discover or create the opportunity, namely, the correlates of *alertness*. One such factor is discussed next.

B. Cognitive Variables

The second most popular trait to be correlated with entrepreneurship is internal locus of control (LOC) (see Shapero, 1975; Borland, 1974; Brockhaus, 1982; and Brockhaus and Nord, 1979). Locus of control is a term given by Rotter (1966) to a generalized belief in the causal structure of the environment. It is the belief individuals have about "whether they exert control over the occurrence of rewards or outside forces exert that control" (Phares, 1976, p. 31). Internal LOC is the belief that one's own effort and skill determine outcomes in one's life, while external LOC is the belief that fate, luck, or powerful others control one's destiny. As a *generalized* belief, LOC characterizes the general approach of people to varying situations in life. However, the concept has also been used to describe the attitudes of people toward a specific situation.

Research on live entrepreneurs has shown them to have significantly more internal LOC than the general population. Moreover, in one longitudinal study (Brockhaus, 1980a), the internal belief was causally related to the degree of success of the entrepreneur in a *later* period. The interesting part of the story is the clear association between internal LOC and alertness to opportunities, an association that was established in numerous experimental studies of a variety of populations. In these studies internals were found to be more attentive to cues in the environment regarding opportunities for gain, much quicker in noticing the potential for new and profitable behaviors, superior in their ability to assimilate and use personally useful information and so forth. Wolk and Ducette (1974) characterize internals as "more active perceivers and utilizers of actual or potential information in the environemnt" than externals. Elsewhere (Gilad, 1981) this author has surveyed the findings of these studies in detail. Here it will suffice to quote a leading researcher on the topic, Herbert Lefcourt (1976), who offered the following statement about the causal link between LOC and alertness to opportunities: "If a person believes that there is nothing he can do to alter [his situation] ... then he will *not be aware nor ready* to take advantage of cues offered [by the environment] regarding possible avenues open for [rewards]" (p. 377; emphasis added).

If internal LOC gives rise to a mental state of readiness to grasp at opportunities, and external LOC reduces such alertness, the antecedents of LOC acquire special significance. Specifically, if LOC can be influenced by economic variables, entrepreneurship may be endogenous to the economic model. Again, space is too limited to expand on the experimental findings regarding the antecedents of LOC, and the interested reader is referred to Gilad (1984). The bulk of these studies confirms the intuitive prediction that the objective locus of control, that is, the true distribution of power over outcomes in the environment, is directly related to the development of the subjective belief regarding control. Most of these findings relate to developmental periods in the life of an individual, that is, they are taken from familial and educational environments, and one should therefore be cautious in generalizing from them. In addition, it is not known how much lack of power is required to instill an external belief in the individual. Despite these difficulties, it is still reasonable to suggest that social-economic megastructures such as a free market or a planned society will have an opposing effect on the LOC beliefs of their respective citizenries. Freedom to choose means and ends is a necessary requirement for the development of internality (see Gilad, 1981). All else being equal, an arbitrary interference in the decisions of the person is detrimental to the feeling of control. A society based on centralized control is therefore inherently more prone to breed a populace with a belief in external LOC.[4]

Moreover, any change in the distribution of power in the environment, from the decision-maker to outside powers, may, in theory, result in cognitive behavior associated with a reduction in internality. An interesting research question is therefore the effect of imposing public regulatory measures on the perception of control of the regulatees. The social cost resulting from "externalizing" entrepreneurs and business executives in a given industry or, alternately, making an industry unattractive to internal individuals is a neglected factor in the social cost-benefit analysis that is traditionally being used in defense of regulations. That does not mean that all regulations are evil. Rather, using regulatory procedures without considering the psychological effects of shifts in control, that is, regulating processes rather than outcomes; allowing for arbitrariness and unpredictability in enforcement, and so on, may hinder rather than improve social welfare.

C. Social Variables

In a series of pioneering articles, Dean K. Simonton applied time-series techniques to analyzing the antecedents of creativity (see individual references in the text). In his transhistorical causal analysis, Simonton paid particular attention to sociopolitical variables and their effect on the emergence of creative people.

While creativity is not identical with entrepreneurship, most major researchers of the latter agree that it involves the former (see Ronen, 1983; Gilad, 1982). Simonton's findings should therefore be of interest to economists who are looking for ways to encourage entrepreneurship (or analyzing proposed policies for their effect on entrepreneurship).

Simonton distinguishes between two phases of a creative person's life. The first, the developmental phase, is the time (usually childhood to early adulthood) during which the creative potential is developed. The second, the productive period, is the time when the person's creative output is actually produced. The segregation of possible social-political influences in accordance with the above distinction allows for a better understanding of the history of creativity.

Simonton found that developmental-period influences are more important than external events operating during the productive period. Essentially, creative productivity was found to be almost immune to outside influences once development was completed. For example, adulthood creativity is immune to personal problems, social reinforcements (e.g., social incentives), civil disturbances, or even cultural persecution. Only war was found to have a negative effect on productive-period creativity, and even then the effect was significant only for balance-of-power wars fought close to the creative individual.[5]

Social, cultural, and political variables did prove influential on creativity when their effects were measured during the incubation period in the life of the creative individual. The following two variables are probably the most relevant to economists.

1. Role-Model Availability. Studies using time-series analysis with lagged variables show that the number of eminent creators in one generation is a positive function of the number of eminent creators in the previous generation. Using a span of 127 generations (each of twenty years' duration), Simonton (1975, 1977) hypothesized that the greater the number of creators available for imitation, the more active is the creative preconciousness in the developmental stage. The result is a positive and significant affect of role model availibility, though b < 1. Additional findings regarding role models reveal that the effectiveness of role models depends on the discipline, that is, creative individuals are mostly influenced by creators in their own field. Furthermore, cross-disciplinary creativity may have adverse effects, such as the "negative role models" provided by religious leaders in one generation for creativity in philosophy in the next generation.

The role of the role models in entrepreneurship is suggested by several studies (see Baumol, 1983; Brockhaus, 1982). Therefore, the findings regarding the developmental-period influences carry a clear implication for public policies and institutional arrangements: If a regime suppresses or reduces the extent of entrepreneurial activity in a given time period, there is no guarantee that the activity can be revived automatically in the next period. In other words, entrepreneurial talent is not "available on demand," and restrictive policies and regulations might cause damage beyond their contemporary impact, by inhibiting the growth of future entrepreneurial talent. Similarily, negative cultural and/or social attitudes toward entrepreneurship may generate a backlash extending well beyond their actual peak. This inference may explain the decline in competitiveness, or "Yankee ingenuity," of the U.S. economy (especially in the 1970s), given the rise to prominence during the 1960s of the idea of the Great Society with its correlates of antibusiness social and political attitudes, and the shift of emphasis from creating wealth to redistributing it. By implication, Strumpel's findings regarding the rise of the postindustrial attitude in Germany may signal a future decline of the West German economy, all else being equal (e.g., barring a sudden influx of immigrants, especially from more entrepreneurial cultures).[6]

A closely related argument regarding the development of future entrepreneurs is based on Simonton's findings about the possible adverse affect of creativity in one discipline on the development of another. To repeat the argument, one can wonder if this century's creativity in social thought did not have an adverse effect on the availability of entrepreneurial creativity, since the shift of social fame to welfare principles and civil rights may have prohibited the development of profit-seeking industrial giants, who under the new social thinking and teaching were seen, at best, as a necessary evil.

2. Political Fragmentation and Civil Disturbances. In two studies, Naroll et al. (1971) and Simonton (1975) found political fragmentation to have a positive and significant effect on the development of creativity. Political fragmentation was defined as the number of independent states in a given civilization, and as the number of sovereign political units increases, the number of eminent creators tends to increase after a lag of approximately 20 years. In addition, the variable of civil disorder (popular revolts, rebellions, and revolutions) was found to be positively related to creative development. Simonton (1978) postulates that the rationale for these effects is that both variables are proxies for cultural diversity, and that the latter encourages the capacity for "divergent thinking...breadth of perceptive and related cognitive attributes required for a fully developed creative potential." Taking this rationale further, the argument can be extended to the issue of immigration as well. Since immigration also raises the cultural diversity to which the local population is exposed, a rise in creativity can be expected. Some indirect evidence to that effect is the finding of a positive effect of migration on contemporary mean IQ (and, by implication, on creativity) in a given population (Lynn, 1979), though this is usually explained by the selective nature of migration (Douglas, 1964; Maxwell, 1969). The implication for public policy is that any cost-benefit analysis of the economic consequences of immigration policy should reckon in the suggested effect of immigration on future economic development, via its effect on the development of creativity and, therefore, of entrepreneurial talent. Being hard to quantify, this effect might be easily ignored, especially at times of economic hardship.

III. SUMMARY AND CONCLUSIONS

This chapter surveyed some of the behavioral research findings regarding entrepreneurs and speculated about their relevance and applicability to economic theory and policy. Not surprisingly, the common flavor of these findings is the "compatibility" of entrepreneurship and freedom in its various forms: economic, personal, and political. Despite the abuse of the concept of freedom, it is still intuitively understood to represent the lack of impediments to the individual's choices: choices of goals and choices of means to pursue them, within the general framework provided by the law. This freedom is a necessary, if not sufficient, condition for the *expression* of a need to achieve, internal locus of control, and other correlates of entrepreneurial behavior. More important, perhaps, is the fact that it also seems to be a necessary condition for the *development* of these traits.

Though the emphasis on freedom as a prerequisite for entrepreneurship is hardly new, the suggestion that future entrepreneurship depends on present role models and social norms renders that emphasis especially urgent. If the development of entrepreneurial talents is discouraged by reckless policies, the incidence of the cost of these policies (e.g., in employment, to which small businesses contribute heavily) will be borne by future generations. Promises of encouraging the "private sector" are meaningless if not accompanied by a whole *zeitgeist* of a free market. If the social/political thrust of a nation moves away from entrepreneurial achievements, reliance on free enterprise, and sanctioning of "economic heroes" to other concerns, one should not be surprised to see a decline in entrepreneurial spirit and behavior later on.

ACKNOWLEDGMENTS

I am very grateful to Lauren Shapiro for her tireless efforts to bring my version of the English language to conform to the standard rules. Any remaining errors, however, are solely mine.

NOTES

1. Compare, for example, Demsetz's satisfaction with the adequacy of the existing neoclassical models, with Teece and Winter's (1984) conclusion: "Neoclassical economic theory has not brought us very far along the road towards detailed explanation, let alone prediction.... It is rare in positive science to find so elaborate a theoretical structure erected on so narrow and shallow a factual foundation" (p. 119). Similarly, a rigorous reply to Demsetz's equation of entrepreneurship and luck can be found in Kirzner (1979, Chapter 10).

2. This should not be interpreted to imply the complete lack of *n* Ach or the denial of the existence of entrepreneurship under a socialistic system. The latter is especially clear in behaviors aimed at beating the system. However, with the premium placed on conformity and obedience, the socialistic system is no match for the capitalistic one in encouraging the development of *n* Ach.

3. G. H. Hardy (1969), one of the greatest mathematicians of all times, observed: "Ambition has been the driving force behind nearly all the best work of the world... .Practically all substantial contributions to human happiness have been made by ambitious men." It is interesting that of all disciplines, economics is the one that has discarded ambition.

4. The very high incidence of alcoholism and drinking in general in the USSR may be one indication of a more external populace, since heavy drinking is associated with the feeling of helplessness, or of feeling like a "pawn."

5. It is probably here that creative production may differ from entrepreneurial production. If creativity is hard to contain once it is developed, entrepreneurship is more easily curbed with external constraints such as changes in the incentive and political system.

However, both entrepreneurship and creativity *potential* share, to a large extent, the same developmental influences.

6. I am greatly indebted to Stanley Kaish for the following insight regarding the limits on the validity of this argument about the intergenerational effect of social/political attitudes. One should be aware that this argument is probably valid only within some specific limits. Thus the current generation of yuppies is definitely more entrepreneurial and materialistic than their parents, the hippies. The hippies, in turn, were the children of bourgeois. This pattern suggests a cyclical trend rather than the linear relation espoused in this paper following Simonton's findings. The two seemingly competing hypotheses can be reconciled by assuming that changes in the social/political attitudes toward entrepreneurship follow a normal distribution. As long as these attitudes are close to the mean, one generation's mores will be reinforced in the next generation, thus pushing the *zeitgeist* toward the tail. Once the social norms are pushed to their extremes, however, a counterreaction will take place, shifting the attitudes back toward the center of the distribution. This cyclical nature of the social/political climate regarding entrepreneurial behavior then sets the limits within which our hypothesis of linearity is valid.

REFERENCES

Baumol, W. J., "Entrepreneurship in Economic Theory," *American Economic Review*, 58, no. 2 (May 1968).

Baumol, W. J., "Toward Operational Models of Entrepreneurship," in J. Ronen, ed., *Entrepreneurship*. Lexington, MA: Lexington Books, 1983.

Borland, C., "Locus of Control, Need for Achievement, and Entrepreneurship." Doctoral Dissertation, University of Texas, 1974.

Brockhaus, R. H., "Psychological and Environmental Factors which Distinguish the Successful from the Unsuccessful Entrepreneur: A Longitudinal Study," *Academy of Management Proceedings*, (1980a).

Brockhaus, R. H., "The Effect of Job Satisfaction on the Decision to Start a Business," *Journal of Small Business Management*, (1980b).

Brockhaus, R. H., "The Psychology of the Entrepreneur," in C. A. Kent, D. L. Sexton, and K. H. Vesper, eds., *Encyclopedia of Entrepreneurship*. Englewood Cliffs, NJ: Prentice Hall, 1982.

Brockhaus, R. H., and W. J. Nord, "An Exploration of Factors Affecting the Entrepreneurial Decision: Personal Characteristics vs. Environmental Calculations," *Academy of Management Proceedings*, (1979).

Casson, M., *The Entrepreneur: An Economic Theory*. Totowa, NJ: Barnes & Noble, 1982.

Cochran, T. C., "The Entrepreneur in Economic Change," *Behavioral Science*, 9, no. 2 (April 1964).

Cole, A. H., *Business Enterprise in its Social Setting*. Cambridge, MA: Harvard University Press, 1959.

Demsetz, H., "The Neglect of the Entrepreneur," in J. Ronen, ed., *Entrepreneurship*. Lexington, MA: Lexington Books, 1983.

Douglas, J. W. B., *The Home and the School*. London: MacGibbon & Kee, 1964.

Gilad, B., "An Interdisciplinary Approach to Entrepreneurship: Locus of Control and Alertness," Doctoral dissertation, New York University, 1981.

Gilad, B., "On Encouraging Entrepreneurship—An Interdisciplinary Analysis," *Journal of Behavioral Economics*, 11, no. 1 (Summer 1982), 132–163.

Gilad, B., "The Case for a 'Partnership Approach' to Public Regulation," *Journal of Economic Psychology*, 5 (1984), 265–280.

Gilad, B., and P. Levine, "A Behavioral Model of Entrepreneurial Supply and its Impact on Corporate Formation." Working Paper no. 220–3, Rutgers University, Newark, 1984.

Hagen, E. E., *On the Theory of Social Change: How Economic Growth Begins.* Homewood, IL: Dorsey Press, 1962.

Hardy, G. H., *A Mathematical Apology.* Cambridge: Cambridge University Press.

Hornaday, J. A., and J. Aboud, "Characteristics of Successful Entrepreneurs," *Personnel Psychology*, 24 (Summer 1971).

Kirzner, I. M., *Competition and Entrepreneurship.* Chicago: University of Chicago Press, 1973.

Kirzner, I. M., *Perception, Opportunity and Profit.* Chicago: University of Chicago Press, 1979.

Kirzner, I. M., "Entrepreneurs and the Entrepreneurial Function: A Commentary," in J. Ronen, ed., *Entrepreneurship.* Lexington, MA: Lexington Books, 1983.

Komives, J. L., "A Preliminary Study of the Personal Values of High Technology Entrepreneurs," in A. C. Cooper and J. L. Komives, eds., *Technical Entrepreneurship: A Symposium (Proceedings).* Milwaukee: Center for Venture Management, 1972.

Lefcourt, H. M., *Locus of Control: Current Trends in Theory and Research.* New York: Wiley, 1976.

Lynn, R., "The Social Ecology of Intelligence and Achievement," *British Journal of Social and Clinical Psychology*, 18 (1979), pp. 1–12.

Maxwell, J., *The Level and Trend of National Intelligence.* London: London University Press, 1969.

McClelland, D. C., *The Achieving Society.* Princeton: Van Nostrand, 1961.

McClelland, D. C., "Need Achievement and Entrepreneurship: A Longitudinal Study," *Journal of Personality and Social Psychology*, 1 (1965).

McClelland, D. C., "Entrepreneurship and Achievement Motivation," in P. Lengyel, ed., *Approaches to the Science of Socio-Economic Development.* Paris: UNESCO, 1971.

McClelland, D. C., J. W. Atkinson, R. A. Clark, and E. L. Lowell, *The Achievement Motive.* New York: Appleton-Century-Crofts, 1953.

McClelland, D. C., and D. G. Winter, *Motivating Economic Achievement.* New York: Free Press, 1969.

McCloskey, D. N., "The Rhetoric of Economics," *Journal of Economic Literature*, 21, no. 2 (June 1983).

Miron, D., and D. C. McClelland, "The Impact of Achievement Motivation Training on Small Businesses," *California Management Review*, 21, no. 4 (Summer 1979).

Naroll, R., E. C. Benjamin, F. K. Fohl, M. J. Fried, R. E. Hildreth, and J. M. Schaffer, "Creativity: A Cross-historical Pilot Survey," *Journal of Cross Cultural Psychology*, 2 (1971), 181–188.

Nelson, R. and S. G. Winter, *An Evolutionary Theory of Economic Change.* Cambridge, MA: Harvard University Press, 1982.

Phares, E. J., *Locus of Control in Personality.* N. J.: General Learning Press, 1976.

Powell, J. D., and C. F. Bimmerle, "A Model of Entrepreneurship: Moving toward Precision and Complexity," *Journal of Small Business Management*, 18, no. 1 (January 1980), 33–36.

Ronen, J., *Entrepreneurship.* Lexington, MA: Lexington Books, 1983.

Rosen, S., "Economics and Entrepreneurs," in J. Ronen, ed., *Entrepreneurship.* Lexington, MA: Lexington Books, 1983.

Rotter, J. B., "Generalized Expectancies for Internal versus External Control of Reinforcement," *Psychological Monographs*, 80, whole no. 609 (1966).

Schultz, T. W., "The Value of the Ability to Deal with Disequilibria," *Journal of Economic Literature*, (September 1975).

Shapero, A., "The Displaced, Uncomfortable Entrepreneur," *Psychology Today* (November 1975).

Simonton, D. K., "Sociocultural Context of Individual Creativity: A Transhistorical Time-series Analysis," *Journal of Personality and Social Psychology*, 32 (1975), 1119–1133.
Simonton, D. K., "Eminence, Creativity, and Geographic Marginality: A Recursive Structural Equation Model," *Journal of Personality and Social Psychology*, 35 (1977), 805–816.
Simonton, D. K., "History and the Eminent Person," *Gifted Child Quarterly*, 22 (1978), 187–195.
Weber, M., *The Protestant Ethic and the Spirit of Capitalism*. New York: Scribner's, 1930.
Teece, D. J., and S. G. Winter, "The Limits of Neoclassical Theory in Management Education," *American Economic Review Papers and Proceedings*, (May 1984).
Wolk, S. and T. Ducette, "Intentional Performance and Incidental Learning as a Function of Personality and Task Dimensions," *Journal of Personality and Social Psychology*, 29 (1974), 90–101.

Section B

Intra-Firm Considerations in Productivity

INTRODUCTION TO SECTION B:
INTRA-FIRM CONSIDERATIONS IN PRODUCTIVITY

The labor-supply curve found in economic models relates hours of labor offered to wage rates. Production functions then convert these hours worked into output. However, an hour is not an hour is not an hour. Both Leibenstein and Tomer amply demonstrate that in this section. In Leibenstein's thinking, X-inefficiency alters the output gained from hours worked. So the average cost curve is not a line but an area. The cost of producing any given output involves more than the mix of labor and capital. It also involves the conditions under which the labor is working, or more accurately, under which it sees itself as working.

In his oft-quoted 1979 review article published in the *Journal of Economic Literature*, Leibenstein suggested in passing that "many organizations allow for conflict resolution through a hierarchical system . . . but despite a hierarchical power structure informal degrees of influence may play a significant role."[1] In the paper published in this collection, Leibenstein has come back to the point that workers in a firm often do not share common goals with either their co-workers or their managers. Management attempts to assure effort toward its purposes through hierarchical sanctions. At the same time, peer pressures of various sorts occur within the worker group. Leibenstein analyzes these through employment of reaction models.

The paper goes to the heart of behavioral economics. The subject matter is in the traditional economic area of productivity. Yet it is clear that group interaction, customarily thought of as a topic in social psychology, has an important role to play. Leibenstein considers that role through the economist's traditional tool of modeling. The result is a paper that is accessible to readers of both disciplines and that casts new light on the basic economic issue of costs and productivity.

Tomer's paper also conveys the message that firms do not all produce at the frontier of their production possibilities because the people who work in them do not. Capital and labor do not automatically combine into an effective production effort. The possibilities of organizational conditions creating personal inefficiencies exist. Where elsewhere in this volume Frantz deals with market conditions effecting efficiency, and Grossbard-Shechtman deals with family conditions, Tomer focuses on organizational conditions and productivity. He points out that the firm derives a return from its investment in organizational capital that is just as real as the return from its investments in human and physical capital.

Economists generally ignore the organizational-capital element. To remedy this situation, Tomer introduces a taxonomy of investment in individuals, organizations, and combinations of the two. He cites three stages of organizational development found in the organizational behavior literature: the entrepreneurial, the mechanistic, and the dynamic organization. As a firm evolves through these stages, its productivity can be described by a curve, with the least productive effort coming from the mechanistic organization and the most productive from the dynamic. Unfortunately, it sounds as if most firms are locked in the mechanistic stage, characterized by routine and hierarchy and lacking the ability to generate the ethic of self-actualization that Tomer feels is so important to an organization. With such great benefits available but left untaken, we may well wonder if management perceives the costs of organizational capital to be higher than they actually are.

NOTE

1. H. Leibenstein, "A branch of economics is missing: micro-micro theory," *Journal of Economic Literature*, 17, no. 2 (June 1979).

INTRA-FIRM EFFORT DECISIONS AND SANCTIONS:
HIERARCHY VERSUS PEERS

Harvey Leibenstein

The focus of this paper is primarily on two related questions: 1) Given that hierarchies can invoke a large variety of sanctions on firm members, why are hierarchies frequently unable to elicit optimal effort levels? and 2) What are the role and nature of the system of formal and informal sanctions imposed by *both* hierarchies *and* peers in determining effort? All firm members are involved in effort decisions. Also, effort is not *uniquely* related to the wage-employment exchange. One way of viewing the matter is to view effort decisions in firms as intracontract decisions. Hence, discretionary elements must be important here.

In a recent book, Alfred Chandler (1980, p. 1) pointed out that large firms in the United States and Europe have at least a six-level hierarchy. It is not our aim to analyze hierarchy in a general sense (see Williamson, 1967, 1975; Chandler, 1977). Rather, we shall only look at some aspects of hierarchy[1] as they relate to possibly nonoptimal effort decisions[2] and be especially concerned with the system of latent sanctions that surrounds individual-effort decision-making. Probably most decision-makers are only vaguely aware of the sanctions involved, since they make their decisions in such a way so that they rarely bump into the sanctions that could be applied.

Although employment contracts are incomplete or fuzzy, they usually permit the firm to apply many types of sanctions. Individuals may be fired, laid off, refused pay increases, refused promotions, and not given sufficient status. Also, salaries may be reduced under some circumstances, demotions are possible, and generally, various privileges can be withheld. Despite its latent power, somehow the hierarchy frequently does not succeed in eliciting as much effort, or quality of effort, as one might expect. We explore in this paper why this should be the case.

I. A BRIEF REVIEW OF BASIC IDEAS

What follows is a list of ideas connected with X-efficiency theory that have been developed elsewhere (Leibenstein, 1976, 1982). They are presented here only to indicate the background that, to some degree, the discussion in the main body of this paper presumes. (Readers familiar with these ideas should skip to the next section.)

We start with a relation between pressure and the degree of effectiveness of decisions. This follows a well-established psychological concept, the Yerkes-Dodson law (Broadbent, 1971), which argues that there exists a performance/pressure relation that is bell shaped. In our use of this law, at low pressure levels, decision procedures are nonoptimal; at intermediate pressure levels, they approximate optimality; but at relatively high pressure levels, they once again are nonoptimal. We will focus on the first category.

Following Herbert Simon's (1978) distinction between procedural and substantive decision theories, we assume that all decisions involve procedures. Many of these procedures are, at times, nonoptimal. We have in mind procedures such as habits, conventions, rules of thumb, quick responses to commands, nonresponses, responses according to a rule book, emulation, and spur-of-the-moment decisions.[3] We assume that, *on the average*, at low pressure levels, such procedures are nonoptimal.

Given the nature of the employment contract, we assume that individuals are allowed some discretion and that, furthermore, they "take" a certain amount of discretion. Thus the effort decision is made within certain discretionary bounds.

Procedures are subject to inertia. Thus a procedure is not altered unless certain independent variables go beyond certain inert area bounds surrounding the procedure. A wide variety of procedures persist despite some change in the environment.

We recognize that there are latent adversarial interests surrounding the management-labor situation. Employees have an incentive to minimize effort directed at firm interests within the discretionary boundaries. The firm has an incentive to obtain maximum effort but minimize the cost of wages and working conditions. This results in a latent Prisoner's Dilemma. There are free-riding incentives with respect to effort on the part of representative employees, and the firm has an incentive to offer as little as possible in terms of wages and working conditions, given any effort level. The Prisoner's Dilemma aspect is intensified by the strength of adversarial feelings between the two sides.

But such latent Prisoner's Dilemma problems are solved by *effort conventions*[4] or other consensual procedures,[5] so that both sides accept the effort-level convention and some related wage and working-condition convention[6] as parameters of the system. However, both the hierarchy and peers will formally and informally attempt to apply sanctions with respect to effort choices and hence set bounds within which effort choice and wage conventions persist. It is this last aspect that we consider in some detail below.

In almost all cases it is impossible to define the effort aspect of the contract explicitly. Hence there will be discretion given. In many cases some discretion will be taken by employees, even if there was no intent to give the particular bit of discretion involved. Some discretion is bound to exist because of knowledge differences. There is little point in a superior trying to learn all aspects of a subordinate's job. The subordinate may have special detailed information in order to tailor the job in a much better way than the superior could possibly fashion. This last is especially true where a high level of professional knowledge is involved. In any event, discretion is a significant element in what follows. The basic question is to what extent the firm can channel the use of discretion or of effort space through the employment of sanctions.

II. THE VOLUNTARILY MOTIVATED EFFORT HYPOTHESIS

We visualize the hierarchy as a pyramidal chain. Those higher up have more power and responsibility and provide more abstract information to those below. The most detailed information is at the lowest level, where employees work directly on the product or service. As we go up the chain, information becomes more abstract, or more summary. A basic asymmetry is that those higher up have greater power to obtain detailed information from those below, while those below have less power to obtain abstract information from those above. Thus, in principle, someone at the top has access to all the detailed information available at the bottom. However, while such an individual may have the power to obtain detailed information on which he explicitly focuses, he does not have the capacity to obtain all the detailed information.

It may be useful to consider the following basic proposition: An individual can perform *voluntarily* at a noticeably higher level than what the individual would do under well-monitored conditions *and sanctions*. The main idea is to draw the distinction between an agreement to do something simply because it is agreed to, under fairly well-monitored conditions, plus sanctions for failure, versus a voluntarily motivated effort level. In other words, there are effort levels beyond the monitored stage that are significant and *could* be achieved, but such levels could not be achieved simply on a monitoring-sanction basis. Notice the word *could*, not *would*. Factors such as morale and team spirit fit this general line of reasoning. While general experience supports this proposition, it is frequently not recognized. The basic phenomena are especially likely to be important where quality aspects of effort are concerned. Not only are there limits to the type of monitoring that could be carried out, including such considerations as the cost of detailed monitoring, but also monitoring may reduce enthusiasm for effort.

Of course, this hypothesis is hardly new. In one form or another it has probably been rediscovered frequently. For instance, in 1858, Henry Varnum Poor wrote about "the grave difficulties of adapting human capabilities and current business practices and institutions to the severe requirements demanded by the efficient operation of such large administrative units." He further worried about the problems resulting from "regarding man as a mere machine, out of which all the qualities necessary to be a good servant can be enforced by mere payment of wages. But duties cannot always be prescribed and the most valuable are often voluntary ones" (see Hayes, 1979). It is important to keep in mind that this hypothesis is not consistent with the idea of a production function or with the idea of the firm as primarily a monitoring entity vis-à-vis production (Alchian and Demsetz, 1972).

To start with, there is likely to be a dilution of purpose, especially in its intensity, as we travel down the hierarchy toward those who carry out basic activities.[7] Thus, once we get to the basic activities level, the message from the top is extremely diluted. In part, this is because those at the top are not aware of the exact direction of their efforts, and at each level firm members have considerable discretion in carrying out their activities. This results in two consequences: (1) skewing of direction from the original purposes, and (2) the possible increase in discretionary powers toward subordinates and away from principals. Of course, the real principals (stockholders) are usually not in a position to state their interests.

There are obviously some monitored levels sufficiently low so that voluntary effort levels would be higher. The obviousness of this proposition is simply that whatever the monitored level is, there is a voluntary response that is at least equal to it. The interesting question is: is there a voluntary level that cannot be equaled by a monitored level?

Consider the highest possible monitored level. We want to show that the overall situation is superior if the same level is achieved on a voluntary basis, namely, that the situation is better and cheaper if it is *not* monitored, or if it is monitored in a somewhat looser fashion than otherwise. To start with, there is the cost of monitoring. Clearly, the overall output level is higher if the cost of monitoring is lower, that is, manpower used for monitoring could be used for other productive purposes. In addition, there is the utility of work to those performing on a voluntary basis. In other words, we assume that there is some negative utility associated with being monitored, and hence there is a positive utility if one achieves what there is to be achieved on a voluntary basis.

Most important, certain characteristics of effort cannot be achieved on a monitoring basis. For instance, it is usually impossible to monitor some aspects of quality, especially whether firm members care about their work so that high-quality output results. The extent of caring about one's effort has value even if the *result* of the work can itself be monitored. In other words, there are reject costs, or "doing-over" costs because of sloppy work, even if the end result of the particular quality is monitorable! In addition, in the course of many jobs (perhaps all), the individual meets unexpected circumstances. While monitoring can usually handle repeatable situations, it often cannot handle special problems.

An element that usually cannot be monitored is information known only at lower levels. This could arise in a variety of circumstances. The basic employee is likely to gain certain information about the details of the production process that may be of value to the hierarchy. He or she will invariably have the discretion to communicate this information or not. The hierarchy has no way of monitoring whether information it does not know about has been communicated. For instance, this may arise in circumstances where there is learning by doing. As a consequence of experience, information that is usable by others may be gathered but not communicated. This may involve knowledge about the possibilities of superior effort or improvements in quality. Such information is not only a determinant of effort of the particular employee involved, but it may also have value in improving the effort levels of all similarly placed employees.

Probably most important is the emotional reaction to monitoring. Inevitably, beyond some point, monitoring sends a message. It usually indicates that the employee is not completely trusted. Lack of trust operates in a wide variety of ways. The way it is most likely to operate is a sense by the individual that exemplary effort, or even effort beyond a minimum, will not be rewarded. The group within which an individual sees himself as a peer-group member may be quite large relative to those, say in the personnel department, who are in a position to arrange rewards. In addition, subordinates may believe that additional effort, once shown, will be expected (by superiors) to persist. Hence the flexibility that an individual may believe he has at low effort levels will seem to disappear or be compromised if a fairly high effort level is revealed as a possibility. All these elements are, of course, augmented by group feelings. If the group as such shows a lack of trust by not believing that greater efforts will be rewarded, this group belief is likely to precipitate resistance to attempts by the higher-ups in the hierarchy to induce, in one way or another, greater effort levels by those lower down.

Many arrangements that initially assume mutual trust are likely to be delicate. Suppose that somehow an arrangement is offered under which employees promise to do their best while managers promise to arrange for the highest payment possible, given the employee's effort. Consider two cases. In the first, the manager has all the power to make such arrangements; in the second, he must check with superiors. The main difficulty is that there is no way of assessing the quid pro quo in this particular situation. If the employee increases his effort in stages, the manager must increase remuneration in such a way so that the employee feels it is a fair and proper increase. In a sense, the manager must give what the employee feels is appropriate. If the manager pays more than he feels is appropriate, he will expect still greater effort from the employee in order to make up for it. Clearly, any misstep in such a sequence is likely to sever the bond of trust that was the basis of the original arrangement.

The existence of a hierarchy creates additional difficulties under such an arrangement. The middle-level managers with whom the basic employees deal are themselves not their own masters. They must check out what they can do with those above them. A fairly pervasive bureaucratic bias for accountability is likely to interfere with any kind of sensible arrangement. As a consequence, the middle-level manager is really hampered in any attempt to deliver on a quid pro quo arrangement. Once the inability to deliver becomes clear to basic employees, the incentive, initially based on trust, disappears, since it is impossible for the employees to judge how relatively unknown and faceless members of the bureaucracy will react.

At the same time, we must keep in the back of our minds that there are some basic underlying incentives for both management and non-managerial employees not to stick to any implicit bargain. For each effort level that representative employees choose, there is an incentive for management to attempt to pay the lowest wages and fringe benefits possible. Similarly, for each set of wages, there is an incentive for employees to put forth the minimum effort level. This is the basic underlying, *latent* Prisoner's Dilemma problem. Effort conventions and wage conventions serve as solutions that frequently hide the Prisoner's Dilemma aspect from view. Nevertheless, the underlying incentives are there even if they are not used when the force of convention and related sanctions are strong enough (see Leibenstein, 1982, for an expanded treatment of these ideas.)

A difficulty frequently inherent in hierarchies is the lack of participatory enthusiasm on the part of those in specific posts in which they are presumed to carry out the firm's objectives. One can think of loyalty and motivation to serve a specific individual, but it is quite different if the person being served happens to be in a particular *post*, in which the individual occupying it may change but the post does not. The nature of hierarchical attachments, whether they are specific or abstract, can determine the degree of an individual's enthusiasm for his tasks. This, in part, involves enthusiasm to discover what his tasks are, or ought to be, in terms of the interests of the principal.

III.   HIERARCHICAL SANCTIONS

We now turn to the examination of the power of the hierarchy over employees and whether the sanctions used are of a type that is likely to elicit high levels of effort. To start with, we consider the situation of a representative basic employee who works on some aspect of the product. We will then change our position and consider the situation faced by members at various levels of the hierarchy (See Simon, 1957, pp. 131–133).

We start with the isolated employee. From his viewpoint the hierarchy will appear to be extremely strong, given the availability of possible sanctions against him, but he will appear relatively weak if, and only if, he considers his position in isolation from others in the enterprise. Thus the possibility of being fired, not having one's salary increased, or having some types of privileges withheld may seem to give the hierarchy overwhelming power to apply sanctions. However, if the individual looks at all his peers as a group, the situation that is reflected is somewhat different. What power does the hierarchy have over *all* the peers simultaneously, or under equal treatment of all peers?

Clearly, the cost to the hierarchy of sanctions against an individual is likely to be quite small. But the cost of sanctions against *all* individuals in a given group is likely to be high. In each instance, the cost is incurred against a single individual, but the sanctions must be applied equally to all individuals if management is not to be perceived as idiosyncratic and unfair. If the individual in question is representative, he can count on the belief that sanctions will not be taken against him when it is not possible for the firm to take sanctions against all others similarly placed.

Hence, from that viewpoint, the hierarchy appears weak. Thus the hierarchy could develop reasonably acceptable sanctions with respect to "abnormal behavior," but not against what is viewed as normal or conventional behavior.

Thus the representative individual who takes into account the power of the hierarchy under equal treatment is aware of sanction limitations. He or she chooses an effort level in relation to what appears to be normal for the group. In fact, the individual may perceive a range and consider going to the lower bounds of that range. What becomes clear from the previous discussion is that history is important. The ideas of normal and abnormal performance will depend on what has been normal in the more recent past and in the distant past. The reasonableness of the sanctions of the hierarchy will depend on the history of performance.

In general, we might conclude that (1) the hierarchy is relatively weak in imposing sanctions in view of the "voluntary-enthusiasm" proposition that we started with. In addition, (2) the hierarchy is weak if it has to move against all peers in the group equally. Also, (3) the hierarchy is likely to be weak if it must consider power and informational divisions within the hierarchy.

This last deserves elaboration. It is one thing for a given "boss" to impose sanctions when that manager is in complete command. But this is not the case in a four- or five-level hierarchy. No member of the hierarchy, even if that individual has considerable responsibility for the monitoring of performance, is likely to be in a position to carry out sanctions according to his own personal whims or according to what he believes are appropriate sanctions. He must take into account the reaction of others at different levels in the hierarchy. Here a basic asymmetry is likely to be significant. Those highest in the hierarchy are likely to have the most power to carry out sanctions. They are also likely to have the least information about the basic employees against whom such sanctions might be carried out. Those closest to the activities of basic employees are likely to have the most information about possible deficiencies in performance, but they are in a position of least power compared with the others in the hierarchy. Thus lower-level hierarchy people can apply sanctions only in accordance with some well-established rules. Such rules will usually have to take into account what has been historically determined as normal versus abnormal, or conventional versus nonconventional, performance.

Finally, it is important to consider that a set of effort/wage cost combinations exists that implies the same profit level. Clearly, the firm seeking to maximize profits would be quite happy with a lower, rather than higher, effort/wage cost combination, so as to avoid some of the resistance to high effort levels obtained by monitoring and sanctions. In other

Figure 1.

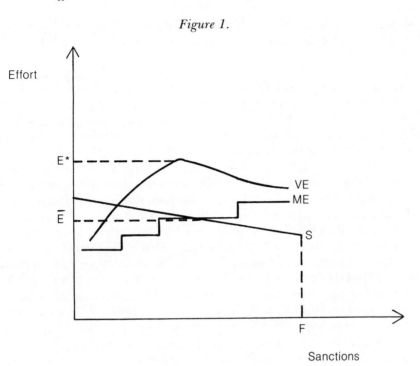

Sanctions

words, at very high effort levels, there is a disutility to obtaining that effort by the higher levels of the hierarchy, and it is easier to live with a lower effort/wage cost combination. Note that this is a comparative statement. We are not referring to a *move* from a high-effort/high-wage level to a low-effort/low-wage level, but rather to comparative static equilibria.

Figure 1 may help to provide a summary of some of the ideas. The abscissa indicates the degree of hierarchical sanctions. These sanctions may run the gamut from mild rebukes, to lesser promotions, to non-promotions, to employees being fired (point F). Curve S is the supply of sanctions for alternative effort levels provided by the hierarchy. Curve ME is the supply of effort, on the average, under monitoring for each level of sanctions.

Sanctions are within boundaries. That is, they are not continuous for every level of effort. Hence we have a step function, and we should expect that employees will have a tendency to place themselves at the lower end of effort for each step. In an effective system these curves (S and ME) will cross prior to sanction level F. If the hierarchy sets the sanction curve too low, it will be ineffectual. If it is set too high, the firm is in a foolish and costly position, since it will either opt not to take any action or have to fire all its employees if it operates in accordance with its sanction scheme. Clearly, setting the curve somewhere in between is the likely level.

The curve marked VE represents the maximum voluntary effort level provided by employees for each level of sanctions. This assumes the provision of the best *positive* motivating forces. The arguments presented (and briefly summarized below) suggest that a number of points exist on VE (or on nonoptimal positive motivator curves below VE) that are significantly above the equilibrium point Ē.

We have presented various arguments in support of the idea that a monitored-sanction effort level will be lower than a voluntary one. Among the important elements that motivate suboptimal efforts under monitoring are: (a) a negative utility associated with the monitoring experience, (b) a lower effort in intrinsically unmonitorable activities, (c) suboptimal unmonitorable information transfer, (d) the shift of effort to observed and away from unobserved activities, (e) the costs of monitoring, and (f) the costs involved in finding replacements for those who are fired or for those who leave because of the monitoring atmosphere.

We noted that the hierarchy is likely to be relatively weak in its attempts to extract very high effort levels through sanctions, although its power may be strong against isolated individuals but not against all peers. In addition, the hierarchy does not speak with one voice, with the same degree of power, or with the same amount of detailed information at all levels. Hence the hierarchy is weaker than would otherwise appear to be the case once we consider internal divisions. At the same time, we must keep in mind that at relatively low monitored levels employees are likely to see sanctions as fair, whereas at high levels they would be viewed as undesirable attempts to extract additional effort.

IV. PEER SANCTIONS AND SANCTION LEVELS

How people behave given the existence of an effort convention will also depend on the nature of peer-group sanctions. We have in mind not only the degree to which people show their displeasure at nonconventional behavior but the nature of allowed behavior within the sanction. In this section, sanctions are classified in various ways, and we consider how particular sanctions influence behavior. In some of the figures below, effort conventions (related to sanctions) are considered simultaneously. However, conventions and sanctions, although connected, are, in principle, separable. We shall consider the conventions only in passing, since the focus of this paper is on sanctions and their influence on effort behavior.

A. No-Group Sanctions

Under this heading we consider the state of affairs under which essentially no peer sanctions exist. There may be a sense of something like average behavior that may have an influence, but firm members feel that there are no sanctions from peers with respect to behavior. In this case, people may emulate the behavior of others whenever it appears to be comfortable to do so simply so as not to stand out. Thus the implicit sanction in this case is conspicuousness. Of course, some personalities may not be concerned about conspicuousness; others may want to avoid it. This general point has been made by Schelling (1960); he argues that nonobservance of an institutionalized behavior pattern carries "the pain of conspicuousness" (p. 91). The idea here is that even though no specific effort level is institutionalized, there is a sense in which the average level will carry some weight in that it serves as an indication of what individuals ought to do.

Under these circumstances, anyone who wants to be an effort-free rider would feel at liberty to do so; hence we shall expect certain personalities to approximate free-riding behavior (up to the point that appropriate hierarchical sanctions permit) and to divert effort to their own interests and away from firm interests. This is illustrated in Figure 2a by two curves. The curve marked FR indicates complete free-riding behavior and reflects the minimal effort level desired by the individual. Curve MFR involves some degree of modified free riding in which an individual attempts to avoid conspicuousness; hence the curve has a slightly upward slope, reflecting the avoidance of conspicuousness. In Figure 2b we show the reaction curve for all individuals. The intersection of the reaction curve and the 45° line represents the equilibrium effort level under which no one will have a desire to change their effort. Of course, around the equilibrium, which shows only the average, there is a distribution of individual levels.

In this particular case, all the nonimplicit sanctions are left to the hierarchy.

B. Upper-Bound Sanction

Under this type of sanction the group indicates that it does not care how low the effort level is but does not want people to put forth too high an effort level. In Figure 3 we show the reaction curve starting above the 45° line; the curve would reflect boredom at very low levels but would rise as the efforts of other individuals rise. However, the curve is close to the sanction level, shown by the point marked S on the abscissa. Up to a point, the higher the sanction level, the higher the equilibrium

Figure 2a.

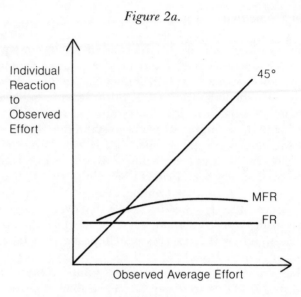

Figure 2b.

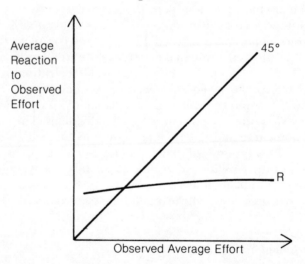

effort convention will turn out to be. Clearly, in this case, there is strong pressure for the effort level not to be above the sanctioned level; if the sanctioned level is low, this would constrain individuals to put in less effort than their desires would dictate under individualistic behavior.

This particular type of sanction may be viewed as the standard defense by peers against attempts by the hierarchy to elicit relatively high effort levels. This type of sanction is symptomatic of industrial relations in the

Figure 3.

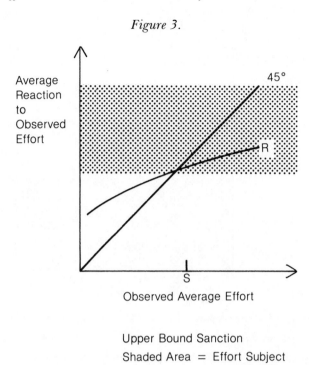

Upper Bound Sanction

Shaded Area = Effort Subject
to Sanction

United Kingdom, but it is also frequently visible in the United States. Whether or not labor is organized is not important in this case. There is a long history of informal sanctions in enterprises without unions.

C. Lower-Bound Sanction

This represents the opposite of the type of sanction considered above. Here others want everybody else to make at least a minimal contribution to effort, although how much of a contribution above the minimum is left to the individual. The reaction curve is shown in Figure 4. If the sanction level is quite low, then voluntary behavior will determine the actual level. Clearly, individuals at the tail end of the distribution, those who would normally produce at low levels, are forced to produce at a higher level, and hence the average is higher than it would otherwise be. The higher the sanctioned level, the higher the average reaction curve. Also, the reaction curve flattens out. Thus in this particular case, the lower the sanctioned level, the steeper the reaction curve and vice versa.

This particular case is likely to be one that is, on the whole, supportive

Figure 4.

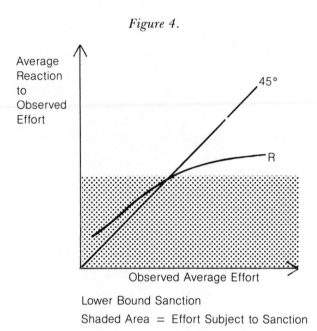

Lower Bound Sanction

Shaded Area = Effort Subject to Sanction

of hierarchical interests whether or not the hierarchy has an additional set of sanctions. It has been asserted that such cases are found in efficient German firms where there is considerable respect for the hierarchy and the system of hierarchy. There is no way of determining whether or not this is a general case.

D. Competitive Contribution Sanctions

This case comes closer to what we find in the *successful* large Japanese firms. The group or faction that each individual belongs to not only requires a minimal contribution but creates an atmosphere in which the minimum rises as others perform. Thus whatever the performance level of others, it is viewed as the appropriate contributing level. The upper limit is determined by the maximum capacity of the average individual. Those who have greater capacities need not be concerned about producing more, but those with lower capacities will always feel that they have not made an appropriate contribution and will attempt to find ways of doing so through longer hours or efforts that could be maintained only in the short run. Clearly, in this case the equilibrium effort level will be high. This is shown in Figure 5. However, it is important to note that the result need not be the maximum. Those who compete easily, for example, those who do not find it difficult to make a slightly above-

Figure 5.   Competitive contributions.

average contribution, may feel or behave in such a way that they do not put forth their maximum effort, even if their actual effort is observably high. Since the maximum contributions are nonobservable, there is no reason for the average outcome of the group to be maximum.

It is important to note that in this version we are likely to have a situation under which both the hierarchy and the peers support the sanction. The hierarchy supports it because they are able to obtain highly satisfactory results from the lower-level group by offering some sense of shared interests between the individual contribution and the interests of the firm. In the Japanese system such interests are augmented by a relatively large bonus system (20 percent to 35 percent of annual income), which supports the incentives and sanctions that exist (see Clark, 1979).

The competitive contribution sanction is likely to have two components. The group operates as a team. As a consequence, individuals compete, at least to some degree, in their contribution toward team effort in the belief that the other members of the group will care about everybody else's contribution and to some extent show disapproval of "low" contributions. But these motivational circumstances are unlikely to persist if there is no reward for higher team performance. Thus this is a system that must be supported and augmented by the hierarchy. As suggested in an earlier section, the hierarchy must recognize differences in team performance and be in a position to deliver appropriate rewards for increased team performance. Clearly, the type of Japanese bonus system, since it is fairly large, will operate in this manner. But it must be noted that it is the persistence of the subgroup as a clearly identifiable group within the organization, with its own small hierarchy, that is an essential part of the system.

This type of sanction can lead to anxiety and neurosis as a result of individuals attempting to achieve unrealistic effort levels under competitive incentives. It has been argued that this is sometimes the case in Japanese firms. However, some simultaneous concern for the welfare of one's peers is likely to lead to a realistic upper-level standard at which the competitive contribution stops. This is probably a situation that is not consistent with utility maximization on the job.

E. Adversarial Sanctions

Where the feelings are adversarial, the outcome is not likely to be much different in general than that under free riding, with the exception that the effort levels will probably be lower than free-riding effort levels. Here we distinguish two possibilities. The first possibility is that the adversarial feelings are individual but are not additionally supported by group sanctions; the second possibility is that there are group sanctions and group support for adversarial attitudes. In general, we should expect that in the group-supported case the effort level would be even lower than it is in the individual adversarial situation.

F. Fear of Victimization

In some cases there may be group sanctions whose reason for existence is to avoid possible victimization by management. This is reported in extreme instances of labor relations in the United Kingdom. Usually there is a variety of work rules and attitudes associated with work rules that involve unusual sensitivity to attempts to increase effort by management. Under such circumstances, there are likely to be extreme sanctions against almost anyone exceeding the upper-bound effort level. The net result is that the average performance will be below those in situations where only an upper-bound focus sanction exists. The extreme sensitivity to going beyond the boundary is the essential element here.

G. The Shape of the Reaction Curve

We have generally drawn the reaction curve so that at low observed levels the reaction is above the observed level, and at high observed levels he reaction is below that level. What does the slope of the reaction curve represent? It appears to represent the degree of deviation from uniform behavior between individuals and the group. If sanctions against any deviation are exceptionally strong, the reaction curve is always along the 45° line until the maximum effort is reached. At the maximum, the curve contains a segment parallel to the abscissa. However, this is unlikely to represent any realistic behavioral circumstances. People may, to some degree, be pressured toward conformity, but they are rarely pressured toward complete conformity. Hence at low levels they are likely to exceed the conformity requirements, and at higher levels they are likely to follow that requirement. The extent of the deviation from the 45° line will depend on the extent to which the sanctions exert pressure toward complete conformity. The equilibrium point will, of course, depend on the nature of the sanction itself. It is of extreme importance to note that all such sanction systems are likely to depend on history. Since at various points members leave and others enter the firm, those who enter will probably, at least initially, determine their effort levels on the basis of information about "how things are generally done" in the organization. Thus firms with different histories are likely to have different reaction curves, different equilibrium effort levels, and different sanctions.

V. CONCLUDING REMARKS

Effort decisions are made within certain boundaries. These boundaries are likely to be determined in part by both hierarchical sanctions and peer-group sanctions. It is worth noting that some peer-group sanctions serve as basic defenses against the possibility or reality of overly ambitious hierarchical sanctions. Nevertheless, the likely situation is that the sum of all sanctions leads to a considerable area of discretion for effort determination.

Not considered here is the possibility that the hierarchical and peer sanctions are basically in conflict. This might be an interesting temporary possibility, but an analysis of this phenomenon would take us too far afield.

The basic conclusion is that sanctions developed by the hierarchy probably leave a relatively wide area of behavioral possibilities beyond which voluntaristic incentives are stronger than the sanctions. I have argued elsewhere that this leads to a latent Prisoner's Dilemma type of situation but that the dilemma is solved by the adoption of what is usually a set of suboptimal effort and wage conventions. At the same time, significant peer-group effort conventions probably exist.

How the peer-group sanctions influence the outcome will depend on whether they are sanctions that (1) *cooperate* with the hierarchy, or (2) are *neutral*, or (3) are essentially *adversarial*. Clearly, cooperative sanctions, which are common in Japanese enterprise, usually lead to relatively high effort conventions compared with the effects of neutral or adversarial types of sanctions.

ACKNOWLEDGMENT

I am indebted to Roger Frantz and Stanley Kaish for helpful comments on a previous version of this paper.

NOTES

1. The role of hierarchies in economics is a large and growing subject. Williamson's *Market and Hierarchies* is probably the most important book in recent years. Some works worth mentioning are Beckmann (1960), Calvo and Wellisz (1978), Chandler (1977), Chandler and Daemes (1980), and Hess (1983). Nevertheless, the penetration of hierarchy concepts into microeconomics is slight. Needless to say, we do not consider hierarchies generally or formally here. In a general sense, the problem of hierarchy has not been solved. All that this paper is concerned with are some limited aspects of hierarchy having to do with the power of hierarchies to elicit effort through sanctions.

2. I have already argued elsewhere that intra-firm decisions are frequently not optimal. The attempt here is not to say anything especially new on this matter but rather to dig more deeply into certain elements.

3. Many of these procedures may be viewed as routines in the sense used by Winter (1975) or by Nelson and Winter (1982). The view of routines in the book by Nelson and Winter (1982) is exceptionally insightful, perceptive and valuable to economists who take a behavioral stance. My use of procedures is in terms of ordinary English, and some items on the list would probably not be viewed as routines from that viewpoint.

4. There exists a formal theory of conventions. This is based on some remarks by von Neumann and Morgenstern on "standards of behavior." For the most part, this has been stimulated by the work of Schelling (1960, p. 178), and the formalization developed by Lewis (1969), which sees conventions as a specific solution to a multisolution coordination problem. Of special importance is the treatment by Ullmann-Margalit (1977). Ullmann-Margalit specifically sees conventions as solutions to Prisoner's Dilemma problems as well as other types of problems. Her work is of special interest, since it recognizes that the solutions need not be of an optimal character. In my view, nonoptimal conventions can persist, since it may be inconvenient or costly for anyone to undertake the reorganization necessary to obtain a shift from a nonoptimal convention to an optimal one. See Schotter (1981) for an optimality approach to the problem of conventions.

5. We may view many of these procedures as "consensual procedures" in the sense that they do not violate any sanctions known to the decision-makers and that they are procedures that relevant others do agree with or are assumed to agree with by the decision-makers.

6. On wage conventions or wage customs, see the article by Piore (1973), especially pp. 378 and 379. For our purposes, it does not matter if the wages are determined by convention, or that they are, in part, guided by competitive considerations in the labor market, so that wages are somewhat similar to what people in a given classification receive elsewhere.

7. See Williamson (1967) on this point.

REFERENCES

Alchian, A. A. and H. Demsetz, "Production, Information Costs and Economic Organization," *American Economic Review*, (1972), 777–795.

Beckmann, M., "Returns to Scale in Business Administration," *Quarterly Journal of Economics*, (1960), 464–471.

Broadbent, D. E., *Decision and Stress*. London: Academic Press, 1971.

Calvo, G. and S. Wellisz, "Supervision, Loss of Control and the Optimum Size of the Firm," *Journal of Political Economy*, (1978), 943–952.

Chandler, A., *The Visible Hand: The Managerial Revolution in American Business*. Cambridge, MA: Harvard University Press, 1977.

Chandler, A. and H. Daems, eds., *Managerial Hierarchies: Comparative Perspectives on the Rise of the Modern Industrial Enterprise*. Cambridge, MA: Harvard University Press, 1980.

Clark, Rodney, *The Japanese Company*. New Haven: Yale University Press, 1979.

Hayes, J. L., "Review of *The Visible Hand: The Managerial Revolution in American Business* by A. Chandler," *Journal of Economic Literature*, (March 1979), 93–96.

Hess, James D., *The Economics of Organization*. New York: North-Holland Publishing Company, 1983.

Leibenstein, H., *Beyond Economic Man*. Cambridge, MA: Harvard University Press, 1976.

Leibenstein, H., "The Prisoners' Dilemma in the Invisible Hand: An Analysis of Intrafirm Productivity," *American Economic Review Proceedings*, 72 (May 1982), 92–97.

Lewis, D., *Convention: A Philosophical Study*. Cambridge, MA: Harvard University Press, 1969.

Nelson, Richard R. and Sidney G. Winter, *An Evolutionary Theory of Economic Change*. Cambridge, MA: Harvard University Press, 1982.

Piore, Michael J., "Fragments of a 'Sociological' Theory of Wages," *American Economic Review*, (May 1973), 377–384.

Schelling, T. S., *The Strategy of Conflict*. Oxford: Oxford University Press, 1960.

Schotter, Andrew, *Economic Theory of Social Institutions*. Cambridge: Cambridge University Press, 1981.

Simon, Herbert A., *Administrative Behavior: A Study of Decision-Making Processes in Administrative Organization*. New York: Macmillan, 1957.

Simon, Herbert A., "Rationality as Process and as Product of Thought," *American Economic Review Proceedings*, 68 (May 1978), 1–16.

Ullmann-Margalit, E., *The Emergence of Norms*. New York: Oxford University Press, 1977.

Williamson, Oliver E. "Hierarchical Control and Optimum Firm Size," *Journal of Political Economy*, (April 1967), 123–138.

Williamson, Oliver E., *Markets and Hierarchies*. New York: The Free Press, 1975.

Winter, S. G., "Optimization and Evolution in the Theory of the Firm," in R. H. Day and T. Groves, eds., *Adaptive Economic Models*. New York: Academic Press, 1975.

PRODUCTIVITY AND ORGANIZATIONAL BEHAVIOR:
WHERE HUMAN CAPITAL THEORY FAILS

John F. Tomer

The Baltimore Orioles, according to a knowledgeable observer, have "a damn good organization." "While some other teams seem to operate a revolving door of players pursuing ever-bigger pay checks, Baltimore has signed much of its team to long-term contracts. In the process, it has bred a strong sense of team play and fan loyalty." Baltimore has thus consciously sought harmony and stability on a close-knit team and has managed to "stay relatively free of clubhouse jealousies" (*Wall Street Journal*, October 5, 1983). Judging from their World Series win in 1983, they are also a highly productive organization.

The commentary above suggests a correspondence between a "good organization" and high productivity, which also seems to be the case for "excellent" U.S. companies such as IBM and 3M, many of the large Japanese companies (see, e.g., Peters and Waterman, 1982), and the Mondragon Cooperatives (Ellerman, 1984). The vast and growing literature on organizational behavior contains many insights on the features of organizations that make for high productivity. While these insights have undoubtedly been underutilized by U.S. companies, they have been virtually ignored by economists. If organizations do much to shape the individual behaviors that are responsible for firm productivity, it is incumbent upon economists to do more to incorporate these insights into their theoretical framework. Thus the purpose of this article is first, to review a number of the most important ideas of organizational behavior writers and second, to indicate the implications of these ideas for changing economic theory, in particular, human capital theory. Where human capital theory fails is that it does not allow for the possibility that productivity potential may be vested in the characteristics of the organization as opposed to being vested in individuals or tangible capital. A type of human capital called organizational capital is a concept that remedies this defect. One variant of the concept of organizational capital was developed by this author (Tomer, 1973, 1981), and a different but related concept was developed by Prescott and Visscher (1980). Previous articles, however, have done little to integrate the new organizational capital idea with orthodox human capital theory in a systematic way. The latter task, therefore, is attempted in the second section of this article.

I. ORGANIZATIONAL BEHAVIOR REVIEW

Insights about organizational productivity can be put into perspective by considering a theory of stages of corporate evolution known as corporate Darwinism (Blake, Avis, and Mouton, 1966). In this view, there are three stages of corporate evolution: entrepreneurial, mechanistic, and dynamic. The entrepreneurial corporation is dominated by the drive and determination of a single entrepreneur who plans, organizes, directs, and controls the activities of subordinates bound to him out of fear and loyalty. While the entrepreneurial company may achieve success and grow, its expansion potential is restricted by the entrepreneur's generally limited ability to personally direct and control a large and growing organization (p. 10).

Thus, unless the organization can take on a mechanistic character, the company's growth will peter out. The mechanistic stage is reached when the corporation introduces systematic business practices, involving such things as budgeting, job descriptions, formal organizational charts, procedures manuals, forecasting, and so on, to achieve greater order, predictability, and control. While these systematic practices do introduce elements of efficiency and control that seem to be necessary in large corporations, they also cause problems to the extent that the "system" saps rather than taps human energies, leading to "frustrations, tensions, strife, sacrificed creativity, and reduction of meaningful accomplishment" (Blake, Avis, and Mouton, 1966, p. 11).

Because of these problems, some corporations have looked for ways to break out of the mechanistic stage into the dynamic stage. "In the dynamic stage of corporate evolution, systematic business practices are retained, even strengthened, but initiative and vigor are restored to the very heart of the organization—its people. The method of restoring this vigor and initiative makes use of behavioral science knowledge of leadership and motivation, management by objectives, involvement and commitment, confronting conflict, teamwork, and so on" (Blake, Avis, and Mouton, 1966, p. 12).

A. The Entrepreneurial Corporation

The entrepreneurial corporation, with its single head and lack of economically significant organizational features, is recognizable in skeleton form as the firm in much of orthodox microeconomic theory. The entrepreneur's role as innovator has also received much attention from economists such as Joseph Schumpeter (1961), who have analyzed the important contributions of innovation to economic growth. Although the entrepreneur is generally viewed as organizing (and compensating) the factors of production, there is little room here for viewing organization as a distinct factor of production. Later economists who analyzed corporate organization have, however, pointed to particular organizational features that are related to productivity and thus have anticipated or implicitly treated organizations as a factor of production. Therefore, we need to consider the most significant organizational characteristics of mechanistic and dynamic corporations and how they contribute to productivity.

B. The Mechanistic Corporation

In the view of Max Weber, the modern (mechanistic) corporation is one that applies the principles of bureaucracy in order to achieve "rational efficiency, continuity of operation, speed, precision, and calculation of results" (Gerth and Mills, 1958, p. 49). For Weber, bureaucratic organization was not only technically superior but it and the rationalization that accompanied it were historically inevitable.

An organization, regardless of type, can be thought of as an intricate human strategy designed to achieve certain objectives. The key element of the mechanistic organization is the formal organization structure or organization chart, which "represents the intended rational strategy of the organization," that is, an attempt "to create a logically ordered world" (Argyris, 1960, pp. 10–11). Among the common principles used as a guide in designing the hierarchy of authority are specialization, unity of command, and span of control (Simon, 1957, Chapter 2). When a large group of workers is necessary to accomplish a task, the task inevitably will be divided up into subtasks, which will be assigned to individuals or groups specializing in these functions. To accomplish the task, the subtasks must be coordinated with each other using integrative mechanisms which, in many cases, do not allow for face-to-face communication. Following Jay Galbraith (1973, p. 10):

> The simplest method of coordinating interdependent subtasks is to specify the necessary behavior in advance of their execution in the form of rules or programs. ... If everyone adopts the appropriate behavior the resultant aggregate response is an integrated or coordinated pattern of behavior ... [without] further communication.

When an organization encounters new situations, the old rules and programs are likely to be unsatisfactory; thus there is a need for additional integrating devices. A satisfactory response to the new situation must consider all the affected subtasks, and this involves a substantial information-collection and problem-solving activity. Hierarchy emerges when subtask managerial positions are created to handle these information- collection and decision-making tasks necessitated by uncertainty, and still higher positions are created to handle those aspects that cannot be handled at the lowest managerial level. "In addition, the hierarchy is also a hierarchy of authority and reward power, so that the decisions of [managerial] role occupants are effective determinants of the behavior of the task performers" (Galbraith, 1973, p. 11). The use of hierarchy as an integrating mechanism adds to, but does not replace, the use of rules and, possibly, other mechanisms such as the use of targets and goal setting. Thus the hierarchy has an important function for the organization, and how well it is tailored to the organization's purposes will determine how effective and efficient the organization is. Further, the formal organization structure (including rules and hierarchy) provides for reliable completion of tasks and goal achievement through its channeling of communications and work activities.

In addition to hierarchy and rules, the mechanistic corporation has drawn greatly on the scientific management tradition of thought stemming from Frederick Taylor (1911) and his disciples. The essence of this tradition is the systematic analysis of work by managers who are responsible for planning the flow of work and the content of jobs in order to increase productivity. Scientific management principles emphasize work simplification and the minimization of worker discretion, thereby reducing the skill required of the worker.

C. The Dynamic Corporation

In the dynamic corporation, the human energies dormant in the mechanistic stage are "unleashed and funneled into finding creative and effective solutions to problems of production, many of which may have plagued the company for years" (Blake, Avis, and Mouton, 1966, p. 12). The problems of the mechanistic corporation that keep productivity below potential are inherent in its use of hierarchy and scientific management. First, its emphasis on the system operating like a well-oiled machine leaves the individual in the position of a cog in the machine and feeling uninvigorated, to say the least. Second, the simple, straightforward application of hierarchy and scientific management fails to achieve potential productivity when novelty and uncertainty are high, since its integrating mechanisms will be inadequate for the magnitude of information processing and problem solving involved. Third, the mechanistic organization may fail to achieve potential productivity because there is a lack of fit between the organization and its members' attributes. In other words, the dynamic corporation is superior to the mechanistic one along three dimensions: the psychological, the structural, and the individual.

1. The Psychological Dimension. Argyris (1960) has led the way in pointing out that "there is a lack of congruency between the needs of healthy individuals and the demands of the... [mechanistic] organization" (p. 14). On the one hand, healthy, mature individuals are "predisposed toward relative independence, activeness, use of their important abilities, [and] control over their immediate work world," while mechanistic organizations tend "to require the agents to work in situations where they are dependent, passive, use few and unimportant abilities, etc." (p. 14). As a result, mature individuals will experience frustration, psychological failure, short time perspective, and internal conflict (p. 15). Further, subordinates in a mechanistic organization are likely to experience (1) rivalry and intersubordinate hostility because of the competition for a limited number of positions at the next higher level in the hierarchy and (2) a tendency "to develop an orientation toward their own particular part rather than towards the whole" (p. 16), because of their being rewarded only for doing their subtask well. Employees will also react to the formal organization by creating informal activities, which may, on the one hand, enable them to defend themselves from the negative psychological aspect of organizational experience but may, on the other hand, run counter to the purposes of the organization and consume substantial energy and other resources (pp. 16–18). Such adaptive informal activities include absenteeism, turnover, quota restriction, slowdowns, trade unions, increasing emphasis on material factors and decreasing emphasis on human factors, noninvolvement, withdrawal from work, and alienation.

Thus, in Argyris's view, motivation is lower than potential in a mechanistic organization, and the same is true for productivity. "It is simply impossible to say that the motivation resides 'in' the individual or 'in' the organization. . . . The motivation of the participant is best understood as a resultant of the *transactions* between the individual and the organization" (Argyris, 1960, p. 21). When the organization enables a member to satisfy his higher needs, especially his need for self-actualization, the amount of psychological energy available for organization tasks will be considerably higher (pp. 22–23). Moreover, there is reason to believe that members' decision-making effectiveness, creativity, and ability to play an effective role in groups are also very much related to their ability to satisfy their needs in the organization (p. 23).

Becoming a dynamic organization in this psychological sense requires not the elimination of hierarchy but the creation of conditions under which healthy individuals have high motivation (and psychological energy) because of their ability to satisfy their needs while working toward the organization's purposes. Transforming an organization in this sense has been called organizational development (OD), the essence of which is changing the organizational climate and interpersonal style. According to Porter, Lawler, and Hackman (1975, Chapter 15), there are two main approaches to OD:

1. Helping organizations build more effective *teams* of organization members, with special attention to issues of participation and leadership within teams.
2. Helping organizations find new and better means of managing interpersonal and intergroup (e.g., department-department or line-staff) *conflict*, with special attention to creating a climate of collaboration throughout the organization (p. 458).

OD specialists or consultants have used many different means in the attempt to help organizations become more dynamic. However, some of the most dynamic organizations (both Japanese and American) seem to become that way not so much through the use of OD experts but through a combination of superior leadership and success in evolving a clearly articulated philosophy or set of convictions (superordinate goals), which is supported by the companies' actions and that employees find is motivating and has implications for their work behavior (see, e.g., Ouchi, 1981; Pascale and Athos, 1981; and Peters and Waterman, 1982).[1] Undoubtedly, an organizational climate that fosters trust and self-expression will be one where harmful conflicts are kept to a minimum and energetic cooperation in the pursuit of common goals will be encouraged.

2. The Structural Dimension. When uncertainty is high, the mechanistic organization, at least in the simple form outlined above, will fail to achieve potential productivity because its information-processing capacity will be inadequate to meet the demands on it. Uncertainty refers to "the lack of or absence of information about what will occur in the future" (Nadler, Hackman, and Lawler, 1979, p. 187). Uncertainty derives from the degree of predictability of the work tasks, the stability or rate of change of the work environment, and the degree to which different task elements making up the larger task are interdependent on each other (pp. 190–191). In the presence of greater uncertainty, more information processing and problem solving must be done to insure the successful completion of tasks. Given the organization of the basic work units and their internal relationships, dealing with uncertainty means either (1) developing coordination and control mechanisms so that the organization's information-processing capacity meets its requirements, or (2) reducing its information-processing needs by (a) manipulating its external environment or (b) settling for lower performance (Chapter 11). Let us consider the former alternative in more detail.

It is useful to think of coordination and control mechanisms on a continum with hierarchy and rules at the low end and vertical information systems and lateral relations on the high end (Nadler, Hackman, and Lawler, 1979, p. 216). Vertical information systems "are mechanisms that collect data about organizational functioning and distribute these data to a predetermined network of organizational members" (p. 207). The creation of lateral relations is a way to exchange information and achieve coordination directly between work units rather than by the movement of information up and down the hierarchy (p. 208). Among the processes for achieving the desired lateral relations are: (1) direct contact between managers, (2) creation of a liaison role, (3) creation of task forces, (4) use of teams, (5) creation of an integrating role, (6) change to managerial-linking role, and (7) establishing the matrix organizational form (Galbraith, 1973, p. 110). Organizations typically face a trade-off in deciding on the appropriate coordination and control mechanism, since the superior information processing of the latter mechanisms involves greater cost and complexity. Another alternative open to the organization is to create new self-contained units that contain all the resources, including types of personnel, necessary for task accomplishment, thereby eliminating the interdependency (and some of the information processing need) with other units. An example of this is the change from a functional organizational form to more or less independent groups based on product lines or geographical areas or markets (Galbraith, 1973, p. 16), as is done in multidivisional corporations.[2] In sum, the dynamic organization will, much more so than the mechanistic organization, be able to survive, grow, and be efficient in industries and environments characterized by high uncertainty and novelty, because they are the ones whose organizations have been tailored with many of the above considerations in mind.

One other structural consideration deserves mention here: the structure of jobs. Recall that in the mechanistic ideal, as found in Taylor (1911), job design involves simplification, specialization, and standardization. However, the debilitating effects of these jobs on individuals is well known. To counteract these unmotivating and unsatisfying effects, the job enrichment approach was developed. The general approach is that work will become much more motivating and satisfying for healthy, mature individuals when jobs are characterized by more variety, higher skill requirements, more automonomy, and more performance feedback to the worker and when the job is a more meaningful whole compared with jobs designed in accordance with scientific management (Nadler, Hackman, and Lawler, 1979, Chapter 5). Another alternative to scientific management-job design is to design work for interacting groups or work teams, an approach that also has the promise of higher motivation and satisfaction (pp. 86–88).

3. *The Individual Dimension.* Organizational behavior can also be improved by changing the attributes of individuals, in particular, their skills and attitudes. Of course, change in either the organizational climate or the organizational structure (the former more than the latter) could cause change in individual attributes. However, the focus here is on activities designed to change individuals directly, in order to attain the desired organizational result.

On-the-job or in-the-organization training is designed to improve work skills and, thereby, worker productivity. According to Simon:

> Training is applicable to the process of decision wherever the same elements are involved in a large number of decisions. Training may supply the trainee with the facts necessary in dealing with these decisions; it may provide him with a frame of reference for his thinking; it may teach him 'approved' solutions; or it may indoctrinate him with the values in terms of which his decisions are to be made. (1957, p. 170)

Besides improving performance by improving ability in these ways, training may lead to better performance via higher motivation, as suggested by Peters and Waterman's (1982, pp. 167–168) analysis of the effect of seemingly excessive training sessions for teenage ticket takers and other "cast members" at Disney World in Florida.

Training, as Simon (1957, pp. 170–171) points out, as an "influence upon decisions has its greatest value in those situations where the exercise of formal authority through commands proves difficult.... Training permits a higher degree of decentralization of the decision-making process by bringing the necessary competence into the very lowest levels of the organizational hierarchy." It thus substitutes for rules and programs as a control mechanism and lowers the need for hierarchy as individuals working responsibly and knowledgably are able to deal in many cases with uncertainty and novelty without resort to managers (Galbraith, 1973, pp. 12–13).

Training within the firm is part of the larger process known as socialization.

Socialization...refers to the whole process by which an individual, born with behavioral potentialities of an enormously wide range, is led to develop actual behavior which is confined within a much narrower range—the range of what is customary and acceptable for him according to the standards of his group. (Child, 1954, p. 655)

In this process of "learning the ropes," the organization makes demands on the individual, and typically a counter-process, individualization, occurs in which the member attempts to exert influence on the organization (Porter, Lawler, and Hackman, 1975, pp. 161–162). Whereas training tends to be a formal process, much of socialization consists of informal social interactions through which members acquire new expectations, beliefs, and attitudes and learn about group norms. It is useful to refer to many of these latter aspects as social learning, as contrasted with technical learning. According to Karl-Olof Faxen (1978, p. 132), social learning is "learning about other people and groups in the work organization, about their motives, reactions, values and ambitions. It also relates to the way in which one perceives oneself and one's role in the organization in such matters as responsibility and authority, operating methods and specific expertise."

According to Edgar Schein (Porter, Lawler, and Hackman, 1975, p. 162), organizational effectiveness depends on socialization: "The speed and effectiveness of socialization determine employee loyalty, commitment, productivity and turnover." John Kotter's research on the joining-up process when new employees are brought into the organization confirms Schein's view. Kotter (1973) finds that when joining-up is managed well, the new member's expectations about what is desired from the organization and what the individual is able to offer will match the organization's expectations about what it can give and what it wants. When this type of "psychological contract" between the individual and the organization has been established, the outcomes are generally higher job satisfaction, higher productivity, and longer tenure with the organization than when joining up results in mismatches in expectations (Kotter, 1973). Another aspect of socialization occurs if an organization should desire to change itself by changing the "types" of people who are members. Organizations could do this by systematically selecting people with the desired characteristics and terminating people who are not the right type (Porter, Lawler, and Hackman, 1975, pp. 441–442). Another approach is to use special types of experiential or other training outside the firm with the idea that when the member "returns" to the organization his attitudes, beliefs, and values will be closer to what the organization desires. Along this line, many corporations have tried such diverse programs as encounter groups and human relations training (as, for example, those offered by the Dale Carnegie Institute). The presumption by firms using these approaches is that the new group of employees or the old employees with new attitudes will add to productivity by enabling the organization to function closer to the desired manner. Dynamic corporations, one suspects, are more likely to use these approaches.

II. ORGANIZATIONAL CAPITAL, HUMAN CAPITAL, AND PRODUCTIVITY

The purpose of this section is to integrate the organizational behavior insights concerning the features of organizations that contribute to productivity (see the previous section) with economic theory. A good part of this task involves integrating the concept of organizational capital with human capital theory.

A. The Key Insight

The key organizational behavior insight is that the behavior of an individual in an organization, even an individual's personality and motivation, cannot be explained simply by his or her personal attributes. Individual behavior, and thus organizational productivity, is the result of an inextricable interaction between the characteristics of the organization and the individual (Argyris, 1960, p. 21). As was indicated in the previous section, the individual's behavior and productivity will be determined by the organizational climate, the structure of the organization, and the organization's socialization processes as well as individual attributes. In this author's view, the concept of organizational capital is extremely useful as a way to incorporate into economic theory the insight that organizations are more than the sum of the people who participate in them. Investment in *organizational capital* refers to the using up of resources in order to bring about lasting productivity improvement through changes in the functioning of the organization. Organizational capital formation could involve (1) changing the formal and informal social relationships and patterns of activity within the enterprise, (2) changing individual attributes important to organizational functioning, or (3) the accumulation of information useful in matching workers with organization situations.[3] Organizational capital is human capital in which the attribute is embodied in the organizational relationship, particular organization members, the organization's repositories of information, or some combination of the above in order to improve the functioning of the organization.[4]

In other words, organizational capital is a factor of production, an element in the production function along with labor, tangible capital, human capital that is unrelated to organizational functioning, and other types of intangible capital (Tomer, 1981, pp. 6–7). A number of prominent economists have used closely related concepts in their writings. For example, Jensen and Meckling (1979, p. 471) use a production function that includes a "generalized index describing the range of choice of 'organizational forms' or internal rules of the game available to the firm." In their view, this variable plays "an important role in motivating self-interested and maximizing individuals to achieve the physically possible output." Alchian and Demsetz (1972) have developed the view that the productivity of a team may be greater than the sum of the separable productive contributions of individual team members. Presumably, in many circumstances the realization of the productivity potential of this teamwork requires considerable time and effort; that is, it requires a substantial investment in organization capital. When organizational investment allows the other inputs to achieve output closer to potential, one can speak of an increase in X-efficiency, following Leibenstein's usage (e.g., 1976).[5,6]

B. The Human-Organizational Capital Spectrum

Becker (1964, p. 1) defined human capital formation as "activities that influence future monetary and psychic income by increasing the resources in people." Since organizations are undeniably composed of people, and because an organizational investment will lose value should a sufficient number of people leave the enterprise, organizational capital is clearly a type of human capital. In my previous writings (1973, 1981), I have at least implicitly juxtaposed the two very different types of human capital: the type vested only in individuals (pure human capital) and the type vested only in organizational relationships (pure organizational capital). However, on further consideration of the realities involved in organizing to achieve higher productivity, it seems appropriate to think of a spectrum of human-organizational capital with the pure human type (H-H) on the far left, the pure organizational type (O-O) on the far right, and the two human-organizational capital hybrids, H-O and O-H, in the middle (see Table 1).

The focus of this section's analysis is on firm-specific human capital. Consider first pure human capital formation due to training. According

Table 1. The Human-Organizational Capital Spectrum

Pure Human Capital	Human-Organizational Capital Hybrids		Pure Organizational Capital
H-H Capital	H-O Capital	O-H Capital	O-O Capital

to Becker (1962, p. 17), "training that increases productivity [of laborers], more in firms providing it" than in other firms, is firm-specific. More generally, firm-specific investment increases productivity more in the firm doing it than in others. A firm-specific factor of production is one that is specific to another factor(s) of production; that is, it is the more flexible factor that is capable of being adapted to or specialized to the other factor(s) through investment, which thereby raises its productivity when the other factor(s) is (are) present. For the purpose of this analysis, the factors of production are (1) technology, (2) employees, and (3) organizations (or organizational capital). *Technology* refers to the firm's particular tangible capital and/or technical activities embodying the current state of technical knowledge. *Employees* refers to the particular workers in the firm along with their different human capital endowments. *Organization* refers to the particular features of the firm's organizational relationships, which reflect investments in organizational capital. Table 2 shows six possible classifications, A through F, that are used below to

Table 2. Classification of Human-Organizational Capital Types According to Function in the Firm

			Vested In	
			Employees	Organization
Specific To	Factors of Production	Technology	A	D
		Employees	B	E
		Organization	C	F

explain how the four types of human capital in the spectrum function. As shown, human capital may be vested or embodied in employees or in the organization, and it may be specific to one or more of the three factors of production.

1. Pure Human Capital. Pure human, or H-H, capital formation is probably best illustrated by training during which the student-worker learns a technical skill such as operating a particular type of machinery. Clearly, the attribute acquired and vested in the employee is related to the worker's productivity, and if the worker should quit, his firm's productivity will be lower until they can hire and train someone else. This is pure human capital because this attribute does not contribute to the functioning of the organization. That is, it is specific to the firm's technology, but it is not specific to the firm's organization, so it is classified in box A of Table 2.[7]

2. Pure Organizational Capital. Pure organizational, or O-O, capital formation, on the other hand, may be illustrated by a change in the formal organizational structure in which the channels of communication and formal relationships between several work groups are changed. Assume for purposes of analysis that these structural changes improve productivity by effectively changing workers' organizational behavior in ways that improve the functioning of the organization; also assume that workers (regardless of their attributes) adapt immediately to the new behavioral patterns so that the orientation time and cost are negligible. This is pure organizational capital formation because it is the characteristics of the organization only that have evoked the desired worker behavior, not any change in workers' attributes, such as would be the case if orientation involving some training/socialization were necessary. Clearly, O-O capital is embodied in the organization. Moreover, since the changed characteristics must be adapted to the other (unchanging) organizational characteristics, it is organization-specific and thus is classified in box F of Table 2. Of course, if the organization's characteristics have been adapted to the firm's technology and employees, the O-O capital is also specific to those factors. In this case, boxes D and E of Table 2 are also correct classifications of O-O capital. Also note that the loss of an individual worker will not change the productivity stemming from the structural change, since this part of the organization's productivity derives from and is vested in the organization and does not stem from an individual attribute. It may, of course, be true that if a high fraction of the organization's members left, the investment in organizational capital would be destroyed or substantially reduced in productive value.

3. H-O Capital. On the left side of the spectrum, but not the far left, is a type of capital that is part human capital and part organizational capital (H-O capital); it relates to individual attributes that contribute to the behaviors important for the functioning of the organization. Most organizational change, for example, will require a significant amount of social learning to acquaint organization members with the new roles required of them.[8] This orientation process may involve changing the attitudes, values, and expectations of individuals who adjust to the new social requirements explicit and implicit in the new situation. Such social learning is likely to be much longer lasting than technical learning (Faxen, 1978, p. 133). To the extent that individual attributes such as attitudes and knowledge change, this is an investment embodied in employees. However, to the extent that the attributes acquired are specific to the organization's characteristics and functional requirements, it is organization-specific and thereby a type of organizational capital. Thus, H-O capital is classified in box C of Table 2; it could also be classified in box A if the organization is, in turn, adapted to the firm's technology.[9]

As Schein (1968) and Kotter (1973) have pointed out, organizational effectiveness depends on socialization. Socialization, particularly by influencing individuals' values, attitudes, and behavioral norms, determines individual responsiveness to organization stimuli. Most organizational changes will require additional socialization. Once the new organization with its new social knowledge and attitudes is created, there will be many who can then serve as orienters to individuals who subsequently enter the organization. The orientation process is resource-using in the sense that the orienter's and the orientee's attention would be elsewhere, presumably on some other productive contribution, if it were not important to orient the new member.

Education and training, even if they occur outside the organization, may have an organizational capital aspect to the extent that the individual acquires attributes directly related to his functioning in an organization rather than related to his technical task performance. Presumably, most such education or training will be general rather than firm- or organization-specific.[10] Consider again the training of a machine operator. If this training includes elements related to the worker's responsibilities for maintaining the machine, insuring safety to himself and others, reporting malfunctions and waste, communicating information on productivity, and other aspects of proper social behavior on the job, these notions will undoubtedly influence his organizational behavior (and the productivity of the organization), as opposed to his technical task performance. Some of the attributes inculcated by education may have a negative effect on organizational productivity. For example, many business organizations hesitate to hire people with Ph.D. degrees, except, of course, where they are necessary (such as in research and development), because the typical Ph.D. is too independent, cognitive, and theoretical in his orientation. Recently, there has been an increasing reluctance to hire M.B.A.s from elite academic institutions because the typical M.B.A. is too aggressive, ambitious, and impatient about mundane tasks and is likely to leave the firm in a few years. On the other hand, education may develop qualities of logical reasoning, good communication, persistence, initiative, responsibility, and good work habits that are extremely valuable to organizations (Reynolds, 1982, p. 118).

4. O-H Capital. On the spectrum between pure organizational capital and H-O capital lies O-H capital, which resembles pure organizational capital more than human capital. O-H capital derives from the firm's investment in information about the actual and desired characteristics of current and prospective employees. Employees' desired characteristics presumably follow from the characteristics of the whole organization as well as the particular organizational settings in which employees are placed. A good part of this information comes to be embodied in the formal repositories of the organization's memory; that is, it is documented in the organization's files and available to decision makers (Simon, 1957, p. 166). The other part is the subtle and less quantifiable information retained in the memories of managers, personnel people, and employees' co-workers. The latter type of employee information is an attribute of these people, while the former is an attribute of the organization.[11]

What I refer to as O-H capital is called organizational capital by Prescott and Visscher (1980).[12] They point out how the organization's information on employee abilities and the characteristics of tasks enables the firm to lower production costs by improving the matches between people and jobs (pp. 447–449). Firms can also improve productivity by utilizing information regarding how an employee's attributes complement those of others in teamwork situations (pp. 448, 456).[13] Another similar source of productivity improvement stems from the use of knowledge about what types of individuals are most compatible with the overall purposes and values of the organization. Such information can be used, as many of the leading Japanese companies do, to guide their selection of entry-level recruits (Clark, 1979, pp. 156–167). While Alchian and Demsetz (1972) do not refer to this information as capital, they recognize that the employer, through his monitoring of employees, acquires "special superior information about their productive talents" and that "efficient production with heterogeneous resources is a result not of having *better* resources but in *knowing more accurately* the relative productive performances of those resources" (p. 793, emphasis in original).

While O-H capital may be embodied in either its employees or in the organization (i.e., formal files), it is invariably organization-specific, since the information on workers' desired characteristics almost always derives

Table 3. The Human-Organizational Capital Spectrum

	Pure Human Capital	Human-Organizational Capital Hybrids		Pure Organizational Capital
	H-H Capital	*H-O Capital*	*O-H Capital*	*O-O Capital*
Examples	Machine operator training, bookkeeping training	Formal socialization of new member of organization	Acquiring information about employees' abilities, compatibility	Changing formal organizational structure
Attribute of (vested in)	Employee	Employee	Organization and/or certain employees	Organization
Specific to	Technology	Organization	Organization	Organization
May also be specific to	—	Technology	Technology, employees	Technology, employees

from some of the features of the organization. Thus, O-H capital is generally classified in both box C and box F of Table 2. To the extent that the information on workers' desired characteristics follows from the characteristics of other employees and/or the technology in the firm, O-H may be classified in the A, B, D, or E boxes as well.

In summary, the preceding analysis has focused on four types of firm-specific capital along the human-organizational capital spectrum: pure human (H-H), H-O, O-H, and pure organizational (O-O). Table 3 contrasts these. First, pure human capital such as results from training a machine operator or bookkeeper is specific to the technology of the firm and is an attribute of an individual. Second, H-O capital such as results from the formal and informal socialization of a new member of the organization is specific to the firm's organization and perhaps its technology but is an attribute of the employee. Third, O-H capital is formed when the firm acquires information that aids in the utilization of its employees; it is specific to the firm's organization and perhaps its technology and employees and is an attribute either of the organization or of certain of its members. Last, pure organizational capital resulting, for example, from a change in the formal organizational structure is specific to the firm's organization and perhaps its technology and employees and is an attribute of the organization.

The perspective illustrated in Table 3 is highly suggestive about what a firm would have to do organizationally to achieve its labor productivity potential, given the initial endowments of its laborers. It would have to (1) adapt the formal and informal aspects of its organization to its overall purposes, (2) develop and utilize information on employees' suitability for tasks and organizational situations, and (3) facilitate the employee socialization processes to help members achieve adjustments to the social and technical demands of the organization. In other words, the firm must make a variety of organizational capital investments; it must make investments in pure organizational, O-H, and H-O capital in order to get the most out of its tangible capital and its laborers with their pure human capital endowments. Any time a firm decides on a productivity improvement program with an organizational aspect, it is probable that the organizational investments involved will fall along several points of the human-organizational capital spectrum. Consider some examples.

On January 10, 1984, General Motors announced "the most extensive restructuring of its U.S. auto operations ever" (*Business Week*, January 23, 1984, pp. 32–33). "The reorganization is . . . designed to: (1) help GM launch its new models on schedule, (2) provide more cost control, (3) boost quality control, . . . and (4) make its divisions build more distinctive models. . . . " The reorganization will involve changes in the formal organization structure and changes in the organizational climate. The latter is indicated by planned changes in General Motors' management style that are intended to make them "less bureaucratic and more team-oriented." The former involves dividing up all General Motors' operations into two groups: (1) small cars, and (2) intermediate and large cars. Further, "GM's engineering will be consolidated, not spread throughout the sprawling corporation, and . . . product development and manufacturing will be more centralized." Although the *Business Week* article does not mention it, it would be very surprising if these relatively pure organizational capital investments could be accomplished without substantial investments in H-O and O-H capital, so that General Motors' employees are able to adjust to and are properly utilized in their new organization settings.

While reorganization of the size and scope of General Motors' may be rare, organizational change is common and important. According to Kotter and Schlesinger (1979, p. 106), "most companies or divisions of major corporations find that they must undertake moderate organizational changes at least once a year and major changes every four or five."

This author recently learned from an auto assembly-line worker at a New Jersey plant of Ford Motor Company of a major organizational change at the plant involving an imitation of the assembly procedures pioneered by Toyota.[14] Under the new approach, workers are held responsible for the quality, not just the quantity, of their assembly efforts and are expected to push a button to stop the assembly line if problems develop that cannot be dealt with in the allotted assembly time. In the event of a problem, correction efforts are initiated by this worker and/ or others. The expected result of the increased worker responsibility and autonomy is not only a higher-quality product but cost savings, because the need for quality inspectors is reduced.

According to my informant, Ford has substantially reduced the number of its inspectors. He went on to suggest, however, that the new system has some "bugs" in it. For example, if workers press the button too many times they are liable to be yelled at, and if they fail to press the button when there is a problem, they are similarly liable. He clearly felt conflicted about this. In his view, this situation stems from the lack of resolution as to whether quantity or quality of production takes precedence, and it reflects the organizational conflict between the production and quality managers. This author's suspicion is that the conflicted feelings of workers on this issue are likely to be reflected in lower-than-potential productivity and, therefore, resolution of this organizational matter would have great importance to Ford. Achieving this resolution means making an additional investment in organizational capital. The worker informed me that the Ford employees involved were treated to a special luncheon during which the proposed change was first explained and that prior to its implementation they also attended several question-and-answer sessions.

Consider the types of investment involved in Ford's productivity improvement program. To begin, there is a tangible capital investment in the push-button system; there is, as well, an investment in new organizational knowledge—Ford learning about the Japanese approach. The latter is quite similar to an investment in new technological knowledge. Then there is the basic organizational change, an investment in pure organizational capital, vested in the organization and specific to both the preexisting aspects of the organization and the tangible capital involved in the push buttons. The Ford meetings to inform and orient their employees are obviously evidence of investment in H-O capital, which is specific to the new organization and presumably to the new tangible capital. Investment in O-H capital, acquiring information about how particular employees perform with their changed responsibilities, may also have occurred. If so, the latter would be specific to the employees involved, the new organization, and the tangible capital.

One other issue deserves mention: namely, who is it that does the investing in organizational capital? Unfortunately, not much in the way of a definitive answer can be given. One could, of course, analyze the investment incentives to owners, managers, and nonmanagerial workers under various assumptions. However, a complete analysis of this sort is beyond the scope of this paper. Nevertheless, a few things should be said. First, firms (and thus owners and/or certain managers) can expect significant increases in income when organizational functioning improves. Presumably, in the General Motors and Ford examples and in countless other similar cases, the companies are investing in the expectation of these returns. In those cases where the attributes necessary for improved functioning are vested in employees rather than in the organization, it is likely that a lower but indefinite percentage of the return will accrue to the firm. The indefiniteness in the breakdown of the return between the employees and the firm is expected in situations where negotiation will determine the outcome and where both uncertainty regarding the source of productivity improvements and opportunism on the part of the bargainers are present. Second, managers, as opposed to owners and nonmanagerial employees, may claim a large portion of the return to organizational capital to the extent that (1) creating this capital is an entrepreneurial contribution, and (2) maintaining its functioning requires scarce talents. Perhaps this is one important explanation for the very high compensation that some top management people receive. Third, it should be considered that part of the return to organization may be psychic income. In some cases, employees may forge better (and more productive) relationships with other employees simply because these relationships are more satisfying. Moreover, employees who strongly identify with the firm may initiate changes in their own attitudes to conform to organization needs (an H-O capital investment) whether or not they expect financial rewards from these actions. In sum, this abbreviated analysis suggests that organizational investment may be initiated on behalf of owners, managers, or employees in response to a variety of expected but somewhat uncertain returns (financial or otherwise).

III. CONCLUSION

One important dimension of the role of organization in determining individual behavior can be appreciated by considering what happens to the behavior of a husband and wife when their marriage goes "bad." Neither may be able to talk or behave civilly to each other, and the family's level of functioning in carrying out basic household tasks may be impaired. However "crazy" the couple's behavior toward each other is, their behavior toward people outside the immediate family may be perfectly "normal." What this suggests is that the marriage relationship has an existence separate from the husband and wife's individual attributes and other relationships. The marriage relationship determines the behavior of the couple toward each other but not their behavior in other contexts. Although the relationships in a work organization are not as intense, they similarly determine their members' behavior and thus exert a powerful influence on the productivity of an organization independently of the attributes of workers, tangible capital, and so on.

Of course, as the review of organizational behavior indicated, the organization of a dynamic corporation, by definition, functions well in a psychological sense in large measure because its structure and socialization processes are well tailored to achieve its goals. Economic theory has, in general, not been well equipped to understand the sources of the productivity of such a dynamic corporation. With the possible exception of some aspects of socialization, human capital theory in particular has not incorporated an appreciation of how organizational features determine productivity. This paper has attempted to show how the organizational capital concept remedies this defect and how organizational capital relates to and dovetails with the human capital concept. It also demonstrates one important way that economists can improve their theory, namely, by drawing on the behavioral insights of other disciplines.

ACKNOWLEDGMENTS

An earlier version of this paper was prepared for presentation at the First Behavioral Economics Conference at Princeton University on May 22, 1984. Benjamin Gilad of Rutgers University, Newark, is notable for his conference invitation and intial suggestions that led to the writing of this paper. Comments by Amyra Grossbard-Shechtman of Bar Ilan University, Israel, and my discussion with her led to a marked improvement in the economic analysis.

NOTES

1. Findings cited by Ouchi and Price (1978, pp. 26–27) indicate that OD efforts are not reliably successful. To achieve organization effectiveness and individual psychological success, Ouchi and Price (pp. 36–44) believe that a corporation needs to develop a humanistic hierarchy, i.e., one characterized by clanlike functioning (cultural homogeneity deriving from a high degree of socialization), thus reducing the negative effects of hierarchy.

2. Alfred Chandler (1962) has ably examined how a number of large U.S. corporations, most notably Du Pont; General Motors; Standard Oil of New Jersey; and Sears Roebuck were among the first to choose the multidivisional form of organization because it fit their corporate strategies, which were, in turn, shaped by market demand patterns.

3. This differs slightly from the definition in Tomer (1981, p. 1).

4. This concept of organizational capital was first developed by Tomer (1973, pp. 267–281).

5. Alfred Marshall (1961) anticipated the concept of organization capital. He stated that it is "best sometimes to reckon Organization as a distinct agent of production" and

that "capital consists in a great part of knowledge and organization" (pp. 138–139). However, he did little to develop the insight further.

6. T.Y. Shen's 1981 article includes a useful review of organizational economic research in which elements of organization are treated as production inputs along with capital and labor. Shen emphasizes that the function of the organizational input is to contribute to the transformation of information. Among others, Shen cites Oliver Williamson, who has analyzed organizational features that are both helpful and harmful in this regard. On the one hand, the growth potential of large organizations is limited, as they are likely to become afflicted by information loss (Williamson, 1967); on the other hand, the organizational structure of multidivisional firms helps by reducing information-coordination needs (Williamson, 1970).

7. It could be argued that pure human capital is specific to the employees embodying it, but this seems trivial, since one cannot conceive of the human capital attribute separate from the individual embodying it. In effect, the employee, along with his attributes, is the flexible factor of production being made specific to the technology or the portion of it related to his job.

8. Although he didn't go further in analyzing the organizational aspects, Becker (1962, p. 17) recognized that "resources are usually spent by firms in familiarizing new employees with their organization."

9. It is possible that an investment in changing the attributes of an employee could be made with the purpose of improving the ability of this employee to interact with particular other employees, given their traits, the expected result being higher productivity through better teamwork. While this is possible, I suspect it is a rare occurrence, and thus H-O capital is not classified as employee-specific.

10. Although general in one sense, education in a particular nation is likely to be specific to the types of organization commonly existing in that country.

11. "The collective memory of [the organization's] participants ... is insufficient for organization purposes, first, because what is in one man's mind is not necessarily available to other members of the organization, and second, because when an individual leaves an organization, the organization loses that part of its 'memory.' Hence organizations ... need artificial 'memories.' ... Among the repositories which organizations may use for their information are records systems, correspondence and other files, libraries, and follow-up systems" (Simon, 1957, pp. 166–167).

12. Prescott and Visscher's (1980) concept of organizational capital includes not only information on employees' suitability for particular tasks and information on employees' ability to work as a team with particular fellow employees but also firm-specific human capital vested in individual employees.

13. Again, although he didn't go further in the analysis, Becker (1962, p. 18) recognizes that firms' expenditures to acquire information on employees are a firm-specific investment. Moreover, "[firms] try to increase their knowledge [of new employees] in various ways—testing, rotation among departments, trial and error, etc.—for greater knowledge permits a more efficient utilization of manpower" (p. 18). Becker also includes, as human capital, firms' accumulation of information as a result of "time employed in interviewing, testing, checking references ... " of prospective employees (p. 18).

14. The informant was my cousin. Having worked in the same Ford plant as a college student during three summers and having recently learned much about Japanese management, I felt particularly able to appreciate the impact of this change.

REFERENCES

Alchian, Armen A. and Harold Demsetz, "Production, Information Costs, and Economic Organization," *American Economic Review*, 62 (December 1972), 777–795.

Argyris, Chris, *Integrating the Individual and the Organization.* New York: John Wiley, 1964.

Argyris, Chris, *Understanding Organization Behavior.* Homewood, IL: Dorsey Press, 1960.

Becker, Gary S., "Investment in Human Capital: A Theoretical Analysis," *Journal of Political Economy,* 50 (October 1962 Supplement), 9–49.

Becker, Gary S., *Human Capital: A Theoretical and Empirical Analysis, With Special Reference to Education.* New York: Columbia University Press, 1964.

Blake, Robert R., Warren E. Avis, and Jane S. Mouton, *Corporate Darwinism: An Evolutionary Perspective on Organizing Work in the Dynamic Corporation.* Houston: Gulf Publishing Co., 1966.

Blaug, Mark, "The Empirical Status of Human Capital Theory: A Slightly Jaundiced Survey," *Journal of Economic Literature,* 14 (September 1976), 827–855.

Chandler, Alfred D., Jr., *Strategy and Structure: Chapters in the History of the Industrial Enterprise.* Cambridge, MA: M.I.T. Press, 1962.

Child, I.L., "Socialization," in G. Lindzey, ed., *Handbook of Social Psychology,* Vol. II. Cambridge, MA: Addison-Wesley, 1954.

Clark, Rodney, *The Japanese Company.* New Haven: Yale University Press, 1979.

Ellerman, David P., "Entrepreneurship in the Mondragon Cooperatives." Paper presented at the Association of Social Economics Conference on the Community Dimension of Economic Enterprise, Milwaukee, June 11, 1984.

Faxen, Karl-Olof. "Disembodied Technical Progress: Does Employee Participation in Decision Making Contribute to Change and Growth?" *American Economic Review,* 68 (May 1978), 131–134.

Galbraith, Jay, *Designing Complex Organizations.* Reading, MA: Addison-Wesley, 1973.

Galbraith, Jay, *Organization Design.* Reading, MA: Addison-Wesley, 1977.

Gerth, H.H. and C. Wright Mills, *From Max Weber: Essays in Sociology.* New York: Oxford University Press, 1958.

Jensen, Michael C. and William H. Meckling, "Rights and Production Functions: An Application to Labor-managed Firms and Codetermination," *Journal of Business,* 52 (October 1979), 469–506.

Kotter, John P., "The Psychological Contract: Managing the Joining-Up Process," *California Management Review,* 15 (Spring 1973), 91–99.

Kotter, John P. and Leonard A. Schlesinger, "Choosing Strategies for Change," *Harvard Business Review,* 57 (March–April 1979), 106–114.

Leibenstein, Harvey, *Beyond Economic Man: A New Foundation for Microeconomics.* Cambridge, MA: Harvard University Press, 1976.

Marshall, Alfred, *Principles of Economics.* New York: Macmillan, 1961.

Nadler, David A., J. Richard Hackman, and Edward E. Lawler, *Managing Organizational Behavior.* Boston: Little, Brown and Co., 1979.

Ouchi, William G., *Theory Z: How American Business Can Meet the Japanese Challenge.* Reading, MA: Addison-Wesley, 1981.

Ouchi, William G. and Raymond L. Price, "Hierarchies, Clans and Theory Z: A New Perspective on Organization Development," *Organizational Dynamics* (Autumn 1978), 25–44.

Pascale, Richard T. and Anthony G. Athos, *The Art of Japanese Management: Applications for American Executives.* New York: Simon and Schuster, 1981.

Peters, Thomas J. and Robert H. Waterman, *In Search of Excellence: Lessons from America's Best-Run Companies.* New York: Harper and Row, 1982.

Porter, Lyman W., Edward E. Lawler, and J. Richard Hackman, *Behavior in Organizations.* New York: McGraw-Hill, 1975.

Prescott, Edward C. and Michael Visscher, "Organizational Capital," *Journal of Political Economy,* 88 (June 1980), 446–461.

Reynolds, Lloyd G., *Labor Economics and Labor Relations*, 8th ed. Englewood Cliffs, NJ: Prentice-Hall, 1982.

Schein, Edgar H. "Organizational Socialization and the Profession of Management," *Industrial Management Review*, 9 (1968), 1–15.

Schumpeter, Joseph A., *The Theory of Economic Development: An Inquiry into Profits, Capital, Credit, Interest and the Business Cycle.* New York: Oxford University Press, 1961.

Shen, T.Y., "Technology and Organizational Economics," in Paul C. Nystrom, and William H. Starbuck, eds., *Handbook of Organization Design, Volume 1, Adapting Organizations to their Environments.* Oxford: Oxford University Press, 1981.

Simon, Herbert A., *Administrative Behavior: A Study of Decision-Making Processes in Administrative Organization.* New York: The Free Press, 1957.

Sobel, Irvin, "Human Capital and Institutional Theories of the Labor Market: Rivals or Complements?" *Journal of Economic Issues*, 16 (March 1982), 255–272.

Taylor, Frederick W., *The Principles of Scientific Management.* New York: Harper, 1911.

Tomer, John F., "Organizational Change, Organizational Capital and Economic Growth," *The Eastern Economic Journal*, 7 (January 1981), 1–14.

Tomer, John F., "Productivity Through Cooperation: The Role of Japanese and Gandhian Development Strategies." Unpublished paper presented at the Third World Congress of Social Economics, Fresno, California, August 18, 1983.

Tomer, John F., "Working Smarter the Japanese Way: The X-Efficiency of Theory Z Management," in Paul Kleindorfer, ed., *The Management of Productivity and Technology in Manufacturing.* New York: Plenum, 1985.

Tomer, John F., "Management Consulting for Private Enterprise: A Theoretical and Empirical Analysis of the Contribution of Management Consultants to Economic Growth in the United States." Unpublished Ph.D. Dissertation, Rutgers University, 1973.

Williamson, Oliver E. "Hierarchical Control and Optimum Firm Size," *Journal of Political Economy*, 75 (April 1967), 123–138.

Williamson, Oliver E. *Corporate Control and Business Behavior.* Englewood Cliffs, NJ: Prentice-Hall, 1970.

Section C

Extra-Firm Considerations in Productivity

INTRODUCTION TO SECTION C:
EXTRA-FIRM CONSIDERATIONS IN
PRODUCTIVITY

The two papers in this section relate to the issue of productivity. The analysis presented, however, involves factors that are typically left outside the realm of the neoclassical analysis of the firm.

Filer's paper relates effort level to motivation and other psychological variables. Both his and Frantz's paper highlight behavioral economics' awareness that production functions need more than quantities of factor inputs to be valid. We must be concerned with the broader picture of human decision making, its complex motivational determinants, the role of perception, and the effect of economic and noneconomic variables on decisions. The framework employed goes beyond crude maximizing, and the result is a richer model of choice—in this case, choices about the level of effort to invest on the job.

The second paper, by Amyra Grossbard-Shechtman, starts out by noting the wage differentials that exist between married and single men and married and single women. In the paper, Grossbard-Shechtman then goes beyond the traditional human capital explanations of wage differentials and points out the additional insights that can be gained from the sociological and marriage and family literature. She gives a hint of the complexity of the questions of productivity, labor supply, and wage determination. One of the paper's most interesting suggestions is that the wife represents an unhired factor of production who is not paid directly but whose productivity is reflected in the higher earnings of the husband. A series of hypotheses is presented to test this argument.

PEOPLE AND PRODUCTIVITY:
EFFORT SUPPLY AS VIEWED BY
ECONOMISTS AND PSYCHOLOGISTS

Randall K. Filer

The issue of productivity has captured much attention in the public consciousness over the past several years. Beginning about 1970, the rate of growth of total factor productivity appeared to decline from its historic level of between two and three percent per year to a substantially lower value. The causes for this decline have been the subject of much debate and hand wringing by both economists and the general public. The potential candidates are far too numerous to discuss here. For a general introduction to this literature, the reader is referred to Nelson (1981) and Maital and Meltz (1981). In general, the work by economists in this area has taken the form of "accounting" studies in which recorded rates of productivity growth are attributed to various components, including changes in input composition and quality as well as technological change.

A parallel literature has developed among industrial psychologists investigating intrafirm strategies that might be followed by individual employers in order to increase productivity (defined as the quantity of output produced by a given number of workers using a given technology). Among such strategies are an attempt to hire a different mix of workers better suited to the job at hand (better use of recruitment and selection procedures), the reorganization of work assignments given to current workers (job redesign), and alteration of incentive structures in order to induce more effort from a given pool of workers (motivation). While these aspects of overall productivity levels are obviously only a small component of the entire picture, they are enormously important and are related to work done by economists.

There is an economic literature on optimal job matching (see, e.g., Carol and Parry, 1968), as well as the structure of work assignments within the firm (see Furobotn, 1976). It should be noted, however, that the ability of an individual firm to increase its labor productivity by hiring a different mix of workers is not tantamount to an inefficiency in the economy. If the original sorting of workers and jobs was optimal, then such an action on the part of one firm must result in a more than offsetting decrease in productivity for the rest of the economy. Thus the link between this aspect of the industrial psychological research and economy-wide productivity is somewhat tenuous. On the other hand, if productivity can be increased by either job redesign or alteration of incentive structures in a way that more than compensates for the costs involved, then clearly both aggregate productivity and economic efficiency have been increased. Indeed, these motivation aspects may provide an insight into the most frustrating result of traditional accounting studies: namely, the presence of an unexplained "residual" even after a seemingly comprehensive set of measurable factors have been taken into account.

The reason for this link is straightforward. All measures of productivity, whether of labor productivity or total factor productivity, define labor input as "hours paid for." Sometimes this measure is adjusted for the discrepancy between hours paid for and hours worked—a discrepancy caused by break time, sick leave, vacations, and so on—but it is never adjusted to take into account the fact that simply being present in the workplace is not enough to produce output. Workers must actually *work* for production to take place.

Working is something that can be undertaken with varying degrees of intensity. A worker devoting maximum possible effort and energy to his or her job will typically produce more output than an otherwise identical worker using the same capital but only "going through the motions" of doing the job. If, over time, the amount of energy and effort devoted to his or her job by the average worker declines, measured productivity (whether calculated as labor productivity or total factor productivity) will decline, because less output will be produced for each measured unit of labor input (each hour worked). In reality, since other factors such as technological change are typically responsible for continually increasing levels of productivity, such a shift in effort provided will show up as a reduced rate of productivity growth from that which one would expect to find on the basis of measured changes in inputs (a negative "unexplained residual," in accounting studies).

Indeed, Kendrick (1980) finds such an unexplained residual of be-

tween −.4 and −.6 percentage points a year and states: "We interpret
the residual as reflecting chiefly changes in the rates of actual to potential
labor efficiency at given levels of technology" (p. 16). Elsewhere (Kendrick, 1976), he has stated: "The degree of labor efficiency relative to
realizable standards or 'norms' affects productivity. Changes in efficiency, so defined, as revealed by work measurement should seem largely
to depend on motivational factors...." (p. 5).

Paul Samuelson has been reported as counting a "weakness of the
hungriness motives" as a major reason for the slowdown in the rate of
economic growth throughout the industrial world during the 1970s,
while Herbert Stein has talked about the effects of "me generation attitudes" on worker behavior. Harvard sociologist David Riesman has
spoken about the spread of the "counterculture" into the workplace as
damaging productivity through the erosion of discipline and a decline
in care and attention to jobs.[1]

There is a limited amount of quantitative evidence regarding the decline in worker effort during the 1970s. Research on effort dimensions
of labor supply has been seriously hampered by lack of objective measures of workers' effort outputs. This has led to most of the work in the
field being based on highly subjective impressions and to the decision
by many economists that the problems are too intractable, leading them
to ignore the area in empirical studies. However, one data collection
effort did ask a question that may give some insight into the changing
willingness to supply effort over time. The Survey Research Center of
the University of Michigan conducted national surveys on the quality of
employment in 1969, 1972, and 1977. In each of these surveys workers
were asked how true they felt the following statement was: "On my job
I am not asked to do excessive amounts of work." If one pays careful
attention to the negative wording of this statement, it can be seen that
a "False" answer implies that the worker feels he or she is being asked
to work too hard (i.e., that the amount of effort demanded by the job
exceeds some internal reference standard regarding what is "too hard").
Similarly, a "True" answer means that the worker feels comfortable with
the amount of effort required. Over time, the proportion of the work
force answering with strong agreement ("True" responses) has continually decreased, while strong negative responses have continually risen.[2]
Assuming there has been no change in workers' willingness to answer
the question honestly, this pattern of results is consistent with one or
both of two explanations. Either workers' internal reference standards
regarding an appropriate amount of effort were falling or the amount
of effort in the typical job was increasing. It would seem that in an age
of rapid technological advance and automation, the latter cannot be the
sole explanation for this consistent trend. Thus we are led to conclude

that it is likely that workers at the end of the decade were less willing to "work hard" than they were at its beginning.[3]

Recent survey evidence indicates that between two thirds and three fourths of all working Americans believe that people do not work as hard on jobs today as they did a decade ago and that work motivations are not as strong today as they were ten years ago (see Yankelovich and Immerwahr, 1983; and Louis Harris Associates and Amitai Etzioni 1981). Yankelovich and Immerwahr claim that the difference between the time workers actually worked and the time they were paid for increased by 10 percent between 1965 and 1975, and that the evidence indicates that American workers are not putting out their full effort to do their jobs well.

There has been a relatively unviolated division of labor between economists and psychologists with respect to the study of labor supply. Economists have focused almost exclusively on hours worked, while psychologists have dealt with the effort provided while on the job. Unfortunately, in this case, division of labor has not increased output but rather has resulted in an unnecessary neglect of important connections that may have seriously hampered our ability to understand an important economic question. There was an awareness of the close connection between economics and psychology at an earlier stage of the development of both disciplines (see Dickinson, 1922), but in recent years the study of these links has been limited. One notable example of an attempt by a well-known psychologist to apply concepts of motivation developed in this field to explain an economic phenomenon is McClelland's work on development (1961).

This essay attempts to persuade economists to take seriously questions of the supply of effort provided by workers while actually on the job. The next section summarizes previous work by economists in this area. The two following sections present a very brief summary of the far larger body of work by industrial and organizational psychologists dealing with motivation and effort in employment settings and an attempt to point out the interconnections among these several strains of analysis. The final section concludes by attempting to draw some lessons for economists from the work found in the psychological literature. The reference list includes only those works cited plus a limited sampling of additional relevant works.

I. EFFORT AS VIEWED BY ECONOMISTS

It is somewhat surprising that effort expended on the job has not received more attention from economists. Given its theoretical import, one suspects that the subject has been shortchanged as a result of the difficulty in carrying out empirical studies due to an inability to gather accurate measures of worker effort. This difference between theoretical importance and empirical analysis can be seen in the fact that one of the most widely used labor economics textbooks (Hamermesh and Rees, 1984) includes effort as one of the four components of labor supply, giving it equal weight with labor-force participation decisions, hours-of-work decisions, and skills-acquisition decisions, while the definitive summary of empirical work dealing with labor supply (Killingsworth, 1983) does not mention effort once in its 480 pages and makes only a passing reference to the fact that the leisure variable "of the model refers to time spent not actually working, and therefore, in principle, includes time spent *at* work that is not devoted *to* work [which] pose[s] problems for empirical studies" (p. 2). Even here, however, the emphasis is on break time rather than variable effort expenditures during actual work periods.

There does exist some work by economists that attempts to analyze effort decisions. Perhaps the best known is that by Leibenstein (1976). His concept of X-Inefficiency is based on the fact that effort is under the control of individual workers and is typically not specified in employment contracts. Leibenstein's work involves some subtle modifications of maximization theory. In very simplified terms, however, he defines *economic efficiency* as occurring when labor inputs measured in terms of hours produce the maximum amount they are capable of producing; that is, when effort is at its output maximizing level. Anything less than this is a form of inefficiency. It is argued that workers will always have an incentive to and a capability of introducing such an inefficiency into their employment situation. The key point is that they explicitly regard effort as a variable under their control. Its determinants, however, are not regarded as the typical economic variables such as wages or working conditions but rather as being grounded in interpersonal relationships on the job. For a full development of this theory, the reader is referred to Leibenstein (1976).

There is also some analysis of effort supply in a more neoclassical vein. Among such studies are those of Stafford and Cohen (1974); Levin, Saunders, and Ulph (1975); Brown, Levin, and Ulph (1976); Tomer (1981); Filer (1984); and Becker (1985). All these studies start with a similar modification of the typical labor supply model that has a great deal of intuitive appeal. Conventionally, individual utilities have been regarded as functions of leisure time and consumption of goods. Implicitly, this means that utility levels are connected with an employee's job only through the income provided by that job and the time the job occupies. What actually takes place *during* the 30 to 50 percent of an individual's waking hours that he or she actually spends working can have no influence on his or her psychic happiness or satisfaction (utility). Even on its surface this is an absurd assertion. It has sometimes been modified by allowing consumption that takes place on the job to be related to utility levels (typically through the introduction of the concept of compensating differentials), but only rarely by explicitly recognizing that a worker who taxes herself or himself with strenuous effort expenditures is likely to be less happy than one who is working at a far more relaxed pace. Thus the appropriate utility function expresses utility as a function of leisure (1), consumption off the job (c), consumption while at work (working conditions [j]), and ease of pace (lack of effort [r]):

$$U = U(l, c, j, r)$$

The presence of compensating differentials implies that choices with respect to working conditions are reflected in wage rates and therefore enter into the individual's budget constraint. Given that there is a link between increased effort supplied and increased output, marginal productivity theory requires that wages be a positive function of effort (a negative function of workers' decisions to "take it easy"). Thus effort decisions are also reflected in the budget constraint. From this point on, the solution of the model is conventional.[4] What is generated are four demand equations for leisure (which implies hours worked), consumption of market goods, consumption of working conditions, and ease of pace (leisure on the job, which implies effort supplied) as functions of the individual's stock of human capital, the price of market goods, the price of working conditions (the magnitude of the compensating differentials), and the price of increased ease of work (in terms of foregone wages).

There are few empirical studies based on this framework. Here the difficulty presented by the inability to measure effort becomes paramount. Levin, Saunders, and Ulph (1975) are reduced to using, as an effort measure, a dummy variable indicating a positive response to the question: "Do you think your bonus system makes you work harder?"[5] Even so, they found that "despite the poor data on effort, the effort variables significantly improve the explanation of hours of work" (p. 24). In addition, effort itself was shown to be significantly determined by conventional economic variables.

Filer (1984) used a somewhat more satisfying measure of effort based on self-reporting of individual effort relative to the maximum possible amount of effort to estimate a model close to the one outlined above.[6] Results of this study showed that effort decisions were strongly related to conventional economic variables. Both nonlabor income and exogenous wage levels (purged of the effect of effort on wages implied by marginal productivity considerations) have a negative effect on effort expended while on the job. Given that offsetting income and substitution effects create a theoretical uncertainty about the direction of the effect of wages on effort (Pencavel, 1977), this says income effects dominate substitution effects, and increasing wages may result in reduced effort levels. Furthermore, the results indicated that estimates of the response of hours worked to changes in wage rates may have been seriously biased in previous studies and that this relationship may be far more negative than previously supposed. Finally, the results indicated that there is a substantial degree of substitutability of ease of work for leisure in the typical worker's utility function. Thus, researchers interested in the determinants of Labor supply should be warned that ignoring an important part of such supply may seriously handicap their investigations.

It is clear from the limited number of studies cited above that almost all of the investigation of effort expended by workers on the job has been carried out by industrial psychologists. It is to these studies that we now turn.

II.   EFFORT AS VIEWED BY PSYCHOLOGISTS

The study of effort expended on the job falls under the heading of motivation. Indeed, work motivation is a subset of the much larger field of motivation in general. We will limit our analysis to this subset as it has been formulated by industrial and organizational psychologists. In doing this we will consciously be excluding some less relevant but perhaps peripherally related areas of psychology.[7]

Theories of work motivation are numerous and have been extensively summarized in several places. Among these are Campbell and Pritchard (1976), Staw (1977), and Mitchell (1979; 1982). Therefore, we will limit the discussion that follows to an introductory summary of some of the major theories, with an emphasis on the aspects that are related to work effort as it would be viewed by conventional labor economists.

Motivation deals with both arousal to action and the direction and persistence of that action. Thus Campbell and Pritchard (1976) define motivation as

a label for the determinants of (a) the choice to initiate effort on a certain task, (b) the choice to expend a certain amount of effort, and (c) the choice to persist in expending effort over a period of time. That is, motivation has to do with a set of independent/dependent variable relationships that explain the direction, amplitude, and persistence of an individual's behavior, holding constant the affects of aptitude, skill, and understanding of the task, and the constraints operating in the environment (p. 65).

Mitchell (1982) presents a similar definition, calling motivation "those psychological processes that cause the arousal, direction, and persistence of voluntary actions that are goal directed" (p. 81).

Theories of motivation can be broadly divided into two classes: *content* theories and *process* theories. Content theories deal with the identification of those variables that influence behavior and pay little attention to the means by which this influence is achieved. Process theories focus on the mechanism by which desires are translated into actions. Process theories tend to be less deterministic and more probabilistic than are content theories. Thus "expectancy" plays a major role in these theories. These two theoretical approaches are rooted in different traditions, with content theorists taking their cue from the clinical approach and process theorists being more strongly grounded in the tradition of experimental psychology. As will become obvious in the discussion that follows, theorists in these two traditions are rather like the blind men describing the elephant, with each focusing only on a part of a more complex overall picture.

A. Content Theories

Most content theories are some form of "need"-based theory of motivation. As such, they are derived from the concept of needs as presented by Murray (1938). Basing his arguments on clinical observations, he hypothesized the existence of over twenty specific needs that human beings attempt to satisfy with their actions. Motivation to undertake an action occurs because an individual can at least partially meet one or more of these needs by taking that action.

In 1954, Maslow postulated that human needs fall into a well-ordered hierarchy of several levels. He believed that needs at one level must be largely satisfied or met before the individual would attend to those at a higher level. Thus at any one time not all needs have an equal ability to motivate an individual's behavior. In addition, different needs motivate behavior for different individuals, even in the same work setting.

The hierarchy proposed by Maslow contains five categories. In order of decreasing potency these are:

1. *Physiological needs*, or the need for food, water, sex, and so on.
2. *Safety needs*, or the need for security and freedom from bodily threat.
3. *Social needs*, or the need for belongingness, friendship, affection, and love.
4. *Esteem needs*, or the need for both self-respect and the respect of others.

5. *Self-actualization needs*, or the drive to achieve fulfillment of one's goals and potentials. (This is obviously the hardest of the levels to define both conceptually and operationally.)

Although Maslow states that each individual in society should be partially satisfied in all levels of needs and never totally satisfied in any of them, he believes that everyone will act so as always to be more satisfied in the lower-order needs (such as physiological and safety needs) than in the higher-order ones (such as self-actualization). This hierarchical behavior makes a good deal of intuitive sense. Imagine an individual recently shipwrecked on a South Sea island. One suspects that the first thing he would do is find sources of food and water (physiological needs), then build a shelter against wild animals and the elements (safety needs). After these are done, he might devote his actions to searching the island for signs of other human inhabitants (social needs). Only after these things had been done would he be likely to sit back and be proud of his ability to survive (self-esteem) and contemplate what he should do with his life in order to become self-actualized.

Alderfer (1972) reformulated Maslow's hierarchy into three basic categories called existence needs, relatedness needs, and growth needs. His theory is often identified from the initials of these three categories as the ERG model. Existence needs are similar to Maslow's physiological needs and are those needs for physical substances that are in limited supply, such as food, clothing, or shelter. Relatedness needs involve the social aspects of human intercourse such as love and communication. Growth needs are similar to Maslow's self-actualization need and are just as difficult to identify precisely. Although the need categories are similar to Maslow's, Alderfer places less emphasis on the hierarchical aspect of the categories. He seems to believe that all three categories must be met for an individual to be content with his or her environment. Alderfer does, however, recognize that existence needs are easier both to identify and to provide for than relatedness or growth needs. Thus these needs tend to be satisfied first.

Akin to the work of Maslow and Alderfer is that of both McGregor (1960) and Argyris (1957). McGregor indicates that human beings may be broadly divided into two types: those who are primarily motivated by a desire to satisfy lower-level needs (called Type X) and those who are self-motivated and seek self-actualization (called Type Y). There is no implication of superiority of one type over the other in McGregor's work (although such an implication frequently seems to exist in the works of those who have attempted to apply it). The point is that Type X individuals will be primarily motivated by external incentives, while Type Y people will be motivated by the work itself. Obviously, the structure of jobs and rewards that will elicit greatest productivity will differ between these two types. Argyris further postulates that the natural course of human development is to progress toward "maturation," defined as increased activity, independence, awareness of and control over self, aspiration for superior (or at least equal) position, and the development of long-range perspectives. Again, the inherent hierarchy of Maslow is reasserted, as well as an implicit "value" judgment.

The final major need-based theory of motivation is the two-factor theory of Herzberg (Herzberg, Mausner, and Snyderman, 1959; and Herzberg, 1966). On the basis of in-depth interviews on the subject of job satisfaction, Herzberg postulated that rewards could be divided into two classes: external (labeled hygienes) and internal (labeled motivators). Among the hygienes (external factors) are such things as pay, job security, physical working conditions, company policies, human relations (especially with one's supervisor), and technical supervision. Among the motivators (internal factors) are achievement, recognition, advancement, and responsibility.

Actually, Herzberg and co-workers were concerned with satisfaction as well as motivation. It was their claim that the absence of hygiene factors would produce dissatisfaction, but that once these needs had been met, their further provision would not increase an individual's satisfaction level. On the other hand, workers would not become dissatisfied even in the absence of motivators, but only increased motivators could increase satisfaction levels. Admittedly, this is a somewhat artificial division between "satisfaction" and "dissatisfaction," and Herzberg never makes clear how concepts that are opposite poles of a continuous scale can be cleanly divided.

In part, this artificial distinction may have come about because of methodological problems with the original study. The data were gathered through the use of "critical-incident" reports. In this technique workers were asked to recall times when they were particularly satisfied or dissatisfied on their jobs. It seems, however, that a basic feature of human nature is to assign blame to others while claiming credit for positive outcomes ourselves. This phenomenon is technically known as attribution bias. A reexamination of the Herzberg methodology and its results suggests that the distinct dichotomy produced is likely to be due to such biases (see Farr, 1977). All the negative incidents were attributed by workers to causes outside their control, such as pay or supervision, while all the positive events were believed to be due to their own actions, such as task achievement. Thus, even though two-factor theory has come to have a wide influence among managers, providing much of the basis for the movement toward "job enrichment,"[8] there appears to be serious scientific doubt as to the validity of the entire construct. Indeed, it has proven to be impossible to recreate Herzberg's dichotomy without using critical-incident techniques and easy to do so when they are used.

In the work environment, need-based theories imply that an individual's actions (especially how well he carries out his work assignments) are determined by how well completion of those assignments satisfies the needs that are uppermost in his or her attention at that time. Thus an employer who wants to increase effort should determine an individual's need status and provide rewards for effort that would satisfy those needs. Individuals who are still primarily dealing with lower-level needs might best be motivated by providing them with increased money (with which they could buy food or housing), but those for whom these needs had already largely been met would be most strongly motivated by recognition and the chance for accomplishment (thus bolstering their self-esteem and self-actualization).

To the extent that the individual and the society associate self-worth with income, added monetary rewards may also help to satisfy these needs. Perhaps this helps to explain the extensive reliance on money as a motivator. It alone, among all possible rewards, can contribute toward the satisfaction of all levels of needs, thereby at least reducing the importance of correctly identifying an employee's current need status. There is evidence from a number of different industries and countries that linking monetary rewards with output can lead to high productivity levels. In their survey of productivity-enhancing experiments in the United States, Guzzo and Bondy (1983) found that "financial compensation is an effective way of elevating productivity" (p. 24). This result held for a wide variety of situations, including several where it might be assumed that workers' lower-level needs had been largely satisfied.

There is also evidence that the structure of any potential needs hierarchy may differ across easily identifiable groups (such as those from various socioeconomic classes) in ways beyond simple differences in the extent to which higher-level needs have been called into play by the satisfaction of lower-level needs (see Friedlander, 1965). Thus, while individuals may have similar structures of their utility functions, the actual functions seem to differ. Economists often attempt to deal with this issue through the incorporation of demographic variables in estimating equations. To the extent that differences in utility functions are related to observed demographic variables, such a procedure may be useful. However, methods generally used to incorporate such variables are highly restrictive in the assumptions they require regarding the ways in which utility functions differ.

Although the concept of need hierarchies has met with wide acceptance among practicing managers, it seems to have lost favor among theorists in recent years. In part this may be due to difficulties in obtaining empirical support for these theories (see Salancik and Pfeffer, 1977). In part it may also be the result of the circularity of the concept. There are some basic needs where one might hope to observe changes in physiological states, but in most cases the only evidence that something is a "need" is that people seem to want to satisfy it. Thus unless one wants to infer a "need" for everything a person does (for example, a need to watch television), structure must be imposed on behavior externally and without any possibility of empirical verification. Just how needs are defined is inherently a subjective judgment. The requirement that needs can only be inferred from behaviors that are then, in a circular manner, interpreted as satisfying these needs seems to bother psychologists but should not be too disturbing to economists used to dealing with utility functions and revealed-preference theory.

In summary, needs-based theories of motivation seem to end up by telling us that individuals are motivated to seek certain things that can provide them with satisfaction by fulfilling some inner need. This need may be either instinctive or learned. The more a need is satisfied, the less important it becomes in motivating behavior. To an economist, this sounds suspiciously like saying that individuals have utility functions that exhibit diminishing marginal returns to consumption of any given item and that there are differing degrees of substitutability among items such that identifiable groups of commodities (that satisfy "needs") emerge. In this context it is interesting to note that the literature on two-stage demand systems (derived from strongly separable utility functions) frequently differentiates these stages as being related to various different "needs" (see, for example, Gorman, 1976). However, it is important to realize that much of the discussion in the psychological literature on needs has focused on psychic and mental areas rather than the strictly physical needs that have been the province of consumer economics.

B. Process Theories

Process theories are sometimes known as cognitive theories of motivation and tend to focus on the expectations people have regarding what is likely to happen in the future if they follow a particular course of action in the present. These theories are based on the work of Lewin (1938) and Tolman (1932), who held that people have expectations regarding the outcomes of their actions and that they have preferences among these possible outcomes. Thus individuals will make choices about current actions based on both the attractiveness of possible outcomes and their relative probability of occurrence. This idea forms the basis for what is currently the most influential theory of motivation—expectancy, or VIE, theory.

Expectancy theory was outlined by Vroom (1964) and attempts to predict both choices among various possible activities (tasks) and choices with respect to the amount of effort expended on those tasks undertaken. These choices are based on two factors: the valence or attractiveness of possible outcomes and the expectancy or belief that a behavior (chosen task and effort level) will lead to the possible outcomes. In between actual task performance and eventual outcomes may lie intervening or intermediate outcomes. These are called instruments, and the relationship they have to the final, desired outcomes is referred to as instrumentality. Thus an individual may believe (perhaps not even consciously) that by increasing effort on the job, he or she will produce more widgets per hour and that this will have two results. First, the person's productivity will increase, leading the employer to pay that worker more. Second, co-workers may come to regard the person as a "rate- buster" and shun him or her at lunch breaks. The eventual decision about whether or not to provide added effort will depend on the perceived value of added pay relative to the experienced "pain" of co-worker resentment (the relative valences), the perceived probabilities that each of these would result from added output (that is, how likely are both the employer and the co-workers to notice and respond to the added output—the expectancies), and finally, the extent to which added effort can produce added output (instrumentality).

Using the initial letters of the three primary concepts in the model (valence, instrumentality, and expectancy), the label VIE theory has been attached to this formulation of motivational theory. One can conceive of a decision tree in which there are several possible, mutually exclusive courses of action. Each action is expected to lead with some probability to each of several possible outcomes, which will, in turn, lead with some probability to desired rewards or undesired punishments. By attaching numerical values to each of the possible rewards and punishments, and numerical combination (and there are several suggestions in the literature as to how to do this) it should be possible to calculate the course of action with the highest satisfaction value attached to its expected outcome(s).

Economists will immediately note that this process may require the existence of cardinal utility levels (here called valences). There is no problem with the theoretical construct as long as it relies on subjective utility functions defined over probabilities of world states. However, when specific decision rules such as "Choose the branch with the highest expected utility" are introduced, calculation becomes impossible without an assumption of cardinality. In addition, there are serious problems with any attempt at empirical verification, since measurement of valences will be impossible.

In addition, it is worth noting that VIE theory is explicitly ahistorical. An individual's past history of choices and the consequences arising from those choices are not incorporated into current actions. As formulated by Vroom, VIE theory does not go into how possible outcomes acquire associated valences. These are taken as givens, although Vroom notes that if the perceived valences of a number of outcomes are highly correlated and an individual responds similarly to all of them, they might be regarded as a need.

Thus, in order to motivate performance under VIE theory, a manager should discover what outcomes (rewards) are most valued by a given worker and how likely that worker thinks such outcomes are as a result of the desired actions. Manipulation of either outcomes or their perceived probability of occurrence should result in altered behavior.[9]

Other versions of expectancy theory have been proposed by Graen (1969) and Porter and Lawler (1968). Graen starts with Vroom's basic model and incorporates the effects of social pressures and the internal drive for superior performance. Thus Graen asserts that effort occurs not only because it might result in increased performance that leads to desired outcomes such as recognition and more pay but also because both society and human nature create pressures for high performance *for its own sake.* Thus the amount of effort provided is a function of all three of these factors.

Porter and Lawler modified Vroom's basic theory by dropping the ahistorical assumption and by using continuous rather than discrete forms for both effort and outcomes. Continuous formulation changes nothing of consequence. The incorporation of feedback loops, however, is a major change. Individuals are assumed to alter their perceived effort/reward contingencies as the result of observation of actual outcomes. Thus reinforcement affects cognition, a process we might call learning. This relationship provides a link to the work of behavioral psychologists. The second feedback process postulated by Porter and Lawler involves the effects on perceived satisfaction that would be derived from a particular reward by past satisfaction of that reward. If this relationship is negative, we are in a world where satisfaction of a need reduces its importance as a motivator (as with Maslow's theory). On the other hand, it is possible that experience with certain rewards increases their valence (habit or addiction).

Finally, there is some research (see, for example, Atkinson, 1957) that suggests that relationships in the VIE framework are not monotonic. Rather, the degree of effort workers expend rises with the probability that increased effort will lead to desired rewards until a certain point where the task becomes so "easy" that it ceases to be a challenge and reward achievement seems almost a certainty. Beyond this point effort will fall off with increasing probability of success. Thus neither a very high nor a very low probability of success will elicit much effort. As will be discussed below, individuals seem to have an inner desire to be successful, to have an effect on their environment. This might provide one explanation for the finding of nonmonotonicity. Situations where either failure or success is almost certain offer little opportunity to learn and improve one's skill level. Thus, if such increments are desired, situations with moderate probabilities of success should provoke the most effort.

Another addition to the basic expectancy theory model involves the influence of relative rewards. Called equity theory, this idea was developed in the context of motivation by Adams (1963a, 1963b). Equity theory finds its basis in the concept of cognitive dissonance. It is frequently asserted that human beings have a fundamental drive toward balance or consistency in their cognitions. When there is an imbalance, we experience "dissonance," or discomfort, and seek to restore balance or consistency by our actions. The dominant principle of Adams' equity theory is that we are motivated to maintain equality in the ratio between the amount of effort we exert and the outcomes it generates and the effort and outcomes of "others" who we feel are a relevant comparison group. Thus no matter what rewards are provided to an individual, if that person feels these rewards are in some sense less than those offered to others who are expending similar effort, he or she will feel dissonance and therefore reduce his or her own effort until "equity" is restored. Operationally, there seems to be great agreement about what individuals will do when they feel themselves to be underpaid, and, indeed, research seems to suggest that they do behave in this manner. On the other hand, results are less clear concerning reactions in cases of overpayment. Attribution bias suggests that people may be more likely to believe they deserve their overpayment, making empirical tests more difficult to devise.

There is an extensive literature that attempts to verify process models of motivation empirically.[10] These studies have been undertaken in a variety of settings (laboratory and field), using a variety of methods (manipulation and correlation) and a variety of measures of dependent variables (including job preference, rated effort, performance, and satisfaction). In general, the track record of these studies is not as positive as the widespread acceptance of the framework might lead one to believe it would be.

Typically, individual components of the framework (expectancies or valences) correlated at about the .2 to .3 level with outcome measures. The use of combinations of all three components as predictors increased these correlations only slightly. Even full models such as those of Graen or Porter and Lawler generated predictor/performance correlations with a maximum value of about .3. Highest correlations were obtained when self-rated effort was used as the dependent variable. With respect to equity theory, the results are somewhat ambiguous, with behavior in response to underpayment occurring in the manner the theory predicts but with no clear pattern emerging under schemes of overpayment.

We are led to ask why expectancy theory has been so difficult to verify empirically. Certainly a finding that it enables one to explain about 10 percent of the variation in performance cannot be considered a resounding success. Is this because of difficulties with the studies or fundamental flaws in the theory itself? There are sufficient problems with the studies that it seems unwise to insist on serious modification, at this point, of what appears intuitively to be a useful paradigm. Much of the difficulty in verifying the theory empirically may be the result of limitations inherent in the data. We have already alluded to the fact that *valence* is really another term for *cardinal utility*. Just as no economist expects that asking individuals the question "How many utils would you attach to a given world state?" and then correlating the answers with some other variable would generate high values, no psychologist is very surprised by low valence/performance correlations. This problem would carry over into the use of any variable that was constructed from valences and other components of the theory. Thus it should not be surprising that researchers have found expectancies to be better predictors than the balance of the model. At least expectancies can be measured, using an interval scale. Indeed, for this and other reasons, Schmidt (1973) suggests that using "weak" data with a very demanding theory may lead to seriously misleading results.

Other data problems may arise from the use of self-reports of vaguely understood concepts that may be only loosely related to the theoretical constructs. In addition, the theory is formulated in terms of *intra*individual behavior, yet most of the empirical work has been done using variations *across* individuals. Thus, without it being explicitly stated, an additional condition that all individuals have identical "utility functions" has been imposed. Economists are well aware of the difficulties this creates. Finally, it should be noted that the model is couched in terms of changes in the dependent variable as a result of changes in independent variables, but almost all the research has been done in terms of levels.

A more fundamental problem with the general model has to do with the fact that it is highly linear in its framework (or, at least, it is monotonic). Yet the world may not work this way. Reinforcement experiments have suggested that behavior is most strongly affected when reinforcement probabilities are positive but not approaching unity. Thus using expectancies in a model in a way that suggests that the partial derivative of performance with respect to expectancies always has a positive sign may not be correct. In addition, as we have seen when discussing need theories, the valence assigned to a given outcome may not be constant. Indeed, economists used to the idea of circular indifference curves may be willing to believe that valences may not even always have the same sign. Depending on the levels already provided, individuals may become satiated with any reward and may even find further units to be aversive.[11] One can imagine receiving so many compliments on one's work from supervisors that it becomes uncomfortable.

C. Intrinsic Motivation

Up to this point, we have been discussing extrinsic rewards that are provided by others to a worker at the end of a process of performance. One of the fastest-growing and exciting areas of motivational research is that of intrinsic motivation. Sometimes called effectance motivation, intrinsic motivation is another form of process motivation. It deals with satisfactions that are internally generated by the worker as a result of performing the task itself. One form of intrinsic motivation (Deci, 1975) focuses on the process of completing tasks rather than the goal of completing them. There are reinforcements that are intrinsic to the task itself and that are obtained, not at the end (as is the case even with Herzberg's intrinsic motivators), but during the doing of the task. Such reinforcements may be either physical or cognitive stimuli that the individual finds pleasurable while the task is being performed. For example, a logger may enjoy the physical feeling that comes from exercise while chopping wood.

In addition, there may be intrinsic motivation that is conditional on task accomplishment. White (1959) proposed that organisms derive pleasure simply from having an effect on the environment. In humans this means that pleasure can be obtained simply by increasing one's competence or ability to bring about changes in the environment. Thus a desire for the satisfaction of accomplishment *for its own sake* may motivate behaviors that are effective even in the absence of any externally administered rewards. Such internal rewards are teleological in that they can be achieved only at the successful completion of a task, but they are intrinsic in that they arise from the interaction between an individual and a task without any intervention by others. This concept is found in the work of Harter (1978) and is best illustrated by the "need for achievement" (in-Ach) of McClelland (1951) and McClelland et al. (1953).

For both these reasons, it is possible that a task may itself provide sufficient reinforcement to induce workers to undertake it even if there are no external rewards upon its completion. While in the past there was a recognition of the satisfaction that may accrue from a task itself, it has generally been assumed that internal motivation provided by the task and external motivation provided by need-satisfying rewards contingent on task accomplishment are "additive" in nature. Recent work (see Notz, 1975) has indicated that this may not necessarily be true. There seem to be instances when the addition of extrinsic rewards reduces the potency of intrinsic rewards. Indeed, in some cases this effect may be so large that it reduces overall performance when extrinsic rewards are increased. This seems to be most likely to occur when individuals are performing tasks for which attention to the process is crucial. What may be happening is that workers refocus their attention on the external rewards, thereby reducing the attention given to the internal rewards (which, since these rewards are inseparable from the production process, means that attention is focused away from this process). Some research suggests that extrinsic incentives may have a leveling effect on intrinsic motivation (McLoyd, 1979; Loveland and Olley, 1979). Thus, if intrinsic motivation for accomplishing a task is high, the addition of extrinsic motivators may reduce this motivation. On the other hand, if initial intrinsic motivation is low (people won't do the task for its own sake), the addition of extrinsic motivation may mean that workers will take added pleasure in the task itself, thus increasing their intrinsic motivation.

In reality, all the theories discussed so far (as well as the many we have had to omit because of space considerations) can explain a *part* of the motivation picture. In general, they are not mutually exclusive. The following section attempts to point out the interconnections among the several theories of motivation that have been presented.

III. TOWARD AN INTEGRATION

The connections between the areas discussed above can perhaps best be by referring to the schematic diagram shown in Figure 1. On this diagram underlying characteristics of individuals are contained in triangles, perceptions are found in circles, and concrete actions or states of the world are located in rectangles. Direct influences are shown by solid lines, while feedback loops are indicated by broken lines. Theory names and other notes in brackets serve to relate portions of the diagram to specific ideas discussed in the previous section.

Individuals start with a set of abilities and personality traits and a set

Figure 1. Schematic representation of motivation process.

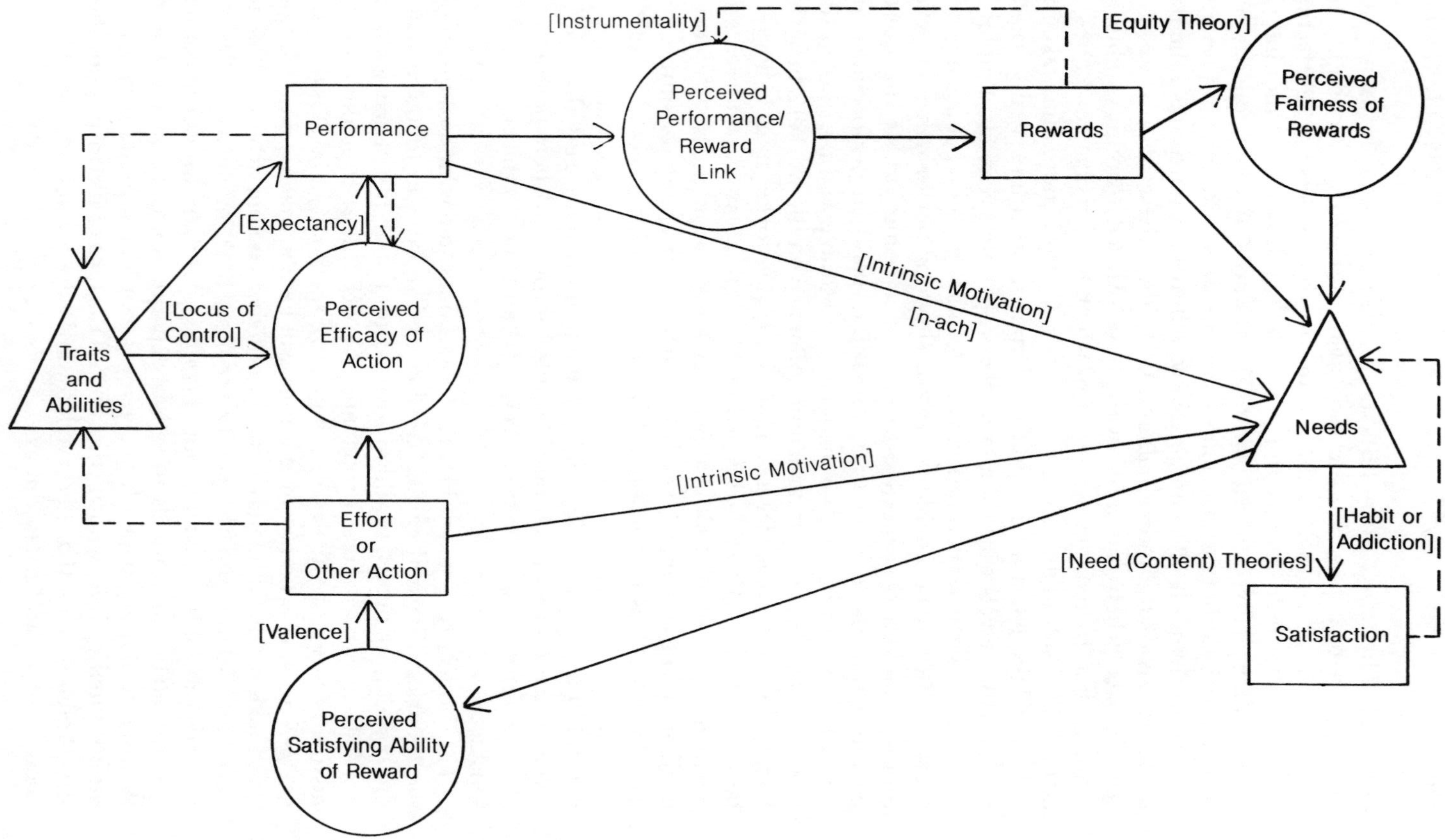

of needs. They seek to undertake a course of action (including how much effort to expend on their job) with an eye toward choosing the set of actions that provides them with the greatest level of satisfaction. The path that links actions and satisfaction is, however, somewhat circuitous. Satisfaction is a function of the rewards that may (or may not) be offered by others as a result of performance, the intrinsic rewards that performance itself generates, how well these rewards meet the particular needs of the individual, and how "fair" these rewards are perceived to be when compared with those offered to others. Thus an individual, in forming expectations of whether a possible new course of action will result in an increase in his or her satisfaction, must take into account all these factors. In addition, there is no guarantee that increased performance levels will result in workers obtaining rewards. Employers may judge performance with a considerable degree of inaccuracy, or they may simply be unable to reward superior performance (as when they are limited by collective bargaining agreements). If the worker perceives that there is only a minimal link between performance and rewards accruing to him, no matter how desirable and fair the possible rewards may be, they can have little influence on the worker's behavior. Finally, for there to be effective motivation, the worker must believe that he is capable of changing his actions in such a way as to increase his performance. Rotter (1966) has pointed out that individuals differ widely in their "locus of control," or belief about their ability to control their environment. If workers doubt that there is a link between their efforts and outputs, or if they believe that ability dominates other factors in determining output,[12] they will see little point in increasing their efforts levels, since there will be no substantial impact on their performance and therefore no increased rewards and no resulting increased satisfaction.

The model presented in Figure 1 points out some relationships among the theories discussed earlier. Maslow and those who followed him in the content, or needs, tradition focused on the ability of particular rewards to satisfy workers. Vroom and the VIE theorists pointed out that no matter how potentially satisfying the rewards might be, it is the worker's *perception* of whether or not they will be obtained as the result of a given action that ultimately determines whether that action will be undertaken. Adams and the equity theorists have made us realize that rewards cannot be evaluated out of context. Humans are social animals, and the ability of rewards to satisfy depends not only on the rewards themselves but on what they convey about one's position relative to others. Finally, those who have advanced the idea of intrinsic motivations have reminded us that observed rewards do not tell the whole story about why we do certain things.

IV. SUMMARY AND CONCLUSIONS

While the preceding survey of motivation as viewed by occupational and industrial psychologists is admittedly very brief, it does indicate some important factors that must be taken into account by economists who wish to deal with the supply of labor effort. In addition, many of these principles carry over into, and should influence, our understanding of economic decisions other than effort supply. Among the most important lessons for economists are:

1. The evidence indicates that effort supply is based on rational choices by workers and that these choices can be predicted using a model that is similar in feeling to the standard utility maximization model of economists. Hedonic self-interest (Bentham) governs valences as formulated by psychologists much as it determines the economist's concept of utility.
2. In addition to goods, other outcomes are important in determining overall satisfaction and therefore choices made to maximize satisfaction. In addition to wages, which can be transformed into consumer goods, workers value working conditions and psychic rewards. Indeed, much of the research suggests that consumer goods are used to satisfy lower-level needs and that these needs rapidly lose their ability to motivate once they have been addressed. This is to say that there is a strong psychological basis for an assumption of a deciding marginal utility of money. On the other hand, nonmonetary rewards do not seem to exhibit such a declining marginal utility. This suggests that as real incomes rise over time, models that are based on monetary factors will become less and less useful in predicting individual behavior as workers shift to attempting to satisfy those parts of their utility functions calling for "psychic" income. Economists have been notably lax in incorporating such factors into our models of consumer maximization.[13]
3. Incorporation of psychic factors into our models may be more difficult to do than simply adding another variable. Unlike physical outputs, which are limited in nature, psychic rewards may not be used up in distribution. Thus models of compensation are more cooperative than zero-sum games. In other words, many of the rewards that matter to individuals cannot be analyzed using traditional tools that focus on exchange processes (such as Edgeworth boxes). In addition, Maslow and others have postulated a quasi-lexicographic form for utility functions, in which "higher-order"

needs do not come into play until "lower-order" needs are substantially satiated.

4. VIE theory makes it very clear that it is individuals' expectations that matter when they determine their behavior. Unlike conventional economists, organizational psychologists have been unwilling to finesse this issue by assuming that all expectations are "rational." Indeed, consumer demand theory (including effort supply) may best be viewed in a Bayesian framework as probabilistic rather than deterministic in nature.

5. Relationships may not be monotonic in nature. Economists have long recognized that there may be satiation in levels of goods and that without free disposal, marginal utilities may even be negative. Now we must also deal with the concept that derivatives with respect to *probabilities* may also change sign. Increasing expectations of an outcome (increasing the expected value of the individual's utility-maximizing position) may or may not be associated with a greater supply of effort. This might roughly be translated as a realization that increased probabilities (of effort leading to better performance or of performance leading to rewards) have both income and substitution effects and that therefore the direction of their influence on choice behavior is uncertain.

6. The strong evidence in support of equity theories of motivation should serve as a warning to economists that we should not be too hasty in discarding either the "relative-income hypothesis" or Veblin effects. Much research indicates that individuals' utilities can be evaluated only in the context of the levels achieved by others. Obviously, this interdependence complicates modeling of consumer choice.

7. Finally, we must hold in mind the fact that utility functions may not be stable and are certainly not identical across individuals.

In summary, the economist concerned with discovering determinants of productivity levels may well find it useful to attempt to model workers' effort-supply decisions. Such decisions appear to exhibit a strong degree of rationality and may be modeled in a manner that is not too alien to neoclassical economists. However, these models will, of necessity, be more complex and interconnected than those we are used to dealing with. Fortunately, the territory is not uncharted and there is a good deal of relevant theoretical and empirical literature upon which we can draw. It is to be hoped that this essay will convince economists to expand the scope of the decisions we allow our consumers to make. Such expansion will not be easy, but the rewards will be great. As was pointed out above, there is a theoretical link between effort-supply decisions and other consumer choices such as hours of work and consumption. Proper modeling of effort choices will also improve our ability to understand these other areas. Without the incorporation of all these factors, we risk serious misinterpretation of any one of them.

ACKNOWLEDGMENTS

Karl Hill proved to be a reliable tour guide through much of the literature summarized. Additional useful comments on earlier drafts of this paper were provided by Michael Berbaum, Robert Filer, Arthur Lewbel, and David Purdy. Any remaining errors (either of commission or omission) are, of course, the responsibility of the author.

NOTES

1. These and other analyses are found in William Bowen, "The Prospects for Productivity," in the editors of Fortune Magazine, *Working Smarter* (1982).

2. In 1969 the response "Very true" was given by 43.1 percent of the sample. This fell to 34.2 percent in 1972 and 27.9 percent in 1977. At the same time, the proportion of the sample who responded either "Not too true" or "Not at all true" increased from 25.3 percent in 1969 to 28.7 percent in 1972 and 33.5 percent in 1977. Given the sample sizes, these differences are statistically significant.

3. "Hard work" is defined here in the sense used by Macarov (1982, p. 15) as "the amount of effort (physical, mental, and psychic) exerted in relation to the amount the worker could presumably exert."

4. However, the fact that observed wages are a function of endogenous effort levels means that they are themselves endogenous to the model and therefore that previous hours-supply estimates that have treated them as exogenous may be seriously biased. For more on this, see Filer (1984).

5. Actually, for poorly explained reasons they used a variable set equal to 2 for workers who answered yes to this question and 1 for those who answered no or who did not work under a bonus system.

6. The effort measure used was similar but not identical to that used by Duncan and Stafford (1980). The model differed from the one presented here only in that it did not incorporate either goods consumption or consumption on the job (working conditions) because of the lack of measures of these factors in the available data. Thus the researcher was forced to rely on an assumption that individuals' utility functions were separable into leisure and consumption.

7. For example, we will have nothing to say regarding Freudian analysis and very little with respect to behavioral psychology or operant conditioning. It should be noted that much of what has recently been called psychological economics has been based on the theory of operant conditioning. There are several works by experimental psychologists (or economists who have read their works) attempting to apply the results of animal-conditioning experiments to the analysis of economic decisions and market behaviors. Among these are Allison (1983), Alhadeff (1982), and, to a certain extent, Lesourne (1977), although this last work also presents some interesting models of human behavior.

8.   Proponents of job enrichment argue that it is impossible to really motivate workers by providing traditional rewards such as higher pay (these are hygienes), and that therefore increased motivation must come about by structuring jobs in such a way as to increase the presence of internal motivators.

9.   The idea that behavior may be altered by manipulation of environments and/or expectations has created disquiet, on philosophical grounds, among some commentators who regard such actions as violations of the individual. It is hard to see how this can be the case, since it is still the individual who assigns the valences, and the manipulations are designed to enable him or her to achieve a higher satisfaction level *as he or she has defined satisfaction*.

10.   For a good summary of the early studies in this area, see Campbell and Pritchard (1976, pp. 84–91).

11.   This is a well-studied phenomenon in the behaviorist literature, where the deprivation/saturation hypothesis holds that anything can serve as either a reward or a punishment (it can have a positive or negative valence), depending on its current rate of administration and the subject's preferred (baseline) rate.

12.   Dunnette (1973) suggests that this is the case in numerous situations.

13.   Works by Atrostic (1982) and Filer (1985) are exceptions to this rule, but there are few others. This is an area where much research remains to be done.

REFERENCES

Adams, J.S., "Towards an Understanding of Inequality," *Journal of Abnormal and Social Psychology*, 67 (1963a), 422–436.

Adams, J.S., "Wage Inequalities, Productivity, and Work Quality," *Industrial Relations*, 3 (1963b), 9–16.

Alderfer, Clayton P., *Existence, Relatedness and Growth: Human Needs in Organizational Settings*. New York: Free Press, 1972.

Alhadeff, David, *Microeconomics and Human Behavior: Toward a New Synthesis of Economics and Psychology*. Berkeley: University of California Press, 1982.

Allison, James, *Behavioral Economics*. New York: Praeger, 1983.

Argyris, Chris, *Personality and Organization*. New York: Harper & Row, 1957.

Atkinson, John W., "Motivational Determinants of Risk-taking Behavior," *Psychological Review*, 64 (1957), 359–372.

Atrostic, B.K., "The Demand for Leisure and Nonpecuniary Job Characteristics," *American Economic Review*, 72 (1982), 428–440.

Becker, Gary S., "Human Capital, Effort, and The Sexual Division of Labor," *Journal of Labor Economics*, 3 (1985), S33–S58.

Bowen, William, "The Prospects for Productivity," in, the editors of Fortune Magazine. *Working Smarter*. New York: Viking, 1982.

Brown, C.V., E. Levin, and D.T. Ulph, "Labor Hours: Married Male Workers," *Scottish Journal of Political Economy*, 23 (1976), 261–278.

Campbell, D.E. "Expectancy Theory of Work Motivation: A Review," *Catalog of Selected Documents in Psychology*, 5 (1975), 255.

Campbell, J.B., and R.D. Pritchard, "Motivation Theory in Industrial and Organizational Psychology," in M.D. Dunnette, ed., *Handbook of Industrial and Organizational Psychology*. Chicago: Rand McNally, 1976.

Carol, A., and S. Parry, "The Economic Rationale of Occupational Choice," *Industrial and Labor Relations Review*, 21 (1968), 183–196.

Chinloy, Peter, *Labor Productivity*. Cambridge: Abt Books, 1981.

Deci, E., *Intrinsic Motivation*. New York: Plenum Press, 1975.

Dickinson, Zenas Clark, *Economic Motives: A Study in the Psychological Foundations of Economic Theory with Some References to Other Social Sciences*. Cambridge, MA: Harvard University Press, 1922.

Duncan, Greg, and Frank Stafford, "Do Union Members Receive Compensating Wage Differentials?" *American Economic Review*, 70 (1980), 355–371.

Dunnette, M.D., "Performance Equals Ability and What?" Technical Report No. 4009, Center for the Study of Organizational Performance and Human Effectiveness, Minneapolis, 1973.

Farr, R., "On the Nature of Attributional Artifacts in Qualitative Research: Herzberg's Two-Factor Theory of Work Motivation," *Journal of Occupational Psychology*, 50 (1977), 3–14.

Federal Reserve Bank of Boston, *The Decline in Productivity Growth: Proceedings of a Conference Held at Edgertown, Massachusetts*, 1980.

Filer, Randall K., "Joint Estimates of the Supply of Labor Hours and the Intensity of Work Effort." Working Paper No. 123, Economics Research Center, Brandeis University, 1984.

Filer, Randall K., "The Influence of Nonpecuniary Compensation on Estimates of Labor Supply Functions," *Quarterly Review of Economics and Business*, 26 (1986), 17–30.

Filer, Randall K., and Anthony K. Lima, "Taxes, Labor Supply and Effort: Will Supply Side Economics Make Us Work Harder?" Working Paper No. 119, Economics Research Center, Brandeis University, 1982.

Fortune Magazine, *Working Smarter*. New York: Viking Press, 1982.

Friedlander, F., "Comparative Work Value Systems," *Personnel Psychology*, 18 (1965), 1–20.

Furobotn, Eirik, "Worker Alienation and the Structure of the Firm," in Svetozar Pejovich, ed., *Governmental Controls and the Free Market*, College Station: Texas A&M University Press, 1976.

Gellerman, Saul, *Motivation and Productivity*. New York: American Management Association, 1963.

Gorman, W.M., "Tricks with Utility Functions," in M. Artin and R. Nobay, eds., *Essays in Economic Analysis*. Cambridge: Cambridge University Press, 1976.

Graen, George, "Instrumentality Theory of Work Motivation: Some Experimental Results and Suggested Modifications," *Journal of Applied Psychology*, 53 (1969), 1–25.

Gruneberg, Michael M., and David J. Oborne, *Industrial Productivity: A Psychological Perspective*. New York: Wiley, 1982.

Guzzo, Richard A., and Jeffrey S. Bondy, *A Guide to Worker Productivity Experiments in the United States 1976–81*. New York: Pergamon, 1983.

Hamermesh, Daniel S., and Albert Rees, *The Economics of Work and Pay*, 3rd ed. New York: Harper & Row, 1984.

Harris, Louis, Associates, and Amitai Etzioni, *Perspectives on Productivity: A Global View*. New York: Sentry Insurance, 1981.

Harter, S., "Effectance Motivation Reconsidered: Toward a Development Model," *Human Development*, 21 (1978), 34–64.

Herzberg, Frederick, *Work and the Nature of Man*. Cleveland: World Publishing, 1966.

Herzberg, F., B. Mausner, and B. Snyderman, *The Motivation to Work*, 2nd ed. New York: Wiley, 1959.

Killingsworth, Mark R., *Labor Supply*. Cambridge: Cambridge University Press, 1983.

Leibenstein, Harvey, *Beyond Economic Man*. Cambridge, MA: Harvard University Press, 1976.

Lesourne, Jacques, *A Theory of the Individual for Economic Analysis*. Amsterdam: North Holland, 1977.

Levin, E., P. J. Saunders, and D.T. Ulph, "Individual Labor Supply Under Weekly Incentive Systems: A Theoretical and Empirical Analysis." Discussion Paper in Economics No. 35, University of Sterling, 1975.

Lewin, K., *The Conceptual Representation and the Measurement of Psychological Forces*. Durham, NC: Duke University Press, 1938.

Likert, Rensis, *The Human Organization*. New York: McGraw-Hill, 1967.

Locke, Edwin A., "The Nature and Causes of Job Satisfaction," in M.D. Dunnette, ed., *Handbook of Industrial and Organizational Psychology*. Chicago: Rand McNally, 1976.

Loveland, K., and J. Olley, "The Effect of External Reward on Task Performance in Children of High and Low Intrinsic Motivation," *Journal of Personality and Social Psychology*, 50 (1979), 1207–1210.

Macarov, David, *Worker Productivity: Myths and Reality*. Beverly Hills, CA: Sage Publications, 1982.

Maital, Shlomo, and Noah Meltz, eds., *Lagging Productivity Growth: Causes and Remedies*. Boston: Ballinger, 1981.

Maslow, A.H., *Motivation and Personality*. New York: Harper & Row, 1954.

McClelland, D.C., *The Achieving Society*. Princeton: Van Nostrand, 1961.

McClelland, D.C, *Personality*. New York: Holt, Rinehart and Winston, 1951.

McClelland, D.C., J.W. Atkinson, R.A. Clark, and E.L. Lowell, *The Achievement Motive*. New York: Appleton-Century-Crofts, 1953.

McGregor, Douglas, *The Human Side of Enterprise*. New York: McGraw-Hill, 1960.

McLoyd, V., "The Effects of Extrinsic Rewards of Differential Value on High and Low Intrinsic Interest," *Child Development*, 50 (1979), 1010–1019.

Mitchell, Terence R., "Motivation: New Directions for Theory, Research and Practice," *Academy of Management Review*, 7 (1982), 80–88.

Mitchell, Terence R., "Organizational Behavior," *Annual Review of Psychology*, 30 (1979), 243–281.

Murray, A.H., *Explorations in Personality*. New York: Oxford University Press, 1938.

Nelson, Richard R., "Research on Productivity Growth and Productivity Differences: Dead Ends and New Departures," *Journal of Economic Literature*, 19 (1981), 1029–1064.

Notz, William, "Work Motivation and the Negative Effects of Extrinsic Rewards," *American Psychologist*, 30 (1975), 884–891.

Pencavel, John H., "Work Effort, On-the-Job Screening, and Alternative Methods of Renumeration," in Ronald G. Ehrenberg, ed., *Research in Labor Economics, Vol. 1*. Greenwich, CT: JAI Press, 1977.

Pinder, Craig C., "Concerning the Application of Human Motivation Theories in Organizational Settings," *Academy of Management Review*, 2 (1977), 384–397.

Porter, L.W., and E.E. Lawler, *Managerial Attitudes and Performance*. Homewood, IL: Dorsey Press, 1968.

Rotter, Julian B., "Generalized Expectancies for Internal versus External Control of Reinforcement," *Psychological Monographs*, 80 (1966), 609.

Salancik, Gerald R., and Jeffrey Pfeffer, "An Examination of Need-Satisfaction Models of Job Attitudes," *Administrative Science Quarterly*, 22 (1977), 427–456.

Schmidt, F.L., "Implications of a Measurement Problem for Expectancy Theory Research," *Organizational Behavior and Human Performance*, 10 (1973), 243–251.

Stafford, Frank P., and Malcolm S. Cohen, "A Model of Work Effort and Productive Consumption," *Journal of Economic Theory*, 7 (1974), 333–347.

Stanton, E.S., "A Critical Evaluation of Motivation, Management and Productivity," *Personnel Journal*, 63 (1983), 208–214.

Staw, Barry M., "Motivation in Organizations: Toward Synthesis and Redirection," in Barry M. Staw and Gerald R. Salancik, eds., *New Directions in Organizational Behavior*. Chicago: St. Clair Press, 1977.

Steers, Richard, and Lyman W. Porter, *Motivation and Work Behavior*, 3rd ed. New York: McGraw-Hill, 1983.

Stern, David, and Daniel Friedman, "Short-Run Behavior of Labor Productivity: Tests of the Motivation Hypothesis," *Journal of Behavioral Economics*, 9 (1980), 89–105.

Sutermeister, Robert, *People and Productivity*. New York: McGraw-Hill, 1976.

Tolman, E.C., *Purposive Behavior in Animals and Men*. New York: Century, 1932.

Tomer, John R., "Worker Motivation: A Neglected Element in Micro-Micro Theory," *Journal of Economic Issues*, 15 (1981), 351–362.

United States Congress Joint Economic Committee, *U.S. Economic Growth from 1976 to 1986: Prospects, Problems and Patterns, Volume I: Productivity*. Washington, D.C.: U.S. Government Printing Office, 1976.

Vroom, V., *Work and Motivation*. New York: Wiley, 1964.

Weiskopf, T.E., S. Bowles, and O.M. Gordon, "Hearts and Minds: A Social Model of U.S. Productivity Growth," *Brookings Papers on Economic Activity*, 14 (1983), 381–450.

White, R.W., "Motivation Reconsidered: The Concept of Competence," *Psychological Review*, 66 (1959), 297–333.

Whyte, William R., ed., *Money and Motivation*. New York: Harper & Row, 1955.

Work in America Institute, *Productivity and the Quality of Work Life: Highlights of the Literature*, 1978.

Yankelovich, Daniel, and John Immerwahr, "The Work Ethic and Economic Vitality," in Michael Wachter and Susan Wachter, eds., *Removing Obstacles to Economic Growth*. Philadelphia: University of Pennsylvania Press, 1984.

Yankelovich, Daniel, and John Immerwahr, *Putting the Work Ethic to Work: A Public Agenda Report on Restoring America's Competitive Vitality*. New York: The Public Agenda Foundation, 1983.

MARRIAGE AND PRODUCTIVITY:
AN INTERDISCIPLINARY ANALYSIS

Amyra Grossbard-Shechtman

I. INTRODUCTION

Married people experience economic activities differently than do singles. Married men work and earn more than single men, married women work and earn less than unmarried women, and people in married households do not consume the same bundles of goods and services purchased by singles. In the United States, married men earn between 8 and 30 percent more than single men, after other factors are accounted for (see Kenny, 1983), whereas married women earn some 3 percent less than single women (Becker, 1981). Similarly, in England, married men earned between 10 and 14 percent more than single men, whereas married women earned 3 percent less than single women (Greenhalgh, 1980). A positive marital-status differential was also found in Sweden by Duncan and Holmlund (1983).

The reasons for these differentials have not been studied adequately by members of the various disciplines to whom this issue is of interest. While offering relatively well-developed empirical estimations of the marital-status differentials, economists explain them using theories of limited scope. Sociologists and sociopsychologists bring a wider range of explanations, but their approach is generally nonquantitative. The most valuable contributions by noneconomists have been made at the micro-level—the study of the organization (family or firm)—by microsociologists (a term coined by Turner [1970]) and social psychologists. This makes generalization difficult.

The underdeveloped state of this area of study derives from the fragmentation of the behavioral sciences. Academic border treaties have assigned one part of the problem—production and productivity—principally to the disciplines that cover economics and business and the other part—marriage—primarily to such other behavioral sciences as psychology, sociology, and anthropology. Within the present incentive structure, academic border crossing rarely pays off (Douglas, 1973; Grossbard, 1978). As a result, the effect of marital status on productivity has received insufficient scholarly attention, and large gains from trade can be reaped through intellectual cross-fertilization.

This paper discusses some of the relevant sociological and sociopsychological literature and compares it to research economists have performed in this area. The emphasis will be on developing testable hypotheses and suggesting directions for further research. Section II reviews economic theories dealing with marital-status differentials, and Section III summarizes some of the sociological theories on the same subject. Section IV gets more specific, in that it concentrates on one particular theory that has been mentioned in both the economic and the sociological literature, namely, wives' investments in their husbands' careers. This section distinguishes different forms such investments can take. Section V presents a theory of occupational differences in marital-status differentials in male productivity. The theory is summarized and extended in the concluding section. The entire discussion focuses on men's benefits from being married. Many of the arguments can be extended to the case of working women.

II. ECONOMIC THEORIES

Economists have explained the observed marital-status differentials in earnings on the basis of five different theories. The most commonly referred to is the specialization theory (see Mincer, 1962; Becker, 1965). As a result of differences in endowments, utility, or both, men and women specialize in the production of different goods and services, which they then trade with each other. Because of their comparative advantage in household production, married women work less and therefore earn less outside the home than do single women, whereas the opposite is true for married men. For a man, marriage implies engaging in an exchange of earned income for household income. Married men therefore specialize in work outside the home more than single men and earn more, even during the same number of working hours. Married men are more productive because of their richer work experience and their stronger need to maintain their earning power in the future (Kenny,1983; Bartlett and Callahan,1984).

While this first theory relates earnings differentials to productivity differentials, other economists have also presented the "perceived-need" hypothesis, wherein employers pay married workers more because such workers need to support a family. Pay scales often reflect such policy, especially in Europe (Bartlett and Callahan, 1984).

A third theory mentioned in the economic literature is that of statistical discrimination (Siebert and Sloane, 1981). According to this theory, employers discriminate against single men and married women because of past statistics relating average productivity and marital status.

Fourth, economists have used the human capital investment theory to provide an alternative explanation for the observed marital-status differentials in productivity and earnings. According to this theory, married men owe their higher earnings to a wife's investments in her husband's human capital (see Benham, 1974). In a similar vein, Marxist economists have written about domestic labor (principally the wife's) as "the care, maintenance and continued socialization of human beings" (Himmelweit and Mohun,1977).

This last theory is closely related to the first one, for the same activities—such as cooking or nurturing—that women specialize in often lead to improvements in human capital; for instance, through better nutrition and physical or mental health. Indirect evidence for such an investment process has been found in the effect of a wife's schooling on her husband's earnings (Benham, 1974), health (Grossman, 1976), and religious practice (Grossbard-Shechtman and Neuman, 1986). Interestingly, the wife's investment theory has not been mentioned in some of the most recent economic literature (Kenny,1983, Bartlett and Callahan 1984).

Finally, economists have theorized that causality does not necessarily proceed from marital status to earnings, but rather from earnings to marital status. Men earning higher wages are more likely to get married either because higher income encourages people to marry (see Becker, 1981; Grossbard-Shechtman, 1984) or because the same desirable and unmeasured characteristics that lead to higher earnings also increase the probability of a worker being married (Kenny, 1983).

III. THEORIES OF OTHER BEHAVIORAL SCIENTISTS

Specialization theory also takes a major place among the explanations sociologists and psychologists have offered for the observed marital-status differentials. Sociologists generally call it role specialization (e.g., Parsons, 1942).

Social scientists attempting to explain the origin of such specialization are divided regarding the relative influence of nature and nurture. Psychologists who specialize in the study of gender differences can be found on both sides of the controversy (e.g., Maccoby and Jacklyn, 1974). Anthropologists and sociologists tend to be particularly interested in demonstrating the dominance of cultural influences (e.g., Mead, 1949), although a few have recently come to emphasize biological factors. According to the so-called sociobiologists (e.g., Wilson, 1975), biological differences in reproduction technology and in the ability to provide for dependents determine gender role specialization observed among all species, including the human race.[1] Most researchers view existing human role specialization as the result of both biologically and culturally determined gender differences.

Sociologists were writing on the wife's contribution to her husband's success at work before economists got interested in the subject (e.g., Whyte, 1956; Moore, 1962). Sociologists differentiate between the wife's *indirect* contribution—her specialization in household tasks, which freed her husband from such responsibilities—and her *direct* contribution.

To designate the wife's direct assistance to her husband's success at work, sociologist Papanek (1973) coined the term *two-person career*. The term implies that both members of a married couple are actually working, although only the man is officially employed.

Sociologists and social psychologists studying wives' contributions to their husbands' success at work generally take a micro perspective in the sense that they focus on one occupation or one organization, mostly the corporation. Their insights often originate from careful observation of workers on the job. In contrast, economists writing on this subject have not paid attention to occupational differences in wives'contributions to husbands' success. Similarly, economists do not study the effect of husbands' occupation on wives' labor supply outside the home, a related subject of research.[2]

Next, I present an inventory of possible investments wives make in their husbands' careers, derived from both the economic and the sociological literature. The subsequent section looks at occupational differences in marital-status differentials.

IV. TYPES OF WIVES' CONTRIBUTIONS TO THEIR HUSBANDS' WORK PERFORMANCE

The following discussion distinguishes between wives' direct contribution to their husbands' work performance by means of (1) assistance in central tasks, (2) investment in husbands' human capital (including organizational capital), and (3) contributions to husbands' peripheral tasks and to the communication of information.

According to Weinstock (1963), a job often includes central and peripheral task specifications. Central tasks are technical requirements of the occupation directly related to performance. Peripheral tasks refer to the "nontechnical, institutionally required social aspects of the job." This distinction is helpful when discussing the two-person career (see Mortimer, Hall, and Hill, 1978), as are the concepts of human capital (Becker, 1964) and organizational capital (Tomer, in this volume).

A. Contributions to Husbands' Central Tasks

Wives sometimes help their husbands by doing the work that could be done by a paid employee. For instance, a saleman's wife may promote sales, or a writer's wife may type his manuscript. According to Kanter (1977a, p.110), the winners of one company's award for exceptional salesmanship all had wives without outside jobs who reported spending a considerable amount of time helping their husbands with sales work. Wives may also aid their husbands' success by acting as "sounding boards," thus helping their husbands think through technical work problems, or by giving concrete advice that will enhance productivity. The latter form of direct help may be more relevant to more complex, generally professional, white-collar occupations.

B. Investment in Human Capital (Including Organizational Capital)

This is the only direct contribution economists have related to (i.e., Benham, 1974). The sociological literature mentions wives' contributions to workers' good nutrition and good physical and mental health. Parsons' (1942) mention of wives' expressive role relates to their help as a sounding board and mental health counselor. Likewise, Lasch's (1977) view of the family as a "haven in a heartless world" centers on the stress-relieving functions of the wife.

In addition, wives can help develop their husbands' motivation to work and organizational capital. The motivation argument restates in part the "marriage-as-need-for-income" argument also mentioned in the economic literature. Using the sociologists' distinction between instrumental (or extrinsic) and intrinsic rewards of work, we see that marriage tends to increase the need for work as an instrument (means) to acquire goods. This is what economists generally mean when presenting this argument.

Sociologists also write of marriage as a means of promoting the intrinsic motivation to work—what economists call the nonpecuniary benefits of work. Turner (1970), for instance, mentions people's need to identify with their job as a major intrinsic, nonpecuniary reward of work. If a husband can get his wife to identify with his work, his own commitment to the job will rise; so will his motivation to work and, consequently, actual productivity.

Whereas workers have intrinsic needs for identity and commitment, organizations also have an interest in promoting such commitment. If the commitment is specific to a firm, it is often called loyalty. Such loyalty can be viewed as organizational human capital, a type of human capital that should be distinguished from technical human capital in that it enhances productivity through better work relations within the organization (see Tomer, in this volume). Loyalty contributes to productivity in two possible ways: by decreasing the likelihood that a worker will quit and by increasing his or her work effort.

The value of loyalty as insurance against a worker quitting follows from conditions of uncertainty and from the relative importance of specific on-the-job training (see Becker, 1964). The value of loyalty as motivation to work hard derives in part from the absence of well-defined property rights. Once a worker has been hired in a team situation, his or her individual extra work effort is a public good.Therefore, individual workers may have an incentive to be free-riders (Leibenstein, 1982) with respect to their team or to the firm as a whole. Loyalty reduces free-riding tendencies by fellow workers or employees and therefore increases workers' productivity[3] (see also Leibenstein in this volume).

Wives can contribute to their husbands' loyalty in marriage. I am assuming here that the propensity for loyalty is an acquired trait, which needs to be learned within an organization. Since it is a general skill, individual firms have limited incentive to teach their workers how to be loyal. The family being such a pervasive organization, it can serve as a teaching ground for loyalty. In turn, the institution of marriage reinforces the loyalty elements in family relations, and women do so more actively than men (see Grossbard-Shechtman, 1982). In other words, marriage can produce loyalty (mostly the wife's contribution to her husband's potential for loyalty toward his employer). A similar argument has been stated by Marxist economists Himmelweit and Mohun (1977, p.16) when they consider the family as a producer of a disciplined working class.

In principle, corporate loyalty and family loyalty can compete with each other. One reason corporations frequently move their employees may be as an attempt to subordinate family loyalty to corporate loyalty. Moreover, Pahl and Pahl (1971, p.184) hypothesize that the company's sponsorship of social events for their employees increases wives' willingness to support their husbands' commitment.

C. Contributions to Husbands' Peripheral Tasks and to the Communication of Information

Workers get involved in activities that do not seem central to their job and are often unrelated at first sight. Examples of such activities are entertaining and participation at public events. A closer look may reveal, however, that such activities often promote a worker's success on the job. Such peripheral tasks often serve to communicate valuable information, and here a spouse can play an important role.

Parties, which can serve as an efficient means of promoting circulation of information within the organization, are often catered by wives. Other peripheral activities enable the employee to communicate personal information of value to the firm that otherwise is hard to gather.

As mentioned earlier, the firm is interested in workers' loyalty and consequent motivation to contribute to joint work efforts, but information on the basic character of a worker is hard to obtain. The wife's behavior often serves as a testimony and a clue to the character and personal side of her husband.

First, a wife makes it possible for her husband to advertise his propensity for loyalty by simply remaining married. Men often tend to advertise their family loyalty at the workplace. Kanter (1977a) reports that in the large corporation she studied, pictures of wives and children adorned men's offices so commonly that they seemed almost mandatory. Such photographs may play the role of advertising loyalty to the family, possibly implying a willingness to be loyal to the firm as well.

Next, husbands working for corporations benefit from their wives' involvement in charitable and community service. Similarly, wives of independent businessmen can help generate business by promoting a favorable public image via their volunteer work. In this case the wives' activities serve the same function as Mobil Oil's funding of a National Geographic special on television. Such wives advertise good will and concern for the community, which can generate direct income for the independent businessman and promotion for the executive contributing to his corporation's sales.

V. WIVES' CONTRIBUTIONS AS AFFECTED BY NATURE OF HUSBANDS' OCCUPATION

Given the types of contributions wives can make to their husbands' success at work, it follows that occupations differ in the degree to which they allow for potential contributions by wives. The following hypotheses were derived from the theoretical considerations discussed in the previous section.

HYPOTHESIS 1. *Marital-status differentials will be larger in occupations with potentially steeper earnings profiles.*

The more a man can earn on his job, the larger the potential differences in earnings, and therefore the larger the potential contribution a wife can make by whatever means are available: indirect assistance by allowing the husband to specialize at work, as well as direct assistance applicable to the work situation. If the husband is an employee, there probably will be more pressure on the wife to contribute to her husband's career the higher the career "ceiling" and the more steps in the ladder (Tausky and Dubin, 1965; Hall, 1975; Mortimer, Hall, and Hill, 1978).

This is one reason executives tend to benefit more from being married than do workers in general, and therefore why executives are more often married than other workers (Whyte, 1956). For instance, in 1969 93.19 percent of the male managers earning $15,000 a year or more (nearly all the managers) were married, 72.25 percent to women not in the paid labor force. As income and status go up, even fewer of the wives hold paid jobs, and even more of the men are married (Kanter, 1977a).

Self-employed men with large potential earnings are also likely to gain large benefits from being married. Independent businessmen or farmers with large growth potential, for example, may experience higher marital-status differentials in earnings than do people of similar background without a growth potential. The hypothesis was tested among resettled farm families given land with growth potential in the Columbia Basin project. The farmers who were most successful were more likely to have wives who conceived of their roles in traditional terms (Straus, 1958).

Although these occupational differences in marital-status differentials have not been tested rigorously, their frequent appearance should lead us to consider this hypothesis seriously. However, the same apparent findings can possibly be explained with the help of additional hypotheses.

When careers have a large growth potential, generally only a small proportion of aspiring ladder climbers ever achieve the highest echelons. This often creates fierce competition and therefore stress, resulting from intensive efforts to move up the ladder. Kanter (1977b) called such careers "absorptive," in the sense that they absorb a large fraction of a person's time and energy. The career-minded husband and his family experience stress in two ways: pressure on the husband's health and pressure on the wife and children, who must put up with many irregular and unpredictable demands of the husbands' job (Turner, 1970). This conclusion leads us to another hypothesis.

HYPOTHESIS 2.   *The more stressful an occupation, the larger the potential marital-status differential in earnings.*

There is more potential for the wife of a husband whose occupation generates a high level of stress to contribute in the sense that there is more need for her to accommodate her husband's work demands; this constitutes an indirection contribution. There also is more room for direct contributions, such as direct assistance in central tasks and assistance in health maintenance. Although careers with high growth potential often tend to be stressful, the two hypotheses are separable to the extent that job stress and absorptiveness are in principle continuous and measurable. Tests can be designed to ascertain how stress level influences marital-status differentials, given a certain pattern of potential growth in earnings. Moreover, in performing such tests one should control for additional aspects of a job that are also likely to affect marital-status differentials.

HYPOTHESIS 3.   *The marital-status differential is likely to be higher in occupations involving more peripheral tasks.*

As was shown in the previous section, one means by which a wife can promote her husband's career is by helping in peripheral tasks such as entertainment and community service. The more such tasks are potentially relevant to an occupation, the more a wife can contribute. Such tasks are more commonly found in high-prestige occupations (Mortimer, Hall, and Hill, 1978, p. 294), in occupations involving extensive personal contacts (Weinstock, 1963), or in occupations highly dependent on the maintenance of a stable clientele (Moore, 1962, p. 84). Therefore, we expect higher marital-status differentials among managers than among engineers of similar ability, and among owners or managers of firms that depend more on their public image because of the type of product they sell.

Again, this hypothesis helps explain the apparently high marital-status differential among corporate managers and independent businessmen. It also explains why wives of university presidents (Clodius and Magrath, 1984), politicians (MacPherson, 1975), officers in the military (Goldman, 1973), and ministers (Taylor and Hartley, 1975) can make important contributions to their husbands' careers.

HYPOTHESIS 4.   *The more complex and potentially substitutable the central tasks of a husband's occupation, the larger the potential marital-status differential.*

Blue collar workers rarely are in a position to delegate any of their central tasks to their wives. But business managers and writers can have their wives do secretarial work, clergymen's wives can run the Sunday school, and wives of storekeepers can tend the store. Wives assisting in central tasks are not necessarily unpaid. Epstein (1971) found in her study of married lawyer teams that the wives did much of the paper work contributing to the husband's success in court or with clients.

HYPOTHESIS 5.   *The more that loyalty contributes to workers' productivity— for example, because of the profitability of investments in human capital— the larger the earnings differential between married and single men.*

As mentioned in the previous section, one of the ways in which wives can potentially contribute to their husbands' careers is by increasing the husbands' propensity to be loyal to the firm. Moreover, the fact that a man is married signals his potential for loyalty.

The potential need for workers' loyalty varies by occupation and by industrial system. Firms need loyal workers more if they consider investing in the workers' firm-specific skills. An industrial system such as Japan sets a particularly high value on loyalty to the firm (Clark, 1979). It is therefore not surprising that employers' discrimination in terms of slower advancement of unmarried workers is more common in Japan than in the United States. In Japan, marriage also serves as a declaration of the willingness to curb individualistic aspirations and to contribute to organizations and to society at large (Hendry, 1986).

VI. SUMMARY AND EXTENSIONS OF THE THEORY

It has been argued here that marital-status differentials in earnings are expected to vary with occupational characteristics such as growth potential, stress and absorptiveness, amount of peripheral and central tasks involved, and need for loyalty. Preliminary evidence based on the sociological literature was offered in partial support of these hypotheses.

The above-mentioned hypotheses all have corollaries, which are derived from the process by which people select marital status, spouses, occupations, and employers. Positions with larger marital-status differentials are more likely to be filled by married men, the result of voluntary selection and possibly encouragement by the employer. Larger marital-status differentials are also likely to lead men to marry women who are particularly adept at contributing in the areas of most importance to their job.

Wives' characteristics that are most likely to contribute effectively to the tasks discussed earlier are a higher education and full-time housewife status. Benham's (1975) finding that the husband's income increases with the wife's schooling even when the husband's own education and years of work are controlled supports this view. Interestingly, he found that the positive contribution of the wife's schooling stops at the point of graduate education, possibly because of the substantially higher percentage of women with graduate degrees who work outside the home.

Further direct evidence of the advantage of a nonworking wife from the husband's point of view has been offered in a study of male engineers and accountants (Burke and Weir, 1976). Husbands of working wives reported more job pressures, expressed more dissatisfaction with their jobs, marriages, and other aspects of their lives, and manifested more symptoms of stress than the husbands of homemakers.

What also needs to be determined in this process of matching by spouses, workers, and employers are the terms of cooperation both at the workplace and in the home. In a period of easy divorce and increasingly attractive opportunities outside the home, it is clear that most women do not invest in their husbands' careers without expecting or actually receiving compensation in return. The more they accept traditional marital roles, implying few personal returns for their investments, the more women are likely to support their husbands' careers. Lopata (1971) found that wives of successful men were more likely to accept traditional marital roles. The more prestigious the husband's occupation, the more likely the wife was to turn the enjoyment of her husband's success into part of her reward (Mortimer, Hall, and Hill, 1978). Some women may, in fact, be caught in a bind, not happy about the compensation they receive for their contribution and unable to find better opportunities through divorce and remarriage. Many corporate wives suffer from marital problems, according to Kanter (1977a, p. 109).

This theory also has implications for employers' policies. First, they may discriminate against unmarried workers. Second, they may select two persons to fill a position that tends to be a two-person career. Employers in fact often interview wives of prospective employees as well as the applicants themselves (Kanter, 1977a). Employers may also organize activities that encourage wives to contribute to their husbands' careers, such as family recreation.

Finally, this theory has implications for divorce and its effect on earnings. Divorce may be less common and remarriage more rapid when men engage in occupations with high marital-status differentials. Bartlett and Callahan (1984) found that men who were divorced or widowed and who had remarried experienced particularly rapid growth in wages.[4] If marriage really contributes as much to earnings as is claimed here, the upward trend in divorce that has characterized recent decades may be one explanation for the downward trend in productivity left unexplained by conventional methods of study.

ACKNOWLEDGMENT

I would like to thank the editors, Shelly Chandler, Roger Frantz, and Ivy Papps for their helpful comments and suggestions, and Hilda Mizrahi and Maureen McDonnell for their efficient typing.

NOTES

1. Economists writing on gender differentiation as it affects labor supply have either ignored the nature-nurture controversy or emphasized biological influences (for instance, Becker, 1981, p. 25). Becker's position on this issue is consistent with his general view of social, legal, and political institutions as promoting long-run individual well-being. According to this view, commonly espoused by economists, socially determined influences on behavior—such as nurturing methods unrelated to natural differences—which do not reflect real factor prices and endowments, would not be socially optimal and would therefore disappear over time. This assumes competition in the broadest sense and the absence of exploitation of one group by another.

2. A critique of the economic literature on female labor supply along these lines can be found in Mortimer, Hall, and Hill (1978).

3. A related discussion of loyalty can be found in Akerloff (1983).

4. This could also possibly reflect the causality discussed in Section I, whereby higher income facilitates remarriage.

REFERENCES

Akerloff, G.A., "Loyalty Filters," *American Economic Review*, 73 (1983), 54–63.

Bartlett, R.L., and C. Callahan, III, "Wage Determination and Marital Status: Another Look," *Industrial Relations* 23 (1984), 90–96.

Becker, G.S., *Human Capital*. New York: Columbia University Press, 1964.

Becker, G.S., "A Theory of the Allocation of Time," *Economic Journal*, 75 (1965), 493–517.

Becker, G.S., *A Treatise on the Family*. Cambridge, MA: Harvard University Press, 1981.

Benham, L., "Benefits of Women's Education within Marriage," in T.W. Schultz, ed., *Economics of the Family*. Chicago: University of Chicago Press, 1974.

Benham, L., "Non-Market Returns to Women's Investment in Education," in C.B. Lloyd, ed., *Sex, Discrimination and the Division of Labor*. New York: Columbia University Press, 1975.

Burke, R.J. and T. Weir, "Relationship of Wives' Employment Status to Husband, Wife, and Pair Satisfaction and Performance," *Journal of Marriage and the Family*, 38 (1976), 279–287.

Clark, R., *The Japanese Company*. New Haven: Yale University Press, 1979.

Clodius, J.E., and D.S. Magrath, eds., *The President's Spouse: Volunteer or Volunteered*. Washington, D.C.: National Association of State Universities and Land-Grant Colleges, 1984.

Douglas, M., "The Exclusion of Economics," *Times Literary Supplement*, (July 6, 1973), 781–782.

Duncan, G.J., and B. Holmlund, "Was Adam Smith Right After All? Another Test of the Theory of Compensating Wage Differentials," *Journal of Labor Economics*, 1 (1983), 366–379.

Epstein, C.F., "Law Partners and Marital Partners," *Human Relations*, 24 (1971), 549–564.

Goldman, N., "Women in the Armed Forces," *American Journal of Sociology*, 78 (1973), 892–911.

Greenhalgh, C., "Male–Female Wage Differentials in Great Britain: Is Marriage an Equal Opportunity?" *Economic Journal*, 90 (1980), 751–775.

Grossbard, A., "Towards a Marriage Between Economics and Anthropology and a General Theory of Marriage," *Papers and Proceedings, American Economic Review*, 68 (1978), 33–37.

Grossbard-Shechtman, A., "A Theory of Marriage Formality: The Case of Guatemala," *Economic Development and Cultural Change*, 30 (1982), 813–830.

Grossbard-Shechtman, A., "A Theory of Allocation in Markets for Labour and Marriage," *Economic Journal*, 94 (1984), 863–882.

Grossbard-Shechtman, A. and S. Neuman, "Economic Behavior, Marriage, and Religiosity," *Journal of Behavioral Economics*, forthcoming, 1986.

Grossman, M., "The Correlation between Health and Schooling," in *Household Production and Consumption*. New York: Columbia University Press, for the National Bureau of Economic Research, 1976.

Hall, R., *Occupations and the Social Structure*. Englewood Cliffs, NJ: Prentice Hall, 1975.

Hendry, J., "Marriage in a Recently Industrialized Society: Japan," in K. Davis, ed., in association with A. Grossbard-Shechtman, *Contemporary Marriage*. New York: Russell-Sage Foundation, 1986.

Himmelweit, S., and S. Mohun, "Domestic Labour and Capital," *Cambridge Journal of Economics*, 1 (1977) 15–31.

Kanter, R.M., *Men and Women of the Corporation*. New York: Basic Books, 1977a.

Kanter, R.M., *Work and Family in the United States: A Critical Review and Agenda for Research and Policy*, New York: Russell Sage, 1977b.

Kenny, L.W., "The Accumulation of Human Capital during Marriage by Males," *Economic Inquiry*, 21 (1983), 223–231.

Lasch, C., *Haven in a Heartless World*. New York: Basic Books, 1977.

Leibenstein, H., "The Prisoner's Dilemma in the Invisible Hand: An Analysis of Intrafirm Productivity," *American Economic Review*, 72 (1982), 92–97.

Lopata, H., *Occupation: Housewife*. London: Oxford University Press, 1971.

Maccoby, E., and C.N. Jacklyn, *The Psychology of Sex Differences*, Stanford, CA: Stanford University Press, 1974.

MacPherson, M., *The Power Lovers: An Intimate Look at Politicians and Their Marriages*. New York: Putnam, 1975.

Mead, M., *Male and Female, A Study of the Sexes in a Changing World*. New York: W. Morrow, 1949.

Mincer, J., "Labor Force Participation of Married Women: A Study of Labor Supply," in *Aspects of Labor Economics*. Princeton, NJ: Princeton University Press, for the National Bureau of Economic Research, 1962.

Moore, W.E., *Conduct of the Corporation*. New York: Random House, 1962.

Mortimer, J., R. Hall, and R. Hill, "Husbands' Occupational Attributes as Constraints on Wives' Employment," *Sociology of Work and Occupations*, 5 (1978), 285–313.

Pahl, J.M., and R.E. Pahl, *Managers and Their Wives*. London: Allen Lane, 1971.

Papanek, H., "Men, Women and Work: Reflections on the Two-Person Career," *American Journal of Sociology*, 78 (1973), 852–872.

Parsons, T., "Age and Sex in the Social Structure of the United States," *American Sociological Review*, 7 (1942), 606–616.

Siebert, W.S., and P.J. Sloane, "The Measurement of Sex and Marital Status Discrimination at the Work Place," *Economica*, 3 (1981), 125–141.

Straus, M.A., "The Role of the Wife in the Settlement of the Columbia Basin Project," *Marriage and Family Living*, 20 (1958), 59–64.

Tausky, D., and R. Dubin, "Career Anchorage: Managerial Mobility Aspirations," *American Sociological Review*, 30 (1965), 725–735.

Taylor, M.G., and S.F. Hartley, "The Two-Person Career: A Classic Example," *Sociology of Work and Occupations*, 2 (1975), 354–372.

Tomer, J.F., "Productivity and Organizational Behavior" in this volume.

Turner, R.H., *Family Interaction*. New York: Wiley, 1970.

Weinstock, S.A., "Role Elements: A Link Between Accumulation and Occupational Status," *British Journal of Sociology*, 64 (1963), 144–149.

Whyte, W.H., *The Organization Man*. New York: Doubleday, 1956.

Wilson, E.O., *Sociobiology*. Cambridge, MA: Harvard University Press, 1975.

Section D

Industrial Organization

INTRODUCTION TO SECTION D:
INDUSTRIAL ORGANIZATION

This section presents two papers dealing with issues that are typically subsumed under the subject of industrial organization. The first paper, by Roger Frantz, reviews 18 years of research on the theory of X-efficiency (XE) as it relates to market structure. The second paper, by Bill Dickens, makes a case for extending public regulation into new areas because of decision-making biases on workers' part.

X-inefficiency, the non-cost-minimizing behavior of firms, is one of the most heavily researched topics in behavioral economics. The theory of XE is rooted in concepts such as motivation for work effort; the Dotson-Yerkes psychological law of the effect of pressure on behavior; the importance of norms, conventions, and habit in creating "inert areas" in behavior, and so on. The crux of the theory is that rational, output-maximizing behavior is only selectively employed by the individual, and the empirical research suggests, moreover, that it is an "inferior good."

While most studies estimate that the welfare loss of allocative inefficiency due to market structure is small, the loss due to X-inefficiency is significant. Competitive pressure increases the attentiveness and care with which a person works and utilizes available resources. Any policy such as tariff or quota that reduces competition reduces welfare. With X-inefficiency included, the welfare loss from monopoly is much greater than when it is measured by allocative inefficiency alone. Frantz's careful documentation of the accumulated evidence regarding the theory re-

305

moves any doubt that XE is of major interest and will be one of the pillars of a unified theory of behavioral economics whenever such a theory is constructed.

Bill Dickens' paper is a classic example of the works that derive their basic tenets from the studies of Kahneman and Tversky. The paper uses insights from the findings of these two researchers on biased judgments and perceptions to question the neoclassical model of occupational safety and to offer an alternative view of the subject. The virtue of the paper is the synthesis it contains of various recent findings about human information processing. These are then applied to economic topics in such a way as to make clear why the old rational model is simply inadequate. One can only wonder whether Friedman's view of the value of realistic assumptions will be shaken by these thoughtfully written arguments. For any economist who is skeptical of simplistic (as contrasted with simple) models of complex environments, this article is extremely convincing.

Last, a note of disagreement. It is Dickens' conclusion that because workers and consumers make biased judgments regarding safety, safety is undersupplied relative to what an informed and unbiased market should demand from producers. He then prescibes policy that calls for education and information, but most important, regulation of safety standards. As long as the intervention is in the form of education and information, there is no question but that intervention in this area is constructive. However, when it comes in the form of outlawing occupations such as boxing, or declaring a wage inadequate to cover the dangers some bureaucrat perceives in a job, we are in trouble. Whose values should prevail? The underpinning of the argument for welfare maximization in the free market is the individual's accurate perception of his own utility surface. If that assumption must be abandoned, as the findings of Kahneman and Tversky suggest and Dickens ably argues, by what objective standard can we tell if government intervention is improving things? Improving the legal procedures for providing workers' compensation may prove, after all, to be a much cheaper solution than government intervention.

X-EFFICIENCY IN BEHAVIORAL ECONOMICS

Roger S. Frantz

I. INTRODUCTION

Jay Gould, in his book *The Panda's Thumb* (1980) writes about Charles Darwin's formulation of the theory of natural selection and the impact a social scientist and philosopher (Auguste Comte), a statistician (Adolphe Quetelet), and an economist (Adam Smith) had on his thinking. About Smith, Gould discusses how Darwin imbibed Smiths' belief that an analysis of the "unconstrained" actions or behaviors of individuals is essential in any study of overall social structure. More recently, Leibenstein has used the concepts of "constrained" and "unconstrained" behavior in discussing X-efficiency (XE). In the context of XE theory, constrained behavior is that behavior which is guided by the "superego," or a desire to adhere to standards. Unconstrained behavior, on the other hand, is behavior guided by the "id," or an unwillingness to adhere to any obligations or standards. The existence of both these aspects in human personality implies at least the possibility of differential motivation or behavior, vis-à-vis single-valued motivation, i.e., maximization. While utility *maximization* in a model of production encompasses behavior, a model allowing for differential motivation seems to contain an added dimension here. That is, not only is effort toward productive efficiency a variable as it is in utility models, but effort toward a maximizing solution per se is variable as well. The behavioral dimension is thus enhanced, as is its link with behavioral economics. The latter, according to Katona (1980), has three major features. First, generalizations about economic behavior emerge from *observations* of behavior under different circumstances. Second, the focus is on the *process* of decision making rather than on the results. Third, the *human* factor is central. The purpose of this paper is to discuss XE theory as a part of behavioral economics while showing how XE is related to market structures in both industrialized and less developed economies.

II. MICRO-MICRO, OR XE, THEORY

What motivates individual firm members and groups within firms? What outcomes do these motivating forces produce? These outcomes may include levels of production, cost, and productivity, as well as technological adoption and input combinations. These outcomes may be cast in terms of efficiency. Yet much of the discussion concerning efficiency has dealt with allocative or price efficiency, and empirical estimates of allocative inefficiency have shown that allocative inefficiency is often trivial. The development of Leibenstein's XE concept emerged from his hypothesis that despite the small estimates reported for allocative inefficiency, efficiency is important. X-efficiency theory is a conceptual framework for thinking about nonallocative efficiency.

Efficiency is concerned with the transformation of inputs into outputs. Measures of efficiency use standards that are applied at different levels of aggregation: macro, industry, and firm. Macro, or allocative, efficiency, uses the welfare triangle analysis to show price and quantity deviations resulting from the economy's movement away from the competitive ideal. Industry-level efficiency utilizes an industry production function or best-practice plant to measure the relative performance of firms in the industry. Here, the most efficient firm *within* the industry group is used as the standard. Firm-level efficiency is concerned with intrafirm resource use. A best-practice technology or engineering standard can be used for judging the firm's level of efficiency, that is, for receiving maximum output (incurring minimum costs) for a given level of inputs. Standards are relative or normative.[1] The standard used by Leibenstein in discussing XE is the excess of actual costs over (technologically given) minimum costs for a given level of output. At times the discussion has also focused on output and technological adoption.

The cost-minimization standard stems from Leibenstein's concern with nonallocative efficiency. That is, apart from the price mechanism or allocative efficiency, do firms make efficient use of the resources placed at their disposal? The conventional assumption implicit in the welfare triangle analysis for measuring the welfare costs of monopoly, as well as in the assumptions of micro theory—value maximization and cost minimization—is that firms are internally efficient. Cost curves are derived from production functions, which implies maximum output from a given set of inputs, that is, cost minimization. Leibenstein's claim is that this assumption has led most economists away from investigating and observing intrafirm environments and thus away from a major (hypothesized) determinant of economic efficiency.

In evaluating XE theory, it is necessary to keep in mind that the theory is most applicable to imperfect markets and to firms that employ a nontrivial number of "nonmarginal product employees"—employees whose value added cannot be (easily) observed. In these cases, Leibenstein finds it useful to be mindful of two extreme sets of circumstances: the one-person owner-manager firm, and the corporation that pays its employees predominantly according to time on the job and that is unusually subjected to employing free-riding firm members. For the one-person owner-manager firm, micro theory merges with micro-micro (XE) theory. Imperfect markets, however, create the potential for discretionary— non-cost minimization–non-profit (value) maximizing—behavior by firm members. Motivations for work effort toward efficiency thus determine both the individual's and the firm's performance. Thus the theory asks, What are the felt pressures for cost minimization-value maximization efficiency? In XE theory, *every* employee contributes, both directly and indirectly, to costs. Cost is thus the *outcome* of individual and group decisions and behaviors.

A more complete statement of the theory, especially a review of the empirical literature, has been presented elsewhere (see Frantz, 1984). Some of the empirical literature will be presented in the next section. Here I will limit my remarks on XE theory to some salient points of the concept of pressure. Pressure has two sources: personality (internal) and the environment (external, or contextual). The personality is seen as having two "sides." On the one hand, we have the desire and the ability to make decisions consistent with the rules for *procedural*, or *process*, rationality (Simon, 1959). We can be calculating, consider alternatives, and, in general, approach our job tasks with care. Leibenstein (1976, Chapter 5) refers to this as constrained or superego behavior. At the same time, we also have the desire and tendency to be unconstrained, to behave according to the dictates of our id or our animal spirits, to give knee-jerk responses to problems, to be unconcerned with or avoid the details necessary for procedural rationality. *Perhaps constrained behavior is simply an "inferior good."* In any case, the basic idea is that we forge a compromise between the two and in the process choose a comfortable level of constraint concern. Thus we may not be willing to submit ourselves completely to constraints, that is, to the tightly calculation precisionlike decision-making techniques necessary to attend to all opportunities for net gain or to void losses. External pressure or circumstances influence an individual's willingness to be constraint-concerned as well; these circumstances include market conditions, goals and structure of the organization, and peer pressures. In addition, they include both "negative" pressures, such as higher unemployment rates, and "positive" pressures, such as direct participation in the firm's decisions and/or higher income. Thus an increase in pressure—internal or external—usually leads to more constraint concern. In contrast to the conventional assumption that the individual is "complete constraint-concerned," that is, rational, Leibenstein assumes that we are "selectively rational," with rational or maximizing behavior and nonmaximizing behavior exhibited at various times under various circumstances. Because he is concerned with processes, hows and whys, Leibenstein's use of the term *rationality* includes a list of its components. That is, rational behavior—procedural rationality á là Simon—stems from a willingness to be calculating and realistic, to learn from experience, just one of several other pertinent personality traits.[2]

Pressure has also been incorporated into the theory via the Yerkes-Dotson law, whereby the quality of decision making is related to pressure in a quadratic function. The implication is that decision making (performance) is related to pressure in such a fashion that only a specific amount of pressure results in the best possible performance. In terms of behavioral economics, the decision-making process, or XE, depends on the level of pressure. Conversely, either too little pressure or too much pressure fail to extract our best efforts. This law, which was first enunciated in 1908, seems "obvious" and has been validated by observation or experimentation on numerous occasions.[3] This pressure-effort relation is a behavioral postulate of XE theory.

The two other behavioral postulates of XE theory are (1) the concept that individual behavior is influenced by norms, conventions, and sanctions used at the workplace, and (2) the concept of inert areas. Once an effort level is established it becomes "optimal," part of the firm's history and tradition, and as such is changed only when the environment (or a personality trait) changes sufficiently to force individuals out of their inert area, or "comfort zone." In XE theory, neither our norms nor our habits will necessarily elicit the procedurally rational behavior necessary for the firm to minimize its cost, that is, to be X-efficient.

X-efficiency is assumed by industrial psychologists. For example, Arnold, Evans, and House (1980, p. 133), psychologists speaking at a conference on lagging productivity, stated that "what Leibenstein . . . refers

to as X-inefficiency is, in fact, an article of faith or belief for organiza-
tional-industrial psychologists. Arguments and data in support of the
existence of X-inefficiency simply do not appear in books on organizational behavior, since its existence is assumed." One example of compatibility between XE theory and theories of organizational behavior is
the VIE, or process, theories of job performance (Vroom, 1964; Porter
and Lawler, 1968; Graen, 1969).[4] VIE theories emphasize the valence,
instrumentality, and expectancy aspects of behavior. The valence, or
importance, can refer either to a particular level of performance or effort
or to a reward contingent on that performance. The instrumentality
refers to the contingency that the value of one variable has for the value
of another. For example, the instrumentality of effort for income is
higher (at least in the short run) for piece-rate workers than for hourly
employees, higher for employees in competitive industries than for those
in monopolies, and higher during periods of relatively high unemployment. For example, free-riders have a lower expectancy than non-free-
riders, other things being equal. Although the specific functional form
varies among authors, they all consider work effort an outcome of these
"process" variables. In terms of XE theory, a high instrumentality of
effort for income or a high expectancy is tantamount to more pressure.
So long as the individual experiences less than "optimum" pressure, the
Yerkes-Dotson law predicts a higher level of XE as a result. In other
words, both XE and VIE theories view (productive work) effort as dependent on the environment.

Let us now state some of the implications of the theory. (1) Firms
minimize costs and maximize profits only as a special case. (2) The cost
of production depends on competition (prices). (3) The form of ownership is an important determinant of costs. (4) Firms do not operate
on their production frontier. (5) Firms can increase both output and job
satisfaction, given current inputs (including technology). Some of the
empirical evidence on XE theory will now be presented.

III. EMPIRICAL EVIDENCE FOR XE THEORY IN BOTH INDUSTRIALIZED AND LESS DEVELOPED COUNTRIES

A. Industrialized Countries

The efficiency effects of rate-of-return regulation and the monopol-
ization of public utilities have received much attention in the literature.
Specifically, this literature cites both allocative and X-inefficiency effects.

However, differences in efficiency are shown to exist between monopoly and duopoly utilities. We will return to this point shortly.

Baumol and Klevorick (1970) are among several writers who have discussed XE and regulation. Baumol and Klevorick state that rate-of-return regulation leads to both Averch-Johnson (AJ) overcapitalization and X-inefficiency by keeping inefficient firms in business. Although AJ overcapitalization has received most of the attention, Baumol and Klevorick state that X-inefficiency *may* be the source of a greater amount of inefficiency. Wilson (1975) and Sherman (1976) have argued similarly on the relative size of the AJ and XE effects of such regulations. Others citing AJ and XE efforts are Muskin and Sorrentino (1977), Cross (1970), Wilder and Stansell (1974), and Leland Johnson (1970). In the related field of health care regulation, Newhouse and Taylor (1970), Baron (1974), and Maynard (1979) discuss XE.

Among public utilities in the United States, some evidence exists for the relative size of the AJ and XE effects. Schmidt and Lovell (1979) estimated a stochastic frontier production and cost functions for a sample of 150 privately owned U.S. steam-powered electric-generating plants. Their results show technical inefficiency, or X-inefficiency, pushing costs 8.5 percent above the cost frontier. In addition, allocative inefficiency— the AJ effect—increased costs an additional 9.2 percent above the frontier. Hollas and Herren (1980) used a sample of 30 municipal electric utility firms that were locally regulated in 1972. Their cost figures are for nonproduction expenses. They report a loss from monopoly ranging from 10 to 16 percent, with X-inefficiency accounting for about 9 percent in either case.

Empirical studies on XE will now be shown to be consistent with several implications of XE theory: cost as a function of (1) competition, (2) price, and (3) the form of ownership. In the first category, Pustay (1978), using Civil Aeronautics Board data, estimated the (relative) efficiency of 11 American air carriers over the period 1965 to 1974. Pustay's estimates show that a cost saving of 12 to 15 percent of the total industry cost would be possible if all carriers performed as well as the most efficient airline. Clearly, Pustay's efficiency index is a relative one; to the extent that the most efficient carriers are X-inefficient, his 12 to 15 percent estimate understates the true cost savings possible from greater X-inefficiency. He attributes X-inefficiency among airlines to CAB regulations, which insulate the airlines from external pressures for efficiency. Carlsson (1972) estimated production frontiers for 26 Swedish manufacturing industries in 1968. Carlsson reports the range of average industry efficiency to be .905–.577. His results also show that higher tariffs are associated with less efficient industries and that, in fact, the ten least efficient Swedish industries are well protected from foreign competition.[5]

Primeaux (1977) compared the average total cost (ATC) of 49 municipally owned electric utility duopolies (in almost every case competing with a private firm) with the ATC of municipally owned electric utility monopolies. His data are for the period 1964 to 1968. His results show that, at the mean, municipally owned duopolies had ATCs 10.75 percent below those of municipally owned monopolies, but that this downward shift was larger for smaller firms. In addition, the benefits of XE outweigh those of economies of scale until annual output (sales) reaches 222 million kilowatt-hours. (In 1962, 3,190 systems had annual sales of 100 million kwh, while 427 had sales exceeding 100 million kwh.)

Stevenson (1982) uses a translog cost function and Federal Power Commission (FPC) data for the years 1970 and 1972 on a sample of 79 electric utilities with generating capacity. Two types of utilities are distinguished: a "combination" utility, which derives at least 15 percent of its revenues from its gas component, and "straight" utilities, which derive less than 5 percent of their revenues from gas. The assumption is that "straights" face more competitive pressure. His results show, at the sample mean, X-inefficiency (cost among straights less than costs among combination utilities) to be of the magnitude of 6.1 percent in 1970 and 8.5 percent in 1972.

Erickson (1976) reported the economic effects of price-fixing conspiracies in the gymnasium-seating, rock-salt, and structural-steel industries. In the gymnasium-seating industry a "careful quantitative examination of orders" shows that the elimination of the conspiracy in 1960 lowered manufacturing costs by 23 percent. This reduction was due in part to an increase in technological change and other cost-reducing programs undertaken with the restoration of competition. In the structural-steel industry, the 1950–1962 conspiracy increased costs of production by "at least" 10 percent. In addition, the inertia caused by the conspiracy allowed two postconspirational entrants to enjoy a cost advantage over the older firms and increase their market share. In banking, Fraser and Rose (1972) and Kunreuther, Kidder, and Juncker (1973) showed that *de novo* entry led to an improvement in the cost position and services rendered by already established banks.

Shepherd (1972) showed declining profitability among "older" firms and industries with increased market share and concentration and found the evidence consistent with XE. McFetridge (1973) found lower price-cost margins among Canadian industries protected by tariffs and hypothesized that the protection afforded by tariffs had caused increases in X-inefficiency. The Food Systems Research Group (1977) at the University of Wisconsin compared profits as a percentage of sales among food retailers with varying degrees of market power. Its findings show the growth of profits fell with increased market power. At the same time, operating expenses as a percentage of sales increased. The research group cites X-inefficiency associated with market power as one possible explanation.

In the second, related category, Gallop and Karlson (1978) tested whether an electric utility's ATC is influenced by its ability to recover fuel cost increases through an automatic fuel adjustment mechanism (FAM). FAM is measured as the ratio of recoverable to otherwise incurred costs and is perceived as having both allocative effects and X-effects. Their sample consisted of 119 privately owned retail or predominantly retail electric utility firms with generating capacity. Cost data for the years 1970 to 1972 came from the FPC. Using translog cost function, Gallop and Karlson separated out the allocative effects from the X-effects for the northeast (NE), coal belt (CB), and Gulf states (GS). Their results show that an FAM value of 1.0 would produce X-inefficiencies of 10, 3, and 5 percent of total costs in the NE in 1971, in the NE in 1972, and in the CB in 1972, respectively. Finally, Gallop and Karlson tried to explain the absence of X-effects in the Gulf states. Gulf-states commissions adjust FAM much more frequently than do their NE and CB counterparts, by raising the base fuel prices against which market prices are evaluated. The utilities are thus cautious because the FAM may become inactive or require payments by the firm. In other words, Gulf-states commissions monitor FAM more closely so as to encourage XE while allowing utilities to recover higher costs during periods of inflation.

Davis (1973) used 1965–1968 hospital cost data showing that neither ATC per admission nor wage rates is affected by the *proportion* of expenses covered by a reimbursement plan. However, both ATC per admission and wage rates increased significantly in the period 1967–1968 (after the introduction of Medicare and Medicaid programs in 1966). Davis hypothesizes that this may reflect an "announcement effect" of reimbursement plans, that is, a one-time upward shift in costs. In other words, the ability to charge higher prices led to higher costs.

In the third category—form of ownership and costs—Bruggink (1982) was concerned with operating costs among public and (regulated) private water companies. Bruggink found reason to believe that public firms are more efficient because they operate in a "unfriendly private-enterprise environment" and must justify themselves with efficient behavior. (Bruggink offered no evidence that pressures are greater on public firms.) He applied American Water Works Association operating-cost data for 1960 to a sample of 77 public and 9 private firms. His results show public firms had operating costs 24 percent lower than those of regulated private firms. As Pustay (1978) did, Bruggink points out that both public and regulated private water companies will operate at costs above minimum; that is, they produce with X-inefficiency. Therefore the 24 percent difference reflects the effects of ownership form on *elevated* levels of costs. Silkman and Young (1982) were concerned with the effects of intergovernmental aid on efficiency in local public libraries and school transportation systems. Their sample consisted of 1,317 school districts and 749 local public libraries. A quasi-minimum total-cost frontier for both services was estimated, accounting for quality and local production (supply) conditions. Their data show that schools on the "frontier" had an average cost per transported student of $67.07, while the average school's cost was $142.72. For local libraries the figures are 24 cents and 78 cents per volume, respectively. They report that when the local revenue share (local "ownership") of local services increased, deviations from the frontier costs fell. For example, a 10-percent increase in local share of transportation and library revenues reduced the deviation from the frontier costs by 2.8 and 3.4 percent, respectively. In an average school district with a population of 20,171, this means a saving of $14,926, or 4.62 percent of total operating expenses for transportation. Intergovernmental aid is thus subject to the "other people's money" effect, or X-inefficiency.

Shelton's data (1967) on restaurants was the first published empirical evidence on XE theory following Leibenstein's 1966 paper. Shelton's sample consisted of a chain of 22 restaurants owned by a nationwide company that operates these restaurants primarily on a franchise basis. Each chain is operated with instructions from the parent company to include the waitresses' manners (what each says upon approaching a table), menus, recipe (cooking instructions) for each menu item, and content (pieces of bacon per order). The accounting records are standardized so as to minimize the need for the franchise or to make decisions and exercise judgment. Shelton evaluated performance differences between franchiser-owners (FO) and franchisor-managers (FM) on the basis of profit as a percent of sales, total sales, and total profits when any single chain underwent a shift from a franchiser-owner to a franchisor-manager or vice-versa. Shelton reports profit margins for FOs averaged 9.5 percent, while for FMs it was 1.8 percent. However, sales among FOs and FMs were almost identical. A parent-company executive commented that "sales aren't much higher under FOs." Rather, they "just watch the little things closer, they utilize the cooks and waitresses better. They reduce waste" (p. 1257).

Other students of this subject are Glassman and Rhodes (1980), who found lower costs in a sample of owner-controlled banks; Monsen, Chiu, and Cooley (1968) who reported higher profits (lower costs) among owner-controlled firms in 12 industries; and McEachern (1978), who discovered higher growth in a way suggestive of greater XE in a sample of owner-managed firms in the drug, chemical, and petroleum industries.

Bradley and Gelb (1981) examined the work environment of the Mondragon Cooperative in Spain. They report that not only was the cooperative economically successful in terms of profits and labor productivity but that, compared with other firms in the region, the "workers" had greater trust in "management," provided more encouragement to co-workers for improving productive efficiency, and had a greater belief that hard work creates success. The authors discuss these findings in terms of the environment's impact on XE—greater work effort *and* more job satisfaction.

B. Less Developed Countries

For all economies, but especially for those of less developed countries (LDC), methods of raising saving, investment, and output levels are crucial. The role of the market (competition) and state-owned enterprises have long been considered (Gillis et al., 1983; H.G. Johnson, 1962). In this section we will present empirical evidence on XE theory as it relates to this issue. In general, this evidence is consistent with that presented for industrialized countries.

Several papers may be cited as discussing XE and competition. A paper by Anderson and Frantz (1984) discusses competition in currency markets and its effect on work effort. On February 19, 1982, the Mexican peso, deregulated by the government, fell in value against the U.S. dollar by approximately 40% (from 27 to 45 pesos per dollar). For border-area residents (which includes Mexicali in Baja California, the city in which the authors gathered data on 46 piece-rate workers in two textile plants over the period November, 1981 to April, 1982), approximately 60 percent of purchases was made in dollars. Thus the workers experienced an immediate 25 percent reduction in real income (per unit of effort). The authors' findings, using OLS, showed that the devaluation had the effect of increasing average weekly output per worker by 15 percent. (The number of hours worked per week was constant.) Conversations with the presidents of both firms revealed their strong belief that this reaction was due in part to the workers trying to maintain their own target income level, in part to their reaction to the increased unemployment in the textile industry following the devaluation, and in part to managements' own increased attentiveness toward their businesses. In this case it was the hardship of a currency devaluation that may be said to have led workers and managers out of an "inert area."

As did Schmidt and Lovell (1979) and Hollas and Herran (1982), Bergsman (1974) estimated the incidence of allocative inefficiency and X-inefficiency due to *trade protection,* among a group of six countries (Brazil, Malaya, Mexico, Norway, Pakistan, and the Philippines). For the six countries the average cost as a percentage of their respective gross national products (GNPs) was 3.48 percent. X-inefficiency alone averaged 3.23 percent. In addition, the two small, relatively open countries, Malaya and Norway, averaged 1.2 percent, much lower than the average for the larger, more industrialized countries Mexico and Brazil (4.5 percent) or the Philippines and Pakistan (4.0 percent) which practice(d) import substitution policies.

The effects of power per se are shown by Wells (1973) in his study of choice of technology among six Indonesian industries. Wells reports that non-cost-minimizing choices were more often chosen not by foreign firms per se but by firms with monopoly power. White (1976) used a sample of 31 Pakistani and U.S. industries in the period 1967–1968 to test for the effects of competition on the use of cost-minimizing capital/labor ratios. As might be expected, Pakistani industries with higher concentration have significantly higher capital-labor ratios even after other variables are controlled for. White interprets these findings as showing that a lack of competitive pressure leads to non-cost-minimizing technology, or X-inefficiency. Finally, he interprets his findings to mean that there is flexibility in capital/labor ratios and that a competitive environment acts as a motivator to have cost-minimizing ratios chosen. Katrak (1980) estimated price-cost margins among Indian manufacturing industries and report they showed rising margins until their concentration rate reached 50 percent and falling margins thereafter. He also reports falling margins as wages per unit of output rose and concluded that X-inefficiency may be responsible for these falling margins. Power is also discussed by Lecraw, although here a multitude of factors emerge. In one study, Lecraw (1977) used data from 40 Thai firms, broken down into 12 industry groups and an aggregate manufacturing group. His findings show that higher projected profits (at the time of investment) increase the deviations from cost-minimizing technology, as do less competition and a firm that is owner-managed (ownership form). Lecraw's explanation for this last finding, based on interviews with Thai businessmen, is that while owner-managers have "engineering-man" motives, nonowner managers are not certain of the owners' preferences and "play it safe" by maximizing profits.

In a second study, Lecraw (1978) analyzed capacity utilization using a sample of 200 Thai firms in 12 four-digit light manufacturing industries. For the entire sample actual, desired, and profit-maximizing capacity utilization levels were 28, 29, and 65 percent, respectively. Lecraw reports that higher projected profits, less competition, and owner-managed firms increase the deviation of actual and desired levels from profit-maximizing levels. Finally, Lecraw (1979) estimated $Q/\hat{Q}$ by finding the parameter values in a CES production function that maximized the correlation between Q and $\hat{Q}$. His sample consisted of 40 firms in 12 five-digit light manufacturing industries. Lecraw reports industry values of $(Q/\hat{Q})$ ranging from .612 to .88 with a twelve-industry average of .77. He also reports lower deviations from the production frontier when a firm faced more competition, expected lower profits, and was not owner-managed.

On the form of ownership, Junaker (1976) estimated the productivity effects of farm owners and tenants in India. Output (efficiency) was measured by the value of main crops. The results show that for large farms (greater than ten hectares or 25 acres), the more land leased the less efficient was the farm. For a given quantity of input, owners produced more output. Tyler (1979) estimated industry production functions for 16 plastics firms and 22 steel firms in Brazil in 1971. Tyler calculated firm efficiency indices using both the Farell (F) index and the nonstochastic frontier production function (NSFPF). The average value for the 16 plastics firms was .65 (F) and .48 (NSFPF). For the five foreign firms, the average values were .72 (FG) and .58. Among the 22 steel firms the values were .57 (F) and .62. For the seven foreign firms they were .64 (F) and .72, while for the five publicly owned firms the values were .48 (FG) and .56. In other words, foreign firms had the lowest average deviation from the frontier, while the publicly owned firms had the highest. Gillis (1982) examined state-owned mining enterprises in Bolivia and Indonesia and reports several cases of X-inefficiency. These include the delaying of the use of superior technologies for years because "things never have been done that way" (p. 16). Other examples of "inert areas" include not changing production procedures in response to a change in tax policy designed to elicit a specific change. State-owned enterprises also were reported using "poorer" accounting procedures with respect to performance evaluation, thus blurring "signal transmission." Also found were seniority rules impacting the superior skills of the most recently trained engineers, limits on compensation that discouraged innovation and the maintenance of mines that did not cover AVC. With respect to these examples, Gillis discusses the difference in the performance of privately owned mines.

IV.   CONCLUSIONS AND IMPLICATIONS

The work on XE theory has increased our understanding of the effects of market structure on the performance of both the individual and the firm. In general, the empirical results seem to show that pressure for productive efficiency brought about through market competition and ownership increases the performance of the firm; that is, it lowers per-unit costs and/or brings the firm closer to its production frontier. In other words, the evidence supports the theory. The results may also be interpreted to show that the individual's mode of behavior varies with market structure; that is, competitive pressure increases the attentiveness and care with which one works and uses available resources. Since there is no a priori reason to believe this lowers job satisfaction or producers' surpluses, we might conclude that individuals maximize under some circumstances but not under others.

Maximization is an assumption in most economic models. Following Friedman, many economists argue that it is a model's ability to make good predictions that counts and that, in fact, the model's power of prediction and the unrealism of the models' assumptions are positively related to each other. A different position is that a model should be coherent; that is, its assumptions should be tied to the world of fact and it should provide both prediction *and* understanding. Perhaps realistic assumptions of human behavior are not of much importance in micro theory—the study of market behavior. Cyert and March, in their book *A Behavioral Theory of the Firm* (1964), address this point when they state:

> The theory of the firm, which is primarily a theory of markets, purports to explain at a general level the way resources are allocated by a price system. To the extent to which the model does this successfully, its gross assumptions will be justified. However, there are a number of important and interesting questions relating specifically to firm behavior that the theory cannot answer and was never developed to answer, especially with regard to the internal allocation of resources and the process of setting prices and output.(p.15)

The psychologists Arnold, Evans, and House (1980) addressed this general issue as well in stating:

> If our dependent variables change from those of neoclassical marginalist theory to the effectiveness and productivity of individual firms or sets of firms, then the adequacy of theory will be directly dependent upon the validity of our description of the behavior of individual economic actors. In order to understand, explain, and predict the relationship between decisionmaking and productivity, we must ensure that we have a good theory of decisionmaking based upon sound knowledge of individual psychological processes.(p. 138)

In other words, micro theory assumes mechanistic behavior such that values are maximized and costs minimized; firms produce on their production and cost functions, and all potentials are realized. There is, in essence, no place for behavior or for that matter, behavioral economics.

In addition, the adequacy of behavioral assumptions will have significant welfare implications. This is because the deadweight loss estimates of inefficiency assume that costs are invariant with respect to market structure. If, however, monopolists have higher per-unit costs than do competitive firms, the social cost of monopoly power includes a transfer of resources from a more cost-conscious to a less cost-conscious sector.[6] Tullock (1976) discussed this possibility for the case of government taxation or the imposition of a tariff by government—the welfare costs of government. Others, most notably Leibenstein, have extended this analysis to private enterprise firms possessing market power. The fact that the allocative-deadweight loss has been estimated to be perhaps .001 of the GNP while including XE and the higher per-unit costs may increase the social cost several times means that the behavioral and cost effects of market power do have serious welfare and policy implications for both industrialized and less developed countries.

NOTES

1. Forsund and Hjalmarsson (1974) discuss this issue in relation to XE theory.
2. Frantz (1980, 1982) has written on Leibenstein's use of the personality concept and its similarity to some modern theories in psychology.
3. See Atkinson and Birch (1978) for a discussion and applications of the Yerkes-Dotson law.
4. These and other theories of work motivation are extensively reviewed in Campbell and Pritchard (1976).
5. Forsund and Hjalmarsson (1974) discuss the shortcomings of using production frontiers for measuring XE.
6. If one assumes utility maximization, then these higher "costs" are actually higher benefits of the "quiet life" and hence involve no social cost. See Parish and Ng (1972) for a discussion of this argument. Many papers relating XE theory and utility theory have been summarized by Frantz (1984).

REFERENCES

Anderson, J., and R. Frantz, "The Response of Labor Effort to Falling Real Wages: The Mexican Peso Devaluation of February 1982," *World Development*, 12, no. 7 (July 1984), 759–766.
Arnold, H., M. Evans, and R.J. House, "Productivity: A Psychological Perspective," in S. Maital and N. Meltz, eds., *Lagging Productivity Growth*. Cambridge, MA: Ballinger, 1980.
Atkinson, J. and O. Birch, *Introduction to Motivation*. New York: Van Nostrand, 1978.
Baron, D., "A Study of Hospital Cost Inflation," *Journal of Human Resources*, 9 (Winter 1974), 33–49.
Baumol, W., and A. Klevorick, "Input Choice and Rate of Return Regulation: An Overview of the Discussion," *Bell Journal of Economics*, 1 (Autumn 1970), 162–190.

Bergsman, J., "Commercial Policy, Allocative Efficiency and 'X-Efficiency,' " *Quarterly Journal of Economics*, 88 (August 1974), 409–433.

Bradley, K., and A. Gelb, "Motivation and Control in the Mondragon Experiment," *British Journal of Industrial Relations*, 19 (July 1981), 211–231.

Bruggink, T., "Public Versus Regulated Private Enterprise in the Municipal Water Industry: A Comparison of Operating Costs," *Quarterly Review of Economics and Business*, 22 (Spring 1982), 111–125.

Campbell, J., and R. Pritchard, "Motivation Theory in Industrial and Organizational Psychology," in M. Dunnette, ed., *Handbook of Industrial and Organizational Psychology*. Chicago: Rand McNally, 1976.

Carlsson, B., "The Measurement of Efficiency in Production: An Application to Swedish Manufacturing Industries, 1968" *Swedish Journal of Economics*, 74 (Dec. 1972), 468–485.

Cross, J., "Incentive Pricing and Utility Regulations," *Quarterly Journal of Economics*, 84 (May 1970), 236–253.

Cyert, R., and J. March, *A Behavioral Theory of the Firm*. Englewood Cliffs, NJ: Prentice-Hall, 1963.

Davis, K., "Theories of Hospital Inflation: Some Empirical Evidence," *Journal of Human Resources*, 8 (Spring 1973), 181–201.

Erickson, W., "Price Fixing Conspiracies: Their Long-Term Impact," *Journal of Industrial Economics*, 24 (March 1976), 189–202.

Foods Systems Research Group, "The Profit and Price Performance of Leading Food Chains, 1970–74." U.S. Congress, Joint Economic Committee, 95th Congress, 1st. Session, April 12, 1977. Washington, D.C.: U.S. Government Printing Office, 1977.

Forsund, F., and L. Hjalmarsson, "On the Measurement of Productive Efficiency," *Swedish Journal of Economics*, 76 (June 1974), 141–154.

Frantz, Roger, "On the Existence of X-Efficiency," *Journal of Post Keynesian Economics*, 4 (Summer 1980), 509–527.

Frantz, Roger, "Worker Motivation and X-Efficiency Theory: A Comment," *Journal of Economic Issues*, 16 (September 1982), 864–868.

Frantz, Roger, "Corporate Management, Property Rights and the Existence of X-Efficiency Once More," *Southern Economic Journal*, 50 (April 1984), 1204–1208.

Frantz, Roger, "X-Efficiency Theory: A Review of the Literature, 1966–1983," Center for Public Economics, SDSU, 1984.

Fraser, D., and P. Rose, "Bank Entry and Bank Performance," *Journal of Finance*, 27 (March 1972), 65–78.

Gillis, M., "Allocative and X-Efficiency in State Owned Mining Enterprises: Comparisons Between Bolivia and Indonesia," *Journal of Comparative Economics*, 6 (March 1972), 1–23.

Gillis, M., D. Perkins, M. Roemer, and Donald Snodgrass, *Economics of Development*. New York: W.W. Norton, 1983.

Glassman, C., and S. Rhoades, "Owner versus Manager Control Effects on Bank Performance," *Review of Economics and Statistics*, 62 (May 1980), 263–270.

Gollop, F., and S. Karlson, "The Impact of the Fuel Adjustment Mechanism on Economic Efficiency," *Review of Economics and Statistics*, 60 (November 1978), 574–584.

Gould, J., *The Panda's Thumb*. New York: Norton, 1982.

Graen, G., "Instrumentality Theory of Work Motivation: Some Experimental Results and Suggested Modifications," *Journal of Applied Psychology Monograph*, No. 53 (1969), 1–25.

Hollas, D., and R. Hereen, "An Estimate of the Deadweight and X-Efficiency Losses in the Municipal Electric Industry," *Journal of Economics and Business*, 34 (1982), 269–281.

Johnson, H.G., *Money, Trade and Economic Growth*. London: Allen & Unwin, 1962.

Johnson, L., "Technological Advance and Market Structure in Domestic Telecommunications," *American Economic Review*, 60 (May 1970), 204–218.

Junaker, P., "Land Tenure and Indian Agricultural Productivity," *Journal of Development Studies*, 13 (October 1976), 42–60.

Katona, G., *Essays on Behavioral Economics*. Ann Arbor: I.S.R., 1980.

Katrak, H., "Industry Structure, Foreign Trade and Price-Cost Margins in Indian Manufacturing Industries," *Journal of Development Studies*, 17 (October 1980), 62–79.

Kunreuther, J., K. Kidder, and G. Juncker, "Competition and the Changing Banking Structure in New Jersey," *Monthly Review, Federal Reserve Bank of New York*, 55 (August 1973), 203–210.

Lecraw, D., "Empirical Test for X-inefficiency: A Note," *Kyklos*, 30, no. 1, (1977), 116–120.

Lecraw, D., "Determinants of Capacity Utilization by Firms in LDC's," *Journal of Development Studies*, 5 (June 1978), 139–153.

Lecraw, D., "Choice of Technology in Low-Wage Countries: A Non-Neoclassical Approach," *Quarterly Journal of Economics*, 93 (November 1979), 631–645.

Leibenstein, H., "Allocative Efficiency vs. 'X-Efficiency'," *American Economic Review*, 56 (June 1966), 392–415.

Leibenstein, H., *Beyond Economic Man: A New Foundation for Microeconomics*. Cambridge, MA: Harvard University Press, 1976.

Leibenstein, H., *General X-Efficiency Theory and Economic Development*. New York: Oxford University Press, 1978.

Leibenstein, H., "X-Inefficiency Xists-Reply to an Xorcist," *American Economic Review*, 68 (May 1978), 328–334.

Leibenstein, H., "A Branch of Economics Is Missing: Micro-Micro Theory," *Journal of Economic Literature*, 17 (June 1979), 477–502.

Leibenstein, H., "Microeconomics and X-Efficiency Theory," *Public Interest*, special issue (1980), 97–110.

Leibenstein, H., "The Prisoner's Dilemma in the Invisible Hand: An Analysis of Intrafirm Productivity," *American Economic Review*, 72 (May 1982), 92–97.

Leibenstein, H., "On Bull's-Eye-Painting Economics," *Journal of Post Keynesian Economics*, 4 (Spring 1982), 460–465.

Leibenstein, H., "Property Rights Theory and X-Efficiency Theory: A Comment," *American Economic Review*, 73 (September 1983), 831–842.

McEachern, W., "Corporate Control and Growth: An Alternative Approach," *Journal of Industrial Economics*, 26 (March 1978), 257–266.

Maynard, A., "Pricing Insurance and the National Health Service," *Journal of Social Policy*, 8 (April 1979), 157–176.

Monsen, R., J. Chiv, and D. Cooley, "The Effect of Separation of Ownership and Control on the Performance of the Large Firm," *Quarterly Journal of Economics*, 82 (August 1968), 435–451.

Muskin, J., and J. Sorrentino, "Externalities in a Regulated Industry: The Aircraft Noise Problem," *American Economic Review*, 67 (March 1977), 347–350.

Newhouse, J., and V. Taylor, "The Subsidy Problem in Hospital Insurance: A Proposal," *Journal of Human Resources*, 43 (October 1970), 452–456.

Parish, R., and Y-K. Ng, "Monopoly, X-Efficiency and the Measurement of Welfare Loss," *Economica*, 39 (August 1972), 301–308.

Porter, L.W., and E.E. Lawler, *Managerial Attitudes and Performance*. Homewood, IL: Dorsey Press, 1968.

Primeaux, W., "An Assessment of X-Efficiency Gained Through Competition," *Review of Economics and Statistics*, 59 (February 1977), 105–113.

Pustay, M., "Industrial Inefficiency Under Regulatory Surveillance," *Journal of Industrial Economics*, 27 (September 1978), 49–68.

Schmidt, P., C.A. Lovell, "Estimating Technical and Allocative Inefficiency Relative to Stochastic Production and Cost Functions," *Journal of Econometrics*, 9 (February 1979), 343–366.

Shelton, J., "Allocative Efficiency versus X-Efficiency: Comment," *American Economic Review*, 57 (December 1967), 1252–1258.

Shepherd, W., "The Elements of Market Structure," *Review of Economics and Statistics*, 54 (February 1972), 25–37.

Sherman, R., "Curing Regulatory Bias in U.S. Public Utilities," *Journal of Economics and Business*, 29 (Fall 1976), 1–9.

Silkman, R., and D. Young, "X-Efficiency and State Formula Grants," *National Tax Journal*, 35 (September 1982), 383–397.

Simon, H., "Theories of Decision Making in Economics," *American Economic Review*, 49 (June 1959), 253–283.

Stevenson, R., "X-Inefficiency and Interfirm Rivalry: Evidence from the Electric Utility Industry," *Land Economics*, 58 (February 1982), 52–66.

Tyler, W., "Technical Efficiency in Production in a Developing Country: An Empirical Examination of the Brazilian Plastics and Steel Industries," *Oxford Economic Papers*, 31 (November 1979), 477–495.

Vroom, V., *Work and Motivation*. New York: Wiley, 1964.

Wells, L., Jr., "Economic Man and Engineering Man: Choice and Technology in a Low-Wage Country," *Public Policy*, 21 (Summer 1973), 319–342.

White, L., "Appropriate Technology, X-Inefficiency, and A Competitive Environment: Some Evidence From Pakistan," *Quarterly Journal of Economics*, 90 (November 1979), 575–589.

Wilder, R., and S. Stansell, "Determinants of Research and Development Activity by Electric Utilities," *Bell Journal of Economics and Management*, 5 (Autumn 1974), 646–650.

Wilson, G., "Regulation, Public Policy, and Efficient Provision of Freight Transportation," *Transportation Journal*, 15 (Fall 1975), 5–20.

SAFETY REGULATION AND "IRRATIONAL" BEHAVIOR

William T. Dickens

I. INTRODUCTION

The standard economic approach to analyzing safety problems begins with the presumption that consumers or workers have well-defined preferences over different states of the world (i.e., healthy, injured, dead) and estimates of the probability of each state, contingent on their purchase of each product or taking each of many jobs. If they are insufficiently sure about these probabilities, or any other characteristics of the products or jobs, they will engage in a search for more information, stopping only when the perceived marginal benefit of additional search is exceeded by the cost. Then the consumers/workers make their choices. These behavioral assumptions, along with some additional assumptions about the nature of preferences and market alternatives, provide the basis for predictions about the welfare implications of government regulation.

Of course, no one believes these assumptions. Nonetheless, economists still feel that they are useful. Even models based on assumptions that are demonstrably false can produce excellent predictions. The name most often associated with this point of view is Milton Friedman (1953). He gives the example of a model of the position of leaves on a tree in which it is assumed that the leaves arrange themselves to maximize their exposure to sunlight. Another example is a model of the shots made by an expert billiard player in which the player uses spherical trigonometry and Newton's laws of motion to plot the optimal paths for the billiard balls (Friedman, 1953, pp. 19–22). The leaves of the tree do not consciously place themselves to receive more sunlight, and the billiard player never performs the trigonometric calculations in planning his shots. Despite this, the models work. In both cases the processes are in some sense sufficiently similar to the models so that the predictions of the model are accurate. According to Friedman, theories should be judged only by the accuracy of their predictions and not by their assumptions.

Unfortunately, Friedman's observations about appropriate methodology are of little use to policy makers planning safety regulations. They need to know, not which theory is "true" or "best" in some absolute sense, but which theory will provide the most accurate assessment of the welfare effects of alternative policies. But these welfare effects are inherently unobservable.[1] Thus the theories must be judged on the basis of their success in predicting phenomena that are not of immediate concern and also on the plausibility of their extension to the phenomenon of interest. This latter type of judgment must involve the examination of the assumptions of competing theories—something that even Friedman (p. 23) allows as a legitimate enterprise. No one would use the "intelligent-leaf" model to explain the position of leaves on the ground. The optimal billiard-player model is unlikely to do well in predicting the shots of a novice. Similarly, the rational economic-agent model may be inappropriate for judging the relative merits of programs for promoting consumer and job safety.

In other applications, approximately rational decisions are supposed to result from competitive selection of more rational agents or from individuals' learning from repeated experience. Firms that do not behave rationally may be driven out of business by those that do. Alternatively, a person who repeats the same task many times has many opportunities to think of better ways to do it and to experiment with alternatives. However, competitive selection may not operate for consumers and workers. Learning may also be inadequate, since adverse safety outcomes are very infrequent for almost all jobs and products. This suggests that there is a prima facie case for further consideration of how peoples' decisions may deviate from the standard assumptions of rationality. In fact, behavioral decision theory researchers have found that individuals (as opposed to groups) making probabilistic judgments about unlikely occurrences, with few opportunities to repeat the judgment and thereby learn from mistakes, are subject to a wide variety of potentially serious biases. Firms' safety decisions may not be perfect, but their decisions are more likely to be made by groups, and their wider range of experience may allow for more learning. Consequently, this analysis focuses on workers' and consumers' decisions. What we need to do is identify the types of judgment errors that might affect individual safety choices. We can then consider how we would expect markets to behave if the errors were prevalent. If market behavior is consistent with such errors, we may consider the policy implications of models that assume that people make serious judgment errors. The rest of this paper follows this line of analysis.

Section II presents a brief review of relevant aspects of behavioral decision theory literature. The conclusion of this review is that a large number of people may act as if they were ignoring safety in making their decisions. Those who do not act in this manner may make decisions that are inconsistent. Section III presents a model of market behavior when economic agents are subject to these judgment errors. Section III also considers whether such a model fits with what we know about implicit markets for job safety. Section IV examines the policy implications of this model, and Section V is a brief summary and conclusion.

II. JUDGMENT ERRORS AND SAFETY DECISIONS

Dickens (1985) contains an extensive review of the behavioral decision theory literature relevant to occupational safety and health decisions. With some minor qualifications, most of that discussion is relevant here. Both occupational safety decisions and product safety decisions involve the same sorts of problems. The major differences are: first, most people purchase a given product more frequently than they change jobs; second, their purchases probably involve consideration of a smaller number of attributes than do job choices, and third, a job is far more important for the survival and comfort of most workers than is almost any single product purchase. For the types of judgment errors discussed below, the first two differences probably work to make product choices more rational than job choices. The effect of the third is hard to judge. The higher costs and benefits involved in job choice may give people incentives to be more rational.[2] On the other hand, they also increase the likelihood of motivation conflict, which can result in less rational behavior. These differences between product choice and job choice may be significant in some cases. Still, for many types of products—automobiles, lawn mowers, children's toys, tires, or power tools—the similarities are sufficient to warrant considering both product safety regulation and job safety regulation together.

One conclusion of my review of problems likely to complicate workers' decisions with respect to job safety is that potentially important deviations from rationality can be divided into three classes. The first and most important is that people often overlook low-probability events in making decisions even when the cost of overlooking them may be great. The second is that when people do pay attention to low-probability events in making decisions, their judgments tend to be inconsistent and subject to a number of biases. Without more information on the specifics of safety choices it is difficult to say what the net direction of all biases is, but what is more important, from the policy perspective, is that these biases affect people differently and will introduce more inconsistency into decisions. This inconsistency can be shown to produce market failures, which cause inefficiencies and can lead to an underprovision of product or job safety in an unregulated market. The third problem concerns decisions made after an initial commitment to a particular job. For several reasons, people may form unrealistically optimistic assessments of the job they are on. This may lead them to make inappropriate decisions about future job changes and self-protection decisions on the current job. What follows is a brief review of some of the evidence for the existence and relevance of these three classes of decision errors.

People often do not use all the information available to them. Kahneman and Tversky (1979) propose a theory of behavior based on their interpretation of laboratory evidence of how people make choices involving probabilistic outcomes. According to the theory, people edit out certain information in choosing among lotteries. For instance, people will not concern themselves with a trait if options are similar with respect to that trait. Also, low-probability outcomes are often ignored.

Job or product choices involving safety are essentially choices among lotteries. With a very high probability, one gets a product that does what one wants or a source of livelihood. With some low probability one may also be injured. Jobs or products may differ substantially with respect to the likelihood of an injury. But if people do not pay attention to low-probability events when choosing between jobs or products, their choices will not depend on relative safety.

The decisions made by Kahneman and Tversky's subjects were very abstract and simple compared with the decisions made by workers and consumers. One might suspect that real-world decisions are not made in the same way as these. On one hand, the fact that real-world decisions are much more complex and involve many more attributes suggests that they may be more subject to error than decisions made in laboratory settings. However, people have a great deal at stake in making purchases and work decisions, and these incentives may make them less prone to error. The evidence for incentive effects on judgment errors of all kinds is mixed. McAllister et al. (1979) show that people facing more significant decisions, or decisions that cannot be reversed, tend to choose more complex and analytic decision strategies. But Grether and Plott (1979) find a slightly higher incidence of preference inconsistency among subjects whose compensation for taking part in an experiment depended on their performance. Similarly, Borgida and Nisbett (1977) found that students making judgments about courses they were planning to take were more likely to make a particular judgment error than students who were not going to take the courses. Finally, Fischer (1982) found that incentives reduce the frequency of extreme overconfidence, though substantial overconfidence persists.

Despite the differences between these abstract decisions and job and product choices, there is some evidence that the tendency to ignore low-probability events carries over to real-world decision problems. A number of authors have remarked on the apparent irrationality of people living in earthquake-prone areas and floodplains in that the majority of them fail to purchase actuarially advantageous government-subsidized insurance. Kunreuther (1978) has argued that the tendency to ignore low-probability events is one of the most important barriers to people making rational decisions about disaster insurance. To demonstrate this, he conducted laboratory experiments involving simulations of fairly complex real-world decisions. Subjects in the experiment played a farm management game. Several times during the game subjects were offered the option of purchasing actuarially fair insurance against hazards with probabilities of occurrence that ranged from .002 to .25 per simulated year. All hazards had the same expected cost (probability times loss). On the average, people in this experiment were much more likely to purchase insurance against more probable but less costly hazards than very costly but improbable hazards. When the subjects were questioned about their decisions, most indicated they did not consider the latter hazards likely enough to warrant further thought (p. 183), even though the cost of these events was relatively high.

The tendency to ignore low-probability events will be exacerbated by another common error. People have a tendency to view themselves as being less likely to have undesirable experiences than statistical evidence suggests they are.[3] In particular, Rethans (1979) found that people believe they are less likely than the average person to be harmed by the products they use. Thus, even if people perceive the average danger of a job or product to be high, they may still ignore the problem because "It can't happen to me."

Even people who do not ignore safety will not necessarily make decisions that consistently approximate the norm of the rational decision maker. One of the most fundamental problems with human judgment about the likelihood of different outcomes is that it is inconsistent. The extent of this problem is illustrated by studies which have shown that, in many situations, simple rules derived from an expert decision maker's behavior performed better than did the decision maker himself.[4] It would be expected that a decision maker could always do at least as well as a simple rule just by applying the rule. It would also be natural to assume that a human decision maker could outperform a rule by taking more factors into account. But this is evidently not the case. It appears that people are either inconsistent in applying their own rules or are overly influenced by unique information not covered by the rules. Thus, even if workers or consumers have sufficient information to form accurate judgments of hazards, their assessments may be subject to random judgment errors.

There are many reasons for this inconsistency. For example, it has been argued that vivid anecdotal information seems to have more of an impact on most people's judgment than more diagnostic statistical information.[5] Vivid information seems to be more easily recalled from memory. To determine how likely an event is, most people seem to try to see how easy it is to recall an instance of that event. Kahneman and Tversky (1979) have labeled this method of judging probability the "availability heuristic." This process is often functional. However, the inefficient use of information will contribute to inconsistency in judgment. To the extent that people differ in their exposure to anecdotes and their ability to recall them, their decisions will differ.

Besides paying too much attention to vivid anecdotal information, people also have a demonstrable tendency to ignore base-rate data in forming expectations.[6] People will take extreme outcomes as being fully representative of the behavior of a process even if they know that such behavior is unusual for similar processes (base-rate information). For example, people may put too much weight on the accident experience of a particular firm, relative to the experience of other plants in the industry, in judging the safety of that plant. Thus inconsistency will be exacerbated if people share base-rate data but have different knowledge of specific problems with particular products or jobs.

Another problem that is likely to induce inconsistency is what Tversky and Kahneman (1982, p. 14) call *anchoring*. Any preconception about the nature of a phenomenon is likely to affect a person's perception of that phenomenon.[7] To a certain extent, such interpretation of evidence is not a problem. In many situations, what people do may be a shorthand for a more complicated and normatively correct filtering of information. But there is substantial evidence that people are overly conservative in changing preconceptions in the face of new evidence.[8] In fact, it has been found that any starting estimate for a judgment task, even one that a subject knows to be completely arbitrary, may affect judgment (Tversky and Kahneman, 1974).

There is other evidence that people do not pay much attention to the quality of information. For instance, it appears that people tend to pay no attention to sample size.[9] Besides the example of random anchoring described above, other situations have been found where nondiagnostic information seems to affect judgment (Nisbett, Zukier, and Lemley, 1981; Edgell and Hennessey, 1980). Thus peoples' decisions may be overly sensitive to small amounts of unique information—even irrelevant information. This, too, will contribute to inconsistency. Finally, it has been argued that people do not discount evidence from biased samples even if they are aware of the bias.[10] In most situations this is probably not important, since the population one wishes to make inferences about is the one with which one is familiar. However, workers who hunt for information about a job by talking to workers who are still on that job, or people who consult current owners of a product for information about that product, may not discount the information received appropriately considering the biased nature of the sample. Workers currently holding a job may see it in a better light than others who have considered the job and not taken it or those who have quit. Similarly, people who purchased a particular brand were those who thought it was the best.

Of course, choices may be inconsistent between individuals with identical tastes even if people are rational, if they have different sets of information. For example, people may form their expectations about the danger of a product or job from the experience of their acquaintances who work on the job or own the product. Since people have different friends with different experiences, they may have different information. These differences will be exacerbated by the decision errors described above. In addition, a nearly universal problem with human judgment is that people tend to be overconfident. When people are asked to say how sure they are of a judgment they have made, they tend to report being more confident than is warranted, given the available data. When people are asked to estimate confidence intervals on their judgments, especially in real-world situations, they generally report intervals that prove to be too tight in the light of subsequent events.[11] The more uncertain one is about a decision, the greater the perceived value of new information. But if people are usually overconfident about their estimates, they may engage in too little information search, further exacerbating the inconsistencies due to unique information.[12]

Once someone is on a job or has purchased a product, he or she may make errors in deciding how much insurance to buy, how careful to be on the job or while using the product, or whether to change jobs or to discard or replace a product. Two factors complicate such decisions. Both may lead people to behave as if they believed that their chosen job or product were safer than it is. Thus people may tend to purchase too little insurance, view carefulness as less worthwhile, and be less willing to replace a product than they should be.

The first problem was discussed above—once someone has formed an opinion about something, that opinion will be resistant to change. Tversky and Kahneman call this anchoring. Evidence that does not fit with a person's beliefs may be ignored or given less credence. Since people usually choose the product or job they feel is best for them, this view may be very persistent. Further, if people choose jobs or products that they initially believe are safe, they may not react as much as they should to new information indicating that their jobs or products are dangerous. Anchoring may not be the only source of this type of problem. Once one has made a commitment to a product or job, motivation conflict may complicate decisions. Motivation conflict results when two or more preferences cannot be indulged at the same time. In this case, the conflict would be between the desire to make later decisions that protect one's safety and the desire to see one's job or chosen product as safe, one's original decision as a good one, and oneself as a competent decision maker. When this sort of conflict occurs, people may change their beliefs about the world in order to accommodate their conflicting desires.

Akerlof and Dickens (1982) have operationalized a model of motivation conflict. They make three assumptions about people's behavior that distinguish their work from the standard economic model. First, people have preferences not only over states of the world but over their own beliefs about the world. Second, people can manipulate their own beliefs. Finally, changes people make in their beliefs can affect their future behavior. Akerlof and Dickens support these assumptions by citing a number of experiments drawn from the literature on cognitive dissonance. Taken together, these three axioms can lead to decisions that while optimal from the point of view of the individual, can produce outcomes in unregulated competitive markets that are not first best. For example, Akerlof and Dickens have developed a model of choice of safety equipment in which workers prefer to believe that their jobs are safe. In order to make correct decisions about future purchase of safety equipment, workers must admit that their job is dangerous. Whether workers do this and suffer the psychic costs or choose to believe that their jobs are safe and fail to purchase safety equipment, they could be made better off by a law requiring them to buy the safety equipment. This model is easily extended to decisions about insurance, job changing, or replacement of a previously purchased product.

Clearly, the behavioral decision theory literature shows that the standard economic model of choice under uncertainty does not predict a wide range of observed behavior that seems relevant to economic decisions in which safety is one of the attributes considered. Can a model based on these behavioral observations explain the behavior of implicit markets for safety as well as the standard model? We turn to this question now.

III. A BEHAVIORAL MODEL OF SAFETY CHOICE— CAN IT FIT THE FACTS?

To begin, let us consider how a product market might behave if some consumers did not pay attention to safety. For ease of exposition, let us assume that the product is provided by a large number of competitive producers. In this case each competitor produces the good at zero profit. Producers may differ in the price they charge and the safety of the good they provide. The heavy curved line (P,C) in Figure 1 shows the minimum average cost of producing the product with each level of safety. There is a least cost point. Providing more or less safety increases the cost. Except for differences in safety, we will assume the products are identical. If a firm sets its price equal to the minimum average cost and produces the necessary volume, it will earn zero profits. Competitive producers must price their products so that the price-safety combinations they offer are on the P,C Curve. Since all consumers are assumed to be attentive to price, if a producer's product fell above the P,C Curve, another firm could enter and offer an equally safe product at a lower price, take away the first firm's business, and still make a positive profit. This possibility is ruled out by the assumption of competition. If a pro-

Figure 1. Implicit market for product safety with attentive and inattentive consumers.

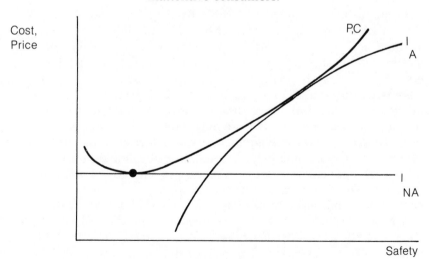

ducer's product fell below the P,C Curve, the firm would be paying more to produce the product than it would be earning from its sale and would go out of business.

Consumers who are attentive to the safety of the product will choose a price-safety pair that maximizes their utility, subject to the constraint that the price-safety pair lies on the heavy curved line. A consumer's choice can be represented as the tangency of an individual indifference curve and the zero profit locus (Rosen, 1974). One such curve (I_A) is depicted in Figure 1.

Consumers who are not attentive to safety will choose to buy the good with the lowest price. These consumers' preferences are represented by the horizontal indifference curve I_{NA} in Figure 1. An economist observing a product market where these two price-safety pairs were offered would see nothing wrong. Apparently people with different tastes are purchasing products offering different amounts of safety. Those who desire less safety pay less for the product. However, the existence of the price-safety trade-off provides no evidence that the market is operating efficiently. Competition and the increasing cost of safety create the trade-off, not differences in preferences.

The apparent existence of such trade-offs in the labor market has been cited as evidence that markets may come close to efficiently allocating job safety.[13] However, an analysis similar to the one presented above can also produce compensating wage differences in a labor market where many workers pay no attention to safety in making job decisions (see the appendix). All that is necessary is that some workers pay attention to safety. How well does such a model fit with other things we know about the implicit market for job safety?

So far we have assumed that some fixed group of workers or consumers are nonattentive to safety. But if we consider who is likely to be attentive and how events might change this, we can get some additional insights into market behavior. For example, we might expect that workers or consumers who experience an accident may be more likely to be attentive. Kunreuther (1978) found that one of the major determinants of whether people purchased disaster insurance was whether they had recently experienced one. If inattentive workers who experience or observe an accident become attentive, they may realize that they would prefer a safer job. Some may choose to quit and find a new job. Thus, all other things being equal, we would expect inattentive workers to have a higher turnover rate than workers who are attentive. Inattentive workers will be in the more hazardous jobs, so we would expect that more dangerous jobs would have higher turnover rates (see the appendix). Viscusi (1979a) found that workers in more dangerous jobs do have higher turnover rates. He suggests that this is the result of job search with imperfect information, but the observation fits just as well with the model proposed above.

It has also been observed that young people are more likely to be injured on the job. It has been suggested that the inexperience of young workers makes them more accident prone. On the other hand, younger workers are also more agile and have better reflexes and more acute senses. From this we might expect them to be less accident prone. The behavioral model provides another explanation. If experience makes people less likely to be inattentive, we might expect young people to be disproportionately represented in dangerous jobs and thus more likely to have accidents.

It was noted above that decisions made by groups are more likely to approach the norm of rational behavior than are decisions made by individuals. From this we might expect that wages negotiated by unions would be more likely to reflect differences in job safety than nonunion wages. Dickens (1984b) reviewed the evidence on union/nonunion differences in compensating wage differentials. That review found that every study of differences in compensation for exposure to deadly hazards shows unions receiving larger compensating differences. Further, only one study found statistically significant compensating differences in the nonunion sector, and I present evidence that suggests that this finding is due to the absence of controls for other job characteristics. The findings with respect to nonfatal hazards are inconsistent. Perhaps the greater frequency of nonfatal injuries increases workers' awareness of the conditions likely to cause them, so that more workers are attentive to them. Alternatively, the evidence for compensating wage differences for exposure to nonfatal hazards is weak (Smith, 1979), and perhaps the inconsistency just reflects the inadequacy of the data. This evidence suggests the possibility that, at least with respect to potentially fatal job hazards, nearly all nonunion workers are inattentive.

This last conclusion seems to be inconsistent with the observation by Viscusi (1979, p. 239) that over half of all blue-collar workers report that their jobs expose them to some danger. In addition, this self-reported job danger is positively related to wages, after controlling for other factors. If we interpret people's reporting that they are exposed to danger as indicating that they are attentive to safety, we might expect that self reported danger would be negatively correlated with wages, after controlling for other factors. If we interpret self-reported danger as being indicative of both attentiveness and above-average danger, we must conclude that nearly all workers are attentive. However, neither of these interpretations is necessarily appropriate. Workers who report that their jobs expose them to some danger may not have considered the danger when they first accepted their current jobs and may not consider it in any future decisions to change jobs. All players in Kun-reuther's (1978) farm game were aware of the possibility of the low-probability–high-cost disasters, and most still ignored them. The mean-ing of the question is further complicated because what people mean by danger may differ among them. Some who report not being exposed to danger mean that they are not exposed to extreme danger. Others who report being exposed may refer to trivial hazards. Finally, when the effect of this self-report variable on earnings is broken down by the union status of the workers, the effect is statistically significant only in the union sector and only in one of the two specifications tried. Thus it is not clear how to interpret this finding. It certainly does not constitute proof that nonattentiveness to safety is not a problem.

Another apparent inconsistency is that many employers offering the most dangerous jobs do spend money on protection. Given the simple model described in the appendix, we would expect that such employers would hire workers who are not attentive to job safety and therefore have no incentive to invest in protection. There are two possible expla-nations for this. First, some jobs may be so dangerous—such as test pilot or race-car driver—that everyone is attentive to safety when considering them. Beyond this, there are other incentives for firms to provide job and product safety. All employers are required to carry workers' com-pensation insurance. Almost all employers can reduce their workers' compensation bills by having their premiums set on the basis of their performance. This gives them an incentive to spend some resources on safety. In the product market, the threat of suits alleging liability for accidents will provide incentives for firms to remove at least the most extreme dangers from their products.

Firms may wish to avoid having a large number of accidents. If they do not, they may develop a bad reputation, so that people dealing with them will be attentive to safety. Workers considering employment in a warehouse where many people they know have been injured may be attentive to safety there. The same workers may not be attentive when considering other employment. In the field of product safety, after the series of serious accidents involving Ford Pintos or those involving Fire-stone 500 tires, people considering buying Ford Pintos or Firestone 500 tires may have become more attentive to safety than they had previously been; they may have become more attentive even in considering other brands.

Finally, employers who wish to retain employees for long periods of time, and producers who want consumers to repeat their purchases frequently, have an incentive to provide more safety. First, the added safety will make it less likely that a worker or consumer will experience an accident that would lead to attentiveness and a change in job or brand choice. Second, those who become attentive will be less likely to change because the safety level would be more acceptable.

Taken together, these other considerations may or may not create enough incentive for firms to provide near optimal amounts of safety. However, they can explain why firms employing inattentive workers may spend some money on safety measures.

Even if workers and consumers are attentive to safety, their decisions may not result in an efficient allocation of safety. In the model used above, those who were attentive to safety worked in jobs or purchased products that offered the best wage/price safety combinations possible, given their tastes and the possibilities offered by the market (see the appendix). However, the evidence presented in Section II strongly suggests that even attentive people will make inconsistent and biased judgments about safety. If they do, how will markets behave?

Considering all attentive people who have similar tastes, each should have the same preference ranking for available jobs or products. The evidence on inconsistency from Section II suggests that they do not. People with similar tastes will order jobs differently because of decision errors. However, we would not expect preference orderings to be completely random. While the decision strategies people use are imperfect, they are functional to some extent in most situations (Klein, 1983). For instance, we would expect that two jobs or products that differed a great deal in their true expected utility would be less likely to be ranked incorrectly than two relatively similar jobs or products. We would also expect that lowering a product's price or paying a higher wage would tend to cause people to rank the product or job higher. Such a model of preference orderings would be indistinguishable from one in which people make random errors in their perception of product or job safety. This is fortunate, since models of this type have been analyzed by Perloff and Salop (1980) and Dickens (1984a, p. 162–166).

The conclusion of these analyses is that market outcomes will depart from efficiency in three ways. First, the fact that everyone has a different view of the desirability of each product or job means that each producer or employer faces a demand/supply curve that is less than infinitely elastic. Consequently, producers/employers will have monopoly/monopsony power. Second, the people who buy a particular product or take a particular job will tend to be those who perceive it as being safer than it is. This may lead them to fail to purchase actuarially fair insurance against the consequences of an accident. Interestingly, the fact that people will systematically underestimate the danger of the job or product they choose does not mean that employers or producers will not have an incentive to produce products with the optimal amount of safety. What matters is not whether people correctly perceive the level of safety but whether the market as a whole correctly responds to changes in the level of safety. The conditions when this will happen are not entirely unbelievable in an information model. However, if people are subject to the sorts of judgment errors described in Section II, it becomes implausible. For example, even people who are attentive to safety may not pay attention to differences between jobs or products they consider to be relatively safe. Since people will tend to choose the products or jobs they perceive as being safer, changes in safety are less likely to be perceived and acted on by the relevant agents. If demand/supply curves do not change at all in response to changes in the provision of safety, there will be no incentives for firms to expend any resources on improving safety.

The analysis above suggests that if either of the first two types of deviation from rationality identified in Section II are common, workers or consumers may be protected by far fewer safety measures than is optimal from an objective cost/benefit perspective, and policy intervention may be productive. In addition, the model of cognitive dissonance described in Section II has obvious policy implications. Section IV considers the possibilities.

IV. POLICY IMPLICATIONS

Although the behavioral model presented above appears to be fully consistent with observed labor and product market behavior and is based on extensive laboratory and observational evidence of the nature of human behavior, serious policy recommendations based on the model are still premature. To have confidence in the model, we would like to have more direct evidence about the salience of the behavioral assumptions. To get this information, additional research should be conducted. A sober call for this type of research would be an appropriate way to end this paper. Alternatively, concluding the paper with some speculation on the policy implications of a behavioral model would be more provocative. Experience shows that such a conclusion would also be more likely to lead to additional research. In this spirit, here are some tentative lessons we might take from the above discussion.

First, even if many people pay no attention to safety in making market decisions, that does not by itself mean that additional government intervention is needed. In Section III a list of several other incentives firms face for providing safety was presented. Before considering new policies, we should examine these incentives to see how close they are likely to bring us to the first best for the provision of safety.

The first incentive discussed above was workers' compensation insurance. From any perspective we would expect this to have some impact on job safety. However, workers' compensation payments do not completely repay workers for medical expenses and lost wages. They certainly provide no compensation for pain and suffering. Thus any incentives firms and insurance companies face are necessarily insufficient to insure that safety levels are efficient. Further, if an attempt was made to increase workers' compensation payments so that they did fully compensate the average worker for accidental losses, the average worker would be indifferent toward having or not having an accident. Workers with higher than average marginal utilities of income would prefer to be injured if their disutility of injury was less than or equal to average. Certainly we do not wish to create incentives so that a large number of people will want to have accidents.

Workers' compensation laws prevent employees from suing their employers for occupational injuries in almost all cases. However, firms have no protection from liability claims by their customers. If the courts could costlessly establish responsibility for accidents and could also exactly determine the dollar value of all damages, firms would have the correct incentives for providing safety even if all consumers were totally inattentive to safety. When the court system is not perfect or costless, outcomes depend on the nature of imperfections, and the incentives provided by legal liability can be perverse. For example, Simon (1980) shows that reliance on torts to insure product quality can have undesirable distributional consequences, if courts are costly and outcomes are risky.

Another constraint faced by firms in both the product and the labor market is the effect of accidents on their reputations. This may be of considerable importance to firms dealing with relatively small groups of consumers or workers. The pharmacist who accidently poisons someone in a small town is likely to go out of business. The pharmaceutical company that produces a drug with serious side effects may be unaffected by any resulting illnesses unless the problem is widespread enough to get attention from the media. Similarly, a firm that draws workers from a sufficiently diverse group of people may not have its reputation damaged by a relatively serious safety problem.

An exception would be firms that need repeat customers to maintain an efficient level of production or one that needs a stable work force to take advantage of specific human capital or the efficiency incentives of age-earnings profiles. As noted above, such firms have an incentive to provide more safety to prevent accidents.

While the above discussion is a relatively complete account of what mechanisms besides premiums in prices or wages may induce firms to provide job or product safety, it does not indicate the quantitative significance of these incentives. We still do not know whether they are adequate to ensure workers' and consumers' safety. However, there is evidence that can be interpreted as showing there may be significant departures from efficiency despite the incentives.

If one believes that a large number of workers are inattentive to safety when they are deciding which job to take, the fact that firms with lower turnover also have lower accident rates indicates that all incentives taken together are not enough to get the high-turnover firms to provide socially optimal levels of safety. Similarly, it is interesting to note that the classes of products for which repeat purchases are most important—food and drugs—were the first to be subject to government safety regulation. This regulation has met with far less resistance than other types of product safety regulation. Most covered firms proudly display their USDA ratings as a sign that they meet high quality standards. Similarly, restaurant inspections are at least tolerated, if not supported, by the affected firms. Producers of consumer products that tend to be less frequently purchased have been far less receptive to regulation. They have put up stiff resistance to the consumer products safety commission and other government attempts to insure product safety and quality. This can be interpreted as indicating that the regulation of products with large numbers of repeat purchases is less of a constraint on producers than regulation of less frequently purchased products.

These observations suggest that if many people are not attentive to safety there are at least some market segments where incentives are inadequate to induce firms to provide optimal levels of safety. For this reason, it is worth considering what the alternatives might be for government intervention.

If inattentiveness to safety is a problem, one obvious solution is to do something to make people pay attention to safety in making product and job choices. Educational campaigns may be one way to do this. But studies suggest that many decision problems are very deeply rooted, and extensive education is necessary to get people to behave in accordance with the rational model.[14]

Another alternative would be to require that firms provide information on product and job safety to prospective customers or employees. This might prompt people to be attentive. If safety information is present in a highly visible form when people are making their decision, they may be more likely to use it. Another advantage of requiring the provision of safety information is that if it is provided in a very accessible form, the second type of problem—the inconsistency of judgment decisions—might be ameliorated.

But if we require the provision of safety information, we must also consider whether there are other sorts of information people should be taking into account. For instance, people may not pay attention to the energy efficiency of electrical appliances or to product durability. Workers may not pay attention to differences in retirement benefits between employers or the security and actuarial assumptions of their pension plans, or they may ignore the long-run career prospects in a particular occupation or industry. If a few important considerations could be identified for each product or job, provision of information might be an adequate solution to this problem. But if there are many equally important things that people do not pay attention to, supplying information would probably be an inadequate response. The more information that is provided, the less likely people are to read it and use it in their decisions. Another possible problem with information provision is that the information may come too late. By the time a person gets to the point of coming to a firm to apply for a job or buy a product, much of the screening of alternatives may have been done already. If this is the case, other remedies would have to be considered. Behavioral decision researchers are skeptical of the usefulness of information for a number of other reasons (see Slovic, Fischhoff, and Lichtenstein, 1982).

Another possibility is the introduction of a system of fines or taxes levied against companies for injuries incurred by workers or users of a firm's product. Also, firms that expose their workers to dangerous chemicals or working conditions might be taxed. A problem with using fines or taxes is that it does nothing to eliminate the monopoly/monopsony power caused by misjudgments and misinformation. This is no problem if everyone is inattentive, but the opposite is true if a substantial number of people do pay attention to safety and are either poorly informed or subject to inconsistency in judgment.

Perhaps the most appealing attribute of direct regulation is that it would eliminate any monopoly power resulting from inconsistent judgments about safety. If regulations are passed to enforce a uniform level of job and product safety consistent with negligible risk, people may be inattentive with no ill effects. The biggest drawback to uniform regulation is that it ignores differences in costs between industries in providing safety. But allowing for flexibility could reintroduce the problems of monopoly and monopsony power. Perhaps the best idea would be to establish uniform standards but then allow firms to violate them if they could provide an economic rationale for doing so and would agree to inform customers or workers about the nature and likely consequences of the violation of the standard. Thus workers and consumers would be protected in most situations and could be inattentive to safety with no ill effects. In cases where there were dangers, their attention would be called to it by information supplied to them when they investigated the job or product. In addition, the information could be designed to aid people in making decisions that were as consistent and rational as possible. Finally, such a regulatory regime would have the efficiency effects, described in Section II, of ameliorating problems caused by motivation conflict.

Of course, one of the major lessons of the OSHA experience has been that setting regulations does not guarantee improvements in safety. Regulations that are not effectively enforced are useless. In a model where workers are not completely rational, inadequately enforced regulation can be worse than useless. If workers believe that regulation is working and become less attentive to safety, regulation might make them worse off. The seriousness of this consideration is suggested by a study by Burton, Kates, and White (1978), which argues that the sense of security generated by flood-control dams has made people who live near them far less cautious and has increased the yearly losses due to floods.

On the other hand, some of the problems with offsetting behavioral responses to safety regulation may be less serious in behavioral models than in models where people are assumed to be rational. In a behavioral model there are at least two reasons we might expect people to be more cautious if safety is regulated. First, if mandated changes are sufficiently noticeable, people who would otherwise have been inattentive to the risk may pay attention and take precautions. For instance, requiring automatic safety belts may cause people to be more conscious of safety when driving. Requiring exhaust hoods and other precautions when people work with dangerous chemicals may make people more careful in dealing with chemicals.

Second, Katona (1965, p. 4) has identified what he calls a "goal gradient" effect. As people get closer to a desired end they work harder to obtain it. From that perspective, people who are in very dangerous jobs may feel they cannot do much to affect their safety. People in jobs where regulation has made them relatively safe may be more likely to put in the effort to prevent accidents.

In addition to these implications for the nature of regulatory law, the behavioral model also has implications for optimal enforcement strategies. The model developed above suggests that firms with high turnover rates or a younger work force are more likely to be underinvesting in safety precautions. Industries with high turnover rates and/or younger workers are therefore good prospects for more intense regulatory overseeing. So are those firms within an industry that operate with less stable or younger work forces. In the product market, items that are purchased infrequently are most likely to present safety problems.

V. CONCLUSION—WHAT IS TO BE DONE?

In choosing an appropriate model for analyzing alternative programs for protecting workers and consumers, it is impossible to compare the predictions of models with respect to the phenomena we care most about—the effects of regulation on welfare. Instead, we must consider how well competing theories can explain other relevant types of behavior. We must also consider whether the assumptions of the theory are likely to produce reasonable predictions about the welfare consequences of regulation.

The preceding analysis strongly suggests that there are many types of behavior relevant to safety regulation decisions that are not consistent with the standard economic model. Further, a model based on behavioral assumptions, which allows for the types of decision errors that have been found in behavioral decision theory research, has been shown to be consistent with most of what is known about implicit safety markets. The analysis of Section IV shows that the policy implications of such a model are distinct in many ways from previously considered models where decision makers are assumed to be economically rational. This would seem to be a very promising research program.

Still, considerable work remains to be done. First, much of the policy analysis presented above is speculative. More analytic examinations of the policy implications of the behavioral model should be developed. The analysis above also raises a number of empirical issues—such as the importance of interindustry differences in the cost of providing job safety. Second, the major source of support for the models developed in Section III was the laboratory evidence for judgment errors. There is some work that is suggestive of the generalizability of these findings to market behavior, but more field studies of these types of behaviors and more simulation studies or laboratory studies that involve decisions that were directly comparable to real-world safety decisions would be useful corroboration of the existing evidence.

Although the analysis presented here is speculative, it is also suggestive of the potential importance of behavioral economics in understanding the appropriate role of government in insuring that its citizens have safe working conditions and consumer products. It is my hope that this line of research will be vigorously pursued.

APPENDIX

A Labor Market Where Some Workers Are Inattentive to Safety

What follows is a simple characterization of a labor market where jobs differ in both wages and safety and in which some workers are attentive to the safety differences and others are not. With a minimum of assumptions it is shown that any equilibrium in such a market must have two characteristics: (1) Any attentive employee who works in a job that is less safe than that held by any other worker must receive a compensating wage differential, and (2) Nonattentive workers must be employed in the least safe jobs.

Description of the Market: An auctioneer calls out a wage for each possible level of job safety. Each firm offers to employ a certain number of workers at one or more levels of job safety. Workers who are not attentive to safety all offer to work at the safety level(s) offering the highest wage. Workers who are attentive to safety offer to work at the safety level(s) that offer the highest utility given the announced wages. Utility is assumed to be strictly increasing in both safety and wages. An equilibrium is said to exist when the number of workers who seek employment at each safety level is equal to the number of job offers at that safety level. Any such equilibrium must have both of the following characteristics:

1.   If the safety level of worker I's job is greater than the safety level of worker J's job, then worker J's wage must be greater than or equal to worker I's. If worker J is attentive to safety, the inequality is strict. To see this, consider first the case where worker J is inattentive. Since all inattentive workers will offer to work only for the highest wage, worker J's wage must be greater than or equal to all other workers' wages. If worker J is attentive and his/her job is less safe than the job in which worker I is employed, then worker J's wage must be strictly greater than worker I's or else J would prefer to work at the safety level that worker I is employed at and would not offer to work at his/her current job.

2.   No attentive worker will be employed in a job that is less safe than any in which an inattentive worker is employed. If an attentive worker is employed in a job that is less safe than any other job, the wage the attentive worker receives must be higher than the wage received by the worker on the safer job (from item 1, above). But all inattentive workers must be receiving the highest possible wage. Therefore, attentive workers cannot be employed in jobs that are less safe than any employing inattentive workers.

ACKNOWLEDGMENTS

I would like to thank the Institute of Industrial Relations at University of California, Berkeley for research support. I would also like to thank Benjamin Gilad,

Kevin Lang, George Lowenstein and Chris Martin for comments on an earlier version of the ideas presented here.

NOTES

1. Since welfare is subjective, we cannot observe it directly. Only under the most extreme perfect market assumptions would we expect people to give meaningful answers to questions about the effects of policy on their welfare. With imperfect information or less than complete rationality, people may not be able to tell how a policy change had affected them or even if it had.

2. Evidence on the importance of incentives is mixed. In some situations, incentives seem to produce less normatively appropriate behavior (see note 7).

3. Akerlof and Dickens (1982) suggest a cognitive dissonance explanation for this tendency. Slovic, Fischhoff, and Lichtenstein (1982, p. 471) review several studies of this phenomenon.

4. See Nisbett and Ross (1981, p. 140–141) for a list of these studies.

5. This problem is extensively discussed in Slovic, Fischhoff, and Lichtenstein (1977), Einhorn and Hogarth (1981), and Nisbett and Ross (1981, pp. 18–24 and several other places throughout the book; see *vividness* and *availability heuristic* in the index).

6. Once again this problem has received considerable attention. See Nisbett and Ross (1981, pp. 25–28, pp. 141–150). Christensen-Szalanski and Beach (1982) show that people may be able to use base-rate information if they have experience with a causal relation between the base rate and the outcome, but that experience with the base rate in the absence of a causal relation between it and the outcome being assessed will not be used.

7. For instance, if we are told before meeting someone that the person is very bright, we will have a tendency to interpret the person's behavior as being indicative of intelligence. Nisbett and Ross discuss the evidence for this phenomenon (1981, pp. 93–101, 168–175).

8. This was one of the early findings of psychological decision theory research. Slovic, Fischhoff, and Lichtenstein (1977) discuss this.

9. This tendency has been dubbed "the law of small numbers" (Nisbett and Ross, 1981, pp. 77–82, 256–260; Slovic, Fischhoff, and Lichtenstein, 1977.) Bar-Hillel (1979) presents evidence that, in some situations, people can be induced to pay attention to sample size but only to the extent that it reflects sample-to-population ratio. In these experiments people were found to be willing to trade sample size for sample-to-population ratio even when it decreased the expected sample accuracy.

10. Nisbett and Ross present an extensive discussion of the evidence for this phenomenon (1981, pp. 82–89, 260–261).

11. Slovic, Fischhoff, and Lichtenstein (1977), Einhorn and Hogarth (1981), Lichtenstein, Fischhoff, and Phillips (1982) and Nisbett and Ross (1981) all offer extensive discussions of the evidence for this problem. Slovic, Fischhoff, and Lichtenstein (1982) review the evidence with respect to real-world decision problems.

12. The problem of information search has been investigated in the behavioral decision theory literature without reference to overconfidence. The general finding is that, depending on the experimental manipulation, people may do too much or too little information search, and the deviations from optimality can be quite large. See Connolly and Gilani (1982).

13. For instance, Smith (1976, p. 30) claims that "the finding that compensating premiums...do exist and that employers do supply safety in response to incentives suggests

that there is a private market for safety that functions more or less like (the market of the standard model)." See also Viscusi (1979b; 1983).

14.   Slovic, Fischhoff, and Lichtenstein (1977) discuss some of the attempts that have been made to teach people to make judgments more in accordance with the normative model. Results suggest that for many types of biases extensive individual attention is necessary to get people to correct their biases on even a small range of problems (see also Fischhoff, 1982). Brehmer and Kuylenstierna (1978) argue that normatively correct behavior in some common situations may be too complex for people to implement even after receiving instructions.

REFERENCES

Akerlof, George A. and William T. Dickens, "The Economic Consequences of Cognitive Dissonance," *American Economic Review*, 79, no. 3 (June 1981), 307–319.

Bar-Hillel, Maya, "The Role of Sample Size in Sample Evaluation," *Organizational Behavior and Human Performance*, 24 (1979), 245–257.

Borgida, E. and R.E. Nisbett, "The Differential Impact of Abstract vs. Concrete Information on Decisions," *Journal of Applied Social Psychology*, 7 (1977) 258–271.

Brehmer, Berndt and Jans Kuylenstierna, "Task Information and Performances in Probabilistic Inference Tasks," *Organizational Behavior and Human Performance*, 22 (1978), 445–464.

Burton, I., R.W. Kates, and G.F. White, *The Environment as Hazard*. New York: Oxford University Press, 1978.

Christensen-Szalanski, Jay J.J., and Lee Roy Beach, "Experience and the Base Rate Fallacy," *Organizational Behavior and Human Performance*, 29 (1982), 270–278.

Connolly, Terry and Naveed Gilani, "Information Search in Judgment Tasks: A Regression Model and Some Preliminary Findings," *Organizational Behavior and Human Performance*, 30 (1982), 330–350.

Dickens, William T., "Occupational Safety and Health Regulation and Economic Theory," in William Darity, ed., *Labor Economics: Modern Views*. New York: Kluwer-Nijhoff, 1984a.

Dickens, William T., "Differences Between Risk Premiums in Union and Nonunion Wages and the Case for Occupational Safety Regulation," *American Economic Review*, 74, no. 2 (1984b), 320–323.

Dickens, William T., "Occupational Safety and Health and Irrational Behavior: A Preliminary Analysis," in David Appel and John Worrall, eds., *Benefit Issues in Workers Compensation*. Ithaca, NY: ILR Press, Cornell, 1985.

Edgell, Stephan E., and Judith E. Hennessey, "Irrelevant Information and Utilization of Event Base Rates in Nonmetric Multiple-Cue Probability Learning," *Organizational Behavior and Human Performance*, 26 (1980), 1–6.

Einhorn, Hillel J. and Robin M. Hogarth, "Behavioral Decision Theory: Processes of Judgment and Choice," *Annual Review of Psychology*, 32 (1981), 53–88.

Fischer, Gregory W., "Scoring Rule Feedback and the Overconfidence Syndrome in Subjective Probability Forecasting," *Organizational Behavior and Human Performance*, 29 (1982), 352–369.

Fischhoff, Baruch, "Debiasing," in Daniel Kahneman, Paul Slovic and Amos Tversky, eds., *Judgments Under Uncertainty: Heuristics and Biases*. Cambridge: Cambridge University Press, 1982, pp. 422–444.

Friedman, Milton, "The Methodology of Positive Economics," in Milton Friedman, ed., *Essays in Positive Economics*. Chicago: University of Chicago Press, 1953.

Goodman, Barbara, Mark Saltzman, and Ward Edwards, "Prediction of Bids for Two-Outcome Gambles in a Casino Setting," *Organizational Behavior and Human Performance*, 24 (1979), 382–399.

Grether, David M., and Charles R. Plott, "Economic Theory of Choice and the Preference Reversal Phenomena," *American Economic Review*, 69, no. 4 (September 1979), 623–638.

Kahneman, Daniel and Amos Tverksy, "Prospect Theory: An Analysis of Decisions Under Risk," *Econometrica*, 47, no. 2 (March 1979), 263–291.

Katona, George, "Private Pensions and Individual Savings." Monograph no. 40, Survey Research Center, University of Michigan, Ann Arbor, Michigan, 1965.

Klein, Norman M., "Utility and Decision Strategies: A Second Look at the Rational Decision Maker," *Organizational Behavior and Human Performance*, 31 (1983), 1–25.

Kunreuther, Howard, *Disaster Insurance Protection: Public Policy Lessons.* New York: Wiley, 1978.

Lichtenstein, Sarah, Baruch Fischhoff, and Lawrence D. Phillips, "Calibration of Probabilities: The State of the Art to 1980," in Daniel Kahneman, Paul Slovic and Amos Tversky, eds., *Judgments Under Uncertainty: Heuristics and Biases.* Cambridge: Cambridge University Press, 1982, pp. 306–334.

McAllister, Daniel W., Terence R. Mitchell, and Lee Roy Beach, "The Contingency Model for the Selection of Decision Strategies: An Empirical Test of the Effects of Significance, Accountability, and Reversibility," *Organizational Behavior and Human Performance*, 24 (1970), 228–244.

Nisbett, Richard E., and L. Ross, *Human Inference: Strategies and Shortcomings of Social Judgments.* Englewood Cliffs, NJ: Prentice-Hall, 1980.

Nisbett, Richard E., Henry Zukier, and Ronald E. Lemley, "The Dilution Effect: Nondiagnostic Information Weakens the Implications of Diagnostic Information," *Cognitive Psychology*, 13 (1981), 248–277.

Perloff, Jeffrey M., and Steven C. Salop, "Firm-Specific Information, Product Differentiation and Industry Equilibrium." Mimeo, University of Pennsylvania and F.T.C., April 1980.

Rethans, A., "An Investigation of Consumer Perceptions of Products Hazards." Ph.D. Dissertation, University of Oregon, 1979.

Rosen, Sherwin, "Hedonic Prices and Implicit Markets: Product Differentiation in Pure Competition," *Journal of Political Economy*, 82, no. 1 (January 1974), 34–55.

Simon, Marilyn J., "Imperfect Information, Costly Litigation and Product Quality," *The Bell Journal of Economics*, 12, no. 1 (Spring 1980), 171–184.

Slovic, Paul, Baruch Fischhoff, and Sarah Lichtenstein, "The Certainty Illusion," *ORI Research Bulletin*, 16, no. 4 (1976).

Slovic, Paul, Baruch Fischhoff, and Sarah Lichtenstein, "Behavioral Decision Theory," *Annual Review of Psychology*, 28 (1977), 1–39.

Slovic, Paul, Baruch Fischhoff, and Sarah Lichtenstein, "Facts Versus Fears: Understanding Perceived Risk," in Daniel Kahneman, Paul Slovic and Amos Tversky, eds., *Judgment Under Uncertainty: Heuristics and Biases.* Cambridge: Cambridge University Press, 1982, pp. 463–489.

Smith, Robert Stewart, *The Occupational Safety and Health Act: Its Goals and its Achievements.* Washington, D.C.: AEI, 1976.

Smith, Robert Stewart, "Compensating Wage Differentials and Public Policy: A Review," *Industrial and Labor Relations Review*, 32, no. 3 (April 1979), 339–352.

Tversky, Amos and Daniel Kahneman, "Judgments Under Uncertainty: Heuristics and Biases," *Science*, 185 (1974), 1124–1131.

Tversky, Amos and Daniel Kahneman, "Judgments Under Uncertainty: Heuristics and

Biases," in Daniel Kahneman, Paul Slovic and Amos Tversky, eds., *Judgments under Uncertainty: Heuristics and Biases*. Cambridge: Cambridge University Press, 1982, pp. 3–22.

Viscusi, W. Kip, "Job Hazards and Quit Rates: An Analysis of Adaptive Worker Behavior," *International Economic Review*, 20, no. 1 (February 1979a), 29–58.

Viscusi, W. Kip, *Employment Hazards: An Investigation of Market Performance*. Cambridge, MA: Harvard University Press, 1979b.

Viscusi, W. Kip, *Risk by Choice: Regulating Health and Safety in the Workplace*. Cambridge, MA: Harvard University Press, 1983.

BIOGRAPHICAL SKETCHES OF
THE CONTRIBUTORS

Bruce J. Caldwell is an Associate Professor of Economics at the University of North Carolina at Greensboro. His publications include the book *Beyond Positivism: Economic Methodology in the Twentieth Century*, an edited book of readings entitled *Appraisal and Criticism in Economics*, and various contributions to the *American Economic Review*, *Journal of Economic Literature*, *History of Political Economy*, *Southern Economic Journal*, and other academic journals. His research interests include the history of economic thought and methodology.

William T. Dickens received his Ph.D. from M.I.T. in 1981 and is currently an Assistant Professor of Economics at the University of California, Berkeley. He has done research on labor productivity, occupational safety and health, and union growth, as well as behavior economics. His current interest is in testing non-competitive theories of wage setting.

Randall K. Filer is Associate Professor of Economics at Hunter College of the City University of New York. He received his Ph.D. from Princeton University and taught at Brandeis University from 1978 to 1986. His research, focusing on earnings, includes published work on affective human capital, male-female wage differences, effort supply and the earnings of artists. Research currently in progress deals with occupational segregation and comparable worth, as well as the determinants of retirement age.

Robert Forsythe is an Associate Professor of Economics at The University of Iowa. He received a B.S. from the Pennsylvania State University and an M.S. in statistics and M.S. and Ph.D. degrees in economics from Carnegie-Mellon University. He has published articles in the *American Economic Review, Econometrica, Journal of Accounting Research, Journal of Finance,* and other scholarly journals. His current research interests lie principally in experimental economics and financial economics.

Roger S. Frantz is Professor of Economics at San Diego State University. He has written extensively on the impact of X-efficiency on worker motivation, corporate management, industrial organization and development. His papers have appeared in the *Southern Economic Journal, Journal of Economic Issues, Journal of Post Keynesian Economics* and numerous other publications. He presently serves as Symposium Editor of the *Journal of Behavioral Economics.*

Benjamin Gilad is Assistant Professor of Management in the Department of Business Administration, Rutgers University, Newark. He holds a B.A. in psychology from Tel-Aviv University, an M.B.A. from Central Missouri State University and a Ph.D. in economics from New York University. His research interests include the interface of psychology and economics, entrepreneurial behavior, and business intelligence systems. He is the co-founder and executive director of SABE, the Society for the Advancement of Behavioral Economics.

Amyra Grossbard-Shechtman is Associate Professor of Economics at San Diego State University. She studied economics, sociology and anthropology at the Hebrew University and the University of Chicago. Her article, "Theory of Allocation of Time in Markets for Labour and Marriage" appeared in *Economic Journal* in 1984, and she has published other articles on marriage in economics (including behavioral economics), anthropology, sociology and Jewish law journals. Her research focuses on the connections between marriage and the labor force.

Harvey Leibenstein is Andelot Professor of Economics and Population at Harvard University. He received his Ph.D. in 1951 from Princeton University. While a professor at the University of California, Berkeley, during 1960–1967, he began working on the X-inefficiency problem and researching firm behavior in developing countries. For the past two decades he has done work on X-efficiency theory.

James N. Morgan is a Senior Research Scientist at the Institute for Social Research, and Professor of Economics at the University of Michigan. He received his B.A. from Northwestern University and his Ph.D. from Harvard. He has conducted survey research on the affluent, the poor, accident victims, injured workers, and philanthropy, and since 1968 has been one of the directors of the Panel Study of Income Dynamics. Ten volumes, entitled *Five Thousand American Families*, summarize its findings. He taught consumer economics for many years and co-authored a text, *The Economics of Personal Choice*. He is interested in developing new environments for older people that would encourage productive activity and mutual support.

John F. Tomer is Associate Professor of Economics and Finance at Manhattan College, Riverdale, New York. His articles have appeared in the *Journal of Economic Issues, Review of Social Economy, Eastern Economic Journal, Public Finance Quarterly*, and *Urban Affairs Quarterly*. He is presently completing work on a book entitled *Organizational Capital: The Path to Higher Productivity and Well-Being* (Praeger, 1986).

W. Fred van Raaij is Professor of Economic Psychology at Erasmus University, Rotterdam, The Netherlands. He studied statistics and psychology at Leyden University and obtained his Ph.D. in psychology at Tilburg University. He was also affiliated with Twente Institute of Technology and the University of Illinois at Urbana-Champaign. He is editor of the *Journal of Economic Psychology*. His research interests include behavior and information processing, advertising, and business cycle effects on spending and saving.

Karl-Erik Wärneryd is Professor of Economic Psychology at the Stockholm School of Economics. He received his M.B.A. from the Stockholm School of Economics and his Ph.D. in psychology from the University of Chicago. He has published books and articles in economic psychology, particularly in the areas of consumer behavior and mass communication. As a member of a Swedish government commission on advertising, he spent several years dealing with every conceivable aspect of advertising.

Sidney G. Winter is Professor of Economics and Management at the Yale University School of Management. He holds a B.A. in economics from Swarthmore College and a Ph.D. in economics from Yale University. He is co-editor of *The Journal of Economic Behavior and Organization*. His interest in the behavioral theory of the firm led to his seminal book,

An Evolutionary Theory of Economic Change, co-authored with Richard Nelson.